Paradigms and Sand Castles

Analytical Perspectives on Politics

Political Science is developing rapidly and changing markedly. Keeping in touch with new ideas across the discipline is a challenge for political scientists and for their students.

To help meet this challenge, the series Analytical Perspectives on Politics presents creative and sophisticated syntheses of major areas of research in the field of political science. In each book, a high-caliber author provides a clear and discriminating description of the current state of the art and a strong-minded prescription and structure for future work in the field.

These distinctive books provide a compact review for political scientists, a helpful introduction for graduate students, and central reading for advanced undergraduate courses.

Robert W. Jackman, *Power without Force: The Political Capacity of Nation-States*

Linda L. Fowler, *Candidates, Congress, and the American Democracy*

Scott Gates and Brian D. Humes, *Games, Information, and Politics: Applying Game Theoretic Models to Political Science*

Lawrence Baum, *The Puzzle of Judicial Behavior*

Barbara Geddes, *Paradigms and Sand Castles: Theory Building and Research Design in Comparative Politics*

Rose McDermott, *Political Psychology in International Relations*

Ole R. Holsti, *Public Opinion and American Foreign Policy, Revised Edition*

Paradigms and Sand Castles

Theory Building and Research Design in Comparative Politics

BARBARA GEDDES

The University of Michigan Press
Ann Arbor

Published in the United States of America by
The University of Michigan Press
Manufactured in the United States of America
♾ Printed on acid-free paper

2010 2009 7 6 5

A CIP catalog record for this book is available from the British Library.

Library of Congress Cataloging-in-Publication Data

Geddes, Barbara.
Paradigms and sand castles : theory building and research design in comparative politics / Barbara Geddes.
p. cm. — (Analytical perspectives on politics)
Includes bibliographical references and index.
ISBN 0-472-09835-7 (cloth : alk. paper) — ISBN 0-472-06835-0 (pbk. : alk. paper)
1. Comparative government. 2. Political science—Research. I. Title. II. Series.

JA86 .G35 2003
320.3—dc21 2003002160

ISBN 978-0-472-09835-4 (cloth : alk. paper)
ISBN 978-0-472-06835-7 (pbk. : alk. paper)

ISBN13 978-0-472-02397-4 (electronic)

To John

Contents

Acknowledgments ix

1. Research Design and the Accumulation of Knowledge 1

2. Big Questions, Little Answers: How the Questions You Choose Affect the Answers You Get 27

3. How the Cases You Choose Affect the Answers You Get: Selection Bias and Related Issues 89

4. How the Evidence You Use Affects the Answers You Get: Rigorous Use of the Evidence Contained in Case Studies 131

5. How the Approach You Choose Affects the Answers You Get: Rational Choice and Its Uses in Comparative Politics 175

6. Conclusion 213

Appendix A 225

Appendix B 233

Appendix C 247

Bibliography 289

Index 307

Acknowledgments

I wrote the first fragment of what has become this book with my youngest daughter, a colicky infant, screaming in the background. She is thirteen now. My first thanks go to her for growing up, turning into a quirky and delightful person, and allowing the resumption of more or less civilized life.

In working on a project that has taken so long, I have acquired more debts of gratitude than I am likely to remember. Over the years, many UCLA graduate students (one of them has tenure now) helped with research on various aspects of the project. I thank Allyson Benton, Hanna Birnir, Kimberly Niles, John Quinn, Tatiana Rizova, and Cathy Sweet for their help and area expertise. Special thanks to Cheryl Schonhardt-Bailey, without whose persistence at the library I could not have written the first fragment during the summer of the colicky baby; and to Eduardo Alemán, Liz Stein, and Marisa Kellam, whose intelligent, conscientious, and good-natured toil at the end made all the difference.

I have been using this book to teach my graduate class in research design since before I started writing it. Many of the ideas in the book emerged in response to students' research projects. The examples, originally developed to convey abstract ideas to the students in these classes, have been honed in response to their questions and bewildered looks. I thank my students for their thoughtful questions and their enthusiastic response to the class. It has been my favorite class to teach for many years.

I have also benefited from the comments of more colleagues than I can remember, both individually and during seminars. I would especially like to thank David Laitin for his challenging and very helpful comments on much of the manuscript; David Collier for his critique of an early version of the selection bias chapter; Bob Jackman for his discussion of an early version of the test of the Lipset and Rokkan argument and for encouragement on the project as a whole; and Ellen Lust-Okar for sharing her expertise on the Middle East. Seminars at UC San Diego, the University of New Mexico, and Yale stand out in my mind as having been especially stimulating, and I thank Miles Kahler, Karen Remmer, and Ivan Szelenyi for arranging them.

Much of the financial support for this project was provided by Dean Scott Waugh of UCLA, and I thank him for this and his many other contributions to the quality of intellectual life at UCLA.

Finally, I thank my greatest fan, John Zaller, who read all of the manuscript and pounded mercilessly at its logic and organization, while at the same time maintaining an exuberant enthusiasm for the project. I thank him for sharing and reinforcing the commitment to "science as a vocation" that motivates this book. And I also thank him for the cheerful, good-natured, and energetic way he shares the other domains of my life.

CHAPTER 1

Research Design and the Accumulation of Knowledge

> 'My name is Ozymandias, king of kings:
> Look on my works, ye Mighty, and despair!'
> Nothing beside remains. Round the decay
> Of that colossal wreck, boundless and bare
> The lone and level sands stretch far away.
> —Percy Bysshe Shelley, "Ozymandias"

The last thirty years have treated students of the politics of developing countries almost as unkindly as the years did Ozymandias. At precisely the moment when the impulse toward authoritarianism had "been fully explained by a variety of converging approaches and [was] therefore understood in its majestic inevitability and perhaps even permanence" (Hirschman 1979, 98), democratization began its sweep through much of the world. In a second and even more unexpected development, governments in every region began to abandon state interventionist economic policies in favor of greater market orientation. On top of everything else, the Soviet empire collapsed. Though scholars have greeted most of these events with delight, few expected them, because theories dominant at the time these changes began did not predict them (cf. Remmer 1995, 103; and Kalyvas 1999).[1]

Confronted by compelling and exciting events in the world, scholars quickly turned their attention to trying to understand them. One of the first fruits of these investigations was the recognition that few of the theories dear to the hearts of students of

1. A number of scholars had analyzed the fragilities and contradictions that eventually contributed to transitions in one or another kind of authoritarianism. See, for example, O'Donnell (1978, 1979) for analyses of the potentially destabilizing tensions among alliance partners within bureaucratic-authoritarian regimes; and Kalyvas (1999) for a summary of the many analyses of the weaknesses and dysfunctional aspects of communist regimes. To my knowledge, however, no one expected or predicted the sweep of democratization and economic reform across much of the developing world that we have witnessed.

comparative development offered much leverage for explaining recent events. The limited usefulness of old theories was noticed early on—sometimes by the authors of earlier studies themselves—in the study of transitions from authoritarianism. Neither the dependency-influenced arguments that had figured so large in explanations for the surge of authoritarianism during the 1960s and 1970s (e.g., O'Donnell 1973; Cardoso 1973a) nor historical accounts of democratization (e.g., Moore 1966) seemed to offer much help in explaining flip-flops between democracy and authoritarianism.[2] Guillermo O'Donnell and Philippe Schmitter eloquently express the inadequacy of standard interest group or class-based approaches.

> During these transitions . . . it is almost impossible to specify *ex ante* which classes, sectors, institutions, and other groups will take what role, opt for which issues, or support what alternative. . . . [These are] choices and processes where assumptions about the relative stability and predictability of social, economic, and institutional parameters—and, therefore, of their descriptive and explanatory power—seem patently inadequate. (1986, 4–5)

Christopher Clapham and George Philip also highlight the apparent indeterminacy of regime transitions: "Patterns of military regime succession are rather like paths through the jungle: there are various trails, all pretty rough going . . . , and most of them not leading where you want to go anyhow" (1985, 24). Processes appear complicated and unpredictable when we lack theories to explain them.

The literature on marketization has faced similar difficulties. Empirical studies find that the staple causal factor for explaining economic policy—interest group influence—accounts for few of the policy changes associated with economic liberalization (see, e.g., Haggard 1990; Haggard and Kaufman 1992, 1995; and Bates and Krueger 1993). Yet no one has discovered or devised a theoretical approach that works better than interest group theories. As a result, analyses of economic liberalization, like

2. Rueschemeyer, Stephens, and Stephens (1992) disagree with this otherwise generally accepted conclusion. They have tried to provide a life-support system for the tradition begun by Moore through a series of substantive revisions and the inclusion of additional variables and contingencies.

those of democratization, remained largely descriptive for many years.[3]

Students of the Soviet empire, in contrast, found it easier to explain its collapse. Their problem was not too few predictions of collapse, but too many. Since at least the 1950s, many analyses of communist regimes have stressed their inherent dysfunctions and contradictions. When the regimes finally broke down, these dysfunctions were invoked as causes. Yet these political systems had lasted forty years in Eastern Europe and seventy in the Soviet Union. An oddity of the transitions literature is that most early analyses of the breakdown of long-lived communist regimes emphasized their contradictions and weaknesses, while few discussions of the collapse of military regimes—which last on average about nine years—focus on inherent sources of regime fragility.[4]

Since the cultural, social structural, and economic theories that had long informed the study of developing countries seemed to offer little help in explaining contemporary events, scholars turned to the study of politics for answers. But the theoretical cupboard was nearly bare. Because of our past failure to theorize the internal workings of political processes in developing countries, most analysts found themselves in uncharted territory when it came to building theories that use political causes to explain political outcomes. The result was the emphasis on contingency and voluntarism found in the early literature on democratization (e.g., O'Donnell, Schmitter, and Whitehead 1986; Diamond, Linz, and Lipsett 1989).

Early analyses of economic liberalization suffered from some of the same rudderless quality, though scholars attempting to explain different countries' responses to the international economic crises of the 1980s and 1990s found more uses for traditional ideas than did those studying democratization. International factors, primarily pressure from international financial institutions, continued to receive attention, as did pressures from domestic economic interests. Conjunctural country circumstances and the idiosyncratic beliefs and commitments of decision makers, however, also

---

3. Economists, for whom the puzzle is why does liberalization take so long, have proposed a number of subtle variations on interest-group theory to account for delayed reforms. See, for example, Alesina and Drazen (1991), Fernández and Rodrik (1991), and Rodrik (1994). Political scientists, however, for whom the political impediments to economic reform seemed obvious and the initiation of reform more puzzling, had more difficulty coming up with new theories or systematic revisions of old ones.

4. O'Donnell (1978, 1979) is the best-known exception.

played a large role in analyses (see Stallings and Kaufman 1989; Haggard and Kaufman 1992, 1995; Bates and Krueger 1993; and Haggard and Webb 1994). Despite some efforts at theory building (e.g., Frieden 1989), this literature, like that on democratization, remained largely descriptive and focused on the details of decision making in different cases. In short, scholars working on two of the topics of highest salience in the developing world during the last quarter century—democratization and economic reform—found old theories wanting.

This did not result from acts of nature or of human contrivance beyond our control. The point of departure for this book is that we have made our own fate through our inattention to basic issues of research design. To be successful, social science must steer a careful course between the Scylla of lovely but untested theory and Charybdis, the maelstrom of information unstructured by theory. Much of the field of comparative politics has failed to keep to this difficult course, veering instead from one catastrophic extreme to the other.[5] The result is a modest accumulation of theoretical knowledge in many parts of the field. Arguments, theories, and even paradigms tend to rise and fall in rapid succession, leaving behind little to show that they ever existed. Like elaborate sand castles, paradigms have been built with great effort and attention to theoretical detail, only to be washed away by the tide of the next generation of graduate students, whose research batters at the weak points of existing paradigms—as it should—until the theoretical edifice crumbles and disappears.

The need to start over with every new current event cannot be attributed to any failure of theoretical imagination among comparativists. Rather, it is the result of our inability to build on, develop, and extend old theories instead of periodically discarding them. This is not to say that we are promiscuous or disloyal to our theories. We cling to them with the same fervor and tenacity as do other scholars to theirs. The problem is that our theories—siren songs composed without systematic checking against facts—eventually disillusion us. Cruel and inconvenient facts, often available at the time of composition but not

5. There are many obvious exceptions to this criticism, including much of the work on West European democracies. Nevertheless, it applies to much of the field, especially that part of it that studies "big" questions such as democratization, development, economic policy reform, and revolution.

used, eventually insist on our attention and force the abandonment of our creations.

As a consequence, we face new happenings in the world with few theoretical tools, condemned to begin from scratch with unstructured, inductive searches for patterns. At their best, such inductive explorations lead to generalizations and correlations, which in turn give rise to theoretical speculations. More typically, however, inductive fact-gathering missions result in a disorganized mass of information. "Only very occasionally . . . do facts collected with so little guidance from pre-established theory speak with sufficient clarity to permit the emergence of a first paradigm" (Kuhn 1970, 16). Though they need not be, in practice theoretical speculations arising from inductive studies tend to be marred by vague, unarticulated first principles and behavioral assumptions that have not been carefully thought through. Apparent relationships between cause and effect may be uncovered within the set of cases examined, but few efforts are made to find out if such relationships also occur among other cases. Sometimes historical detail substitutes for causal argument, and the adumbration of events leading up to outcomes takes the place of explanation. Authors may carefully hedge their tentative arguments with caveats about the need for further testing, but most readers ignore the caveats and attribute to such arguments the status of established findings. As a result, sturdy, long-lived theories all too often fail to emerge from inductive work.

The central message of this book is that we could steer a course through that narrow channel between untested theory and atheoretical data more successfully, and thus accumulate theoretical knowledge more rapidly, if certain research norms were changed. Although research norms are changing, basic principles of research design continue to be ignored in many studies. Common problems include inappropriate selection of cases from which to draw evidence for testing theories and a casual attitude toward nonquantitative measurement, both of which undermine the credibility of evidence gathered to support arguments. The failure to organize and store evidence in ways that make it accessible to others raises the costs of replication and thus also slows theoretical progress. Uncritical acceptance by readers of theories that have not undergone systematic empirical tests exacerbates the problem.

Granted, we work in a harsh environment for the development of solid theory because of severe information limitations, but harsh environments sometimes lead to useful innovations. This study will suggest some innovations and some ideas borrowed from other fields. The book deals with several of the widespread methodological practices noted above, showing their unfortunate consequences and making suggestions for their improvement. It begins with a controversial subject: the translation of fascination with "big structures, large processes, huge comparisons" (Tilly 1984) into useful and replicable research. It then moves to relatively well understood issues such as case selection and concept operationalization. Finally, the book concludes with a discussion of the characteristics that a good theory should have and highlights the uses and limitations of the rational choice framework as one possible approach to theory building.

The Rise and Fall of Paradigms: An Example

Although a great deal of excellent research has been done on developing countries, the methodological faults noted above have also been quite common in the study of less industrialized countries. To illustrate how weak research norms can cause the sandcastle effect, I sketch the history of one prominent theoretical tradition in the field of comparative development. The intellectual history reprised here, of the rise and fall of the modernization and dependency paradigms, will be familiar to most comparativists. Hundreds of us reviewed it ourselves on qualifying exams. The basic arguments and concepts will be novel only to the young. I use an important and well-known, though now outdated, debate for this example in order to show the centrality of the problems I address later in the book.

The history of the study of the relationship between economic development and democracy can be periodized by the rise and fall of paradigms in much the same way that the history of many developing countries themselves can be periodized by the rise and fall of regimes. My use of the word *paradigm* differs slightly from Thomas Kuhn's (1970), in that he defines a paradigm as the dominant understanding of a particular class of phenomena at a particular time. As Mattei Dogan (2001) notes, political science is in Kuhn's terms prescientific. Consequently, no Kuhnian hegemonic paradigm has existed. The collections of theories, hypotheses, applications, and favored methodologies I refer to as paradigms do, however, have most of the other features Kuhn attributes to paradigms. They encompass a set of factual and explanatory knowledge claims, in other words, theories, that are widely accepted by adherents. And they structure further research: determining which facts are theoretically salient; defining what constitutes a paradox and what questions urgently require answers; identifying which cases need to be examined and what kinds of evidence are considered meaningful.

Like regimes, paradigms are sometimes overthrown by well-organized, coherent, mobilized opposition—as, for example, modernization "theory" was toppled by dependency "theory." At other times, paradigms fall because of their own internal contradictions and their inability to deal with the inconvenient facts thrown up by the world—the fate of dependency theory in the early 1980s. When this happens, paradigms, like regimes, are succeeded by periods of chaos and contention. Such a phase followed the fall of dependency theory.

To achieve success, paradigms need to have the same characteristics as successful ideologies. Ideologies simplify the world, explain what we see around us in a compelling way, and identify what needs to be done. The basic ideas need to be simple, yet applicable to a broad range of puzzling questions. They need to have the "aha!" factor—that is, to lead the newly exposed individual to exclaim, "That has to be right! Why didn't I think of it?" And finally, paradigms need to be fruitful; the theories they contain need to explain previously unexplained regularities and to create new paradoxes and puzzles. As ideologies imply needed political action or policies, a successful paradigm implies a research frontier of puzzles and paradoxes on which scholars need to work. Among the theory-induced paradoxes of note, the vast outpouring of work on voter turnout spawned by the theory of collective action plays the same role within its intellectual framework as did the vast outpouring of work on false consciousness within the Marxist framework. In both instances, real-world phenomena that might otherwise have been considered thoroughly unremarkable—that is, citizens vote and workers fail to rebel—have been subjected to intense scrutiny and debate because basic theoretical premises render them puzzling within their respective theoretical worldviews.

The brief history below demonstrates the relationship between evidence and paradigm shifts. Each paradigm lost its power to structure research when evidence of gross inconsistency between expectations arising from theories within the paradigm and real-world events became impossible to ignore. This is the usual mode of progress in science: earlier theoretical understandings are first undermined by inconsistent facts and then replaced by newer theories that can accommodate both old and new evidence. The claim here is thus not that theories or paradigms are overturned in some unusual way in the subfield, but rather that evidence was available that should have called them into question at the time of their creation. It should not have taken decades to notice the plethora of inconvenient facts.

When developing countries first began to receive concentrated attention from political scientists after World War II, central questions for the emerging subfield were (and remain today): what causes democracy? and what impedes economic development? Scholars not only scrutinized events and processes in developing countries themselves, but also returned to the study of the historical development of the more industrialized countries and compared different political and economic routes to development. The paradigm that emerged was the loose collection of assumptions, generalizations, and hypotheses referred to, generously, as modernization "theory." I label modernization theory a paradigm because the generalizations, hypotheses, and theories of which it was composed formed a more or less consistent and logically coherent body.

The modernization paradigm reflected the times in which it developed, as do all paradigms. Some of its central ideas drew on observations of the world during the 1950s, a time when technology and democracy seemed to be spreading rapidly from the North Atlantic countries to the rest of the world. Observers assumed they could extrapolate their own time into the future. Other ideas in this paradigm derived from contemporary academic theories, especially pluralist understandings of politics and neoclassical economics.

The pluralist image of political life contributed to expectations that change would come about incrementally and peacefully through the interplay of societal interests (cf. Binder 1986). Neoclassical economics supplied theoretical support for a view of the international economy as simply the medium through which trade could occur, enabling resources to flow to their most efficient use and all parties to capture the gains of specialization based on comparative advantage.

With nearly a half century of hindsight, we can see that the parts of modernization theory that were tested carefully (by the standards of the 1950s) have survived the test of time fairly well, though they spent some time in the dustbin of history before being fished out, dusted off, and put back on the academic shelf. One of the most important of these is the correlation between democracy and economic development (Lipset 1959; Jackman 1973), interpreted then as support for the argument that development causes democracy.[6] Many of the arguments drawn from economics have also survived. Quite a few of the most basic ideas of modernization theory were never tested, however. A central one was that the diffusion of values that had originated in Western Europe would lead to the rapid transformation of traditional societies and cultures into modern ones (Levy 1966). Expectations about the effects of diffusion were based on historical experience in northwestern Europe and the rapidity with which developing societies embraced certain material innovations, such as vaccinations and modern methods of transportation, during the immediate postwar period. Plausible as the values argument was to those steeped in Weberian ideas, it was never tested. That is, no one attempted to measure the diffusion of values and show that changes in them affected development.[7]

Ideas about the effects of the diffusion of technological innovations also remained untested. Observers believed that the diffusion of technology, which they saw happening rapidly, would lead to quick economic development, and that cultural and societal modernization would follow automatically as a result of changes in status, expectations, and roles brought about by the resource mobility required by industrialization (Moore 1963). This emphasis on technological innovation as the deus ex machina that would bring profound social, political, and cultural changes was consistent with Marx's interpretation of European modernization. The consequences of the real diffusion of technology, in which some innovations spread much faster than others—for example, vaccinations faster than birth control—were not measured, and the expectation that technological diffusion would cause cultural and social changes was not tested.

---

6. The relationship between economic development and democracy is one of the most thoroughly tested in comparative politics. The interpretation of the relationship is still disputed, however (see Przeworski and Limongi 1997; and Przeworski et al. 2000).

7. A few pioneering studies did demonstrate the existence of differences in values between citizens in developing and industrialized countries (e.g., McClelland 1961).

Early modernization theorists differed from Marx in giving scant attention to the struggle among conflicting interests vested in different stages of development, or to the possibility of violence, rebellion, and revolution as means to overcome interests vested in the traditional order. Their expectations of incremental, relatively peaceful change reflected late-nineteenth-century experience in Britain and North America and were consistent with the pluralist image of politics dominant at the time. They failed to take into account the more violent and conflictual histories of most of the rest of Europe (and earlier periods in Britain and the United States), as well as the many examples of stalled or retarded development in other parts of the world. As with the diffusion hypothesis, the experience of a few developed countries made these expectations plausible, but neither the basic argument nor the mechanisms underlying it were tested. Not only was the number of cases examined small, but they were selected from among the most developed countries. As will be shown below, selecting cases for study from one end of the outcome continuum we hope to explain increases the likelihood of reaching mistaken conclusions.

The failure to subject many of the basic ideas of modernization theory to careful empirical tests had two consequences. First, those aspects of the theory that were inconsistent with reality were not winnowed out from the parts of it that, fifty years later, continue to structure our thinking about development. Second, anomalies that might have led to abandonment of some ideas and minor revision of others could instead be interpreted as challenging the whole paradigm. Because there was no large barrier of supportive empirical findings to be gotten over before jumping to that conclusion, the discovery of some anomalies led to the repudiation of the whole paradigm by most scholars in the field. The intellectual rejection of the paradigm also helped legitimize the abandonment by policymakers in most developing countries of economic policies supported by neoclassical economic theory.

Challenges to modernization theory arose as a result of observations by scholars from developing countries and by Northern scholars engaged in research in these countries. The "modernization" that the theory sought to explain did not seem to be occurring. Instead of a new crop of prosperous and democratic societies, observers saw what they interpreted as the stunted and malformed offspring of a careless and exploitative intercourse between advanced and backward nations.

The uneven diffusion of innovations from advanced to developing countries had a number of consequences unforeseen by modernization theorists. Modern industrial techniques implanted in enclaves by foreign investors failed to spread to the rest of the economy. Agricultural production for the domestic market trailed behind industrialization and urbanization, leading to pressure on food supplies and an increasing dependence on imported food. Industry drew too little labor out of the unproductive agricultural sector to improve the distribution of income, and the income gap between the rural poor and the rest of society increased. Economic growth failed to generate adequate self-sustained domestic investment, and consequently developing countries remained dependent on foreign sources of capital and technology. Continued dependence on imports led to recurrent and increasingly serious balance of payments crises. The spread of medical innovations without compensating increases in agricultural productivity led to fears of deepening poverty as population outstripped growth. These things were happening as modernization theorists were producing and disseminating their ideas, but the unexpected outcomes were not incorporated into revised theories because so few of the early theorists engaged in careful efforts to test their ideas.

In the political sphere, military interventions and the consolidation of single-party rule outpaced the creation of stable democracy. The introduction of Northern political forms into societies in which traditional modes of personal and political interaction still prevailed resulted in political systems characterized by nepotism, corruption, and clientelism even where democracy maintained a tenuous hold. In many countries, the line between public and private resources seemed hopelessly blurred.

Scholars doing field research in particular countries noticed these developments and reported them in case studies that are still among the most useful sources of information about those times and places. Since research norms at the time did not stress the importance of testing theories across a range of cases, however, their insights made little impression on those producing high theory.

The very real ills afflicting developing countries discredited the benign expectations of modernization theory. The observation that many of the predictions associated with the modernization paradigm were not being fulfilled—when this realization finally filtered into the halls of North American academe—left the paradigm vulnerable to overthrow by a new approach that was, like the ancien régime, logically coherent, plausible, in tune with its times, and untested: dependency theory.

Dependency theory turned modernization theory on its head. It attributed development problems to the consequences of integration into the international capitalist economy and to exploitation by foreign economic and political interests. Dependency theorists hypothesized two broad causes of economic difficulties: impersonal economic forces arising from the dependent country's position in the international economy; and the pursuit of their own interests in opposition to national interests by transnational corporations and their domestic allies (see, e.g., Sunkel 1972, 1973; dos Santos 1970; Frank 1967, 1970; Cardoso 1973b; and Brown 1963).

The characteristics of a backward country's position in the international economy that *dependencistas* assumed to be detrimental to development included disadvantageous terms of trade for raw materials (Prébisch 1950; Cardoso and Faletto 1979, 155), excessive vulnerability to changes in international prices of their few exports, and reliance on few trading partners and suppliers of aid, investment, and loans.

Dependency theory assumed a conflict between the interests of transnational corporations and the developmental needs of host countries. Often, *dependencistas* pictured transnationals and their host-country allies as the organizations and individual actors through whom international economic forces influenced domestic economic outcomes. Within the dependency paradigm, slow growth, bottlenecks in the economy, continued dependence, and balance of payments crises were attributed to the resource drain resulting from such transnational practices as repatriation of profits, transfer pricing, preference for imported over domestic inputs, and the maintenance of a monopoly on new techniques and the development of innovations (Baran 1957; Evans 1979, 19–38; Leys 1974, 8–18).

Dependency theory relied on the structuralist critique of neoclassical economics for economic theory and interpretations. Central to the structuralist critique is the claim that the distribution of the gains from trade between more and less developed economies disadvantages the less developed (Prébisch 1950; Singer 1950). The fundamental mode of analysis used by *dependencistas* draws on Marx; dependency theory treats classes as the most salient social actors and class struggle as the means through which political change occurs. Its view of the international economy descends from writings on imperialism by early neo-Marxists (e.g., Lenin [1916] 1968).

Much of the evidence supporting these arguments was anecdotal. Where they were supported by quantitative evidence, analysts inferred far more than the data would actually support. The famous Prébisch thesis, for example, is supported empirically by a time series showing Argentine terms of trade during several decades when the international price of wheat, Argentina's main export, was falling. From the experience of one country, exporting a handful of agricultural products during one time period, came the argument that the terms of trade for primary products as a general category were falling and that international trade generally disadvantaged the exporters of such products. Analysts failed to notice disconfirming empirical studies.[8]

The anomaly that eventually undermined the early stagnationist version of dependency theory came not from scholarly studies but from events in the real world too large for the next generation of scholars to ignore. The early dependency paradigm achieved its greatest influence during the 1960s and early 1970s, precisely when most developing countries—contrary to the theory's expectations—were growing rapidly. Between 1960 and 1979, the yearly GNP growth rate in Latin America, whose experience had spawned the dependency argument, averaged 3.3 percent per capita. This compares favorably with an average in the industrialized countries (excluding Japan) during the same period of 2.9 percent per capita.[9] Moreover, since the rate of population growth in Latin America was two to three times as high as in the industrialized countries, the difference in absolute as opposed to per capita growth rates was much greater.

In other words, the stagnation and slow growth that early dependency theory had sought to explain had certainly vanished from Latin America, if it had ever existed. Postindependence growth rates in sub-Saharan Africa came closer to fulfilling the

8. Other studies show that the terms of trade for raw materials vary depending on which time period and which commodities are examined. The international economy does not invariably disadvantage the producers of primary products (Gonçalves and Barros 1982; Brown 1974, 242–48; Haberler 1961, 275–97). A review of most of the early quantitative attempts to test arguments subsumed under the label *dependency theory* can be found in McGowan and Smith (1978).

9. These figures were calculated from data in World Bank (1981, 134–35).

expectations of the dependency/neocolonialist arguments. The average annual per capita increase in GNP between 1960 and 1979 (excluding South Africa) was only 1.6 percent there—low by international standards for that time period. Nevertheless, even in Africa, positive per capita growth rates disconfirmed the more extreme stagnationist predictions. Meanwhile, several trade-dependent Asian countries were growing at remarkable rates. Those who had proposed the early dependency arguments had failed to do rudimentary fact checking, and many scholars in the comparative development field accepted their knowledge claims despite the paucity of systematic evidence to support them.

In response to the incontrovertible evidence of growth in most developing countries, dependency theory was revised. Industrializing countries continued to experience very serious economic and political problems despite respectable growth rates, and dependency theorists were understandably reluctant to abandon such an intuitively appealing and deductively compelling set of ideas. Practitioners modified dependency-influenced arguments and used them to explain erratic and crisis-ridden growth, a dual economy resulting in unequal distribution, political instability, and authoritarianism.

Analysts working in the dependency tradition argued that the "structural" causes of inflation and balance of payments crises inhere in the dependent relationship. Inflation, in the structuralist view, stems largely from two phenomena: reliance on the export of primary products to earn foreign exchange, and the existence of a dual economy in the developing country. Reliance on primary product exports, they contend, carries inflation into the domestic economy and causes balance of payments problems as a result of deteriorating terms of trade and because primary products are subject to very wide and rapid international price swings.

Dependencistas linked the development of the dual economy to the history of foreign domination of production and trade in dependent countries. The defining features of a dual economy include low productivity in a large traditional agricultural sector and a severely skewed income distribution. The traditional agricultural sector appears to ignore market incentives. In consequence, food production lags behind industrialization, urbanization, and population growth. The increased food imports that then become necessary contribute to the balance of payments problem. Profits in the traditional agricultural sector, which should contribute to capital accumulation, remain low. The skewed distribution of income contributes to the balance of payments problem by intensifying the demand for luxury consumption goods, which, even if manufactured inside the country, use imported inputs, imported technology, and imported capital. Dependency theory blamed the persistence of these problems, despite rapid industrial growth, on the prevalence of foreign corporations in the economies of the dependent countries (Sunkel 1973; Cardoso 1973a, 146–48).

Most of these arguments were supported by illustrations rather than tests. A small number of cross-national statistical studies did confirm claims that economic dependence caused skewed income distribution and other problems (Chase-Dunn 1975; Bornschier, Chase-Dunn, and Rubinson 1978), but, as with earlier dependency theory, cross-national studies that challenged the implications of the revised dependency paradigm were ignored (e.g., Kaufman et al. 1975; McGowan and Smith 1978; Jackman 1982). In fact, some prominent dependency theorists rejected the idea that testing was possible or desirable (Cardoso 1977).[10]

When developing countries fell victim to dictatorship, *dependencistas* and others influenced by their work blamed authoritarianism on conditions peculiar to dependent countries' interaction with the international capitalist economy. Several arguments were advanced linking authoritarianism to dependency. The best known, often called the bureaucratic-authoritarian model, hypothesized that late, dependent industrialization differed from industrialization in the early modernizers in that it encompassed two distinct economic-political stages: an easy phase of import substitution based on the production of relatively simple consumption goods, during which the amount of capital needed to industrialize is small; and a "deepening" phase, when the demand for simple consumption goods has been met and opportunities for further import-substitution industrialization lie in the production of goods requiring much larger infusions of capital. During the easy phase of industrialization, relatively small capital requirements allow workers to share the benefits of growth and

10. Duval (1978) argues that Cardoso and others who make similar statements mean that the situation of dependency (an unequal exchange relationship) determines the domain of a set of arguments, but that dependence itself should not be treated as a variable within arguments. Thinking of dependency theory in this way, however, does not imply that the arguments expected to apply within the domain should not be tested.

participate in the inclusive political systems that result. As the easy phase is exhausted and capital needs become more urgent, however, the interests of owners and workers diverge. Capitalists then support exclusionary authoritarian regimes that can repress unions and suppress wages in order to accumulate capital more rapidly (O'Donnell 1973).

The interest of domestic capitalists in wage reduction coincides with the interest of foreign corporations in a concentrated income distribution, which creates a larger market for their upper-income consumer products (Cardoso 1973a). Fear of communism gives the military an interest in repressing working-class political mobilization and encouraging capital accumulation in order to increase the growth rate. Growth is doubly desired by the military. On the one hand, it is expected to undercut the appeal of communism to the poor; on the other hand, it is expected to lead to higher geopolitical status and a more secure base of military power (Stepan 1971).

This convergence of interests provides the basis for a coalition of the domestic bourgeoisie, the international bourgeoisie, and the state—dominated by the military and technocrats—that supports the bureaucratic-authoritarian regime and its policies (Evans 1979). The bureaucratic-authoritarian argument thus offers an explanation for why several of the more advanced developing countries succumbed to authoritarianism in the 1960s and 1970s, when modernization theory would have predicted an increased likelihood of democracy. In contrast to much that had gone before it, O'Donnell's elaboration (1973) of the bureaucratic-authoritarian argument did not select cases for examination from only one end of the outcome continuum: he compared countries that had experienced military intervention with countries that had not. He also showed evidence of various kinds to support his critique of modernization theory. This more rigorous research design greatly increased the persuasiveness of his argument. Though based on the experience of a small number of Latin American countries, the study was quite methodologically sophisticated. Many viewed it as a definitive disconfirmation of modernization theory.

As can be seen even in this very incomplete sketch of scholarship influenced by the dependency paradigm, this set of ideas was remarkably fruitful. By the early 1980s, however, a plethora of inconvenient facts had forced themselves on scholars' attention. For neo-*dependencistas,* the most inconvenient facts came from the Asian newly industrializing countries, which, despite being among the most dependent in the world, had experienced about twenty years of rapid, relatively stable growth unmarred by the severe inflationary and balance of payments crises that plagued other developing countries. What's more, they had increased agricultural productivity and maintained relatively equitable income distributions while doing so.

Meanwhile, the bureaucratic-authoritarian argument also faced a challenge: bureaucratic authoritarianism was vanishing. The original bureaucratic-authoritarian regimes were experiencing rapid democratization even though the capital squeeze that had been proposed as the underlying cause of their emergence had become far worse in the early eighties.

Causes of the Fragility of Theories and Paradigms

The main reason these appealing theories and paradigms were discarded in such rapid succession is, I argue, the unfortunate failure of many comparativists working on developing areas to make use of all available information in the formulation of theories in the first place, together with the willingness of consumers to accept theories without strong supporting evidence. Let me reiterate that the problem is not that new theories and paradigms supersede old ones as new information becomes available. That is the normal way the accumulation of knowledge progresses. Nor is it that researchers working in earlier decades failed to make use of analytical tools that have only more recently become widely used. Rather, it is that a bit more simple fact checking prior to the dissemination of theories and a bit more skepticism on the part of consumers of theoretical ideas prior to acceptance could have made possible more careful decisions about which theories to reject and thus a more rapid development of knowledge. Perhaps we could have sifted through these ideas in a few years rather than taking decades to do it. The parts of modernization theory that now appear robust might have remained standing during the heyday of dependency theory—as might the parts of dependency theory that may yet return to claim our attention, though they now lie discarded along the road to the Washington consensus.

Analysts did not ignore evidence, but they used it selectively to develop, support, or test theories. Many of the arguments within the modernization paradigm, for example, used evidence from only a few North Atlantic countries. Early versions of dependency theory, which sought to explain stagnation in developing countries, ignored readily available evidence of rapid growth. Later extensions of dependency theory recognized that growth was occurring but ignored evidence from East Asia of growth without most of the crises and distortions associated with development in Latin America and Africa. Few scholars working on these issues either collected systematic evidence on the actual performance of countries in different situations or used such evidence as had been assembled by others.

The general inattention to evidence slowed down the emergence of a better understanding of economic development that might have usefully informed policy choice. It caused a failure to notice that policies commonly pursued as part of government strategies to foster industrialization actually caused many of the economic problems characteristic of late developing economies. Overvalued exchange rates, used to transfer resources from the agricultural to the industrial sector, caused recurrent balance of payments crises and decreased production for export. High tariffs encouraged the growth of internationally uncompetitive manufacturing sectors. Urban bias in policies aimed at fostering industrialization worsened income distribution. By the late 1960s, some development economists understood the connection between import-substitution development strategies and these unintended consequences, and their arguments were readily available to political scientists in published sources—though these arguments too were untested—(e.g., Hirschman 1968; Fishlow 1971; Leff 1968, 77–88; Kuczynski 1977). Yet arguments in the dependency tradition continued to attribute these problems to structural features of the relationship between late developing countries and the international capitalist economy, and arguments in the modernization tradition continued to attribute developmental difficulties to culture. Because governments were assumed in both traditions to reflect societal interests, government actions and their consequences rarely became the focus of research.

As Robert Merton (1957, 16) observes, a paradigm can be transformed "from a sociological field-glass into a sociological blinker" (cf. Kuhn 1970). Observers may note the existence of some trait or phenomenon, describe it, perhaps discuss it at length in an ad hoc way, but never incorporate it or its implications into theories, because in the context of the prevailing paradigm it is considered epiphenomenal or unimportant.

Such was the case for both modernization and dependency

theorists who failed to treat systematically the effects of government policy on economic performance, even though everyone recognized that nearly all Third World governments intervened heavily in their economies. Scholars described at length government efforts to promote development. Descriptions of policies and their effects figure prominently in numerous case studies of developing countries. Observers also recognized that the interests and ideologies of state leaders affected the content of these policies and thus the distribution of the fruits of growth to various groups. Both paradigms, however—drawing on pluralist and Marxist worldviews, respectively—assumed that these state interests and ideologies reflected societal interests. Hence, many observations languished as untheorized descriptions.

Analysts from both schools, for example, interpreted populist policies as reflecting the distribution of societal interests at the stage of development when the working and middle classes had reached significant size but could not yet threaten the most fundamental economic interests of property holders (e.g., di Tella 1965; Weffort 1965; Ianni 1968; Cardoso and Faletto 1979). Several studies described the role of parties and individual political leaders in shaping and mobilizing the expression of popular-sector interests (e.g., Powell 1971; Skidmore 1967; Collier and Collier 1979). But these descriptions did not find a place in dominant theories. Instead, theories continued to emphasize structural causes—especially the growth of the popular sector associated with industrialization—as leading more or less automatically to government decisions to embrace particular development strategies.

When the economic outcomes that resulted from policies apparently designed to appeal to the interests that made up the populist coalition failed to deliver all the benefits expected, causes for this failure were sought either in culture traits thought to be inhospitable to economic endeavor, or in the machinations of foreigners and small but powerful domestic interest groups able to pursue their goals through informal or corrupt means. The possibility that economic difficulties could be caused by honest policy mistakes was not seriously considered. Nor was the possibility that the political realm has a systematic rationality of its own, partly independent of societal economic interests. Consequently, although "the state" figured in many dependency-influenced arguments as the enforcer of the "pact of domination" (Cardoso 1973a) or as a coalition partner with dominant interests during periods of authoritarianism (Evans 1979; O'Donnell 1979), few political scientists made any effort to assess the independent effect of state policies on economic outcomes. Instead, most analysts seem to have uncritically accepted governments' claims that import-substitution industrialization strategies served a national interest in development.

Of course, one of the purposes of theory is to simplify the world and direct attention to some phenomena while leaving others in obscurity. Understanding is impossible without such simplification, and the theories embedded in the modernization and dependency paradigms did not differ from other theories in providing it. When theories are tested and found wanting, however, analysts feel driven to search for other explanations of the outcomes the theory had seemed to explain. In the course of this search for alternative explanations, they try out the explanatory potential of other phenomena they have noticed. If students of developing countries had been more fully engaged in the normal-science routine of proposing hypotheses, testing them with evidence, revising or replacing initial hypotheses, testing again, revising or replacing again, and so on, they might well have taken seriously the relationship between government policy and economic outcomes much earlier. The real point, then, is that if analysts follow the standard prescriptions of research design, paradigms can serve as blinkers only temporarily.

In this book I focus on research norms, but of course ideology, preconceptions, and aesthetics also contribute to the disregard for available information. As numerous indignant observers have pointed out, the ideological dispositions of scholars play a role in determining which theories they find inherently plausible. Modernization theory had considerable intuitive appeal for many North American social scientists but seemed ethnocentric, condescending, and disingenuous to many Third World scholars, who saw it as a rationalization for an exploitative international division of labor. Dependency theory, in contrast, which placed the blame for underdevelopment on the shoulders of exploitative external forces, held much more appeal for many in the Third World. As Robert Tucker (1969) noted, Marx's most powerful image of society as polarized between the property-owning few and the immiserated masses has much more resonance for Third World observers who live in societies that approximate this description than for citizens of advanced industrial societies, who have greater familiarity with more complex class structures.

In short, the intuitive, emotional, and ideological appeals of different theories certainly increase their persuasiveness among different groups. When a theory fits with personal experience, preconceptions, and ideology, it seems highly plausible. Scholars feel less motivated to go to the trouble of digging up facts to confirm such a congenial theory and, as a result, fail to unearth the facts that would disconfirm it. Stronger research norms in the profession, however, would reduce the effects of ideology on scholarship. Although, as Dick Sklar has noted, theories are conceived in ideological sin rather than scientific virtue,[11] norms of testing and replication would cause the rapid abandonment of theoretical ideas inconsistent with evidence.

A research community that rewarded the creation of theory but also had strong traditions of testing claims against the best available information—and of systematically collecting the evidence needed to do so—would not so easily be led astray by elegant and ideologically appealing but also, unfortunately, wrong theories. Such a community would be more receptive to evidence when it surfaced, from whatever source. In short, although ideology and taste will always play an important role in scholarship, strong research norms can keep their influence within bounds.

The Uncertain Future of the Field

For the last decades, no paradigm in the sense used here has prevailed in the subfield of comparative development. Instead, multiple "approaches" compete for adherents. The distinction I am making here between a paradigm and an approach hinges on the role of explanatory hypotheses in each. A paradigm, as I have used the term here, is a set of more or less consistent theories and hypotheses that explain various aspects of reality and which, taken together, form a coherent worldview.

In contrast, an approach involves, first, a claim that certain factors—for example, states, classes, or political leaders—deserve attention, without articulating specific hypotheses about them; and, second, the belief that certain research methodologies are the most useful and appropriate means of gaining understanding. I would, for example, call historical institutionalism (sometimes called the new institutionalism), with its emphasis on

11. Personal communication. For an elaboration of his views, see Sklar (2002).

the importance of the state and other institutions and its advocacy of the comparative historical method, an approach rather than a paradigm. It identifies entities to examine and privileges certain techniques for doing so, but the hypotheses advanced about different aspects of reality need not form a coherent whole. Rational choice is also an approach. It emphasizes the centrality of individual actors and assumes they pursue their goals rationally, given a particular political and institutional context. Its favored research style involves an initial elaboration of the deductive logic expected to determine individual behavior, followed by an empirical investigation of whether individuals actually behaved as expected. Rational choice is not a paradigm, as the term has been used here, and certainly not a theory, because it includes uncountable numbers of hypotheses and theories, many of which are inconsistent with each other.[12]

The current multiplication of approaches can be traced to two causes: the disconfirmation of many of the central arguments of earlier paradigms; and the emergence in the world of urgent questions that so far have seemed inexplicable by the kind of simple, elegant theories on which successful paradigms rest.

As factual knowledge accumulates, it becomes harder and harder to come up with simple theories to explain the kind of large-scale, long-term outcomes on which comparative politics has traditionally focused. Advocates of comparative historical sociology accept this and, in consequence, defend complicated, highly contingent, inelegant explanations as the only kind likely to reflect accurately the causal complexity of the world. In my judgment, this position is tantamount to giving up on the "science" in our ambitious name for ourselves; I do not think we should settle for such a compromise.

We cannot avoid this compromise, however, unless we are willing to change some of our traditional practices. The difficulty accumulating theoretical knowledge will continue to plague us as long as we ignore the basic principles of research design. Although much of this book focuses on the concrete details of empirical research, its primary goal is to aid theory building.

A new theory is like a river in spring. Rushing down from the high ground, it cuts a narrow channel through the wilderness of

12. One of the oddities of Green and Shapiro's critique (1994) of rational choice is that they sometimes treat it quite literally as a single theory and thus believe that if a particular rational choice hypothesis is disconfirmed, analysts should reject all possible rational choice hypotheses.

complexity. When it encounters factual obstacles too large to sweep along, it should be diverted into a new, equally rapid and narrow course. In our subfield, however, old theories, modified by many collisions with inconvenient facts, are like rivers that have reached the delta after crossing a broad, flat plain. They dissipate into numerous small channels meandering through swamp until they merge gradually and imperceptibly into the "wide Sargasso Sea" of thick description. Better research practices offer a way out of the swamp.

Plan of the Book

Traditionally, comparativists have been fascinated by big questions of immense real-world importance such as what causes democratization, economic development, or ethnic conflict. These are the questions that attracted most of us into the field. The choice of a big question for study does not translate automatically into a feasible research design, however. Chapter 2 deals with the relationship among questions of interest, research strategy, and theory building. Among the methodological practices that most impede the development of a body of theoretical knowledge in comparative politics, I argue, is our standard approach to explaining these big, complicated outcomes. I suggest an alternative approach. When trying to get some theoretical leverage on compound outcomes (otherwise known as big questions), it is often more useful to divide the big question into the multiple processes that contribute to it and propose explanations for the separate processes rather than the compound outcome as a whole. Implications drawn from the explanations proposed can then be tested. Another way of putting this idea into words is to say that although multiple regression is an excellent tool for testing hypotheses, it is not always a good image to have in mind when trying to explain something complicated, because it focuses attention on the identification of causal factors rather than on how the causal factors work. Chapter 2 articulates a strategy for approaching big questions that focuses on the theorization of the multiple processes that combine to produce complex, world-changing events. It then uses an extended example to demonstrate how implications can be drawn from such theorizations and then tested.

Another of the methodological practices that impede the accumulation of knowledge is the selection of cases on the dependent variable—that is, choosing cases for study that have all experienced the outcome of interest, or that cluster at one end of the possible outcome continuum, rather than selecting cases that have experienced the full range of possible outcomes so that they can be compared. No amount of evidence gathered from cases selected on the dependent variable will confirm most hypotheses (King, Keohane, and Verba 1994). Chapter 3 deals with case selection and related issues. It demonstrates how selection bias has affected the conclusions in several well-known studies. It also discusses issues related to selection bias that can arise in time series and longitudinal case studies. The final section of the chapter shows how regression to the mean—the inadvertent selection bias that occurs when only cases at the extreme end of some continuum of interest experience some event—can affect research conclusions in comparative politics.

Most of the examples in chapter 3 and elsewhere use quantitative forms of evidence to demonstrate the claims I make. I use quantitative evidence because it often makes a point especially clear, not because I think this form of evidence is always superior to nonquantitative forms. In advocating greater attention to research design and hypothesis testing, I am not suggesting that all comparativists can or should become number crunchers. In fact, chapter 4 explicitly focuses on nonquantitative hypothesis testing.

Chapter 4 demonstrates how to use the kind of evidence found in case studies to test arguments. It also discusses deriving criteria from the argument itself for setting the boundaries of the universe of cases within which an argument should apply. It delves into the intricacies of operationalizing complicated concepts that have been expressed only verbally in the argument being tested. In addition, it considers the criteria for selecting appropriate time periods in which to assess concepts used as variables in the argument. In many comparative historical arguments, decisions about which periods of time fit within the domain of the theory can be as difficult and contentious as decisions about operationalizing key concepts.

The emphasis throughout chapter 4 is on the thoughtful elaboration of concrete criteria for determining the cases and time periods to which an argument can be expected to apply, the concrete operationalization of concepts, and the careful delineation of categories to which nonquantitative variables are assigned. Informed scholars can disagree about such criteria, and in many situations the "correct" choice is not obvious. The criteria on which all of these decisions are based should be written down and made public along with the research conclusions, so that readers can, on the one hand, decide whether they consider the criteria appropriate and, on the other, replicate the study. Readers of the research conclusions should be able to see when and where conclusions depend on particular operationalizations and other choices, and they should be able to estimate how conclusions would be changed by modifying operationalization and classification decisions. Chapter 4 uses an extended example on party development to illustrate how this might be done.

Chapter 5 moves from issues related to the testing of theories to those related to the creation of theories. If one accepts the argument that a focus on process and on the fundamental units of action—in most cases, individuals—will increase the likelihood of accumulating a sturdy body of theory, then rational choice, among the main approaches now competing for adherents, offers a good deal of promise. I would not argue that it is an ideal approach or the only possible one, but it is both simple and well developed. It thus offers not only the shoulders of giants (or at least tall people) to stand on, but a step stool to use to get up there. Of course, rational choice arguments, like those associated with any other approach, have their characteristic limitations. They can cross the line from simple to simplistic, from "creative tautology"—in Brian Barry's words (1970)—to mere tautology. Rational choice arguments do, however, focus on individual actors. They do lead to concentration on process rather than correlations. And they do routinely generate testable propositions, even though practitioners sometimes fail to engage in the arduous work of testing, as Donald Green and Ian Shapiro (1994) have noted. For these reasons, the rational choice approach has considerable potential for leading to development of theory.[13] Chapter 5 reviews the rational choice approach, identifying the areas of inquiry in which it can be expected to offer the most and the least leverage.

The main purpose of the chapter is to introduce the basic features of the rational choice approach to comparativists who

13. Prospect theory may well supplant rational choice in time, since it combines more descriptively accurate assumptions about human motivations with deductive logic and a focus on individuals and process similar to that in rational choice. At present, however, most efforts to apply prospect theory to empirical situations in political science are at an early, ad hoc stage and are likely to remain that way for some time because of the daunting level of modeling skill needed to use it in a rigorous way.

may not have had much experience with it or who may have misconceptions about it. The chapter also reviews the many substantive areas in which rational choice arguments have been used, so that those interested will know where to find out more. I do not seek to proselytize for the rational choice approach. Instead, I use it as an example of an approach that incorporates many of the features that contribute to theoretical fruitfulness. We should keep these features in mind as we search for approaches that suit particular subjects better than rational choice does.

The choice of approach logically precedes the proposal of hypotheses and testing, though one may, of course, test hypotheses drawn from multiple approaches. If the order of chapters in this book followed this logic, the chapter on approaches would come near the beginning. I put it at the end, however, because I do not want rational choice to frame the whole book. I believe the methodological suggestions made here are relevant and useful to anyone who seeks to explain political outcomes, regardless of approach.

The book covers a narrow and perhaps idiosyncratic range of topics. Certainly there are other aspects of research design that deserve attention. I do not claim that if we follow the advice in this book, scholars in other disciplines will stop responding to the term political *science* with amusement. We have a long way to go before the wishful thinking embodied in that label approaches reality, and some believe that the aspiration displayed in that name is not only unrealistic but undesirable. For those who find "science as a vocation"[14] a compelling goal, however, the advice in this book aims to prevent casual, uninformed, or unintended ventures off the long path leading to that goal. It aims not to provide a set of clear and mechanical rules of research design, but rather to foment thoughtful and innovative ways of using the inadequate and fuzzy evidence we actually have in order to build theories.

14. "Science as a Vocation" is the title of Max Weber's inspiring essay on the pursuit of knowledge (Weber 1958, 129).

CHAPTER 2

Big Questions, Little Answers

How the Questions You Choose Affect the Answers You Get

For the scholar who wants to contribute to the accumulation of knowledge, the first step in the process is choosing a question to investigate. This chapter makes some suggestions about how to shape research questions to increase the likelihood that they will yield compelling and robust theories. The early part of the chapter is an attempt to articulate some of the values and emotions that I believe motivate good scholars. These values and emotions undergird much research, but they are rarely expressed. On the contrary, the advice given to beginning scholars often implies the opposite values. Here I discuss the role of curiosity, indignation, and passion in the selection and framing of research topics.

In the second and much longer part of the chapter, I suggest a change in the way we usually think about the kinds of big, world-transforming subjects that comparativists often choose to study. Large-scale phenomena such as democratic breakdown, economic development, democratization, economic liberalization, and revolution result from the convergence of a number of different processes, some of which occur independently from others. No simple theory is likely to explain such compound outcomes. In principle, a complex, multifaceted theory might successfully do so, but in practice the task of constructing such theories has daunted most analysts. I propose changing the way we approach these questions. Instead of trying to "explain" such compound outcomes as wholes, I suggest a focus on the various processes that contribute to the final outcome, with the goal of theorizing these processes individually and generating testable propositions about them. In contrast to much of the methodological advice given in this book, the suggestions in this chapter do not derive from the logic of quantitative research. I cannot make any claim that this research strategy is more "correct" than any other. My argument rests, rather, on the judgment that it is a more effective route to an accumulation of theoretical knowledge. The proof of the pudding is in the eating, however, and until we have some pudding, we cannot taste it. The last part of the chapter is an extended example of how to break up a big question into multiple processes, theorize one of them, and then test one of the implications of the theory thus devised.

"Science as a Vocation," Not Just a Job: Choosing a Research Topic

Students are often advised to choose research topics by looking for holes in the literature or by reading the ads in the *Personnel Newsletter* of the American Political Science Association to see what topics are hot. This advice conveys the impression that the search for research topics can and perhaps should be methodical and instrumental. This impression is false, and the advice, if followed, leads to a number of perversities: taking The Literature seriously whether it merits it or not; the selection of a topic that will become outdated before the dissertation is done; boredom.

Curiosity, fascination, and indignation should guide the choice of research topic. Emotion has been banned from most of the research enterprise, and properly so. But one place it should remain is in the choosing of research topics. The standard advice on how to choose a topic leaves out the role of such emotions as commitment, irritation, and obsession.

An especially thoughtful version of the standard advice is articulated by Gary King, Robert Keohane, and Sidney Verba (1994, 15–17), who advise students to pick topics that are important in the world and that contribute to an identifiable scholarly literature. Beginning scholars are advised to:

1. Choose a hypothesis seen as important by scholars in the literature but for which no one has completed a systematic study. . . .
2. Choose a hypothesis in the literature that we suspect is false (or one we believe has not been adequately confirmed) and investigate whether it is indeed false. . . .
3. Attempt to resolve or provide further evidence of one side of a controversy in the literature—perhaps demon-

strate that the controversy was unfounded from the start.

4. Design research to illuminate or evaluate unquestioned assumptions in the literature.
5. Argue that an important topic has been overlooked in the literature and then proceed to contribute a systematic study to the area. (16–17)

It would be difficult to disagree with any of this advice, and it is probably very useful to students in the sciencelike parts of social science. It assumes, however, that the relevant literature really does contain a considerable accumulation of theory and stylized facts. It thus fails to take into account the real state of a good deal of the literature in comparative politics. The literature on some subjects contains only a few arguments generally accepted as true; many controversies in which the hypotheses on both sides lack both clarity and strong empirical support; and large amounts of opinion and conjecture, unsupported by systematic evidence but nevertheless often referred to as theory. Such a literature creates a fuzzy research frontier. The reader finds not well-defined holes in the literature but swampy quagmires. Students who wade into these literatures often find themselves sinking into the quicksand of contested definitions and chasing after nebulous dependent variables that flit around like will-o'-the-wisps.

Consequently, good research in the field is more often motivated by curiosity about the world and intuition about cause-and-effect relationships than might be true in a field with more accumulated knowledge and a more clearly defined research frontier. Much of what is eventually judged to be exciting research in the comparative field either addresses subjects not covered in the literature or addresses old subjects in very novel ways, rather than extending the existing literature.

Contrary to the advice about looking for holes in the literature, good research in the comparative field often begins either with an intense but unfocused curiosity about why some event or process has happened or with a sense of sputtering indignation at the patent idiocy of some particular argument advanced in the literature. Sometimes political commitments or an aroused sense of injustice drive this curiosity or indignation. Potential researchers who feel little curiosity, intuition, or indignation in response to the social world and the arguments published about it should consider the possibility that they have chosen the wrong job.

The literature does play a role in the choice of a research topic, but not in the mechanical way suggested by the standard advice.

It stimulates the indignation, annoyance, and irritation that often fuel good research. When one reads an argument, finds it utterly implausible, and believes that one can find evidence to demonstrate that it is wrong beyond the possibility of refutation, one has indeed found a hole in the literature. Generally, however, these holes are not found through coolheaded searches. Instead, our gut-level response of irritation causes us to pause and notice them while we are reading for some other purpose. Moreover, such holes cannot be found unless the reader has sufficient background knowledge of facts to notice that the argument seems inconsistent with reality.

Arguments in the literature also create expectations about how events will play out in as yet unexamined cases. When we have some information about such cases that leads us to believe they may not meet expectations, our curiosity is aroused. Cases and outcomes may capture our interest because they differ from other cases or from what theory has led us to expect. Such outcomes call for explanation because they are anomalous when compared with other known or apparently understood instances. At this stage, the comparison may be entirely implicit, and the analyst may focus on the anomalous case; but without the implicit comparison, there would be no basis for considering the case interesting or puzzling.

I emphasize the emotional aspects of choosing research topics because these emotions contribute to the intense commitment to finding out what really causes things to happen that leads to good research. As Max Weber asserted, "Without this strange intoxication, ridiculed by every outsider; without this passion . . . you have *no* calling for science and you should do something else" (1958, 135).

Fostering Creativity

In the same essay, Weber also stressed the importance of the nonmethodical aspects of thought—intuition and inspiration. He emphasized the importance of having ideas, that is, of creativity:

> Certainly enthusiasm is a prerequisite of the "inspiration" which is decisive. Nowadays . . . there is a widespread no-

> tion that science has become a problem in calculation, fabricated in laboratories or statistical filing systems just as "in a factory," a calculation involving only the cool intellect and not one's "heart and soul". . . . [but] some idea has to occur to someone's mind . . . if one is to accomplish anything worthwhile. And such intuition cannot be forced. It has nothing to do with any cold calculation. (1958, 135)

Creativity is distributed as unequally among us as everything else, and very little is understood about it. Nevertheless, I believe that the way we train ourselves in graduate school and for the rest of our lives determines how much combustible material our creative sparks will find to ignite. Weber stressed that the soil in which ideas grow is normally prepared by very hard work. I will go further and suggest that some kinds of hard work are more likely to bear fruit than others.

Original ideas grow out of having individual and autonomous reactions to the world. We can have such reactions only on the basis of our own inner sense of how the world works. The task of the apprentice scholar, therefore, is to develop this inner sense. This process can be helped along in a somewhat conscious and systematic manner. Good scholarship arises from the interaction of observation and conjecture. We can intentionally increase the amount of observation we have to draw upon and thus deepen our ability to speculate fruitfully; we do this by exposing ourselves to large amounts of information, whether by wide reading about many countries and over long historical periods or via the scrutiny of masses of quantitative data. However it is done, the scholar is filling his or her stores with information within which to hunt for patterns and with which to probe the plausibility of hypotheses. I would urge all students to get into the habit of creating formal or informal "data sets," that is, collecting and storing in some place other than their own fallible brains large quantities of factual information. (For some kinds of information, Excel spreadsheets are the perfect storage medium, but in other situations there may be no substitute for old-fashioned index cards.)

The kind of information that should be collected, of course, depends on the scholar's interests. Whatever the topic, however, it is always useful to find out about it in countries and times outside one's primary area of expertise. For example, if the student's interests center on how oil wealth has affected government in Middle Eastern countries, he should also stockpile some information on forms of government and uses of oil revenues in countries of other regions. The student interested in the effects of political institutions on the development of party systems in new democracies should resist the temptation to base her speculations on the experience of the countries most thoroughly covered in the literature—for example, Chile, Argentina, and Brazil—and should make sure she knows basic facts about electoral institutions and party systems in the small, less studied countries of Latin America and, if at all possible, in the new democracies of the rest of the world.

Having this kind of factual knowledge base helps the scholar to avoid making unfounded claims about the uniqueness of particular events, processes, or countries and also to avoid mistaking the simplified portraits of events often found in the literature for realistic descriptions. Much of the literature on many subjects in the comparative field is dominated by descriptions of events in a few much-studied countries. Much of the transitions literature on Latin America, for example, focuses on Brazil, Argentina, and Chile (along with Spain). Scholars working on transitions in other parts of the world assume that this literature accurately describes the general transition experience of Latin America, but it does not. Transitions have also occurred in Bolivia, Ecuador, Paraguay, Peru, and most of Central America. In some ways, the transitions in most of these latter countries more closely resemble those of African countries than those of the more often studied and more industrialized Southern Cone countries. If one's knowledge of Latin American transitions comes solely from the best known transitions literature, conclusions about differences between Latin American transitions and those in other regions will be inaccurate. Increases in factual information, however, improve the chance of finding the patterns that really exist.

A second aid to creativity arises from becoming fluent in the use of various kinds of models. When models—even such simple ones as the prisoner's dilemma—enter our imaginative repertoires, they make possible interpretations of information that simply would not have occurred to us otherwise.

A model is a simplified representation of a process. Its purpose is to illuminate a basic logic underlying the process that might not be perceptible from observation of the entire complicated reality overlaid, as all reality is, with multitudinous irrelevant details. A good model—one that is useful, fruitful, or exciting—shows both its creator and those who are exposed to it something about the process that they had not perceived before.[1] When a model seems to fit the essential features of a situation, it enables the analyst to understand that situation more clearly and deeply than before. It also aids in communicating this understanding to others.

The collective action problem, usually expressed in purely verbal terms, is probably the best-known example of a model that simply changed the way we understand the world. Prior to the dissemination of the idea that individuals will not find it rational to expend their own resources in order to secure public goods for groups of which they are members, the failure of various disadvantaged groups to organize politically was considered puzzling. Much ink was spilled explaining false consciousness. Since Mancur Olson's very striking articulation (1965) of the collective action problem, our baseline expectations about political mobilization have been inverted. We now find it puzzling, and hence worthy of explanation, when large groups do manage to organize in order to press for some public good.

Another widely used model is the idea of evolutionary selection. The central idea here is that outcomes may occur in the absence of intentional decision making because the actors, organizations, states, parties, or other entities that fail to behave in certain ways will lose office or go out of existence. Thus the only ones that remain will be those that did behave as required, even though they may not have understood their situation or made conscious decisions about it. Probably the most famous example of the use of this logic comes from Richard Nelson and Sidney Winter (1982), who found that managers of firms do not really think much about maximizing profit. Nevertheless, they argue, firms behave as though their managers sought to maximize profit, because the firms of those managers who deviate greatly from what they would do if they were maximizing profit go bankrupt. The same logic can be used to explain the prevalence of contiguous territorial states as the main large-scale form of governance in the world today. At one time, many rulers laid claims to noncontiguous pieces of territory, and they did not decide to give up outlying bits in order to concentrate on consolidating their rule in the contiguous areas. Instead, wars, uprisings, and the

1. For an extensive and wonderfully useful discussion of models in the social sciences, see Lave and March (1975).

spread of nationalism led to the consolidation of contiguous states that were relatively large (compared to what preceded them) at the expense of smaller and more scattered ones. In other words, even though rulers may not have consciously sought to limit their domains to contiguous areas, competition among them eliminated noncontiguous areas, which were much more difficult to defend militarily, and allowed the rulers of large contiguous areas to consolidate their territorial claims at the expense of others'.

The two models described here can be applied using only words. There are many others that usually need to be expressed mathematically or graphically because the processes they examine are too complicated to be captured easily by words alone. Widely used models include divide-the-dollar games, which illuminate how different rules and time horizons affect the outcome of bargaining over distribution; signaling models, which describe the effect of costly symbolic actions on the perceptions of others; information cascades, which describe the diffusion of changes in information or perception of risk; spatial models of preferences, used to think about voting behavior, policy choice by legislators, and lots of other issues; prospect theory, which models the effect of prior gains and losses on risk aversion; and contagion models, which can be used to think about anything from the diffusion of technological innovation to the spread of religious fundamentalism. The internal logic of these models is too complicated to be fully and simply articulated in words. In such arguments, equations and graphical representations are used in addition to verbal descriptions as a way of making all aspects of the logic precise and clear.

Even if the student has no interest in becoming proficient in the use of such models, exposure to them enriches the theoretical imagination. It improves the quality of our speculations, which are, in the words of Charles Lave and James March (1975, 2), "the soul of social science."

A form of hard work that seems to me much less likely to fertilize the soil in which the imagination may grow is the kind of reading that is often considered preparation for qualifying exams. Being able to read the introductions and conclusions of "great books" in order to summarize the main argument in a few sentences is a skill in its own right, a skill often rewarded in graduate school. But it does not seem to be correlated with the ability to do imaginative research.

When one reads, whether in preparation for qualifying exams or not, one should ponder and even brood over the discussions of *why* one thing causes another. This, not the simple identification of cause and effect, is the crux of a work of scholarship, and the reader needs to think about whether it rings true, whether it fits with what he thinks he already knows about the world. If individuals are not the unit of analysis in the argument, it is very useful to think through which individuals would have to be motivated, in what way, and to do what in order for the argument to hold. If individuals are the main actors in the argument, it is useful to ask oneself whether the motivations implied by the argument seem to be plausible accounts of how, on average, people behave.

Readers should also scrutinize the evidence the author offers to support the argument. They should never accept an author's assertion that evidence supports the claims made without looking at the evidence and thinking about it. One cannot assess the evidence supporting arguments without reading the middle parts of books. If one does not have time to read everything one should—and one never does—it is better to read carefully what one can of the evidence than to read only the introduction and conclusion for a summary of the argument.

Although it is all-important to absorb both information about the world and models of how information can be organized and interpreted, this is not enough. Scholars must also constantly, though often implicitly, ask themselves the question, What do I think? Do I believe this? Students cannot develop an autonomous reaction to the world by constantly worrying about what others think. They must worry about what they think themselves, and make sure they think something. The vocation of science is not for the other-directed. The gradual accretion of thoughts entertained in response to information and models will be the basis of one's own creative ideas and scientifically important discoveries.

The Mentor's Role

I turn now to the delicate subject of mentors. Having an apprentice relationship with an experienced scholar can be a very useful training experience. The student can learn how a seasoned scholar approaches intellectual puzzles and how to make practical use of the statistical and modeling tools acquired in classes. Typically, an experienced researcher has figured out, stumbled on, and borrowed lots of tricks and efficiencies over the years that can be passed on to students. The student also gains professional socialization and sometimes a leg up in the job market via coauthored publications. These are the advantages of a close mentoring relationship, and they are very substantial.

The mentoring relationship can be intellectually seductive to the student, however. Graduate students, like the peasants described by James Scott (1976), feel powerless in an unpredictable world. Among other survival strategies, students often attempt to cultivate patron-client relationships with faculty members, who they hope can protect them from the various hazardous forces of nature they face.[2] In this environment of situationally induced dependence, students may become so imbued with the mentor's worldview and research project that they dismiss evidence that conflicts with the mentor's arguments. Students may even experience something akin to hostage syndrome, in which they come to identify completely with the mentor's point of view, feeling that all the adviser's opponents and all other ways of thinking are wrongheaded or even contemptible. Such narrow-minded partisanship is a rather common but perverse result of the mentoring relationship. Students should guard against it, and mentors should make all possible efforts to limit students' natural impulse toward partisanship. When students rely so heavily on the mentor, they may be unable to conceive of research projects other than subsets of the mentor's research.

Advisers may, through inertia or inattention, seem to want students to defer to all their ideas, but what good advisers really want is for their students to be unafraid to challenge them in sophisticated and well-informed ways. The best scholars are not the best research assistants in graduate school, but rather those who challenge, extend, and go beyond their teachers, and good advisers know that.

By the dissertation stage, a student should be perched on the mentor's shoulder, having absorbed what the mentor has to teach and poised to take off in independent flight. He should not be huddled under the mentor's protective wing. It is part of the mentor's job to push reluctant fledglings out of the nest if necessary.

Just as young people in the West do not allow their parents to

2. Students also make use of the "weapons of the weak" noted by Scott—gossip, slander, ostracism, and shirking—to punish the village notables who fail to perform their allotted roles in the departmental moral economy.

choose mates for them, students should not allow advisers to choose their dissertation topics. They should listen carefully to the adviser's advice, as one listens to parental advice, but ultimately the scholar must feel an intense fascination in order to sustain the commitment needed for such a massive research endeavor. The average comparativist lives with a dissertation topic for between eight and twenty years, from starting to think about it to publication of the dissertation-book and possible spin-offs and extensions. That is as long as many marriages last. Many comparativists continue working on their dissertation subject for the rest of their careers. No one but the person who will be putting in this massive amount of time and effort is really qualified to choose the subject.

Romantic Questions, Reliable Answers

Having allowed passion, fascination, or indignation to influence the choice of topic, the researcher then faces a very different kind of task: devising a research strategy. Many of the classic works in the comparative field focus on big, romantic questions, and the same kinds of questions draw many into the field. The choice of a strategy for investigating such topics requires methodical thought as well as romantic attraction. Outcomes such as democratization, the collapse of empires, and revolution result from the convergence of a number of different processes, some of which may occur independently of others. Insufficient attention to research strategy when approaching such big questions accounts for quite a few sand castles.

Because the complex outcomes are rare and undertheorized, inductive research strategies prevail. Either researchers immerse themselves in the history and social structure of a few cases that have experienced the outcome of interest and come up with a list of events and characteristics that predate the outcome, or they cull indicators of potential causes from large public data sets and plop them into statistical models. Thus, the implicit or explicit model of explanation, even for those who reject quantitative research, turns out to be a kitchen-sink regression. But correlation is not causation, even in nonquantitative research.

At its best, this unstructured inductive approach to investigating complex social outcomes is analogous to that of medical researchers who try to understand the onset of cancer by amassing data on all the dietary and environmental factors that correlate with an increased incidence of the disease. These studies are useful. They lead to the accumulation of hypotheses, some of which are ultimately confirmed and some not. "But though this sort of fact-collecting has been essential to the origin of many significant sciences," Thomas Kuhn notes that anyone who examines famous instances of pretheoretic work "will discover that it produces a morass" (1970, 16). It does not by itself lead to an understanding of the process through which cancer develops. For that, researchers have had to step back from the aggregate outcome, the diseased person, and focus instead on basic mechanisms—for example, the factors that regulate cell division and death. They must concentrate on the units within which the process occurs (the cell and the gene) rather than on the outcome (the diseased organism).

In a similar manner, students of comparative politics need to seek to understand underlying political processes rather than to "explain," in the sense of identifying the correlates of, complex outcomes. What I am proposing here bears a resemblance to the research strategy that Robert Bates et al. have called analytic narratives. I concur with their belief that we need to

> seek to locate and explore particular mechanisms that shape the interplay between strategic actors and that thereby generate outcomes. [We need to] focus on the mechanisms that translate such macrohistorical forces into specific political outcomes. By isolating and unpacking such mechanisms, analytic narratives thus contribute to structural accounts. (1998, 12–13)

In order to unpack these mechanisms, we need to focus on the fundamental unit of politics, in most cases individuals. We need to break up the traditional big questions into more precisely defined questions about what individuals do in specific situations that recur often enough to support generalizations about them. I depart from Bates et al., however, in that I see "analytic narratives" as an essential part of the research enterprise, but not its end product. A carefully constructed explanatory argument built up from fundamentals usually has multiple implications, at least some of which are testable. The research effort is not complete until empirical tests have shown that implications drawn from the argument are consistent with reality.

Figuring out the implications of an argument involves repeatedly asking, "If this argument were true, what would I see in the real world?" Some scholars seem impelled by intuition to engage in this kind of reasoning, but anyone can train himself to do it as part of a regular routine. To demonstrate deriving implications from an argument, let us use Barrington Moore's famous aphorism "no bourgeois, no democracy"[3] (1966, 418) as a simple example. Since there are no contemporary societies that are literally without a bourgeoisie, and since the aphorism is stated in absolutes but the world is probabilistic, it can be restated in social sciencese as: "The likelihood of democracy increases once the size of the bourgeoisie has passed a certain threshold." If *bourgeois* is taken to refer to the commercial and industrial bourgeoisie but not government bureaucrats, the implications of this argument include the following:

- Democracies would not be expected to occur before the industrial and commercial revolutions.
- The establishment of democracies would be expected first in the countries that industrialized first.
- In the contemporary world, democracy would be more likely in more industrialized countries.
- Democracy would be less likely in countries in which wealth comes mainly from the export of mineral resources (because comparative advantage might be expected to reduce industrial investment).
- The likelihood of democracy would decline as state ownership of economic resources rose.
- Democracy would be less likely in countries in which foreigners or pariah capitalists excluded from the political community own most enterprises.

The point of this rather simpleminded exercise is that to test the famous aphorism, one need not count the members of the industrial and commercial bourgeoisie in each country and then correlate the count with the Freedom House democracy scale. Instead of, or in addition to, a direct test of an argument, one can figure out some of its observable implications and test them. Some of the implications of any argument will be consistent with more than one theory, but if enough implications can be drawn,

3. This academic sound bite is Moore's summary of Marx, not of his own argument. It is useful in the current context because it is so simple, not because it captures Moore's argument.

not all will be consistent with both the proposed argument and the same rival hypothesis. Although one cannot test all arguments and cannot always reject alternative interpretations for given sets of findings, one can, through tests of multiple implications, build support for a particular causal explanation one brick at a time.

If instead of the aphorism—which is itself an assertion about a correlation—I had used an argument that, like those advocated by Bates et al., showed the moving parts in the causal mechanism, the number of implications would have been multiplied. Implications can be drawn from every link in the logical chain, not just from the hypothesized relationship between initial cause and final effect. Big, romantic, untestable ideas can be made amenable to rigorous investigation by first breaking them up into their component processes and then theorizing these processes one at a time. In the example below, I demonstrate drawing implications from causal mechanisms.

Breaking up the traditional big questions of comparative politics into the processes that contribute to them would make possible the construction and testing of theories. I would not label this shift in the focus of analysis as a move from grand to mid-range theory. A persuasive theory, backed by solid evidence, about one of the several processes that combine to lead to a transformational outcome strikes me as very grand indeed.

An Example of Breaking Up a Big Question into Processes

Abstract methodological prescriptions are rarely compelling or even fully intelligible. In an effort to move from the abstract to the concrete and thus make a more persuasive argument for a change in research strategy, the rest of this chapter focuses on transitions from authoritarianism as an extended illustration of both the problems associated with big questions and the usefulness of disaggregation into multiple processes as a research strategy. It will also demonstrate the leverage that very simple models can bring to bear on a question and show the usefulness of collecting a large mass of information about a subject.

When we read research results in books and journals, we usually see only the finished product reporting the encounter between argument and evidence. Often, however, the most difficult part of research comes before any evidence is collected, during the stage when the analyst has to figure out how to think about the problem in a fruitful way. This example goes through those initial steps in considerable detail.

I chose transitions as an example because of its normative and academic importance. During recent decades, the last authoritarian holdouts in capitalist Europe, nearly all countries in Latin America and Eastern Europe, and some countries in Asia and Africa have democratized. At the beginning of 1974, the year identified by Samuel Huntington (1991) as the start of the "third wave" of democratization, dictatorships of one kind or another governed 80 countries.[4] Only 15 of these dictatorships still survived at the end of 2000. During these years, 93 authoritarian regimes collapsed (some countries endured more than one dictatorship during the period). These transitions had resulted in 40 democracies that survived at the end of 2000, some quite flawed but many stable and broadly competitive; 9 democracies that lasted only a short time before being overthrown in their turn; and 35 new authoritarian regimes, 15 of which lasted into the new millennium.[5] No one knows if these will be the last transitions for these countries, but so far, contrary to initial expectations, new democracies have proved fairly resilient. The study of these transitions has become a major focus of scholarly attention.

Some of the finest minds in comparative politics have worked on this subject. The body of literature on transitions now includes hundreds, perhaps thousands, of case studies of particular transitions, dozens of comparisons among small numbers of cases, and at least half a dozen important efforts at theoretically informed generalizations. A number of descriptive generalizations have become rather widely accepted. One example is the observation that "there is no transition whose beginning is not the consequence—direct or indirect—of important divisions within the authoritarian regime itself" (O'Donnell and Schmitter 1986, 19); a second is that pacts between competing elites facilitate the successful transition to democracy (Karl 1986, 1990; Higley and Gunther 1992).

---

4. Figures here and elsewhere in this chapter are drawn from a data set I have collected that includes all authoritarian regimes (except monarchies) lasting three years or more, in existence at any time since 1946, in countries with a million or more inhabitants. If monarchies and countries with less than a million inhabitants were included, the number of authoritarian regimes would be larger. See Geddes (1999a) for more details about the data set.

5. Outcome numbers exclude regimes in countries created as a result of border changes during transitions, thus they do not sum to 93.

These and similar inductive generalizations emerging from studies of particular groups of countries have added to our factual knowledge, and they have forced the abandonment of some dearly held preconceptions. These are important advances. Nevertheless, despite the passage of more than twenty-five years since the current wave of democratization began and the sacrifice of whole forests to the production of literature on the subject, few new theories of democratization have been created. When fine scholars—several of whom have in the past constructed theories of great elegance and plausibility—seem to have backed away from theorizing about this topic, it behooves us to think about why.

A part of the difficulty, I believe, stems from certain common choices about research design. Of the fifty-six volumes on transitions reviewed in the *American Political Science Review* between 1985 and 1995, thirty-one were studies of single countries, and many of the others were edited volumes made up of individual case studies of several countries but lacking a theoretical synthesis of the different experiences. In nearly all these books, the cases were selected on the dependent variable; that is, authors sought to explain one or more cases of political liberalization or democratization without comparing them to cases in which change had failed to occur. Many of these studies supply readers with valuable factual information, but the research design chosen prevents their authors from testing their theoretical claims.

Furthermore, in the majority of the studies, the outcome of interest (liberalization, transition, or consolidation) had not yet finished happening when the study was written. The desire of authors to write about the most important political events of the time, and of publishers to publish things at the peak of interest in them, is understandable. This rush to publish, however, has devastating effects on the accumulation of theoretical knowledge. There is no way to test causal arguments if the outcome being explained has not yet happened at the time the study is done. Becoming embroiled in controversies over the causes of something that has not happened is like arguing about what the angels dancing on the head of a pin look like without first having made sure that at least one angel really performs there.

These would be short-term problems, with theories emerging over time, if analysts continued working on the same problems after the outcomes had become clear and if readers treated very tentative conclusions with appropriate skepticism, but most do not. Around the time it became clear that transitions to democracy really had occurred in a large number of countries, many scholars shifted their attention to trying to explain the consolidation of democracy, which of course had not yet happened. Interest in transitions declined at precisely the time when enough experience had accumulated to make theory building possible.

The rush to publish is not unique to the study of regime change, of course, and thus cannot carry all the blame for its modest generation of theory. A further cause, I suggest, arises from the choice of a compound outcome—that is, an outcome that results from the confluence of multiple causal processes—as the object of study, while maintaining an approach more suited to simple outcomes.

To show exactly what I mean, in the pages that follow I develop a concrete research strategy that begins with the disaggregation of the big question—why democratization occurs—into a series of more researchable questions about mechanisms. The second step is a theorization of the specific process chosen for study—in this case, the internal authoritarian politics that sometimes lead to transition. The third step is the articulation of testable implications derived from the theorization. Decisions about the domains of different testable implications constitute the fourth step. The fifth is the actual discovery or collection of evidence on which to test the implications; the sixth is the testing itself; and the seventh is the interpretation of and response to test results.

What I am aiming for here, and in other examples in this book, is the self-conscious articulation of steps in the research process that, like the values discussed above, occur in the practice of good scholarship but are rarely described in detail. At various points, I shall step back from the description of the steps involved in setting up the research question to comment on why I made certain decisions, to mention where ideas came from, or to reiterate methodological points. The example in this chapter emphasizes steps one through three as outlined in the previous paragraph, leaving detailed discussion of issues involved in testing to later chapters.

Theory-Based Disaggregation

The first issue that confronts the researcher attempting to follow the research strategy suggested here is figuring out how to disaggregate the processes leading to the compound outcome. There will always be multiple ways to do this, some more fruitful than others. The only general advice that can be given is that the disaggregation should be based on theoretical intuition and that more than one should be tried. The paragraphs below sketch an example of the process involved based on my theoretical intuitions and fairly wide reading about transitions. Another observer's intuitions might be different and at least equally useful.

The Intuition

A regime transition is a change in the basic institutions that determine who will rule, how rulers will be chosen, and how basic distributive decisions will be made. When such a change in institutions occurs as a result of revolution or violent seizure of power, a standard way of simplifying reality for the purpose of theory building is to focus attention on the winning and losing groups in the power struggle, assuming implicitly that institutions chosen will reflect the interests of the winners and that any bargaining that occurs over institutions is bargaining over details among winners. Then, to explain such regime changes, we try to understand why groups concluded that the old regime had become intolerable and how they developed the organizational strength and popular support needed to overthrow it.

Our intuitions about regime change in general seem to derive from observing such forcible seizures of power, but these are not, as it happens, very useful for understanding most transitions to democracy. The breakdown of an authoritarian regime need not lead to democratization, but when it does, the transition involves bargaining and negotiation. Unlike revolutionary victories and authoritarian seizures of power, transitions to more participatory forms of government cannot be accomplished entirely by force, and the institutions that emerge during such transitions reflect compromises among groups, not domination by a single group. Even when the authoritarian regime is overthrown by the military, bargaining is necessary in order to complete the transition to democracy. No single group wins and imposes its institutional choices on all others. Furthermore, this bargaining occurs over a period of time, during which the identity of particular negotiators can change. Institutional changes may be accomplished in increments. It is only at the end of the process that the observer can look at the set of institutional changes and make a judgment about whether democratization has occurred. In short, bargaining over institutions is a central feature of regime change.

Several different processes can affect this bargaining. Political competition and rivalry within the authoritarian elite can cause splits that may increase the willingness of factions to bargain, as Guillermo O'Donnell and Philippe Schmitter (1986) have noted. Members of the upper class who had initially benefited from regime policies may become critical of later policies or performance and may withdraw their support and their investments, thereby destabilizing the economy and the regime. Economic crisis or some other disaster may push ordinary citizens into clamorous opposition, despite its risks. Such societal changes can strengthen opposition bargainers and weaken elites. Changes in the international economy or the influence of powerful neighbors may alter the cost-benefit calculations of both leaders and led about the feasibility of regime change. Not all these processes will be salient in every transition, but often several of them are. They may interact with each other, but they may also be independent.

The theoretical disaggregation that begins the research strategy should focus on such possibly independent processes identified by the researcher. The disaggregation I suggest places the bargaining over institutions at the center of analysis and seeks to explain how these processes affected bargaining among different actors at different times during the transition.

The Topics

With these ideas in mind, a possible set of topics would include the following:

1. The politics within authoritarian governments, that is, how political rivalries, policy disagreements, and bargaining within different kinds of authoritarian regimes affect the incentives of authoritarian rulers to liberalize[6]

6. Except for discussions of hard-liners and soft-liners who cannot be identified a priori (e.g., Przeworski 1992), this is a topic that received little attention in the early analyses of regime change. Przeworski (1991) has even asserted that characteristics of the old regime do not affect outcomes in the new one. Remmer (1989) and Bratton and van de Walle (1994, 1997), however, have argued that different kinds of authoritarian regimes dissolve in characteristically different ways, which has consequences both for the likelihood of transition and for the kind of regime likely to emerge as a result. For a review of some of these issues, see Snyder and Mahoney (1999).

2. The determinants of upper-class support for authoritarian rule and the effects of loss of such support on bargaining between government and opposition, and hence on regime maintenance[7]
3. The causes and risks of mass expressions of discontent and the influence of mass mobilization on bargaining between government and opposition[8]
4. The effect of the relationship between opposition elites and masses on bargaining between government and opposition[9]
5. The relationship among (*a*) the timing of institutional choices, (*b*) the interests of the bargainers at particular times, and (*c*) extent of democratization[10]
6. The relationship between economic modernization and citizen influence on regime choice[11]
7. The effect of international economic and geopolitical shocks on the decisions and actions of regime leaders, regime supporters, and ordinary citizens

---

7. Many case studies note the fickleness and ingratitude of bourgeois and other upper-class supporters of authoritarian regimes, along with the role these groups have played in opposition to authoritarian governments. Cardoso's study (1986) of the Brazilian bourgeoisie during democratization is one of the earliest and most insightful.

8. Many case studies describe the effect of demonstrations and other mass actions on the decisions of authoritarian rulers. In addition, several authors have emphasized the importance of popular opposition in bringing about transitions (e.g., Bratton and van de Walle 1997; Casper and Taylor 1996; Collier 1999; Collier and Mahoney 1997; Bermeo 1997). These studies are largely descriptive, however. Though initial theoretical steps have been taken from several different directions to account for why large numbers of people, after having suffered oppression and poverty for long periods of time, suddenly rise up to voice their indignation (Przeworski 1986; Geddes and Zaller 1989; Lohmann 1994), much more work remains to be done. Furthermore, to my knowledge, no one has offered a compelling explanation of why authoritarian regimes sometimes respond with coercion to mass protests and at other times hasten to compromise.

9. It should be possible to extend work on nested games (Tsebelis 1990) to deal with this subject, though adaptation will be required to accommodate the institutional fluidity characteristic of transitions.

10. Much of the work on this subject has focused on pacts (e.g., Higley and Gunther 1992; Karl 1986, 1990). This topic has only begun to be more fully and systematically explored (e.g., Przeworski 1991; Geddes 1995, 1996; Mainwaring 1994).

11. The correlation between economic development and democracy is one of the best established in comparative politics (Bollen 1979; Bollen and Jackman 1985; Przeworski et al. 2000; Burkhart and Lewis-Beck 1994; Barro 1999). The causes of this relationship, however, continue to be debated.

Though different researchers would break up the big question in different ways, any disaggregation into constituent processes should have some of the characteristics of the topics on this list. Each topic is posed as a general comparative question. We would hesitate to propose an argument about any of these topics based on the experience of only one country. Research on these topics seems, on the contrary, to demand comparison across cases. None of these topics imply selection bias, that is, none imply limiting studies to those countries that have completed transitions. All governments face opposition, and the absence of bargaining in particular times and places requires explanation; it is not a reason to exclude cases from examination. I will return to issues related to appropriate selection of cases in later chapters. For now, the important thing to note is that each topic listed here is worthy of a project in itself. When processes are described separately in this way, it becomes clear why it might be difficult to theorize transitions as a whole.

Some of these topics, especially 2 and 3, have received considerable attention in the case study literature. The next step in developing research strategies to investigate them would be to build theories that subsume and explain the observations made in the case studies. In the extended example below, I examine the first topic, to which somewhat less attention has been paid. I propose an argument about the incentives facing leaders in different kinds of authoritarianism that helps to explain, first, why some authoritarian governments initiate liberalization when they face little societal pressure to do so; and, second, why and when the factions that always exist within dictatorships may contribute to democratization. This argument thus offers an explanation for two elements in the process of regime change that a number of studies note without explaining, but it does not try to account for the final outcome of democratization itself.

A Theorization of One Process: Politics in Authoritarian Regimes

O'Donnell and Schmitter's observation (1986) about the importance of splits within authoritarian governments, noted above, alerts us to the importance of individuals near the center of power during the transition process. Although political factions and disagreements can be found within any authoritarian government,[12] *every* transition is not actually a *consequence* of "important divisions within the authoritarian regime itself" (O'Donnell and Schmitter 1986, 19). The Salazar-Caetano dictatorship in Portugal did not fall as a result of internal splits (though such splits existed, of course), unless that regime is defined as including the midlevel military officers who had spent most of their careers in Africa and who forcibly overthrew the dictatorship. Arguably, a number of other dictators (such as Somoza in Nicaragua and the Shah in Iran) fell not because of divisions within the regime itself—meaning splits among those with decision-making power—but because of desertions from the societal and military coalition originally supporting them. And, though O'Donnell and Schmitter had no way of knowing it at the time they wrote, the collapses of communist regimes in countries such as Bulgaria and East Germany were not caused by splits within the regime, unless those regimes are defined as including not only high officials of the Bulgarian and East German communist parties but also their Soviet allies. Nor, according to Michael Bratton and Nicolas van de Walle (1992, 1997), has the initiation of liberalization in many African countries been a consequence of splits internal to regimes.

It is nevertheless true that in a large number of the recent transitions from authoritarianism, the initial steps toward what became democratization were taken by those in power, for reasons internal to the ruling elite rather than in response to pressure from either supporters or opponents in the larger society. The observation of this pattern in a number of cases surprised observers who were accustomed to thinking of institutional changes as consequences of power shifts, not as the causes of them.

One of the reasons that regime transitions have proven so theoretically intractable is that different kinds of authoritarianism break down in different ways. The beginnings of some can be traced to splits within the regime, but others begin in other ways. Dictatorships can differ from each other as much as they differ from democracy, and these differences affect the way they collapse. They draw on different groups to staff government offices and on different segments of society for support. They have different procedures for making decisions, different characteris-

12. Numerous descriptions exist of factionalism within authoritarian regimes in every region of the world; see, for example, Stepan (1971); Fontana (1987); Sandbrook (1986); and Waterbury (1973).

tic forms of intraelite factionalism and competition, different ways of choosing leaders and handling succession, and different ways of responding to societal interests and opposition. Because analysts have not studied these differences systematically, what theorizing exists about authoritarian regimes is posed at a highly abstract level, and few authors have considered how characteristics of dictatorships affect transitions. These differences, however, cause authoritarian regimes to break down in systematically different ways, as I show below.

To explain the first incremental institutional changes that set some countries on the path toward democratization, we need a theory of politics within authoritarian regimes. Where do we get one? Standard theories of politics in democratic regimes begin with two simplifying assumptions: first, that officials want to remain in office; second, that the best strategy for doing so is to give constituents what they want. Much of the literature on democratic politics concerns how different political institutions affect the survival strategies of politicians. The analysis of transitions requires an analogous investigation of the effects of differences among various kinds of authoritarian institutions.

To begin the task of investigating the effects of authoritarian institutions, we need first to assess the plausibility of the standard assumptions, and then, possibly, to revise them. Most obviously, in the absence of routine ways for citizens to remove authoritarian leaders from office, empirical investigation is needed to answer questions about who exactly the constituents of dictators are, how satisfied they have to be, and what factors besides satisfaction with regime performance affect constituents' acquiescence. These questions cannot be answered in the abstract, nor can answers be assumed, as in the study of democratic politics. Topics 2, 3, 6, and 7 as outlined above deal with these issues.

Less obviously, it should not be assumed that the officers, parties, and cliques supporting authoritarian leaders always want to remain in power. Military officers, in contrast to cadres in single-party and personalist regimes, may not want to. If there are circumstances in which they can achieve their ends better while out of power, as I will argue there are, then we can expect them to return voluntarily to the barracks. Furthermore, the costs of leaving office vary for different kinds of authoritarian leaders. Military officers can return to the profession that called them in the first place, usually without suffering punishment for actions while in office. Cadres in single parties lose their monopoly on the advantages of office, but they also usually remain free to compete for office after a transition and thus to continue their chosen profession. The allies of a personalist leader, however, generally find it hard to continue the life to which they have become accustomed. Compared with other kinds of authoritarians, they are more likely to lose the opportunity for future office, and possibly also their property and lives, in the wake of a transition.

To begin building an understanding of authoritarian politics, I focus on rivalries and relationships within the entity from which authoritarian governments are drawn: the officer corps, the single party, the clique surrounding the ruler, or some combination of these. Most of the time, the greatest threat to the survival of the leader in office—though not necessarily to the survival of the regime—comes from within this ruling group, not from outside opposition. In normal times, most of what we would call politics, namely, the struggle over office, spoils, and policy decisions, takes place within this ruling group.

Politics within the ruling group tells only part of the story of regime change, but it is a part about which we understand little. Opposition from outside the ruling coalition and exogenous shocks, such as the Soviet collapse, the international economic crisis of the 1980s, and the economic reforms induced by that crisis, have affected regime survival, sometimes decisively. By focusing on the political dynamics within different kinds of authoritarian regimes, however, I aim to show why some forms of authoritarianism are more vulnerable than others to exogenous shocks and popular opposition.

The Classification of Authoritarian Regimes

Before we can use differences among authoritarian regimes as the basis for elaborating theoretical arguments about the consequences of these differences, we need to develop a simplifying classificatory scheme of regime types and clear criteria for assigning cases to categories. Without this kind of simplification of reality, we would be inundated by complexity and unable to see the patterns underlying it. The aim here is to "carve nature at its joints," that is, to find the places in the complicated whole at which elements seem to divide naturally. As with carving a chicken, we must know a fair amount about the basic structure of the beast in order to find the right places to hack. Because I consider the most important differences among authoritarian regimes to be qualitative, I create a typology for "measuring" regimes rather than a scale or index. Typologies are theoretical constructs used when variables can only be measured nominally. Like other theoretical constructs, they are useful or not useful rather than true or false. To be useful, they have to capture differences that are essential to the argument being made.[13]

In this section, I discuss the bases for assigning regimes to one category or another.[14] I initially classified regimes as personalist, military, or single-party. In military regimes, a group of officers decides who will rule and exercises some influence on policy. In single-party regimes, one party dominates access to political office and control over policy, though other parties may exist and compete as minor players in elections. Personalist regimes differ from both military and single-party in that access to office and the fruits of office depend much more on the discretion of an individual leader. The leader may be an officer and may have created a party to support himself, but neither the military nor the party exercises independent decision-making power insulated from the whims of the ruler (cf. Bratton and van de Walle 1997, 61–96; Chehabi and Linz 1998, 4–45; and Snyder 1998). I had to add intermediate categories to this classification scheme after discovering how many of the cases simply resisted being crammed into one or another of the original categories.

My initial guess about what kind of classification would best capture the important differences among authoritarian regimes grew out of reading about many such regimes. Let me again emphasize the importance of collecting information about a wide range of cases. Although I had to hunt for information in a much more systematic way further on in the research process, the initial ideas that motivated this study came from reading military sociology and descriptions of events in many countries during transitions just because I was curious.

In this classification scheme, a military regime, in contrast to a personalist regime led by a military officer, is one in which a group of officers determines who will lead the country and has some

13. Typologies have been much and justly maligned in the comparative field because their creation was at one time seen by some as an end in itself, and scholars used to waste their time comparing them and arguing about them. They have a useful role, however, as a way of categorizing causes and effects that cannot be measured using numbers.

14. The classification of individual cases is a "measurement" issue. Measurement will be discussed later in this chapter and in chapter 4. Here I am concerned with creating an overall "coding scheme."

influence on policy. In an institutionalized military regime, senior officers have agreed upon some formula for sharing or rotating power, and consultation is somewhat routinized. Examples of military regimes include that of Brazil (1964–85), in which senior officers, in consultation with a small number of civilian allies, picked each successive president in keeping with rules specified by the institutions of the authoritarian regime; and that of Argentina (1976–83), in which, despite intense factional struggle and the efforts of some military presidents to renege on precoup agreements establishing an elaborate arrangement for consultation and predictable rotation in office, senior officers did not permanently lose control of succession and policy.

Many regimes headed by a military officer are not, however, really controlled by a group of senior officers. It is common for military interventions to lead to short periods of collegial military rule followed by the consolidation of power by a single officer and the political marginalization of much of the rest of the officer corps. These are personal dictatorships, even though the leader wears a uniform. Regimes such as that of Rafael Trujillo in the Dominican Republic (1930–61) and Idi Amin in Uganda (1971–79) are somewhat extreme instances of the transformation of a military intervention into personal tyranny. Other regimes, such as that of Augusto Pinochet in Chile (1973–89) and Sani Abacha in Nigeria (1993–99), are harder to classify; the military institution retained some autonomy and influence, but the concentration of power in the hands of a single man prevents them from being categorized simply as military.[15] I classify regimes on the margin between the two categories as military-personalist hybrids.

Since most dictators form parties to support themselves, distinguishing between "real" and nominal single-party regimes involves the same difficulties as distinguishing between military regimes and personalist regimes led by military officers. In real single-party regimes, a party organization exercises some power over the leader at least part of the time, controls the selection of officials, organizes the distribution of benefits to supporters, and mobilizes citizens to vote and show support for party leaders in other ways. Examples of single-party regimes include that of the Institutional Revolutionary Party (PRI) in Mexico, the Revolutionary Party of Tanzania (CCM), and the Leninist parties in

15. This classification of Pinochet is supported by Remmer's analysis (1989) and by Huntington (1991). The classification of Abacha is supported by Obasanjo (1998).

various East European countries. Regimes in which the leader himself maintains a near monopoly over policy and personnel decisions despite the existence of a support party—such as those led by Manuel Odría in Peru and Etienne Eyadema in Togo—are personalist.

Personalist dictators range from vicious psychopaths to benevolent populists. Institutionally, what they have in common is that although they are often supported by parties and militaries, these organizations have not become sufficiently developed or autonomous to prevent the leader from taking personal control of policy decisions and the selection of regime personnel. The fear of potential rivals leads such rulers to undermine these and other institutions that might serve as power bases for potential challenges. They rely instead on informal, and sometimes quite unstable, personal networks—sometimes based on kinship, ethnicity, or region—within which particularistic favors are exchanged for support. Typically, regime personnel are rotated frequently to prevent them from developing autonomous bases of support, and erstwhile supporters who become rivals or dissidents are quickly and unceremoniously deprived of office, influence, and sometimes their lives (cf. Bratton and van de Walle 1994).

Leaders' Interests and Intraregime Politics

In order to build a theory about particular actors, one must first have some knowledge about their goals. I have argued that the goals of leaders in different kinds of authoritarian regimes typically differ from each other. In this section, I discuss their different interests and the evidence supporting my assessment of these interests.

The dictator who leads a personalist regime after having clawed his way to the top in intense and often deadly struggles among regime insiders can reasonably be assumed to have a strong and abiding determination to remain in office. No similar assumption can be made, however, about most of the officials of military regimes. Some individual leaders, especially those who have managed to scramble to the very top during the early chaos of military takeovers, undoubtedly feel as intense a desire to remain there as any other leader, but many officers do not. The discussion below describes the interests of members of the primary supporting institution or informal group in each type of regime, starting with military.

Research on the attitudes and preferences of military officers in many different societies finds that officers in different countries come from different socioeconomic, ethnic, and educational backgrounds. They have different ideologies and feel sympathetic toward different societal interests. No generalizations can be made about the societal interests or policies they are likely to support. According to the scholarly consensus, however, most professional soldiers place a higher value on the survival and efficacy of the military itself than on anything else (Janowitz 1960, 1977; Finer 1975; Bienen 1978; Decalo 1976; Kennedy 1974; Van Doorn 1968, 1969).

This corporate interest implies a concern with the maintenance of hierarchy, discipline, and cohesiveness within the military; autonomy from civilian intervention in postings and promotions; and budgets sufficient to attract high-quality recruits and buy state-of-the-art weapons. Officers also value their nation's territorial integrity and internal order, but the effective pursuit of these goals requires unity, discipline, and adequate supplies (Stepan 1971; Nordlinger 1977; Barros 1978). Such preferences might result from socialization in military schools (Stepan 1971; Barros 1978) or from a rational calculation of the effect of the health of the military institution on the officer's own career prospects. For the purposes of this study, the source of these preferences does not matter.

In countries in which joining the military has become a standard path to personal enrichment (as, for example, during some time periods in Bolivia, Nicaragua, Nigeria, Thailand, Indonesia, and the Congo), acquisitive motives can be assumed to rank high in most officers' preferences. Such motives will occupy first place for some officers and rank second or third for others, if only because the continued existence of lucrative opportunities for officers may depend on the survival of the military as an effective organization. Where acquisitive motives have swamped concern for corporate survival and effectiveness, however, the professionalism of the military deteriorates, and the officer corps is less likely to serve as a successful counterweight to ambitious political leaders.

Where corporate interests prevail, most officers agree to join coup conspiracies only when they believe that the civilian government prevents the achievement of their main goals. Many officers, in fact, will join only if they believe that the military institution itself is threatened. These preferences are consistent with the observations by Alfred Stepan (1971) and Eric Nordlinger (1977) about the importance of threats to the military as an institution in the decisions of officers to join coup conspiracies. They are also consistent with the observation that coups do not usually occur in fully professionalized armies until a consensus exists among senior officers (Stepan 1971; Valenzuela 1978), since the worst possible outcome for the military as an institution is a civil war in which part of the military fights on each side.

Consequently, the most important concern for many officers in deciding whether to join a coup conspiracy is their assessment of how many other officers will join. What Nordlinger, Stepan, and others are describing resembles a classic battle-of-the-sexes game. The insight behind this game comes from the following scenario: One member of a couple would prefer to go to a movie and the other would prefer the symphony, but each would prefer doing something together to doing something alone. Going to either event together is a potential equilibrium, but no dominant strategy exists, since the best outcome for either player always depends on what the other chooses.

The logic of decisions about seizing power or returning to the barracks is the same. Some officers always want to intervene, others have legalist values that preclude intervention except in the most extreme circumstances, and most are located somewhere in between—but almost all care most about the survival and efficacy of the military and thus want the military to move either in or out of power as a cohesive whole. Figure 2.1 depicts this set of preferences as a game.

In the figure, the two numbers in each cell represent the respective payoffs to the two factions, the first number being the payoff for the majority faction and the second number the payoff for the minority faction.[16] In the game depicted, the majority prefers that a united military remain in the barracks. The payoffs to both factions for remaining in the barracks are shown in the lower right cell. The upper left cell shows the payoffs for a successful intervention carried out by a united military. The minority is better off than it was in the barracks, but the majority is slightly worse off since it would have preferred not to intervene.

The minority faction prefers to intervene, but it would be far worse off if it initiated an unsuccessful coup without support

16. I have used numbers in this and other matrices because I think they are easier to understand. The specific numbers used here, however, have no meaning. The logic of the game would be the same for any numbers that maintained the same order.

		Minority Faction	
		intervene	barracks
Majority Faction	intervene	4, 5	2, -10
	barracks	3, -10	5, 4

Fig. 2.1. Game between military factions

from the majority than if they remained unhappily in the barracks (payoffs for this outcome are shown in the lower left cell).[17] Participants in an unsuccessful coup attempt face possible demotion, discharge, court-martial, or execution for treason, so their payoff is shown as negative. The majority faction that opposed the coup is also damaged by the attempt, since the armed forces are weakened and the government is likely to respond with greater oversight, reorganization, and interference with promotions and postings to try to ensure greater future loyalty, all of which reduce military autonomy.

The final possible, though unlikely, outcome is a successful coup carried out despite minority opposition (payoffs are shown in the upper right cell).[18] In this event, the minority that remains loyal to the ousted civilian government is likely to face the same costs as unsuccessful conspirators: demotion, discharge, exile, prison, death. The winners achieve power, but a weakened military institution reduces their chances of keeping it. Future conspiracies supported by those demoted or discharged after the coup become more likely. Once factions of the military take up arms against each other, it takes years or decades to restore unity and trust.

This is a coordination game: once the military is either in power (upper left cell) or out of power (lower right cell), neither

17. The use of *majority* and *minority* here is not meant to imply that the success of coup attempts is determined by which side has the most support. Support affects the likelihood of success but is by no means decisive. For ease of exposition, however, I describe the majority faction as successful if it attempts a coup and the minority faction as unsuccessful. A more realistic game would introduce uncertainty about the likelihood of a successful coup, but the payoffs in the off-diagonal cells would remain lower for both actors than those in the upper left and lower right cells regardless of the outcome of the coup attempt.

18. Since the majority prefers not to intervene, it is hard to imagine anything other than profound misinformation that would lead to this outcome. Even if the majority preferred intervention, however, their payoff for intervening without full support would be lower than for remaining in the barracks.

faction can improve its position unilaterally. Each faction must have the other's cooperation in order to secure its preferred option. When the military is out of power, even if the majority comes to believe it should intervene, it cannot shift equilibria without cooperation from the minority.

There are two ways to solve coordination problems: one is to negotiate until consensus is reached, and the other is to make a credible first move that confronts the second mover with the choice between joining the first mover or receiving the payoff associated with a divided choice. Some military decisions to seize power have been carefully negotiated over a period of months until rules for sharing power have been hammered out and the last legalist holdout has either given in or retired. Such negotiated interventions occurred in Argentina in 1976, Brazil in 1964, and Chile in 1973 (Fontana 1987; Stepan 1971; Valenzuela 1978). Since extended negotiations carry considerable potential for discovery, however, most military interventions have employed a first-mover strategy in which a small group of conspirators seizes the presidential palace, the airport, television and radio stations, military installations in the capital, and perhaps a few other key buildings. It then announces that it has taken power and counts on the rest of the armed forces to go along (Nordlinger 1977). They usually do—but not always.

For the first-mover strategy to work, the first move has to be credible, meaning that other officers have to be convinced that the seizure of power is irreversible. The attempted coup of 1981 in Spain is an example of a failed first-mover strategy. The coup plotters seized the requisite number of installations in Madrid and had reason to believe that garrison commanders in the rest of the country would go along with them. King Juan Carlos, however, immediately began telephoning the garrison commanders, telling them that he opposed the intervention and that if they joined it, they would be guilty of treason. He also went on television to rally citizens against the coup. Once the king had taken such a strong stand, the first move lost its credibility, and most of the military refused to go along. Josep Colomer reports that one of the coup conspirators, when interviewed later, said, "Next time, cut the king's phone line" (1995, 121). Colomer suggests that had the king not been able to use television and the phone to rally support, the first-mover strategy might well have worked, because many in the officer corps sympathized with the goals of the conspirators (110–23).

When the military controls the government, the logic remains the same. Most officers will go along with a credible move by one faction to return to the barracks. Strong disagreements among leading officers over how to respond to economic difficulties or who among them will next occupy the presidency lead to intense factionalization. When this happens, one group is likely to prefer returning to the barracks as a way of avoiding institution-damaging conflict. Observers see splits in the officer corps at the time of the first moves toward democracy because the concern over divisions within the military causes some factions to prefer a return to the barracks. Both hard-line and soft-line factions can use the first-mover strategy, however. Military presidents can make quite credible first moves heading back toward the barracks, and most officers will go along. Hard-liners can also chance first-mover strategies, ousting more moderate military presidents. Again, if the move is credible, most of the officer corps will go along.

For the officer who ends up as paramount leader of the post-coup junta, the game may change after a successful seizure of power, as it did for Pinochet and those like him in other countries who sought to concentrate power in their own hands; but other officers usually see their situation as resembling a battle-of-the-sexes game, even in the most politicized and factionalized militaries. Repeated coups by different factions, as occurred in Syria prior to 1970 and Benin (then called Dahomey) before 1972, would not be possible if most of the army did not go along with the first mover, either in seizing power or in handing it back to civilians.

This analysis demonstrates the usefulness of having some simple models in one's theoretical toolkit. The military's concern about professional unity has been described verbally by a number of scholars, but using the game to show the logic of the situation demonstrates the consequences of this concern in a very clear and stark manner. The comparison between this game and the ones to be developed below will show the effects of differences in the interests of cadres in different kinds of regimes more clearly than could a verbal comparison alone. These models are not, of course, the endpoint of the analysis. After the models have been described, they will need empirical confirmation.

The preferences of party cadres are much simpler than those of officers. Like democratic politicians, party cadres simply want to hold office. Some value office because they want to control

		Majority (Leader's Faction) in office	Majority (Leader's Faction) out of office
Rival Faction	in office	8, 10	5, 1
	out of office	3, 9	0, 0

Fig. 2.2. Game between factions in single-party regimes

policy, some for the pure enjoyment of influence and power, and some for the illicit material gains that can come with office. The game between single-party factions is shown in figure 2.2. The insight behind this game is that everyone's cooperation is needed in order to achieve a desired end, and no one can achieve it alone. In this game, no one ever has an incentive to do anything but cooperate to remain in office.

In this game the best outcome for everyone is for both the majority faction and the rival faction to hold office (payoffs are shown in the upper left cell). The worst outcome occurs when both are out of power (shown in the lower right cell). The upper right cell shows the payoffs when the party has lost control of government but the minority faction still fills some seats in the legislature or holds other offices as an opposition to the new government. The minority's payoff when in opposition is lower than when its party holds power because the opposition has fewer opportunities to exercise influence or line pockets. In the lower left cell, the minority faction is excluded from office, but the dominant faction of the party still rules. In this case, the minority continues to receive some benefits, since its policy preferences are pursued and party connections are likely to bring various opportunities, but members of the excluded minority receive none of the specific perquisites of office. The majority is also worse off, because exclusion gives the minority an incentive to try to unseat the majority. Combatting the minority is both risky and costly for the majority.

Factions form in single-party regimes around policy differences and competition for leadership positions, as they do in other kinds of regimes, but everyone is better off if all factions remain united and in office. This is why co-optation rather than exclusion characterizes established single-party regimes. Neither faction would be better off ruling alone, and neither would voluntarily withdraw from office unless exogenous events changed the costs and benefits of cooperating with each other (and hence changed the game itself).[19]

In contrast to what happens in military and single-party regimes, the political fate of the close allies of a personalist dictator is tied to the fate of the dictator himself. "[I]nsiders in a patrimonial ruling coalition are unlikely to promote reform. . . . Recruited and sustained with material inducements, lacking an independent political base, and thoroughly compromised by corruption, they are dependent on the survival of the incumbent" (Bratton and van de Walle 1997, 86). Personalist dictatorships rarely survive for long after the death or ouster of the dictator, perhaps because dictators, in their efforts to defend themselves from potential rivals, so assiduously eliminate followers who demonstrate high levels of ability and ambition.

In personalist regimes, one leader dominates the military, the state apparatus, and the ruling party, if there is one. Because so much power is concentrated in the hands of this one individual, he generally controls the coalition-building agenda. Consequently, the game between factions in a personalist regime must be depicted as a game tree instead of a two-by-two matrix in order to capture the leader's control over first moves.[20] As shown in figure 2.3, the leader's faction has the initiative, choosing to share the spoils and perks with the rival faction or not. The choice I have labeled "hoard" can be interpreted either as limiting the opportunities and rents available to the rival faction or as excluding some of its members altogether. In the example shown in this figure, the amount of hoarding is small (the payoff to members of the rival faction for continued cooperation despite hoarding by the ruler's faction is 6); perhaps members of the rival faction are not offered the choicest opportunities, or perhaps a few of its members are jailed but the rest continue to prosper. If the whole rival faction were excluded from all benefits, their payoff for continued co-

---

19. The economic shocks of the 1980s and 1990s changed these costs and benefits in many countries, reducing the incentive of potential rivals to cooperate with ruling-party leaders and thus destabilizing regimes. The game used here shows the incentives to cooperate during good times. A different game would be needed to capture the choices facing single-party cadres after serious exogenous shocks.

20. Two-by-two matrices, often used to depict simple prisoner's dilemmas, battle-of-the-sexes games, chicken games, and so on, assume simultaneous decisions by the players or a lack of information about how the other has chosen. More complicated games, including those in which one player chooses first and the second chooses knowing how the first has chosen, have to be depicted using a game tree or equations.

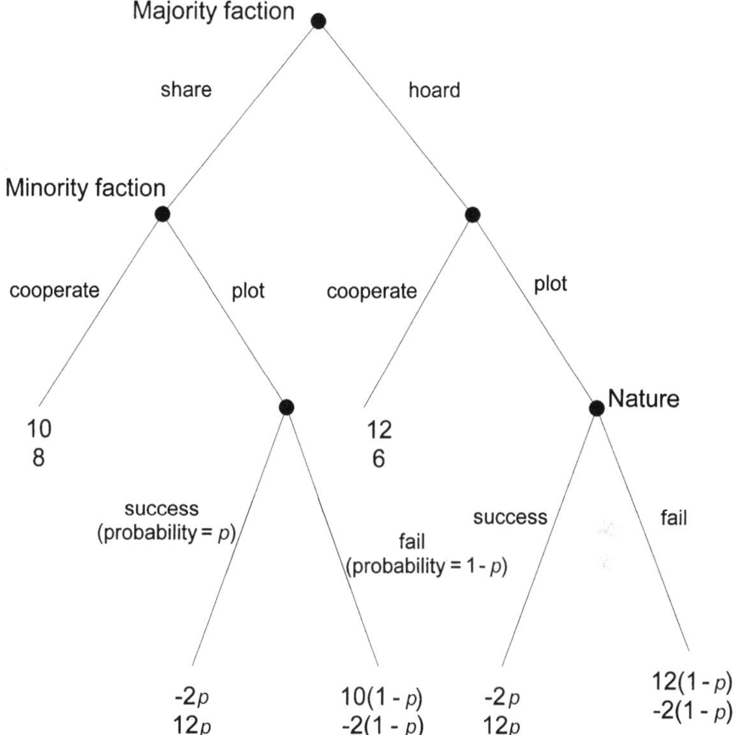

Fig. 2.3. Game between factions within personalist clique

operation would be much lower, but rarely lower than the payoff for refusing to cooperate.

After the leader's faction has chosen its strategy, the rival faction must decide whether to continue supporting the regime or not. During normal times, it has strong reasons to continue. Because its members "face the prospect of losing all visible means of support in a political transition, they have little option but to cling to the regime, to sink or swim with it" (Bratton and van de Walle 1997, 86).

Unlike in single-party regimes, the leader's faction in a personalist regime may actually increase benefits to itself by excluding the rival faction from participation. Where the main benefits of participation in the government come from access to rents and illicit profit opportunities, the payoff to individual members of the ruling group may be higher if these benefits need not be shared too widely. It may also be easier to keep damage to the economy below the meltdown threshold, and thus increase the likelihood of regime survival, if the predatory group is relatively small. Hoarding by the leader's faction is thus likely. If the hoarding is not too extreme, as in figure 2.3, the rival faction is better off continuing to cooperate, and most of the time that is what they do.

If the rival faction withdraws its support and begins to plot the leader's overthrow, its members risk life, liberty, and property. The rewards of a successful overthrow are high, but so are the costs of detection, betrayal, or defeat. In the game, the uncertainty over the outcome of plots is shown as a play by Nature. The plot succeeds with probability p, usually a low number, and fails with probability $1 - p$. The rival faction decides whether to continue its support for the leader's faction by comparing its payoff for support with its expected payoff from a plot. Two considerations thus affect the choice: the benefits being derived from the status quo and the potential plotters' assessment of the risk of plotting. As long as the personalist ruler seems powerful enough to detect plots and defeat coup attempts, the rival faction will continue to cooperate if it gets some benefits from the regime. The leader's faction has an incentive to reduce the benefits to the rival faction to a level just above that needed to prevent plotting. This system is very stable as long as the ruler can distribute the minimum level of benefits needed to deter plotting and can maintain control over an effective security apparatus and loyal military. The situations in which these conditions become less likely are discussed below.

By drawing on some rudimentary game theory, I have begun to develop insights into how the interests of cadres in different kinds of authoritarian regimes might play out in different contexts and how resilient to stress the cadres' loyalties to regime leaders might be. These insights motivate the analysis in the next section.

The Consequences of Differences in Interests

The interests described above provide a starting point for figuring out whether the splits and rivalries that exist within all kinds of governments will lead to regime breakdown. Because most military officers view their interests as following a logic similar to that of a battle-of-the-sexes game, they acquiesce in continued intervention regardless of whether military rule becomes institutionalized, the leader concentrates power in his own hands, or a rival ousts the original leader. The officer corps will not, however, go along with disintegration of the military into openly competing factions. If elite splits threaten military unity and efficacy, some factions will opt for a return to the barracks. If the soft-line faction can make a credible first move in that direction, most other officers will go along.

Military regimes thus contain the seeds of their own destruction. When elite rivalries or policy differences intensify and these factional splits become threatening, a return to the barracks becomes attractive to most officers. For officers, there is life after democracy, because all but the highest regime officials can usually return to the barracks with their status and careers untarnished and their salaries and budgets often increased by nervous transitional governments (Nordlinger 1977; Huntington 1991).

Leaders of single-party regimes also face competition from rivals, but most of the time, as in personalist regimes, the benefits of cooperation are sufficient to ensure continued support from all factions. Leadership struggles and policy disagreements occur, but they do not affect the desire of most cadres to remain in office. For them, life after democracy would require some unpleasant changes in lifestyle. They would have to compete for the benefits they have become accustomed to monopolizing. During leadership struggles, most ordinary cadres just keep their heads down and wait to see who wins. Thus, leadership struggles within single-party regimes usually do not result in transitions.

The close allies of personalist dictators have even less reason to desert the ship in normal times. If the ship goes down, they are likely to go with it. As long as the dictatorship is able to supply some benefits and has a sufficiently competent repressive apparatus to keep the probability of successful plotting reasonably low, they will remain loyal.

These differences explain why the early transitions literature, drawing insights primarily from the transitions from military rule in Latin America, emphasized splits within the regime as causes for the initiation of democratization though later studies did not. In other parts of the world, where rule by the military as an institution is less common, factions and splits could be identified within authoritarian regimes, but they did not result in transitions. Instead, observers emphasized the importance of other factors in bringing down long-standing dictatorships: economic crisis (Haggard and Kaufman 1995), foreign pressure (Huntington 1991), and popular protest (Bratton and van de Walle 1992,

1997; Casper and Taylor 1996). In short, the theorization of intra-authoritarian politics makes it possible to subsume the findings of a number of studies with differing regional foci. In regions where the military led most of the authoritarian regimes that broke down, the first steps toward democratization could be traced to splits within the military leadership, but where single parties or personalist autocrats tended to rule, pressures of various kinds external to the ruling party or clique played larger roles.

The many studies of transitions, most of which draw essential insights primarily from one part of the world, bear some similarity to the parable about five blind men encountering an elephant. Each offers a useful and insightful description of the part of the elephant he touches, but cannot describe the whole. The early studies could not do so because they were trying to explain a process that had barely gotten under way, though of course they had no way of knowing how many countries democratization would eventually affect. Later studies either have made no attempt to survey all cases or, in their attempt to set their own region in the broader context, have misinterpreted studies of some of the most frequently examined cases in particular regions as being representative of the general experience of that region. To repeat two of the most basic pieces of advice in this book: lots of factual information is always good; and it is hard to explain an outcome that has not yet finished coming out.

Drawing Testable Implications from the Argument

In this section, I detail the derivation of testable implications from the analytic argument above. As is often the case in comparative politics, it is not feasible to test in a rigorous way the argument about cadre interests proposed here. To gather the necessary detailed information about the internal politics of a large number of authoritarian regimes would require learning many languages and traveling to many places. Although numerous books and articles have been written about authoritarian governments in the larger, more developed, and for other reasons more "interesting" countries, it is difficult to find even detailed descriptions of events in smaller, less developed countries such as Burkina Faso, Niger, and Laos, especially those in which democratization has not taken place. In situations like this, one must rely on tests of the *implications* of the argument, which can sometimes be done with less detailed information than would be needed to test the argument itself. Testing implications in this kind of situation can make it possible to avoid the selection bias that would almost inevitably arise in an attempt to test the argument itself.

The argument sketched above claims that because officers see their interests in terms similar to a battle-of-the-sexes game, military regimes break down more readily than do other types of authoritarianism in response to internal splits, regardless of the cause of the splits. If that is true, we should expect military regimes to last less long, on average, than other forms of authoritarianism.

We should also expect economic crisis, which weakens support for all governments, to have a stronger disintegrating effect on military governments because of their underlying fragility. This suggestion might at first seem surprising, since most military governments hold no elections and tend to be more insulated from societal interests than other types of dictatorship. Thus, we might suppose them less vulnerable to pressures emanating from citizens unhappy with the regime's economic performance.

The cadre-interests argument, however, implies that officers may decide to step down even without the inducement of overt public pressure. Officers and cadres are aware of their government's economic performance, and they are linked to society via their families and friends. Typically, when officers perceive their government's performance as unsuccessful, some of them advocate intensifying the economic strategy being pursued while others advocate changing it. The backers of each policy prescription support the presidential aspirations of a different officer, and competition between them intensifies, sometimes leading to coups and countercoups. A split over economic strategy has the same effect as any other kind of split: if it threatens to get out of hand, most officers prefer to return to the barracks.

Observers such as Bratton and van de Walle (1997) note the importance of material inducements to loyalty in personalist regimes. We might suspect that where loyalty depends on the leader's ability to deliver individual benefits, economic crisis would cause regime breakdown, but that would be an insufficiently cynical view. Run-of-the-mill poor economic performance hurts ordinary citizens but does not preclude rewarding supporters. It takes a true economic disaster to do that. We should thus expect personalist regimes to be destabilized by economic catastrophe but, in comparison to military regimes, less affected by ordinary poor economic performance. Recent African experience suggests that reforms reducing state intervention in the economy, and hence the rents and corruption opportunities often used to reward supporters, may be as destabilizing to personalist regimes as economic crisis itself.

Because officers tend to decide to return to the barracks for reasons relating to internal military concerns rather than being forced out of office by popular protest or external events, we should expect them to negotiate their extrication. When officers decide to withdraw from power, they enter into negotiations with civilian political leaders to arrange an orderly transition and to safeguard, if possible, their own interests after the transition. We should thus expect that military regimes will be more likely than other kinds of authoritarianism to end in negotiation.

Because of the *internal* sources of fragility in military regimes, we should expect them to be overthrown by armed insurgents or ousted by popular uprisings only rarely. Demonstrations against them occur, but most of the time such demonstrations persuade factions of the military to initiate a transition before popular opposition develops into rebellion. Coups are common in military regimes, but they rarely end the regime. They are usually leadership changes, the analogue of votes of no confidence in parliamentary systems. Coups that bring a liberalizing military president to power often precede transitions in military regimes; such coups can be interpreted as first-mover strategies. They demonstrate that a shift in officer opinion has occurred and that a substantial faction prefers to return to the barracks.

In strong contrast to military officers, the leaders of personalist regimes generally fight tooth and claw to hang on to power. In Bratton and van de Walle's words, "They resist political openings for as long as possible and seek to manage the process of transition only after it has been forced on them" (1997, 83). If they are forced—by foreign pressure, for example—to negotiate with opponents, they renege on agreements at the first opportunity.[21] Military governments rarely renege on the agreements they make, not because they cannot, but because agreements are made at a time when most officers want to return to the barracks.

The cadre-interests argument claims that in normal times, the

---

21. Note, for example, the way Mobutu of Zaire (now Congo), Eyadema of Togo, and various other long-ruling African leaders manipulated electoral rules and intimidated opponents after agreeing, under pressure from international aid donors, to initiate multiparty elections.

members of a ruling personalist clique have little reason to desert their leader or oppose the regime. We should expect to see elite desertions of the regime only if rents and opportunities can no longer be distributed to supporters or if the leader loses control over the security apparatus and armed forces, thus reducing the risk of plotting his overthrow. Loss of control of the security apparatus can happen for various reasons, but one obvious and usually insurmountable reason is the death or physical incapacity of the leader. Dead or incapacitated leaders are replaced in all political systems, but the demise of the leader does not usually end other forms of authoritarianism. Because control of the armed and security forces is usually concentrated in the dictator's hands in personalistic regimes, however, his death or serious illness often reduces the risks of opposition. A testable implication of this argument is that the death of the leader is more likely to lead to regime breakdown in personalist than in other types of authoritarian regimes.

According to the cadre-interests argument, most of the military prefers to return to the barracks in some circumstances. Even for those officers who would prefer to remain in government, the cost for most of resuming a more ordinary military career is low. The cost of losing office is higher for cadres in a dominant party, but not, on average, devastating. Many prominent politicians in post-transition democratic regimes were once cadres of the formerly dominant party. Although the cadres of a single-party regime cannot be expected to desert when times are good, if it looks as though the party's hegemony will soon end, those cadres who think they possess the skills to make a success of democratic politics and whose ambitions are frustrated within the ruling party can be expected to form or join opposition parties. Even those who remain in the ruling party to the bitter end need not despair of life after democratization. Many previously dominant parties continue to function as effective political actors after democratization (cf. van de Walle and Butler 1999). In fact, in a number of ex-communist and African countries, such parties have achieved executive office in the second free and fair election after democratization.

The members of personalist cliques, however, have fewer options. Joining the opposition prior to a transition can have very high costs, and many who desert the regime must go into exile in order to protect their lives and liberty. From exile, they may plot and organize, but few who remain at home are willing to risk public opposition. Those who stick with the regime to the bitter end are much less likely to find a respected place in the post-transition political world than are the close supporters of single-party and military regimes. For these reasons, the end of a personalist regime is more likely to be violent in one way or another than is the end of a single-party or military regime. Thus, another testable implication of the cadre-interests argument is that personalist regimes should be more likely than other forms of authoritarianism to end in the assassination of the leader, popular uprising, armed insurgency, civil war, revolution, or armed invasion (cf. Skocpol and Goodwin 1994).

Violence and upheaval do not segue naturally into democratic elections; consequently, transitions from personalist rule should be more likely to end in renewed authoritarianism than are transitions from other forms of authoritarianism. Transitions accomplished by uprisings, invasions, or assassinations often allow the consolidation of power by those who overthrow the old regime. In contrast, negotiations during transitions usually set a time for elections and hammer out rules for how they will be conducted. Thus, competitive regimes are more likely to succeed military regimes than other forms of authoritarianism.

Like members of personalist cliques, cadres in single-party regimes have few reasons to desert in normal circumstances. Furthermore, because power is less concentrated in single-party regimes, they are less vulnerable to the death or illness of leaders. Thus, we should expect single-party regimes to last longer than either military or personalist regimes.

Because the dominant strategy of the ruling coalition in single-party regimes is to co-opt potential opposition, such regimes tend to respond to crisis by granting modest increases in political participation, increasing opposition representation in the legislature, and granting some opposition demands for institutional changes. They attempt to give the opposition enough to deter them from risky plots and uprisings while continuing to hang on to power.

In the most common kind of regime crisis—one caused by poor economic performance leading to antiregime demonstrations—the ruling elite in any kind of authoritarian regime tends to divide into intransigents and moderates as they struggle to respond. In military regimes, that division itself tends to persuade many officers that the time has come for a return to the barracks. In personalist regimes, the ruling coalition narrows as the intransigents circle the wagons and exclude moderates from access to increasingly scarce spoils. Former regime moderates may then join the opposition because they have been excluded from the distribution of spoils (cf. Bratton and van de Walle 1997). Ruling parties, however, attempt to distract citizens from their economic grievances by granting them modest political rights. This strategy works only sometimes, but it works often enough to extend the average life span of single-party regimes.

Hypotheses Derived from Implications of the Argument

To summarize, we can list a number of expectations about what we would see in the real world if the basic logic of how elite politics works in different kinds of authoritarian regimes were correct. Compared to other kinds of authoritarianism,

- military regimes survive less long;
- military regimes are more quickly destabilized by poor economic performance;
- military regimes are more likely to end in negotiation;
- military regimes are more likely to be followed by competitive forms of government;
- personalist regimes are more likely to end when the dictator dies;
- personalist regimes are more likely to end in popular uprising, rebellion, armed insurgency, invasion, or other kinds of violence;
- personalist regimes are more likely to be followed by new forms of authoritarianism;
- single-party regimes last longest, on average.

Testing the Implications: "Measurement"

Since this is a book on research methods, I include here many details about case selection and classification that might ordinarily appear in the appendix of an article or book. To test the implications discussed above, I have collected basic information about all authoritarian regimes (except monarchies) lasting three or more years that existed or began between 1946 and 1996, in countries with a population of more than a million that became independent before 1990. Authoritarian regimes already in existence in 1946, such as those in the Soviet Union, Mexico, and Turkey, are included, with their length of time in office calculated from the time they actually took power. Countries that became independent after 1945 enter the data set at the time of independence (if authoritarian). Countries that have achieved independence since 1990 because of the breakup of the Soviet Union and other communist states (and that remain authoritarian) have not been included, because the inclusion of a fairly large number of countries with severely truncated regimes might have biased conclusions.

The purpose of the three-year threshold is to distinguish regimes from temporary authoritarian interventions and periods of chaos. Regimes are defined as sets of formal and informal rules and procedures for selecting national leaders and policies. Under this definition, periods of instability and temporary "moderating" military interventions (Stepan 1971) are considered interregnums, not regimes. That is, they are periods of holding customary rules in temporary abeyance, struggle over rules, or transition from one set of rules to the next. The three-year threshold is simply a way of excluding such periods from the data set. This cutoff was chosen—after considerable empirical investigation of very short-lived authoritarian interludes—because it introduced the least misclassification into the data. A lower threshold would lead to the inclusion of a few moderating interventions and interventions that never managed to establish a new set of rules. The military governed during most of these interregnums. If they were included in the data set, the findings I report below would be stronger. A higher threshold would lead to the exclusion of some authoritarian governments that have been included in other literature on transitions.

I use a dichotomous measure of regime type (authoritarian versus not authoritarian) to identify cases for inclusion in the study, because the hypotheses I want to test require being able to identify the endpoints of regimes. Zachary Elkins (2000) argues that continuous measures of regime type are better, and for some purposes they are. In this study, however, they would add nothing. The argument makes no predictions about whether regimes are moving incrementally toward somewhat more press freedom or allowing minority parties a few seats in the legislature. It does make predictions about the conditions that cause regimes to end. To test those, I need to be able to identify unambiguously when an authoritarian regime has ended. I could have dichotomized an available continuous indicator such as the Freedom House index rather than "measuring" the cases myself, but Freedom House indices are made up of measures of citizens' political and civil rights. Since I define regimes as the sets of rules for choosing leaders and policies, Freedom House and other commonly used measures of democracy do not seek to measure the concept I have in mind.

Measurement decisions should derive from definitions of concepts in the theory being investigated and from the needs of particular tests of hypotheses. The usefulness of different indicators depends on their purpose and cannot be judged in the abstract.

In this data set, most decisions about whether governments were sufficiently authoritarian to deserve inclusion were easy, but a few were not. A significant complication was that norms for defining countries as democratic vary by region. Few Latin Americanists would classify Mexico as democratic before 1997, and some would not do so until the PRI finally lost the presidency in 2000. Among Africanists, however, Botswana, in which the ruling party has never lost control of the executive and at least two-thirds of the seats in parliament, is always called democratic. Needing a single standard to apply across regions, I classify regimes as authoritarian if opposition parties have been banned or subjected to serious harassment or institutional disadvantage, or if the ruling party has never lost control of the executive and has controlled at least two-thirds of legislative seats in all elections before 1985. Once a regime is labeled authoritarian, I do not consider it fully democratized until one turnover of executive power has occurred. Where it appears that conclusions might be affected by the stringency of these criteria, I also show results using less demanding rules.[22]

A basic point to be made about using concepts with contested definitions (such as authoritarianism) in research is that the concrete criteria used for classifying cases or observations need to be clear. The researcher must take care to apply the same criteria to all cases. Where these "coding" decisions are complicated or

22. These regime type classifications are similar to those of Huntington (1991), and my "coding" judgments are very close to his. My decision rule for determining whether a political system had crossed the threshold to democracy is essentially the same as that of Przeworski and Limongi (1997). The biggest difference between my classification scheme and that of Linz and Stepan (1996) is that I collapse what they call "sultanistic" and "civilianized" regimes into one category—personalist.

require careful judgment, I suggest using a written coding scheme and reporting the classification of all cases along with the research findings.[23] If one suspects that the concrete criteria used to assign cases to categories will be controversial or that decisions about classification drive results, one should also show results using alternative classificatory criteria.

The rationale for the stringent classification rule used here is that a party (or clique) that has concentrated great power in its hands over the years can, like the current Malaysian government, very quickly and easily reinstate strict limits on opposition when threatened. Such a regime contains few institutionalized limitations on the power of rulers, even if the rulers have not previously felt the need for repressive measures and hence have not relied on them. The consequence of this rule is that a few cases that are sometimes considered democratic—notably, Botswana, Tanzania, Malaysia, and Taiwan (before the election in 2000)—are classified as single-party regimes here. Classifying these countries as democracies would reduce the average life span of single-party regimes by about a year.

To classify authoritarian regimes as military, single-party, personalist, or hybrids of these categories, I relied on the following criteria. Military regimes were defined as those governed by an officer or retired officer, with the support of the military establishment and some routine mechanism by which high-level officers could influence policy choice and appointments. Single-party regimes were defined as those in which the party had some influence over policy, controlled most access to political power and government jobs, and had functioning local-level organizations. Regimes were considered personalist if the leader, who usually came to power as an officer in a military coup or as the leader of a single-party government, had consolidated control over policy and recruitment in his own hands, in the process marginalizing other officers' influence and/or reducing the influence and functions of the party. In the real world, many regimes have characteristics of more than one regime type. When regimes had important characteristics of more than one pure regime type, especially when the area specialist literature contained disagreements about the importance of military and party institutions, I put them in hybrid categories.

In all cases, I attempted to rely on a regime's actual rules for

23. Devising a "coding" scheme is discussed in more detail in chapter 4.

selecting leaders and making allocative decisions rather than formal designations of regime type. In practice, many regimes have characteristics of more than one of these classifications, and many move from one category to another over time even though the same person holds the highest office.

Dictators sometimes succeed in transforming the regimes they lead from one kind to another. As noted above, the transition from military to personalist occurs frequently. I did not count these transformations as regime changes, since that would artificially reduce the length of what we in everyday language call regimes, and one of the implications I want to test involves length of survival. If an early period of uncertainty or transition was followed by consolidation of a different regime type, I assigned the regime to the category in which it seemed to stabilize. Some cases, however, had to be assigned to intermediate categories.

In deciding whether a regime led by the single leader of a single party should be classified as personalist or single-party, I gave more weight to the party if it existed prior to the leader's accession to power, especially if it had organized the fight for independence, a revolution, or some equivalent mass movement, rather than being formed by the leader after his accession; the heir apparent or the successor to the first leader already held a high position in the party and was not a relative or a member of the same tribe or clan as the leader; the party had functioning local-level organizations that did something important, such as distributing agricultural credit or organizing local elections; the party either faced competition from other parties or held intraparty competitive elections for some offices; and party membership was more or less required for government jobs. I gave the party less weight if its membership seemed to be almost all urban (with little or no grassroots organization); its politburo (or equivalent) served as a rubber stamp for the leader; all members of the politburo and assembly were in effect selected by the leader; its membership was dominated by one region, tribe, clan, or religion (in heterogeneous societies); and the dictator's relatives occupied high offices.

To classify a regime led by an officer as either military or personal, I leaned toward military if relationships within the junta or military council seemed relatively collegial; the ruler held the rank of general or its equivalent; the regime had some kind of institutions for deciding succession questions and for routinizing consultation between the leader and the rest of the officer corps; the military hierarchy remained intact; the security apparatus remained under military control rather than being taken over by the leader himself; succession in the event of the leader's death was in hierarchical order; the officer corps included representatives of more than one ethnic, religious, or tribal group (in heterogeneous countries); and the rule of law was maintained (perhaps after rewriting the laws). I treated the following as evidence of greater personalism: seizure of executive office by an officer who was not a retired or active duty general (or the air force or navy equivalent); disintegration of military hierarchy; dissolution of military councils and other military consultative institutions; the forced retirement or murder of officers within the leader's cohort or from tribes or clans other than the leader's; the murder or imprisonment of dissenting officers or of soldiers loyal to them; the formation of a party led by the leader as an alternative base of support for himself; and the holding of plebiscites to legitimize the leader's role. See appendix A for a summary of the regime classification criteria.

Most of the time it was not hard to distinguish between military and single-party regimes, though a few cases, especially in the Middle East, were problematic. Probably the most difficult decisions in this data set involved the current Egyptian regime and post-1963 Syria. Egypt posed a problem because the regime that took power in 1952 has gone through a series of changes. In my judgment, it began as a military regime under Naguib and the Free Officers but was transformed when Nasser consolidated his personal power beginning in 1954. Though the military continued to support the regime, Nasser—and Sadat to an even greater extent—increasingly marginalized it (Springborg 1989). Beginning under Nasser, efforts were made to create a single party; this party achieved some real importance in the mid-1960s but was then undermined by Nasser (Waterbury 1983; Richards and Waterbury 1990). The Nasser period thus seems primarily personalist. Under Sadat, the party became more important, though his government also retained large personalist elements (Hinnebusch 1985). The dominant party has played a more important role as the regime has gone through a modest liberalization. In the Syrian case, some experts refer to the period after 1963 as a Ba'athist regime (Ben-Dor 1975; Perlmutter 1969; Richards and Waterbury 1990), while others emphasize the personal power of Hafez al-Asad until his death (Hopwood 1988; Ma'oz 1986, 1988; Rabinovich 1972). As in the Egyptian case, the military is an important supporter of the regime but seems to have been excluded from most decision making. The best way to deal with these difficult cases seemed to be to put them, along with the regimes of Suharto in Indonesia, Stroessner in Paraguay, and Ne Win in Burma (or Myanmar), into a triple hybrid military/personalist/single-party category. The second section of appendix A lists all the regimes used in the data analysis and their classifications.

How long an authoritarian regime lasts is not always obvious. The beginning is usually clear, because dictatorships start either with an illegal seizure of power or with a change in rules—such as the banning of opposition parties—that in effect eliminates meaningful competition for the top national office, though opposition parties may be allowed minority representation. But the end of an authoritarian regime may be less clearly demarcated. I counted an authoritarian regime as defunct if either the dictator and his supporters had been ousted from office or a negotiated transition resulted in reasonably fair, competitive elections and a change in the party or individual occupying executive office. Where ousters occurred, I used that date as the endpoint. Where elections occurred, I used the date of the election, but I did not include the case unless the winner of the election was allowed to take office. Elections did not have to be direct, but the body electing the executive had to be made up mainly of elected members. Cases in which elections deemed free and fair by outside observers have been held but have not led to a turnover in personnel are not treated as transitions because, until they actually step down, we do not know if long-ruling parties such as the United Malay National Organization (UMNO) or the Revolutionary Party of Tanzania (CCM) really will relinquish power if defeated.[24] The 1992 Angolan elections were deemed free and fair by outside observers, but few would have called Angola a democracy in subsequent years. Several of the countries in which long-ruling parties have won officially free and fair elections, however, probably have taken irreversible steps toward democracy. Since observers disagree about the classification of these "free and fair" countries, tests should be done classifying them first as continuing authoritarian regimes and then as

24. In a study of transitions in Africa, van de Walle and Butler (1999) show that a strong relationship exists between executive turnover and scoring at the democratic end of the Freedom House scale, which suggests an additional reason for not treating democratization as complete until a turnover in power has occurred.

authoritarian regimes that ended at the time of the "free and fair" election. In this data set, these reclassifications make no substantive difference in the results.

Some of the most difficult classification decisions involved judgments about whether successive authoritarian governments should be considered one regime (defined as a set of formal and informal rules and procedures for choosing leaders and policies) or not. Authoritarian regimes often follow one another, as, for example, the Sandinista regime followed the Somozas in Nicaragua. Data sets that simply identify regimes as authoritarian or democratic create the impression that authoritarian regimes are more stable and longer-lived than they really are, because they fail to note that one has broken down and another taken its place. This problem may undermine some of the findings in a series of studies by Adam Przeworski and coauthors on the relationship between regime type and growth (e.g., Przeworski and Limongi 1993; Przeworski et al. 2000). In putting together their data set, they simply coded each country as democratic or not in December of each year. If a country was coded authoritarian two years in a row, the regime was considered to have survived, regardless of whether one authoritarianism had been replaced by another or a democracy had been formed and then overthrown during the intervening year.[25]

I relied on a number of decision rules to avoid this problem. Where a period of democracy intervened between two periods of authoritarianism, I counted the authoritarianisms as separate entities. Where one kind of authoritarian regime succeeded another, as with Somoza-Sandinista, I counted them as separate. Some of these decisions were much more difficult. In a number of cases, periods of collegial military rule were succeeded by one officer's consolidation of his personal power. These I classified as single regimes undergoing consolidation, unless there was persuasive evidence that the support base of the regime had changed. Where a coup—especially if accompanied by a change in clan or tribal dominance or a substantial move down the military hierarchy (e.g., a coup by sergeants against a government led by the

25. This coding decision does not affect their main finding about the robustness of democracy at high levels of development, but it does undermine conclusions about the effect of economic performance on authoritarian stability, since ousters of dictatorships followed by renewed authoritarian rule within the year are coded as on-going regimes.

high command)—led to the change in most of the leadership, I counted it as a regime change. Where one individual who was already part of a governing junta overthrew another but most of the rest continued, I counted it as a single regime.

In any study, but especially when the project involves complicated or contested decisions about how to classify cases, it is important to carry out the analogue of sensitivity analysis in statistics. That is, one should reclassify the cases and see if it affects conclusions. This might involve including or excluding cases from the data set, as in the decision about how many years a dictatorship has to survive in order to be classified as a regime. If I had followed the usual practice of including every period of authoritarianism that lasted a year or more, military regimes would appear even more fragile than they do in the results below, because most of these very short interventions are military. The three-year threshold seems to me theoretically correct in that it derives from the definition of a regime as a set of rules, but it is also a methodologically conservative decision. If the empirical investigation turns out to support the argument even though the most short-lived military interventions have been excluded from the data set, then we can have greater confidence in the argument, because changing that decision rule would only strengthen the findings.

The reclassification of cases could, alternatively, involve moving them from one category to another on one of the variables. For this project, I classified a number of rulers who are often described as military—for example, Barrientos in Bolivia and Ershad in Bangladesh—as personalist because, although they were officers and came to power in coups, the military was not their primary constituency; they organized civilian support and held popular elections to legitimate their rule. If I were to eliminate this criterion for discriminating between personalist and military rule, a certain number of cases would move from the personalist to the military category. The changes would not affect conclusions about the length of military rule, because most of the cases that would be affected were quite short-lived. The reclassification would, however, increase the number of regimes classified as military that ended in violence, and this could affect conclusions about another of the implications of the cadre-interests argument not tested here: that personalist regimes are more likely than others to be violently overthrown.

TABLE 2.1. Durability of Different Types of Authoritarian Regime

Regime Type	Average Length of Rule (years)[a]	Average Age of Surviving Regimes[b]	Percent Regimes Surviving in 2000
Military	9.5 (33)	10.0 (2)	5.7
Military/personalist	11.3 (12)	12.7 (3)	20.0
Personalist[c]	15.5 (46)	18.0 (12)	20.7
Single-party hybrids[d]	19.6 (14)	25.2 (6)	30.0
Single-party (stringent transition criteria)[e]	29.0 (21)	34.0 (13)	38.2
Single-party (less stringent transition criteria)	27.9 (24)	35.4 (9)	27.3
Triple hybrid	33.0 (3)	43.5 (2)	40.0

Note: Regimes maintained by foreign occupation or military threat are excluded. Number of observations on which averages are based is shown in parentheses.

[a]Includes only regimes that had ended by December 2000.

[b]Includes regimes in existence in 1946, or that have come to power since then, that still survived at the end of 2000.

[c]The Rawlings government in Ghana held elections deemed free and fair by international observers in 1996 (and elections boycotted by the opposition in 1992), and voters reelected Rawlings. Many then considered Ghana democratic, but by the criteria used for this study its transition was completed in 2000. If Ghana were classified as having made a transition in 1996, this change would have no effect on the average length of personalist regimes.

[d]Category includes both military/single-party and personalist/single-party regimes.

[e]Six countries in this category have held elections deemed free and fair but nevertheless returned the ruling party to power. The results if these countries are classified as having democratized at the time of the first free and fair elections are shown in the next row.

Testing One of the Implications

Here I describe a test of the first implication above: that military regimes should be expected to survive less long than other kinds of authoritarianism.[26] Preliminary evidence bears out the expectation that sources of fragility endogenous to military regimes cause life spans shorter on average than those of other forms of dictatorial rule. Table 2.1 shows the average life spans of both the pure and hybrid regime types. Among regimes that had ended by December 2000, military regimes lasted on aver-

26. Tests of some of the other implications of the cadre-interests argument are reported in Geddes (1999a).

age 9.5 years,[27] personalist regimes 15.5 years, and single-party regimes (excluding those maintained by foreign occupation or threat of intervention) 29 years.[28]

Another way to assess the durability of different regime types is to compare their current survival rates. As shown in column 3 of table 2.1, the proportion of surviving military regimes is quite low. Only 5.7 percent of those that once existed still survive. In contrast, 20.7 percent of personalist regimes remain in existence, and 38.2 percent of single-party regimes still survived in 2000 if stringent transition criteria are used to determine regime endpoints (27.3 percent if less stringent criteria are used).[29] Military regimes that had come to power by 1997 and still survived had lasted an average of 10 years by 2000. Single-party regimes that remained in power, on the other hand, had lasted an average of 34 years (35.4 if less stringent transition criteria are used).

Although these differences in the average length of different types of regime are quite large, we cannot be sure that they are really caused by regime type. Military regimes are more common in Latin America, where levels of economic development are relatively high, and personalist regimes are most common in Africa, where countries tend to be poorer. It might be that the stronger demand for democracy by citizens of more developed countries accounts for the shorter duration of military regimes. Alternatively, it might be that military regimes last less long because they are responsible for worse economic performance

---

27. Reminder: authoritarian interludes lasting less than three years have been excluded from the data set. The military ruled during most of these interludes. If they were included, the average length of military rule would be reduced. Nordlinger, who did not exclude them from his calculations, found that military regimes last five years on average (1977, 139).

28. Regimes maintained in power by direct foreign occupation or the threat of military intervention have been excluded from the calculation of average life span here and from the statistical analysis below because their longevity depends on external events. The excluded regimes are those in Afghanistan, 1979–92; Bulgaria, 1947–90; Cambodia, 1979–90; Czechoslovakia, 1948–90; German Democratic Republic, 1945–90; Hungary, 1949–90; and Poland, 1947–89. The average length of these regimes is 34 years.

29. The stringent criteria for determining the end of an authoritarian regime require not only that competitive elections be held but also that the executive change hands. The less stringent criteria count authoritarian regimes as ended if competitive elections are held and are considered free and fair by outside observers, regardless of who wins.

than other kinds of authoritarianism. To test for these possibilities, I have carried out statistical tests of the effect of regime type on the probability of regime breakdown, controlling for level of development, growth rate, and region.

I use a hazard model to assess these rival arguments. Hazard models are used in medical research and other areas to predict the survival of individuals with certain conditions, given various treatments. This type of model also seems appropriate for explaining the survival of a different kind of entity. A logit model produces the same substantive results, so they do not depend on the particular specification.

To rule out the possibility that the apparent relationship between regime type and length of time in office might really be caused by level of development, the statistical analysis includes an indicator of development, the natural log of GDP per capita. Since a number of studies have found that current economic performance affects the likelihood of regime breakdown, an indicator for growth is also included in the models as a control variable. The measure of growth used is change in GDP per capita in the prior year. I use the prior year because credit or blame for the prior year's economic performance is unambiguous. In years in which a transition takes place, the outgoing regime might be responsible for only part of the year's performance. Furthermore, economic performance is often erratic in transition years. It can plummet in response to government instability, but it can also improve rapidly during the euphoria that sometimes accompanies a transition. Thus, the previous year's growth seems a better indicator of the regime's recent economic performance. Adam Przeworski and Fernando Limongi (1997) also found, after trying a number of possibilities and lags, that growth during the prior year was the best predictor of regime change.

Economic data are from the Penn World Tables, the longest time series for the largest number of countries I have been able to find. For most countries, it covers 1950–92, which means that regime years prior to 1951 and after 1992 are excluded from the statistical analysis. In addition, no economic data are available from Albania, Cambodia, Cuba, North Korea, Libya, Vietnam, and South Yemen, and there are some years missing from a few other countries. Since the period covered is quite long and I cannot think of any reason to believe that transitions during the years covered would be different from those in the years immediately before and after, I do not think the years excluded introduce bias into the results.

The countries left out of the data set, however, differ from those included. Most had or have single-party or personalist/single-party regimes. Their regimes have lasted an unusually long time (excluding Cambodia, 32.1 years on average). Dictators still rule in five of seven, and nearly all the countries are very poor. If they were included in the data analysis, they would probably further strengthen the coefficient for the effect of single-party regime and reduce the effect of level of development on the probability of regime stability. Since the data set is large, however, and not very many cases have to be left out, I do not think their exclusion has much effect on conclusions.

Region is used as a quasi–fixed effects estimator.[30] Fixed effects estimators are used to hold constant aspects of history and culture that might affect the outcome of interest but that cannot be directly measured. I have used region to hold constant some of the possible effects of colonial history and cultural heritage.

Because regime types are nominal categories, they are entered into the model as dummy variables: if the regime is, for example, military, it is coded "one"; otherwise, it is coded "zero." The left-out regime type is personalist, the middle category in terms of longevity. Thus, the hazard ratios reported should be interpreted as referring to differences between the effect of the type of regime associated with a particular ratio and the effect of personalist regimes.

Hazard ratios have a simple intuitive interpretation. Ratios above one mean that the variable associated with them increases the probability of regime collapse. In the first column of table 2.2, the hazard ratio for military regime is 2.81, which means

30. Usually, country dummy variables are used as fixed effects estimators, but they could not be used to analyze this data set because they cause countries with only one regime to be dropped from the analysis. In this data set, half the countries have had only one authoritarian regime, either because one stable regime remained in power for several decades or because the country is usually democratic and had only one postwar authoritarian interlude. A more serious problem than the loss of cases per se is that regimes in the cases with only one regime, are, on average, unusually long-lived, and they are especially likely to be single-party regimes. The use of country fixed effects estimators eliminates 60 percent of the single-party regimes from the analysis. When the analysis was done using country fixed effects estimators, the coefficient for the effect of military regime was artificially strengthened (since the longest military regimes were eliminated), and the effect of single-party regime was greatly weakened (since most of the single-party regimes were eliminated, leaving an unrepresentative set of mostly African cases).

that, all else being equal, military regimes are nearly three times as likely to break down as personalist regimes. Hazard ratios between zero and one mean that the variable reduces the probability of breakdown. In column 1, the hazard ratio for single-party regimes, .39, means that, all else being equal, single-party regimes have about 40 percent the chance of collapsing that personalist regimes do.

As can be seen in column 1, military regimes break down more readily than all other types. The hazard ratio for the military regime variable is substantively large and statistically significant. The two intermediate regime types, military/personalist and single-party hybrid (in which personalist/single-party regimes predominate, since there are very few military/single-party regimes), are, not surprisingly, not very different from personalist regimes. Single-party regimes, however, are more resilient than personalist regimes to about the same extent that military regimes are less resilient, and this difference is also statistically significant. Finally, the triple hybrid regimes, which combine characteristics of single-party, personalist, and military regimes,

TABLE 2.2. Effect of Regime Type on Authoritarian Survival (Weibull regression, log relative-hazard form)

Dependent Variable: Regime Collapse (hazard ratios)

	Model 1	Model 2	Model 3
Military	2.81**	2.83**	10.26**
Military/personalist	1.31	1.15	2.07
Single-party hybrids	1.24	1.47	3.44*
Single-party	0.39**	0.38*	0.59
Triple hybrid	0.04**	0.00	0.00
Log GDP per capita	0.53*	0.54*	0.40
Growth GDP per capita	0.02*	0.02*	0.004**
Asia	1.22	0.97	0.19
Central America, Caribbean	0.99	0.98	0.23
Eastern Europe[a]	0.18*	0.16	0.00
Middle East	7.46	3.29	0.40
North Africa	0.42*	0.15	0.01**
South America	3.44	3.95	0.35
Sub-Saharan Africa	0.61	0.41	0.05**
Percent Muslim		1.01*	1.02**
Dependence on oil			1.02
Dependence on minerals			1.00
N of observations	1,694	1,627	861

Note: Left-out regime category is personalist; left-out region is Southern Europe.
[a]Excludes regimes maintained by foreign intervention.
* Statistically significant at .05 to .01; **statistically significant at .01 or better.

are the strongest of all. An alternative to the substantive interpretation of this category is that it simply serves the purpose of controlling for five very long-lived and unusual regimes that might otherwise inflate the apparent longevity of single-party regimes.

The control variables used in the regression also show some interesting effects. As the level of development rises, authoritarian regimes, like democratic ones, become more stable. This finding is consistent with that of John Londregan and Keith Poole (1990, 1996), who found that the best predictor of coups, in both democratic and authoritarian regimes, was poverty. It raises some questions, however, about traditional demand-centered explanations for the relationship between increased development and democracy. It is inconsistent with the idea that the citizens of more affluent countries are more likely to demand democratization. Rather, it suggests that when authoritarian governments manage the economy well over the long term, regime allies remain loyal and citizens remain supportive, or at least acquiescent. That interpretation is reinforced by the very strong negative effect of short-term economic growth on the probability of regime breakdown. In other words, both long- and short-term economic performance affects authoritarian stability.

In light of various arguments about the effects of religion, culture, and colonial heritage on the development of democratic values, it is somewhat surprising that most of the region variables show little effect. The left-out region here is southern Europe (Portugal, Spain, and Greece), and we might have expected the regions most culturally distinct from Europe to exhibit differences in the likelihood of regime transition. The only two regions with statistically significant hazard ratios in model 1, however, are Eastern Europe and North Africa. Since the governments kept in place by the threat of Soviet intervention have been excluded from these tests, the East European region contains only the Soviet Union, Romania, and Yugoslavia (Albania had to be excluded because of missing economic data). Controlling for level of development, growth, and regime type, regimes in these countries were unusually resilient. There are internal reasons for this resilience, but in the context of the full data set, this region dummy variable in effect controls for the very unusual longevity of the Soviet regime and prevents it from inflating the apparent effect of the single-party regime type.

The unusual resilience of authoritarian regimes in North

Africa leads to speculations about other possible causes of authoritarian stability that might have been left out of these tests. Several studies have shown that countries with large Islamic populations are less likely to be democratic, and Michael Ross (2001) shows that oil wealth is associated with authoritarianism. North African exceptionalism might be caused by Islam or by oil wealth, though it should be noted that the hazard ratio for the Middle East is not only insignificant but suggests the opposite effect.

The results of tests of these possibilities are shown in columns 2 and 3 of table 2.2. For the hazard model used in column 2, the percentage of the population that is Islamic was added as an additional control variable. The first thing to notice is that the inclusion of this control variable has virtually no effect on the relationship between regime type and breakdown. Those relationships look as strong as ever, and the hazard ratios for growth and level of development are also unaffected. The absence of change increases our faith in the importance of the variables of interest.

The effect of percent Muslim population on the probability of breakdown would be quite interesting in its own right if we believed it. It is statistically significant, though the effect is the opposite of that expected. As Muslim population increases, the probability of regime collapse becomes more likely. This finding does not, of course, mean that democratization is more likely in Islamic countries. Authoritarian regimes collapse and are followed by other authoritarian governments. If this finding were to be replicated in additional tests, it would disconfirm the idea that authoritarianism is more stable in Islamic countries because of an affinity between Muslim culture and authoritarian values. The results so far have to be considered quite tentative, however, because of the exclusion of monarchies from the data set. Since most of the extant monarchies are both long-lived and in predominantly Muslim countries, their inclusion might well cause the disappearance of this finding.

Adding dependence on oil and minerals to the model (column 3) reduces the number of observations by about half and causes the hazard ratios to bounce around quite a bit. Statistical significance is harder to achieve in the smaller data set. Because of peculiarities in the set of cases for which data on oil exports are available, findings from the third model should probably not be taken too seriously.[31] For what they are worth, however, the hazard ratio for military regimes is still statistically significant and remarkably large, growth still reduces the likelihood of breakdown, and percent Muslim has about the same effect as before. Single-party regime and level of development still reduce the probability of breakdown but have lost statistical significance. Dependence on oil apparently has no effect on authoritarian stability, contrary to much that has been written in the literature on rentier states, though here also the exclusion of monarchies renders the conclusion suspect. In short, these findings are mostly consistent with expectations drawn from the cadre-interests argument, though if we had faith in the quality of the data on which the findings are based, the loss of statistical significance for the single-party variable would be cause for concern.

To summarize the findings, the hypotheses about the average duration of different types of authoritarian regime have been mostly confirmed by statistical analysis, holding constant the most obvious challenges to the apparent relationship. Growth was found to have the expected effect of reducing the probability of regime breakdown. Higher levels of development also probably reduced the likelihood of authoritarian breakdown. In short, empirical investigation of the first implication of the cadre-interests argument about authoritarian breakdown has failed to disconfirm expectations.

A series of methodological observations can be made about the empirical test described above. The first observation, though obvious, may need restating: this was a test of an implication of the argument, not of the argument itself. The implication is quite simple and, once the data had been collected, easy to test. Nevertheless, its confirmation adds to the persuasiveness of the argument, and if the other implications listed above also proved consistent with reality, we would be pretty much convinced that the argument captures a key aspect of the explanation of the breakdown of authoritarian regimes.

31. For nearly all African countries, most years after 1983 are missing, which means that most African transitions are missing. In other words, the missing cases are almost all from the poorer half of the data set, which is probably the reason that level of development loses significance. The later years of a considerable number of long-lived African single-party regimes are also left out.

Second, in order to test the implication, evidence had to be gathered about a large number of cases, although the kind of evidence needed was not complicated. It is not always necessary or feasible to include the whole universe of cases, as I did here. If examining the whole universe is infeasible, however, the whole universe nevertheless needs to be identified so that cases from within the universe can be selected at random or in some other way that does not bias conclusions. (Figuring out the domain of an argument is discussed in chapters 3 and 4.) Cases should be selected to ensure that the outcome of interest varies across them. (Case selection is treated in detail in chapter 3.) Cases that have been studied repeatedly by other scholars are, on average, larger, more developed, and more geopolitically important than the cases that have not been studied, and conclusions based on experience in such cases are therefore unlikely to be representative of the whole group.

The number of cases used to test an argument needs to be reasonably large, since it is very hard to be sure that a result has not been caused by chance events when only a few cases are examined. The more arguments one can think of other than the one of interest that could also explain an apparent relationship, and the more factors one thinks need to be held constant in order to exclude the effects of irrelevant forces on the relationship of interest, the more cases need to be examined. The possibility of spurious correlation—that is, the possibility that what appears to be a relationship between some cause and effect really results from some outside factor that causes both of them—can rarely be dismissed without using statistics, and not always even then.

All data sets, whether gathered by the researcher or taken off the shelf, contain some missing data and some mistakes. The researcher should always think carefully about how the missing cases differ from the cases included in the study and how their inclusion, if it could be managed, would affect conclusions. When using an off-the-shelf data set known or rumored to contain mistakes, the researcher should try to figure out whether the mistakes are likely to affect conclusions. The Freedom House democracy indicator, for example, is rumored to contain a pro-Washington bias, especially during the early years. For some purposes, this bias would not matter, but for others it might seriously undermine the credibility of findings. One would want to use a different indicator of democracy in the latter situation.

Conclusion

This chapter began with the claim that one of the practices hindering the accumulation of theory in comparative politics is the way we usually go about trying to explain compound outcomes such as democratization. I argued that greater progress could be made toward actually understanding how such outcomes occur by examining the mechanisms and processes that contribute to them, rather than through inductive searches for the correlates of the undifferentiated whole. Coherent deductive arguments can be devised to explain constituent processes, and hypotheses derived from the arguments can be tested.

I attempted to demonstrate the usefulness of this approach with an extended example. After identifying seven constituent processes of the large, complicated phenomenon of democratization, I proposed a deductive argument based on the individual interests of regime insiders to explain why elite splits play a larger role in some instances of authoritarian breakdown than others, and why some authoritarian regimes initiate political liberalization in the absence of societal pressure to do so. Although this argument as a whole is not testable, it was a simple matter to derive implications of the argument that could potentially be falsified.

The only impediment to testing these hypotheses was the need to gather an appropriate data set. Data gathering was a major and time-consuming effort, but once the data had been gathered, it was possible to show not only that predicted differences existed, but that they were quite large and statistically significant.

I make no grand claims for the cadre-interests argument itself. It may not be true. It is possible that when other variables are taken into consideration, the relationship that seems apparent now between regime type and longevity will disappear. Even if true, the argument explains only one element of the compound process of regime transformation. I do claim, however, that an argument from which an implication has been tested on evidence from a large number of cases is more likely to prove of lasting value than untested arguments induced from a handful of cases. And once data have been gathered, more implications can be tested. If those tests also conform to expectations generated by the argument, our confidence that the argument is true will increase. I also claim that to tack down an explanation of one process that contributes to a compound outcome of great theoretical and real-world importance such as democratization would constitute serious intellectual progress.

While inductive explorations of instances of transition may have been the only possible research strategy at the beginning of the current wave of democratization, we now have enough basic information to move on to theory building. I have tried to show here that the theoretical edifice can best be built one deductive brick at a time, testing as many of them as possible using evidence from a large number of cases.

CHAPTER 3

How the Cases You Choose Affect the Answers You Get

Selection Bias and Related Issues

Comparative politics, like other subfields in political science, has norms and conventions about what constitutes an appropriate research strategy and what kind of evidence makes an argument persuasive. Although the norm has begun to change, for many years one of our most durable conventions was the selection of cases for study from one end of the outcome continuum we wished to explain.[1] That is, if we want to understand something—for example, revolution—we select one or more occurrences and subject them to scrutiny to see if we can identify antecedent events or characteristics as causes.

Most graduate students learn in the statistics courses forced upon them that such selection on the dependent variable often leads to wrong answers, but few remember why, or what the implications of violating this rule might be for their own work. And so, comparativists often ignore or forget about it when undertaking or assessing nonquantitative research.

This chapter demonstrates the consequences of violating the rule. It does so by comparing the conclusions reached in several influential studies based on cases selected on the dependent variable with retests of the same arguments using samples not correlated with the outcome. All the studies discussed in this chapter are intelligent, plausible, insightful, and possibly correct in their knowledge claims. All have been advanced by highly respected social scientists. The effort here is not to discredit arguments or belittle authors—who are, after all, working within accepted conventions—but to demonstrate the deficiencies of the conventions themselves.

1. Comparative politics is not the only field bedeviled by problems with selection bias (see Achen and Snidal 1989).

These conventions affect not only authors but readers of comparative politics. Authors, including some of those discussed below, are frequently aware of the tentativeness of the evidence supporting their arguments and indicate their awareness in the caveats they attach to them. Readers, however, tend to ignore the caveats and give greater weight to unsystematic evidence than it deserves. Many studies in which authors have carefully hedged their explanatory claims are discussed in seminars, cited in literature reviews, and summarized in qualifying exams as though the tentative arguments advanced were supported by solid evidence. The purpose of this chapter is as much to decrease the credulity of readers as to increase the sophistication of researchers.

The message of the chapter is not that the examination of cases selected because they have experienced a particular outcome is never warranted, but rather that the analyst should understand what can and cannot be accomplished with cases selected for this reason. Some kinds of tests of conditions proposed as necessary or sufficient for explaining outcomes can be carried out using only cases that have experienced an outcome, although assessment of what Braumoeller and Goertz (2000) refer to as trivialness requires at least some information about the rest of the universe of cases.[2]

The close examination of an anomalous case with a particular outcome can also serve a useful role in either generating a proposed revision of current theory or suggesting domain conditions not previously understood. A test of the proposed revision or domain condition would require examining a wider range of cases, however. Although the proposal of a revision is a useful

2. As Dion (1998) has pointed out, selection on the dependent variable does not undermine tests of "necessary but not sufficient" or "necessary and sufficient" arguments. Braumoeller and Goertz (2000) propose a series of tests that, taken together, would increase confidence in a necessary or sufficient argument. Carrying out these tests requires: (1) being able to estimate the error in the measurement of both proposed causes and effects; (2) including enough cases selected to have the outcome so that an appropriate statistical test can reject the null hypothesis (with no measurement error, the minimum number is seven; as measurement error increases, so does the required number of cases); (3) collecting enough information about the full universe of cases to assure oneself that there is enough variation in both purported cause and outcome to avoid trivialness. The issue of trivialness is discussed below. It refers to proposed necessary conditions that are theoretically meaningless because they vary little if at all. Braumoeller and Goertz note, for example, that the argument that democratic dyads are necessary for peace is trivial before 1800 because there were no democratic dyads then.

contribution to knowledge building, the revision should not be accepted until it has been tested and confirmed on a representative sample of cases.

The Nature of the Problem

The adverse effects of selecting cases for study on the dependent variable stem from the logic of inference. When one sets out to explain why countries A and B have, say, developed more rapidly than countries C through I, one is implicitly looking for some antecedent factors *X* through *Z* that countries A and B possess in greater degree than do countries C through I. The crux of the difficulty that arises when cases are selected on the dependent variable is that if one studies only countries A and B, one can collect only part of the information needed, namely, the extent of factors *X* through *Z* in countries A and B . Unless one also studies countries C through I (or a sample of them) to make sure they have less of *X* through *Z*, one cannot know whether the factors identified really vary with the outcome under investigation.

The problem becomes more obvious when shown in graphs rather than expressed in words. Suppose a universe of developing countries A through I, where A and B are among the fastest growing. On the basis of an intensive study of A and B, one concludes that factor *X* is the cause of their success. In concluding this, one implicitly assumes that if countries C through I were examined, they would turn out to have less of factor *X* than do A and B, and that one would observe the relationship shown in figure 3.1.

Yet if one examines only countries A and B, it is possible that the full range of cases would look more like one of the scatterplots in figure 3.2. That is, it is possible that there is no relationship

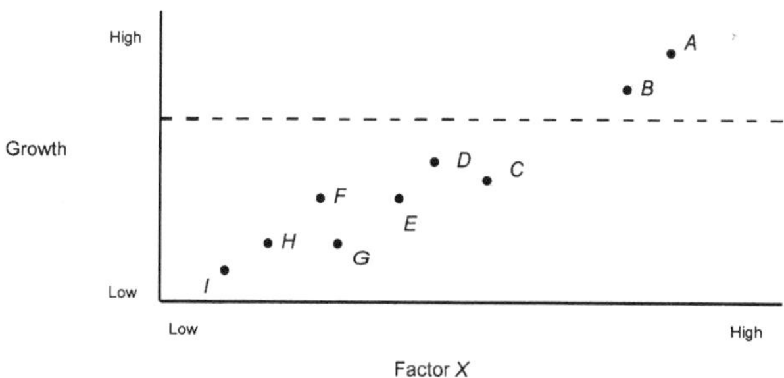

Fig. 3.1. Assumed relationship between factor *X* and growth

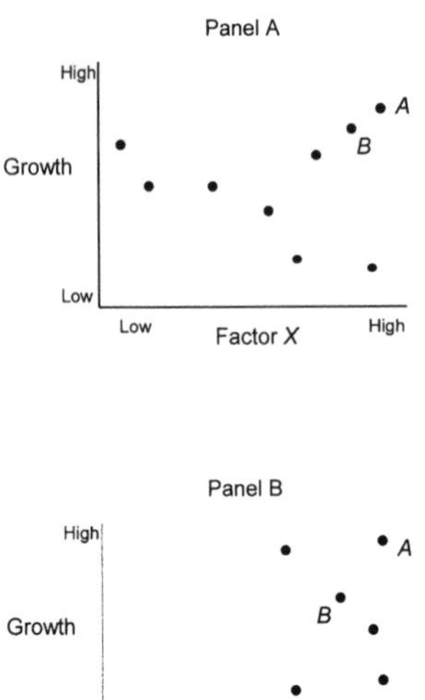

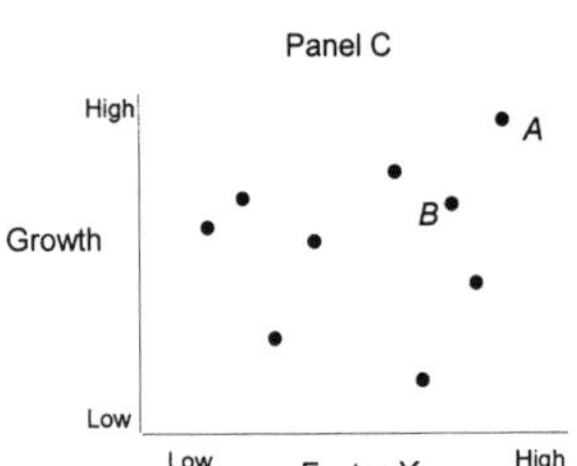

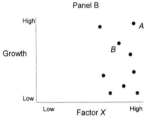

Fig. 3.2. Alternative possible relationships between factor *X* and growth

between *X* and the rate of development. The only things that can actually be explained using a sample selected on the dependent variable are differences among the selected cases.

When one looks only at the cases above the broken line in figure 3.1, two kinds of mistaken inference can occur. The first involves jumping to the conclusion that any characteristic that the selected cases share is a cause. The other involves inferring that relationships (or absence of relationships) between variables *within* the selected set of cases reflect relationships in the entire population of cases.

In the statistical literature, attention has focused on the second kind of faulty inference (Achen 1986; King 1989). If the true relationship between factor *X* and the dependent variable is that shown in figure 3.1 but one selects cases in a manner that results in the examination only of cases located above the broken line, statistical procedures carried out on the selected cases may indicate that no relationship exists or even that the relationship is the opposite of the true one. Selection on the dependent variable biases statistical results toward finding no relationship even when one does, in fact, exist.

In nonquantitative work, however, the first kind of faulty inference is at least as common as the second. If the main causes of the dependent variable are factors *R* through *T,* not including *X,* and one selects cases from one end of the dependent variable, *X* may appear to be important in the selected sample either because of random variation or because it explains some of the differences among cases still remaining in the data set even after the selection has limited it (or because it is correlated with some other factor that explains the remaining differences). In the former situation, the true relationship might look like one of the panels in figure 3.2, but the analyst—on the basis of bits and pieces of information rather than a systematic check—assumes that cases C through I are located in the lower left quadrant and concludes that factor *X* causes the outcome of interest even though, in fact, no relationship exists. In the latter situation, factor *X* makes a minor contribution to the outcome, but the analyst overestimates its importance. An example should help to make these points clearer.

A Straightforward Case of Selection on the Dependent Variable

Analysts trying to explain why some developing countries have grown so much more rapidly than others regularly select a few successful new industrializing countries (NICs) for study. Prior to the debt crisis, which began in 1982, the cases most often examined were Taiwan, South Korea, Singapore, Brazil, and Mexico (see, e.g., Haggard 1990). In all these countries, during the periods of most rapid growth, governments exerted extensive control over labor and prevented most expressions of worker discontent. Having noted this similarity, analysts argue that the repression, co-optation, discipline, or weakness of labor contributes to high growth. Chalmers Johnson (1987, 149), for example, asserts that weak unions and "federations of unions devoid of all but token political power are real comparative advantages in international economic competition." Frederic Deyo (1984, 1987) argues that an export-led growth strategy depends on cheap skilled labor and, consequently, a disciplined and quiescent labor force. Hagen Koo (1987) claims that labor control is needed in order to attract foreign investment.[3]

These claims draw additional plausibility from their convergence with arguments made in studies aimed not at explaining growth but at understanding authoritarian interventions in the more developed countries of Latin America. Among the best known of these is Guillermo O'Donnell's argument (1973) that the transition from the easy stage of import-substitution industrialization to a more capital-intensive stage creates a need for reduced consumption and, hence, a demand for the repression of labor.[4] In the same vein, Fernando Henrique Cardoso (1973a) and Peter Evans (1979) argue that labor repression helps attract foreign investment.

Whatever the details of the argument, many scholars who have studied the NICs seem to agree that repression or co-optation of the labor force contributes to growth. Taiwan, South Korea (especially between 1961 and 1986), Singapore (after 1968), Brazil (1967–81), and Mexico (before 1982) all had repressed and/or co-opted labor forces and relatively high growth rates. In other words, all have the outcome of interest and all exhibit another common trait—labor repression—so analysts conclude that labor repression has caused the outcome.

But that conclusion is unwarranted. Perhaps there are other countries in which labor suffers at least as much repression as in the high-growth countries examined but that have failed to prosper. In order to establish the plausibility of the claim that labor repression contributes to development, it would be necessary to select a sample of cases without reference to their position on the dependent variable (growth), rate each case on its level of labor repression, and show that, on average, countries with higher levels of repression grow faster.

To be persuasive, theories must be tested on at least a few cases other than those examined in the initial development of the

3. Haggard (1986, 354–56) provides a careful and nuanced review of several of these arguments.

4. The dependent variable in O'Donnell's study is regime type, not growth, and its research design is exemplary. O'Donnell compared the two countries that had experienced military intervention with a set of other Latin American countries that, at the time he wrote, remained democratic.

idea. At the stage of theory development, it is virtually impossible to avoid "overfitting," that is, tailoring arguments to fit the circumstances found in particular cases. Testing arguments on other cases allows the analyst to discover which factors proposed as possible causes during the discovery stage of theory building really do have general causal influence and which should, in the context of a general argument, be thought of as part of the "error term." The "error term" contains all those serendipitous, conjunctural, and other kinds of factors that contribute to particular outcomes in particular cases but that do not *systematically* influence outcomes.

Domain of the Argument

To test this or any other hypothesis, one must first identify the universe of cases to which the hypothesis should apply and then find or develop measures of the hypothesized causes and effects. The theory or hypothesis being tested determines the appropriate unit of analysis and the universe of potential observations.

If a theory suggests a relationship between some cause and individual behavior, the test of hypotheses derived from that theory should be based on observations of individuals. Where the unit of analysis is the individual, valid inferences can often be made in studies of single countries or even single towns, because, unless the town has been chosen precisely because the particular kind of individual behavior to be explained prevails within it, observing a range of individuals within a town does not entail selection on the dependent variable. The full range of individual variation may well occur within a town. Thus, for example, the research design used in William Sheridan Allen's *The Nazi Seizure of Power* (1973) avoids selection bias by including both individuals who embraced Nazism and those who resisted, and also by including change in individual attitudes over time.[5]

If, however, the hypothesis predicts country-level outcomes, as those linking labor repression and growth usually do, one should test it on a set of countries that reflects a reasonable range

5. In his critique of King, Keohane, and Verba (1994), Rogowski (1995) has noted that Allen's thoughtful study of one town in which Nazism enjoyed an early and substantial success deepens and enriches our understanding of the rise of Nazism. In the comparative field, we are inclined to equate cases automatically with territorial entities, but the unit of analysis used by Allen is clearly the individual, not the town, and thus he did not select on the dependent variable.

of variation on the country-level outcome. In short, the cases on which an argument is tested should reflect the level of analysis at which the argument is posed.

In everyday language, a case is a single entity, most often a country, but possibly a city, region, agency, administration, social movement, party, revolution, election, policy decision, or virtually anything else that involves interacting human beings. The more technical definition of a case is a unit within which each variable measured takes on only one value or is classified in only one category (Eckstein 1975). Many everyday language case studies include multiple technical cases, otherwise known as observations. Much of the disagreement in the literature over the usefulness of case studies has arisen from a confusion between, on the one hand, the everyday usage of the word *case* to mean (usually) a country; and, on the other hand, the more technical usage of *case* to mean an observation—the sense intended by those who give methodological advice, such as King, Keohane, and Verba (1994).

The appropriate universe of observations on which to test a hypothesis depends on the domain implied by the hypothesis. In other words, the domain depends on the substantive content of the theory or hypothesis itself, not necessarily on the author's statements about where the argument should apply. If an analyst proposes a theory about the effects of industrialization on late developing democratic countries, then tests of the theory can and should be carried out on a sample of countries drawn from the universe of *all* late developing democratic countries. Theories can contain substantive elements that limit their domain to particular regions of the world or time periods, and, if so, those limitations should be kept in mind during testing. Theories are not, however, automatically limited to the domain within which they were first proposed. Authors sometimes fail to realize that their arguments might apply to countries with which they are unfamiliar.

Well-intentioned scholars can disagree about what constitutes the appropriate domain of a theory, but their disagreements should derive from different interpretations of the implications of the theory. Tests of hypotheses in controversial domains can be useful in establishing clearer limits to the domain, extending it, and suggesting new hypotheses about why the domain has the limits it does. It is also legitimate to test arguments in domains outside those implied by theories to see whether the theories have greater generality than their creators realized, though negative results in such tests fail to disconfirm the argument within its original domain.

If the whole universe of cases is too large to study, examination of a random sample is usually recommended as a means of ensuring that the criteria of selection do not correlate with the dependent variable. One can, however, make valid inferences from any sample selected in a way that does not inadvertently result in a set of cases clustered at one end of the outcome continuum. Moreover, randomization does not guarantee the absence of correlation. If, at a particular time, the universe contains only cases that have passed a certain threshold of success because "nature" has in some fashion weeded out the others, then even random or total samples will, in effect, have been selected on the dependent variable. If, for example, potential states that failed to adopt a given military innovation in the fifteenth century were later defeated and incorporated into other states, one would not be able to find evidence of the importance of this innovation by examining a random sample of the states that existed in the eighteenth century. All surviving states would have the innovation.[6]

Some theories have implications that apply to only one end of the dependent variable. To test hypotheses based on these implications, the analyst must, of course, choose cases from the relevant part of the outcome continuum. This may appear at first glance to entail selection on the dependent variable, but it does not. The outcome relevant for the test of a particular implication is the outcome predicted by this hypothesis about that implication, not the outcome explained by the theory. The full range of variation in the outcome predicted by the hypothesis may be contained at one end of the outcome predicted by the theory. For example, one of the implications of the cadre-interests argument described in chapter 2 is that military governments are more likely to negotiate their extrication from power than are personalist regimes. One way to test this implication is to compare the incidence of negotiation by different kinds of dictatorship during the years in which breakdown occurs. In other words, only regimes that had experienced breakdown would be included in the test (one end of the breakdown versus

6. An extensive and thought-provoking discussion of selection by nature can be found in Przeworski and Limongi (1993).

persistence outcome continuum), but the hypothesis actually being tested is about the incidence of negotiation during transitions, not about the causes of breakdown. The outcome continuum relevant for testing this hypothesis is the negotiation versus no negotiation continuum, not the breakdown versus persistence continuum.

For the hypothesis that labor repression contributes to growth, different arguments about the specific reasons a weak labor force might have this effect imply different domains for the argument. One possibility is that the domain should simply include all developing countries. In one of the tests of the argument below, I have included all developing countries for which the Penn World Tables collected data between 1970 and 1982, except those with communist governments, those embroiled in civil war for more than a third of the period covered, and those that are extremely small (fewer than 500,000 inhabitants).[7] Communist countries are excluded because the various theories apply only to countries with capitalist or mixed economies. The other exclusions involve countries with characteristics not related to labor repression that could be expected to affect greatly their growth rates and thus might distort the apparent relationship between labor repression and growth. In the second test, I narrow the domain to conform to arguments associated with O'Donnell and others who expect labor repression to contribute to growth once a certain threshold of development has been reached.

Measurement

The outcome to be explained, growth rate, presents no measurement problems; various measures are readily available. For this test, I used the Penn World Tables to calculate growth in GDP per capita between 1970 and 1982, since most of the studies of development strategies focus on the period before the debt crisis. A further test of the hypothesis that included economic performance in the far more adverse post-1982 international economic environment would also be interesting and useful.

The hypothesized cause—labor repression, co-optation, or quiescence—is more difficult to measure. Standard indicators are not available, and labor repression can take different forms

7. Developing countries are defined as those with per capita income below $4,200 in 1979. This cut-off point excludes wealthy oil exporters (per capita income above $4,200), Saudi Arabia, Kuwait, Libya, and the United Arab Emirates.

in different contexts, for example, state co-optation in one country and private violence against workers in another. To deal with this difficulty, I developed criteria for ranking each country on labor repression, using the *Country Reports on Human Rights Practices* prepared for congressional committees on foreign relations (U.S. Department of State, 1979–83), *Amnesty International Annual Reports* (1973–83), and many studies of labor in particular countries.

Eighty-four developing countries were given scores between zero and one for every year between 1970 and 1981 on five factors expected to contribute to the ability of workers to defend their interests:

- The extent to which unions are legal and free to function
- The autonomy of unions from government or ruling-party control or manipulation
- The right to bargain collectively and to strike
- The degree of political participation allowed to workers and the organizations that represent them
- Freedom from violence, arbitrary arrest, and other forms of repression

When these factors are combined, possible scores range from zero to five, with high scores indicating extreme control and repression and low scores reflecting freedom to organize, independence from ruling parties, legal protection of the right to bargain and strike, freedom to participate in politics, and protection from violence and repression. Countries with very low scores include Fiji, Mauritius, and Jamaica. The highest scorers are Uganda, Haiti, and Iraq. The countries included and their average labor repression scores are shown in appendix B.

In countries that experienced regime changes, policies toward labor usually changed along with the government. Yearly scoring of each country allowed those changes to be tracked. The coding sheet that was used to keep track of information while consulting multiple sources is shown in appendix B, along with the coding scheme. The coding scheme gives careful rules for translating the information gathered into numbers.

The purpose of coding sheets and coding rules, discussed at greater length in chapter 4, is to help make sure that the same factors are assessed in every case and that they are all judged using the same criteria. While it is obvious that some such aid to memory is required for dealing with eighty-four cases, explicit coding rules also increase the precision of studies that focus on only a few cases. I would urge getting into the habit of writing down explicit coding rules, no matter what the number of observations. It helps the analyst stick to the same rules across countries and time, and it also helps readers understand exactly what the analyst means when she makes assessments of key causal factors. The phrase *labor repression* no doubt has somewhat different connotations for scholars with different areas of expertise, but the person who has read the coding scheme in appendix B will have a very clear idea of what is meant by the term here.

Although the indicator of labor repression created in this way is an imperfect measure of a complex set of phenomena, and experts might have small disagreements about the placement of a few cases, this measure is at least as precise as the verbal descriptions available in the literature. It seems, therefore, adequate to the present task of demonstrating a methodological point.

Tests of the hypothesis linking labor repression to growth using these data are shown in figures 3.3, 3.4, 3.5, and 3.6. Figure 3.3 shows the relationship between average labor repression and average growth from 1970 to 1981 for the sample of NICs most frequently studied (Taiwan, South Korea, Singapore, Brazil, and Mexico). This scatterplot reflects the most commonly chosen research strategy for studying the NICs in the 1970s and 1980s. It shows that repression and growth were both relatively high in all five countries. Analysts assumed, without checking carefully, that most of the cases they had not examined would lie in the lower left quadrant of the figure. From data like these—but in verbal form—researchers have concluded that labor repression contributes to growth. The plot shown here actually lends some plausibility to the argument because, using the quantitative measure of labor repression I created, it is possible to show small differences in labor repression that are not discernible in the verbal descriptions. Original statements of the argument did not distinguish levels of repressiveness among these cases of relatively high repression.

Note that the faulty inference expressed in the literature on the NICs is the opposite of the one that a thoughtless analyst using statistical methods would have drawn. A number cruncher might have concluded, on the basis of these data points, that

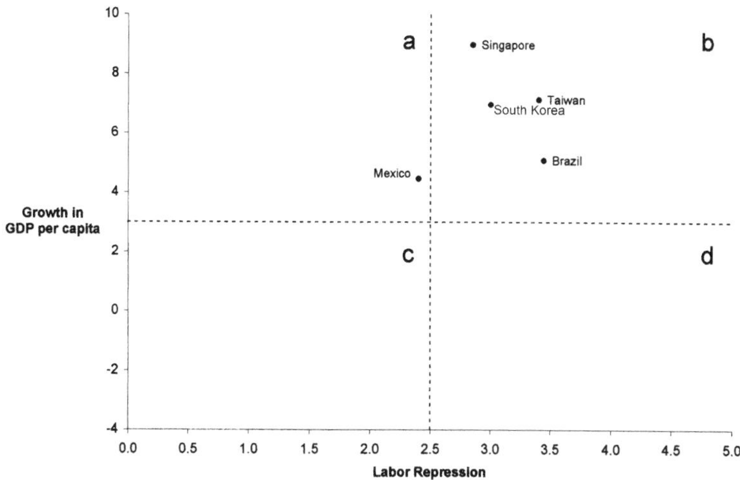

Fig. 3.3. Labor repression and growth in the most frequently studied cases, 1970–81. (GDP per capita from Penn World Tables.)

repression did not cause growth, because the variance in repression explained little of the variance in growth rate within this high-growth sample; on the other hand, the nonquantitative comparativist would conclude that since all cases are high on both growth and repression, repression must be a cause of growth. But, in fact, no conclusion can be drawn from figure 3.3. It simply contains too little information.

Scholars working on East Asia, where the fastest-growing NICs have historically been located, played an important role in developing the argument linking labor repression to growth. If, rather than selecting the five industrializing countries most frequently described in the literature, we examine the cases most familiar to East Asia specialists, it appears that repression does indeed contribute to growth, as shown in figure 3.4.

Based on an image of the world drawn from a few countries in one part of the world, some analysts advanced general arguments about the role of labor repression in growth, implying that the relationship that seemed apparent in Asia would also characterize the entire developing world. Such an inference cannot be justified, because the selection of cases by virtue of their location in East Asia biases the sample just as surely as would selection explicitly based on growth rates. This is so because, on average, growth rates in East Asia are unusually high. (See table 3.1.) Geographical area is correlated with growth, and consequently

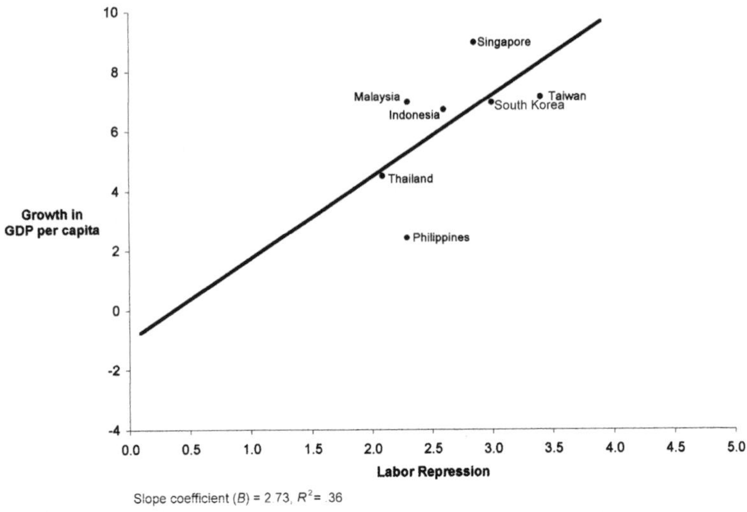

Fig. 3.4. Labor repression and growth in the Asian cases, 1970–81. (GDP per capita from Penn World Tables; for Thailand, from World Bank 1984.)

the selection of cases by geographical location amounts to selection on the dependent variable.

When one looks at the relationship between average labor repression and average growth for a larger sample of countries that includes slow-growing as well as fast-growing ones, the apparent relationship shown in figure 3.4 disappears. As figure 3.5 shows, the slope is approximately flat, and the R^2 is near zero. In other words, level of labor repression has no discernible effect on growth in the larger sample.

It might be objected that several of the arguments linking labor repression to growth were never intended to apply to the entire Third World. Rather, their logic depends on tensions that develop only after industrialization has progressed to a certain

TABLE 3.1. Average Country Growth Rates by Region

	1960–82 (% per capita)	1965–86 (% per capita)
East Asia	5.2	5.1
South Asia	1.4	1.5
Africa	1.0	0.5
Latin America	2.2	1.2
Middle East and North Africa	4.7	3.6

Source: Calculated from data in World Bank (1984, 1988).

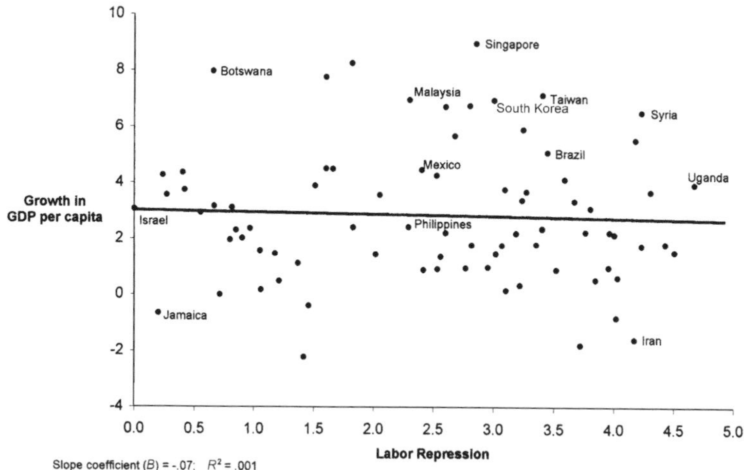

Fig. 3.5. Labor repression and growth in the full universe of developing countries, 1970–81. The countries included, and their labor repression scores, appear in appendix B. (GDP per capita from Penn World Tables.)

stage. Since the literature is unclear about exactly what level of industrialization countries would need to achieve before labor repression would be expected to contribute to growth, I had to decide on a reasonable cutoff point. I used the level of development in South Korea at the beginning of the 1970s as the threshold, since South Korea was the least developed of the countries often discussed as successful examples of labor repression and growth. Figure 3.6 shows the relationship between average labor repression and average growth in the subset of countries that were at least as developed as South Korea in 1970. As figure 3.6 shows, there is no linear relationship between labor repression and growth, even in this subset of cases. The slope is only slightly positive, and the R^2 remains near zero.

In this set of cases, the country with the lowest average growth is Iran, which also scores very high on labor repression. Since Iran's growth rate was depressed toward the end of this period by the revolution, it could be argued that it should be removed from the data set, even though its civil war did not last very long. If this is done, the slope coefficient rises to 0.27, but it remains far from statistical significance, and the R^2 remains near zero. Thus, even with Iran removed, the analysis fails to support the claim that labor repression contributes to growth.

It has been suggested that not labor repression per se but the repression of a previously well organized and mobilized working

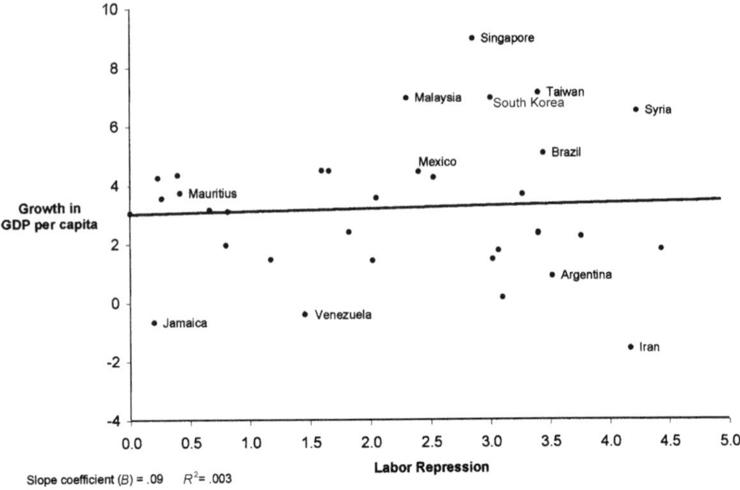

Fig. 3.6. Labor repression and growth in higher-income developing countries, 1970–81. The countries included are those from appendix B whose GDP per capita in 1970 was greater than that of South Korea. (GDP per capita from Penn World Tables.)

class would improve economic performance (O'Donnell 1973; Collier 1979). To test whether increasing repression increases growth, I have estimated time-series models of the effect of yearly labor repression on growth in the following year. In one of the models, two factors that might also be expected to affect growth—oil exports and level of development at the beginning of the period—are controlled for. In the other model, instead of trying to identify the various things that might be expected to affect growth, country fixed effects estimators are used to hold constant all the various country-specific factors that could affect growth rates. When country fixed effects estimators are used, coefficients can be interpreted as reflecting the effect of changes in the variable of interest—here, labor repression—within each country, rather than cross-country differences.

Table 3.2 shows the results of these two regressions. In the model with control variables, the effect of labor repression on growth is both minuscule and statistically insignificant. In the model using fixed effects, the coefficient for labor repression is positive, but not statistically significant. If the coefficient were reliable, it would indicate that for each unit of increase in the labor repression score, a little under a third of a percentage point of extra growth could be expected. The low R^2 for the model

TABLE 3.2. The Effect of Changes in Labor Repression on Growth

Dependent Variable: Annual Growth in GDP Per Capita

	OLS with Control Variables[a]		OLS with Fixed Effects[a]	
	Coefficient	$P > \|Z\|$	Coefficient	$P > \|Z\|$
Labor repression (range 0–5)	.018	.917	.288	.286
Oil exports	.008	.850		
Development level	−.000	.751		
R^2	.000		.099	

[a]Panel corrected standard errors.

shows that even with the inclusion of seventy-nine country fixed effects,[8] the regression explains almost none of the variance in growth.[9]

The point of this exercise is not to demonstrate that the hypothesis that labor repression contributes to growth is false. It may have a small positive effect. It might be that the addition of appropriate control variables or an elaborate lag structure would make clear a relationship that does not show in the simple tests done here. These tests do show, however, that the strong relationship that seems to exist when the analyst examines only the most rapidly growing countries is hard to find when a more representative sample of cases is examined. If analysts interested in the success of the NICs had examined a more representative sample, they would probably have reached different conclusions about the relationship between labor repression and growth. As figures 3.5 and 3.6 show, labor is as often repressed in slow-growing Third World countries as in fast-growing ones.

To sum up, the first example above (fig. 3.3) demonstrates selection bias in its simplest form: the cases are selected precisely because they share the trait one wants to explain. In the second example (fig. 3.4), cases are selected on the basis of a characteristic—geographical region—that is correlated with the dependent variable. In both instances, the hypothesized relationship was a simple, direct one: a higher level of X (labor repression) seemed to result in a higher level of Y (growth).

Not all causal arguments are so simple. Researchers sometimes posit arguments with complicated structures of prior and

8. Four countries had to be excluded because of missing data.

9. Other models were tried using different error specifications and corrections for autocorrelation, even though the regressions reported in table 3.2 disclosed no autocorrelation. In none did the coefficient for repression reach statistical significance.

intervening variables that are more difficult to test rigorously. The consequences of selection on the dependent variable, however, are the same no matter how complicated the argument. The next section will consider another frequently encountered variation on this theme: selection on the dependent variable in a complicated, contingent historical argument.

Selection on the Dependent Variable in a Complicated Historical Argument

Theda Skocpol's stimulating and thoughtful book *States and Social Revolutions* (1979) combines selection on the dependent variable with a complex historical argument. She wants to explain why revolutions occur, so she picks the three most well known instances—the French, Russian, and Chinese revolutions—to examine in detail. She also examines a few cases in which revolution failed to occur, using them as contrasts at strategic points in her chain of argument. The use of cases selected from both ends of the dependent variable makes this a more sophisticated design than the studies of the NICs.

Skocpol argues that external military threats cause state officials to initiate reforms opposed by the dominant class. If the dominant class has an independent economic base and a share of political power, its opposition will be effective and will cause a split in the elite. If, in addition, peasants live in solidary communities autonomous from day-to-day landlord supervision, they will take advantage of the elite split and rebel, which will lead to revolution. (This argument is schematized in fig. 3.7.) This explanation, according to Skocpol, mirrors the historical record in

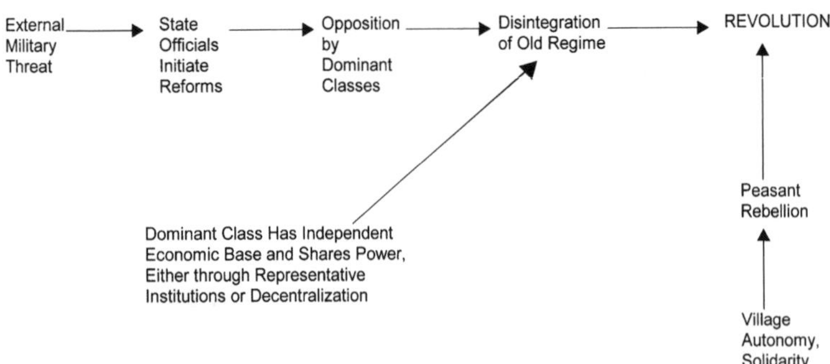

Fig. 3.7. Schematization of Skocpol's argument

France and in the parts of China controlled by the Communists during Japanese occupation. The Russian case differs from the other two in that the upper class lacked the independent economic base necessary to impede state-sponsored reforms. Consequently, the elite remained unified, and revolution failed to occur after the Crimean War. Nevertheless, defeat in World War I caused elite disintegration, which opened the way for revolution in 1917.

At two points in the chain of argument, Skocpol introduces contrasting cases to strengthen her contention that structural features identified as causes in these three cases have general significance. In an examination of Prussia during the late eighteenth to early nineteenth century and Japan during the late nineteenth century, she finds that dominant classes lacked the independent economic base necessary to obstruct state reforms. Both Prussia and Japan faced military threats at least as severe as that facing France, but elites remained unified, and revolution failed to occur. She also looks at Britain during the Civil War and Germany in 1848 and finds levels of village autonomy low. In both cases, elites split, but peasants failed to take advantage of the situation; as a result, revolutions did not occur. These comparisons are summarized in figures 3.8 and 3.9. As the figures show, the cases she examines appear to provide strong support for the argument.

There is no question that the examination of contrasting cases makes the argument more persuasive than it would otherwise be, though an assessment of the argument based on a few cases selected from the other end of the dependent variable carries less weight than would a test based on more cases selected without reference to the dependent variable. Nevertheless, examination of contrasting cases is a solid step in the right

	Elite Split	Elite Cohesive
Dominant Class Economically Independent, Shares Power	France China, after Taiping Rebellion	
Dominant Class Dependent, Excluded from Power	Russia, World War I	Prussia Japan China, before Taiping Rebellion Russia, before World War I

Fig. 3.8. Given external threat, the effect of dominant-class power on the likelihood of an elite split

	Revolution	No Revolution
Village Autonomy	Russia France China, in area controlled by Communists	
Village Dependence		Britain, 1640-60 Germany, 1848 China, before Communists

Fig. 3.9. Given an elite split, the effect of village autonomy on the likelihood of revolution

direction and one of the reasons that Skocpol's study has been considered so persuasive.

Skocpol makes no effort, however, to test other links in the chain of argument with comparable care. In particular, she offers no contrasting cases to strengthen her claim that

> developments within the international states system as such—especially defeats in wars or threats of invasion and struggles over colonial controls—have directly contributed to virtually all outbreaks of revolutionary crises. (23)[10]

This claim, which looms large in the overall thesis, seems especially problematic if we accept her implicit definition of "threatened," that is, as threatened as late-eighteenth-century France. France—arguably the most powerful country in the world at the time—was certainly less threatened than its neighbors.

Most countries in the world have suffered foreign pressures as great as those suffered by prerevolutionary France, and yet revolutions occur infrequently. This raises the question, Are revolutions infrequent because of the absence of appropriate structural conditions, as Skocpol's argument implies, or because foreign threats have less causal impact than Skocpol believes? To distinguish between these two possibilities, one would need to choose a set of cases in which the structural conditions identified by Skocpol did in fact exist (in effect, holding the structural condi-

10. Note that "contributed to virtually all" is a probabilistic statement, not a statement that foreign threat is necessary but not sufficient to explain revolution. Other statements of this argument, however, can be interpreted as meaning that external threats are necessary but not sufficient causes of revolution (Dion 1998).

tions constant). Within this set of countries, one would then need to assess the relationship between level of threat and revolutionary outcome. If threat and occurrence of revolution tended to go together in this set of cases, we would have greater faith in the correctness of Skocpol's argument. If, however, high levels of threat did not seem to increase the likelihood of revolution within this set of cases, we would feel more skeptical about it.

To carry out this test, as with the prior one, we first need to establish the appropriate domain of the argument. The question of what would constitute an appropriate domain for testing Skocpol's argument is controversial. Skocpol herself is extremely modest about the domain for her argument, stating at one point: "Can [the arguments presented in this book] be applied beyond the French, Russian, and Chinese cases? In a sense, the answer is unequivocally 'no'. . . . [T]he causes of revolutions . . . necessarily vary according to the historical and international circumstances of the countries involved" (288). Skocpol does not eschew generalizability entirely, however, since she evidently considers seventeenth-century England, eighteenth- and nineteenth-century Prussia, and mid-nineteenth-century Germany and Japan within the domain of her argument. But she does explicitly limit her argument to "agrarian states," which I take as including countries in the early stages of industrialization (since all the cases included in her study had begun to industrialize) but excluding fully industrialized countries and preagrarian primitive societies. She also limits the argument to countries that have never been colonized; wealthy, "historically autonomous and well-established imperial states" (288); and countries "whose state and class structures had not been recently created" (40).

In the face of such modesty, the rest of the scholarly community has two options in assessing the study. One is to accept the self-imposed limitations suggested by the author and try to test the argument on the set of cases implied by them. The broadest interpretation of these limiting criteria suggests that the appropriate universe thus defined would include, besides some (but not all) of those actually used by Skocpol, only the larger and wealthier pre–World War I states of Europe: Belgium, the Netherlands, Spain, Portugal, Sweden, Lithuania before 1795, Poland before partition, Austria, the Austro-Hungarian Empire, and the Ottoman Empire. This universe includes a fair number of nonrevolutions, so it would be quite possible to retest the argument on this set of cases.

Limiting the argument to this domain does, however, restrict its interest, since twentieth-century revolutions, with the exception of the Russian revolution, have occurred in poor countries that had been at least partly colonized and would thus be outside the domain of Skocpol's argument. Moreover, Skocpol's own selection of cases casts some doubt on the appropriateness of the domain she describes. Japan was not a "well-established imperial state" in the mid-nineteenth century. Nor was China in the twentieth. Germany's state structure, though not affected by colonialism, had been recently created in 1848. China, Japan, and arguably Russia were poor. The time period and geographical location identified by Skocpol as those in which the Chinese peasantry had the autonomy to rebel were precisely the time period and area of Japanese colonization. In short, many of Skocpol's cases violate her own criteria for limiting the domain of her argument.

The alternative approach is to derive the domain of the argument directly from the substantive claims of the argument itself. If we do this, the appropriate domain would seem to include all independent, not fully industrialized states (and possibly empires). These restrictions are necessary because the argument seems to require (1) the existence of an indigenous state elite and dominant class; and (2) a peasantry. Skocpol herself is most adamant about excluding colonized nations from the domain (288–90). This seems a reasonable exclusion during the period of colonization (when the state elite and often the dominant class as well are not indigenous) and perhaps for some limited time—a decade or two—after independence.[11] The claim that any country that has ever been colonized should be forever excluded does not seem to flow from anything in the argument itself, however, and also seems to ignore the role of conquest in the development of the states included in the original argument. After all, England was once colonized by the Normans, large parts of Russia by the Mongols and Tatars, and China by the Mongols. In all three, aspects of subsequent state organization and development are commonly traced to the effects of these conquests.

11. If we think of the domain as derived from the argument itself rather than from Skocpol's somewhat ad hoc comments about it, then her inclusion of China during the time that much of the country was colonized by Japan seems less puzzling. Throughout the Japanese occupation, an indigenous Chinese state elite and dominant class continued to exist in southern China, and it was they whom the Chinese Communists eventually defeated, not the Japanese.

Skocpol also argues that small countries should be excluded because revolutions in them may be caused or prevented by outside intervention (289). This is a legitimate concern. It should not lead to the blanket exclusion of all small countries, however, since we know that outside intervention has failed to prevent revolution in a number of them. Yet it might be reasonable to eliminate some cases in which a persuasive argument can be made about the decisiveness of intervention.

Ideally, a test of Skocpol's hypothesis about the effects of military competition would examine all independent, not fully industrialized states characterized by the structural features—village autonomy and a dominant class with an independent economic base and access to political power—that she identifies as necessary to complete the sequence from military threat to revolution. Then one could determine whether revolutions occur more frequently in countries that have faced military threats.

In practice, identifying the universe of cases that meet these structural criteria is probably impossible. It would require extensive knowledge about every country in the world from the English Civil War to the present. Nonetheless, moderately serious tests of her argument are possible, and one is shown below.

As it happens, several Latin American countries (Mexico, Guatemala, El Salvador, Honduras, Nicaragua, Ecuador, Peru, Bolivia, and Paraguay) have the structural characteristics she identifies and so can be used as a set of cases on which to test the hypothesis linking military threat to revolution. These cases are obviously not selected at random, but since their geographical location is not correlated with revolution, geography does not serve as a proxy for the dependent variable (as occurred in the test of the relationship between labor repression and growth among the East Asian NICs).

In all these countries, dominant classes had an independent economic base in land and/or mining from the nineteenth century until well into the twentieth. They also shared political power. Thus, they had the economic and political resources that Skocpol identifies as necessary to oppose state-sponsored reforms successfully and so pave the way for revolution.

These countries also all contained (and most still contain) large, severely exploited indigenous and mestizo populations, many of whom lived in autonomous, solidary villages. Spanish colonial policy reinforced, and in some areas imposed, corporate village structure. After independence, changes in property rights reduced village control over land, but this reduction in the functions that had contributed to building village autonomy and solidarity was at least partially offset by the increase in absentee landlordism that accompanied increasing commercialization.

Much of the land in these countries was held in large tracts. Some peasants lived on the haciendas, but many lived in traditional villages, owned tiny parcels of land or had use rights to communal land, and worked seasonally on the haciendas. These villages often had long histories of conflict with large landowners over land ownership, water rights, and grazing rights. Villages governed themselves in traditional ways. Landlords have rarely lived in villages in these countries. In short, the rural areas of these Latin American countries approximate Skocpol's description of the autonomous, solidary village structure that makes possible peasants' participation in revolution. Differences of opinion are, of course, possible about whether peasants in these countries were really autonomous enough from day-to-day landlord control to enable them to play the role Skocpol allots to peasants in bringing about social revolutions. Perhaps the best evidence that they were is that revolutions have in fact occurred in several of these countries, and peasant rebellions have occurred in most of them.

With these structural features on which the outcome is contingent held constant, it becomes possible to test the relationship between external threat and revolution. In the test below, I have used a higher level of threat than that experienced by France in the late eighteenth century. I wanted to choose a criterion for assessing threat that would eliminate arguments about whether a country was "really" threatened enough, and I found it hard to establish an unambiguous criterion that corresponded to the "France threshold." Consequently, the criterion used here is loss of a war, accompanied by invasion and/or loss of territory to the opponent. With such a high threat threshold, finding cases of revolution in the absence of threat will not disconfirm Skocpol's argument, since the countries may have experienced external pressures sufficient to meet her criteria even though they did not lose wars. If, however, several countries did lose wars (and the structural conditions identified as necessary by Skocpol are present) but have not had revolutions, this test will cast doubt on her argument.

Figure 3.10 shows eight instances of extreme military threat that failed to lead to revolution, two revolutions (if the Cuban

	Revolution	No Revolution
Defeated and Invaded or Lost Territory	Bolivia (1935), revolution 1952	Peru (1839) Bolivia (1839) Mexico (1848) Mexico (1862-66) Paraguay (1869) Peru (1883) Bolivia (1883) Colombia (1903)
Not Defeated within 20 Years	Mexico, revolution 1910–17 Nicaragua, revolution 1979	All Others

Note: The Cuban Revolution is not, in Skocpol's terms, a social revolution because it did not entail massive uprisings of the lower classes.

Fig. 3.10. Relationship between military defeat and revolution in Latin America (with Skocpol's structural variables held constant)

revolution of 1959 is not counted, because it does not fit Skocpol's definition of a social revolution as entailing massive uprisings of the lower classes) that were not preceded by any unusual degree of external competition or threat, and one revolution, the Bolivian, that fits Skocpol's argument. I do not think any foreign power deserves credit or blame for any of the revolutions that have occurred, and thus the finding that two revolutions occurred without unusual foreign threat is not undermined by foreign influences on revolutionary outcome. The United States may deserve credit or blame for the nonoccurrence of revolution in El Salvador and Guatemala, but if these revolutions had been successful, they would have increased the number of cases in which revolutions occurred in the absence of unusual foreign threat and thus added to the evidence undermining Skocpol's argument. In short, among these cases there is little support for the claim that foreign threat increases the likelihood of revolution. If we accept the idea that the domain depends on the argument itself, then these findings suggest that if Skocpol had selected a broader range of cases to examine, rather than selecting on the dependent variable, she would have reached different conclusions.

This test does not constitute a definitive disconfirmation of Skocpol's argument. Competing interpretations of all the concepts used in the argument—village autonomy, dominant-class independence, military pressure—exist, and different operationalizations might lead to different results. In particular, my operationalization of threat fails to capture the complexity of Skocpol's idea, and a different operationalization might put Nicaragua and Mexico in the threat-revolution cell. Any indicator of threat that identified Nicaragua in 1979 and Mexico in 1910 as threatened, however, would add hundreds of other country-years to the threat–no revolution cell, because the amount of U.S. pressure experienced by these countries at these times was not at all unusual in the region. In short, despite some deficiencies in operationalization, this cursory examination of cases not selected on the dependent variable does cast doubt on the original argument.

Arguments about Necessary Causes

Some have interpreted Skocpol's statements as meaning that she sees external threat as a necessary but not sufficient cause of revolution. As Douglas Dion (1998) and others have noted, the logic underlying tests of arguments about necessary causes differs from that described above. Methods for testing arguments about necessary causes have only begun to be developed, but Dion suggests a Bayesian approach.[12] Bayesian analysis provides a way of assessing the impact of new information on one's prior beliefs about the likelihood that a particular theory is true. If, in order to keep things simple, we set aside the possibility of measurement error and think of only one rival hypothesis to the one being tested, Bayes rule can be expressed as:

$$P_{osterior}(WH|D) = \frac{P_{rior}(WH)\,P(D|WH)}{P_{rior}(WH)P(D|WH) + P_{rior}(RH)P(D|RH)},$$

where

$P_{osterior}$ (WH|D) is the probability that the working hypothesis (the one being tested) is true, in light of the new evidence collected in a study.

P_{rior}(WH) is the analyst's belief about whether the working hypothesis is true before conducting the study.

P(D|WH) is the probability that the data uncovered in this study would turn up *if* the working hypothesis were true.

P_{rior}(RH) is the analyst's belief about the likelihood that the rival hypothesis (the most likely alternative to the working hypothesis) is true prior to conducting the study.

12. See Baumoeller and Goertz (2000) for a careful non-Bayesian approach.

P(D|RH) is the probability that the data uncovered in this study would have emerged *if* the rival hypothesis were true.

If we interpret the Skocpol argument as one about the necessity of external threat, then the appropriate initial research strategy is to choose cases that have experienced revolutions and then check to see if an external threat preceded the revolution. The information about these external threats is the new data that will be used to update the assessment of the likelihood that the working hypothesis is true. Note, however, that the only way to assess the likelihood of observing the new data given that the *rival* hypothesis is true is to know enough about the whole relevant universe of cases (not just those that experienced revolution) to be able to estimate the probability of observing these events (in this case, external threats) if the rival hypothesis better describes reality. In other words, we need to know something about the frequency of the hypothesized preceding event in the universe as a whole.

In order to use Bayes' rule, it is also necessary to state a level of prior belief that the working hypothesis is true. These prior beliefs come from prior research on a subject. When little prior research has been done on a subject, it has become conventional to treat prior beliefs as neutral between the two competing hypotheses, that is, to set P(WH) = P(RH) = 0.5.

To return to the Skocpol example, if we use "as threatened as France" as the appropriate threat threshold, then I would estimate that 95 percent of all countries that would otherwise fit within the domain of the theory have experienced such a threat at some time, many of them repeatedly. With this estimate, the probability of observing the data (external threat) in any particular country between 1600 and the present, given the rival hypothesis that external threat does not cause revolution, can be calculated.

Skocpol examined three cases and found external threats in all three. The probability of seeing these data, *if* the working hypothesis is true (and there is no measurement error) equals one. If the rival hypothesis is true and 95 percent of the countries in the domain of the argument have experienced similar levels of threat at some time, then the probability of observing three instances of threat if the rival hypothesis is true equals $0.95 \times 0.95 \times 0.95 = 0.857$. Plugging these numbers into Bayes' rule, we get:

$$P_{osterior}(WH|D) = [0.5(1)] / [0.5(1) + 0.5(0.857)] = 0.539$$

In other words, when the hypothesized necessary cause is very common in the world, the increase in one's level of belief in the argument is increased only very modestly (from 0.5 to 0.539) when a few new cases are examined. If the hypothesized necessary cause only occurred in ten percent of the cases in the appropriate universe, then examining three cases and finding the data expected would increase our prior belief in the argument to above 99 percent. Thus the number of observations needed to affect posterior beliefs about a hypothesis depends very dramatically on the general distribution of the hypothesized necessary cause.[13]

From the point of view of research design, this discussion of Bayesian inference leads to two conclusions that have not been much emphasized in the literature on testing arguments about necessary causes. First, the Bayesian approach requires that the data used to assess the likelihood that the theory is true be newly observed. It must come from cases observed for the purpose of testing the argument, not from the cases from which the hypothesis was induced. The original cases, along with other research and general knowledge about the world, influence the observer's prior beliefs about whether the argument is true. Bayes' rule provides a way of judging how much more convinced by an argument we should be after seeing new data, not how much faith we should put in a plausible but untested argument.

Second, although arguments about necessary conditions can be tested using only cases selected on the dependent variable, the use of Bayesian logic to assess how much has been learned from the test requires gathering enough information about how often the hypothesized necessary cause occurs in the world more generally in order to estimate the probability that the data that were actually observed would have been observed if the rival hypothesis were true. In the non-Bayesian approach suggested by Braumoeller and Goertz (2000), this issue has been addressed under the label trivialness. Braumoeller and Goertz argue that to be non-trivially necessary, the hypothesized necessary cause must be shown to vary more than a little in the full

13. Dion (1998) provides a chart showing how many cases would be needed to reach 95 percent confidence that an argument is true, given different prior levels of belief and different estimates of the likelihood of observing the data if the rival hypothesis is true.

relevant universe. Whatever amount of variation is deemed sufficient for non-trivialness, we cannot discover it without examining at least some cases not selected on the dependent variable. If the hypothesized necessary cause occurs infrequently, then examining only a few additional cases would suffice to meet their condition.

Time Series, Case Studies, and Selection Bias

Case studies, perhaps the most common form of research in the comparative field, can often be thought of as nonquantitative time-series research designs. They usually examine a single country over a period of time, often for the purpose of explaining some outcome at the end or showing the effects of some change that occurred during the time examined. Case studies are often criticized as single data points and hence incapable of revealing anything about cause-and-effect relationships, but most can be more reasonably thought of as a series of observations of the same case at different times. In fact, most of what are called case studies actually include unsystematic observations at multiple levels of analysis (for example, individuals, government administrations, and parties) and observations of multiple entities at the same level of analysis (for example, several parties in one country) as well as observations over time. For now, however, let us focus on the simplest kind of case study—say, a study of the evolution of one party over time.

Such case studies are subject to several methodological pitfalls, solutions to which are discussed at greater length in chapter 4. Here I want to note the methodological issues related to selection bias that can arise in the context of case studies and single-case quantitative time series. In the typical study of a single case, a country, organization, or group is chosen for examination because it has experienced something unusual, sometimes because it is considered typical of a group of cases that have experienced the unusual. The variation on the dependent variable is supplied by observations of the same case at other times (when it was not experiencing the unusual). Whether such a research design involves actual selection bias depends on whether the variation over time within the case reflects the full range of outcomes in the relevant universe. Often it does not. When the selection of multiple observations of a single case results in a truncated sample relative to the appropriate universe, the result is inadvertent selection on the dependent variable, and selection bias can be expected to have the same results noted above.

The key concern for the researcher, then, is identifying the universe relevant to the question being asked or hypothesis being tested. Only when that has been done can he assess whether outcomes vary widely enough within the single case to avoid selection bias. Here, as elsewhere, the question under examination determines the appropriate universe. Sometimes one wants to understand the effect of a particular policy change in a particular setting. In this situation, one is not asking "What caused outcome *Y?*" but rather "What was the effect of cause *X?*" If cause *X* occurred only in one setting, then a one-country time series or case study is the appropriate research design (Campbell and Ross 1968). If *X* occurred in multiple places, the analyst would be wise to examine its effects in all of those places or a sample of them. Otherwise, he risks the possibility of attributing to *X* anything that might have happened in the chosen country during the time following *X.* When the analyst wants to know what caused outcome *Y,* it is always risky to examine only one entity in which *Y* occurred, even if he cares only about why it happened in a particular place and time. A case study of the particular place and time of interest may not provide the answer.

The reason it might not is that it is quite possible that selecting multiple observations of the same case will have the effect of holding constant or near constant some of the true causes of the outcome of interest, even if the dependent variable spans a considerable range. At the same time, whatever potential causal factors do vary within the single case over time will seem to explain differences in the outcome. These causes of the within-case variation can be less important causal variables that belong in a complete explanation, or they can be idiosyncratic factors that affect this case but not others and therefore do not belong in a general explanation. The analyst has no way of knowing. Either way, he will be tricked into focusing on these factors while giving short shrift to causal factors that may be changing slowly and not very noticeably during the time under study but that nevertheless explain the general trend in the outcome.

This problem is caused by inadvertent selection on one or more causal variables. Case studies are highly vulnerable to inadvertent selection from one end of the continuum of potential causes because so many factors remain constant or change slowly over time in a single entity. In statistical work, selection on the dependent variable leads to biased estimates of the effects of causal factors, but the practical result is usually a failure to demonstrate a causal relationship that actually exists, because within the truncated sample there is little variation in the outcome for differences in the causal factors to explain. Selection on the independent variable, as often happens in case studies, does not lead to biased estimates in statistical work. Nevertheless, in practice it is hard to show that a relationship between a cause and effect exists if the cause varies little within the sample. Whether observations are quantitative does not affect the logic of the research design. In either case, it is quite possible to overlook factors of real causal importance, because they do not vary much over time or follow an incremental trend that country observers take for granted.

If one knows quite a bit about the underlying causal model, a single-case time-series design can be a good way to assess the effect of one potential cause while holding many other things constant (because they do not vary within the single case), but it will be less useful in the more typical situation where the analyst does not know the underlying model. The analyst will then fail to identify any causal factor that varies little within the case and will tend to overemphasize serendipitous contributors to the outcome.

As an example, let us contemplate Albert Hirschman's careful and insightful study of inflation in Chile (1973). In this essay, Hirschman reviews Chile's major bouts of inflation between the nineteenth century and 1961. He reconsiders the role of foreign experts in Chilean policy formulation and shows the importance of dogmatic economic ideologies and policy mistakes in causing inflationary episodes. Hirschman argues in this study, and in the book of which it is a part, that policymakers gradually learn to resolve persistent problems, that the search for solutions has positive externalities in that it brings hitherto unnoticed issues to policymakers' attention, and that reformism, though messy and often emotionally unsatisfying, leads over time to significant improvements. Hirschman describes first the intermittent difficulties with inflation that Chile experienced between 1870 and 1939, and then the persistent and worsening inflation of 1940 to 1959. At each point in the story, Hirschman, with his customary flair and sensitivity to detail and context, discusses the policy mistakes and other factors that increased inflation. During the early period, inflationary episodes were caused by wars and civil wars, serious policy mistakes, and business expansions, all of which

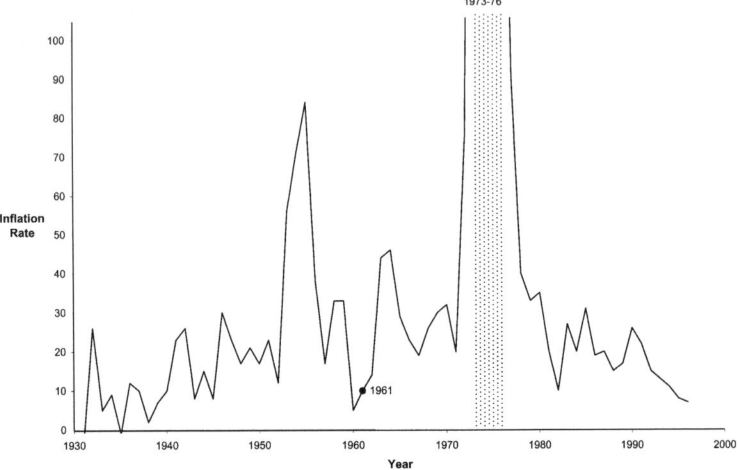

Fig. 3.11. Inflation in Chile, 1930–96. (Data for 1930–61 from Hirschman 1973; 1962–63, Corbo Loi 1974; 1964–96, IMF 1997.)

seem to have been largely self-correcting. Beginning in 1940, however, inflation became more persistent and more serious. It no longer returned to normal between episodes, and the trend line, though masked by zigzagging, began a determined upward slope (see fig. 3.11). Between 1940 and 1959, inflation averaged 28 percent per year (Hirschman 1973, 160). Chilean inflation rates are shown in table 3.3.

Hirschman attributes this worsening mostly to the effects of specific policies, especially the failure to restrict credit to the private sector and the routinization of wage adjustments. The emphasis throughout the essay is on the details of policy and the political context that influenced them. In explaining the control of inflation, which appeared to have been achieved in Chile in 1960–61, Hirschman stresses the intense political struggle over ending automatic wage adjustments—accomplished during an inflationary peak in 1956 (203–5)—and strengthening the system of credit control under President Jorge Alessandri in 1959 (219).

Although Hirschman mentions general economic factors such as fiscal deficits and exchange rates, the reader is left with the impression that Chilean inflation was caused by some fairly discrete policy mistakes. This impression is strengthened by the low inflation rates of 1960 and 1961, caused by specific policy changes introduced by the Alessandri administration. The reader never sees the bigger and more general picture: that the policy strategy of state-sponsored import-substitution industrialization (ISI), which was initiated in Chile in 1939 and varied little during the next thirty-five years, caused increasingly serious inflation.

Although the general policy strategy remained stable and was not subjected to the kind of intense political debate that accompanied the policy changes emphasized by Hirschman, its implementation over time entailed increasingly distortionary tariff and exchange rate policies. These policies led to the same problems with balance of payments crises and inflation that afflicted so many other developing countries. Inflation plagued all developing

TABLE 3.3. Chilean Inflation, 1930–96

Year	Inflation Rate (%)	Year	Inflation Rate (%)
1930	−5	1964	46
1931	−4	1965	29
1932	26	1966	23
1933	5	1967	19
1934	9	1968	26
1935	−1	1969	30
1936	12	1970	32
1937	10	1971	20
1938	2	1972	75
1939	7	1973	361
1940	10	1974	505
1941	23	1975	375
1942	26	1976	212
1943	8	1977	92
1944	15	1978	40
1945	8	1979	33
1946	30	1980	35
1947	23	1981	20
1948	17	1982	10
1949	21	1983	27
1950	17	1984	20
1951	23	1985	31
1952	12	1986	19
1953	56	1987	20
1954	71	1988	15
1955	84	1989	17
1956	38	1990	26
1957	17	1991	22
1958	33	1992	15
1959	33	1993	13
1960	5	1994	11
1961	10	1995	8
1962	14	1996	7
1963	44		

Source: 1930–61, Hirschman (1973); 1962–63, Corbo Loi (1974); 1964–96, World Bank (2002).

countries that followed state-led import-substituting development strategies. The average inflation rate for low- and middle-income countries between 1970 and 1978, a time when virtually all but the most backward were following state-led ISI strategies, was 18 percent per year, compared to about 9 percent per year for industrialized countries (World Bank 1980, 110–11). Hirschman is, of course, entirely correct in noting that discrete policy mistakes worsen inflation; they account for some of the zigzags so apparent in figure 3.11. Nevertheless, the reader interested in understanding why Chile suffered from recurrent and worsening bouts of inflation for nearly four decades after 1939 will not have recognized the main underlying cause after reading this essay.[14]

In fairness, let me note that Hirschman did not aim to explain inflation in this essay. Rather, he sought to show that inflation, like other seemingly intractable problems, could be gradually conquered as policymakers learned to understand it and took advantage of occasionally propitious political circumstances to initiate reforms. When the primary underlying cause of something has not been identified, however, identifying and "fixing" less important and less systematic causes may not result in long-term improvement. The last measure of inflation in Hirschman's study is for 1961, when it appeared that policymakers had at last brought inflation under control. The apparent cure, however, turned out to be a very brief remission.

As is apparent in table 3.3 and figure 3.11, Chilean inflation did not begin its long-term downward trend until the abandonment of state-sponsored import-substitution development policies during the Pinochet administration. The extremely high inflation rates of the Allende years and their immediate aftermath cannot be blamed on development strategy, but if those years are excluded, it is still clear that the conquest of inflation in Chile began in the late 1970s. Current Chilean economic policy-making—and low inflation—demonstrates that Hirschman was correct in believing that human beings, including policymakers, learn. But in Chile, inflation was not finally conquered by reformist muddling through and discrete policy changes, as Hirschman had hoped. It was conquered by traumatic policy changes that reversed four decades of basic economic policy strategy.

---

14. In another essay, written a few years before the one on Chile and drawing on the experiences of several Latin American countries rather than only one, Hirschman (1968) was one of the first to identify a number of the systematic ill effects of the import-substitution strategy of industrialization, including its tendency to cause inflation.

The methodological point is that even if one cares only about what caused inflation in Chile, the best research strategy for discovering these causes may require examining other cases. Important causes, such as the basic thrust of development strategy, may not change very much within a few decades in a single country. Consequently, analysts may overlook their importance and instead concentrate attention on less important causes or on conjunctural factors that turn out to have no general causal effect. Case studies generally help to explain zigzags in the trend line, but they sometimes offer little leverage for explaining the trend itself.

Case Studies, Time Series, and Regression to the Mean

The remainder of this chapter focuses on some less obvious pitfalls that face the researcher who must choose not only which cases to examine but also the beginning and end points of the study. If either the starting or ending dates of a case study or time series are chosen because of their extreme scores, the analyst must be concerned about the effects of regression to the mean, in addition to the other possibilities for mistaken inference associated with selection bias. Because extreme outcomes typically result from a combination of extremes in their systematic causes and extreme unsystematic influences (what would be called the error term in quantitative work), terrible conditions at the initiation of a study are likely to improve with the passage of time, and wonderful situations are likely to deteriorate—even if there has been no change at all in the systematic factors causing them. Such changes in the unsystematic influences on outcomes lead unwary analysts to attribute improvement or deterioration to their favorite hero or villain among intervening events, even though the only real change that has occurred is in the random factors that influence everything in social science and the rest of the world.

Regression to the mean is the name given to the tendency of any extreme situation, score, outcome, or event to be followed by one that is less extreme simply because fewer extreme random factors happened to influence things the second time. Regression to the mean causes the mismeasure of systematic change in outcomes over time. After having misunderstood the amount of change that has actually occurred, the analyst often then compounds the mistake by building an argument to explain the changes that never occurred.

Regression to the mean has been most fully analyzed in the context of educational research. The classic example involves researchers trying to assess the usefulness of a new technique for teaching remedial reading. Students' reading ability is tested. Those who score below some threshold are selected to receive special help, using the new technique. After some time has elapsed, they are tested again, and the rest of the class is also retested as a control, since all students are expected to be increasing their skill over time. The students who received special help always make greater gains than the group that did not receive help, no matter what technique is tried. Illiteracy has not disappeared, however, because at least some and perhaps all of the gain demonstrated by these students is an artifact caused by regression to the mean, not a genuine effect of the remedial reading techniques. The students who scored lowest on the first test did so for two reasons: they read less well than others; and, for unsystematic reasons such as being sick or tired, they did especially badly on the first test. The second test, like the first, measures both the systematic component of reading ability and also random factors such as sickness and tiredness. Since it is unlikely that the same children would be sick or tired during both tests, on average the scores of the remedial group would not include extreme unsystematic elements the second time, and thus they would score higher even if their reading ability had not improved.

Regression to the mean has two sources, one conceptually trivial but practically very important in the social sciences, and the other both conceptually and practically important. The first is that every measurement contains an element of error. For simple physical measurements of things, such as temperature and length, the small element of error in the measure is usually of no practical consequence, but in social science most of the things we want to explain can be "measured" only very inadequately. One of the unsystematic contributors to every outcome is thus measurement error—simply the inaccuracy of all measures, whether quantitative or not. Every outcome is also affected by happenstance, by events that will never occur again and have no theoretical importance, by luck, by the particular skills, failings, and longevity of certain individuals, and so on. These unsystematic contributors to outcomes are also, if the research goal is systematic explanation, part of the "error term." That is, both real measurement error and serendipitous factors contribute to every assessment of an outcome. They are the causes of the statistical artifact, regression to the mean.

Any time that cases are selected for study or "treatment" on the basis of high (or low) scores on some variable, the analyst unintentionally selects a sample with unusually positive (or negative) "error terms," in both senses discussed above. When the selected cases are measured a second time, the inaccuracy in their measurement is no more likely to be positive than negative, and the serendipitous events that affect the outcome then are also no more likely to be positive than negative. In consequence, cases with especially positive outcomes in a first measurement will look as though they are doing less well in a second one, and cases with especially negative outcomes in a first assessment will seem to improve over time—even if *nothing* systematic has changed.

Because most of the work on regression to the mean has occurred in the context of educational and psychological testing, students of comparative politics are sometimes unaware of its implications for their own work. Consider the following hypothetical study. The analyst wants to know what effect structural adjustment loans from international financial institutions have on the economic performance of developing countries. To answer this question, she compares the growth rate per capita in the countries that have received such loans with the growth rates of developing countries that have not. She needs to compare the countries of interest with another set of countries during the same time period as a means of controlling for international factors that affect growth all over the world. Since, however, structural adjustment loans went to countries with economies in crisis, and since these crises are caused by bad luck, bad weather, and unrepeatable events as well as by more systematic factors, their economic performance can be expected to improve, on average, whether or not the loans help. Thus, the unwary researcher who simply compares changes in the performance of countries receiving loans with changes in those that did not may be misled about the effect of the loans, since a certain amount of improvement in the countries with the worst performance could have been expected in any case.

Whenever research focuses on comparison of growth rates over time, the analyst needs to be attentive to the possibility of regression to the mean. The underlying causes of economic performance, such as resource endowment, human capital, savings

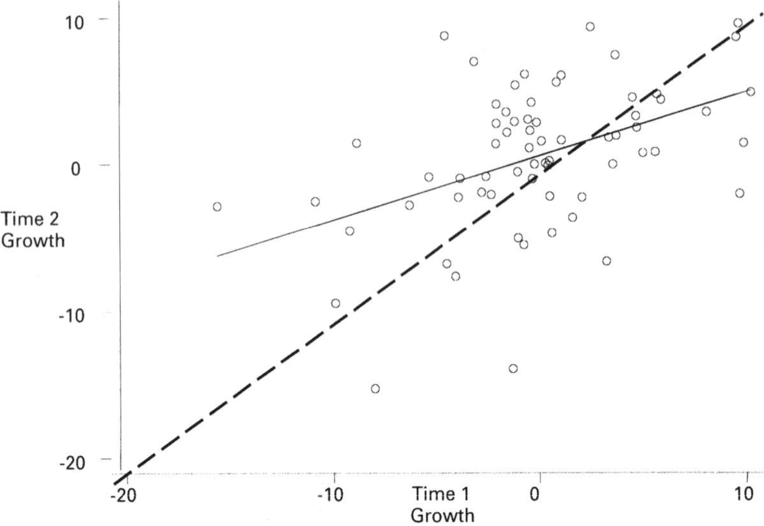

Fig. 3.12. Regression of growth in GDP per capita for 1991 on growth in GDP per capita for 1990 for developing countries. (GDP per capita from Penn World Tables.)

rate, competence of policymakers, and basic thrust of economic policy, do not change much from year to year in most countries. Consequently, we would expect a high correlation between rates of growth from one year to the next, and our casual observation that most Asian countries grow rapidly almost every year and most African countries do not supports that expectation. At the same time, unsystematic factors and measurement error contribute to the observed growth rate in every country every year. This unsystematic component of measured growth always leads to the appearance of faster growth in countries with the worst performance in an earlier time period and slower growth in countries with the best performance.

Figure 3.12 shows the relationship between growth in 1990 and growth in 1991 for developing countries.[15] The solid line is the regression line, which shows the estimated growth rate in 1991 given any particular growth rate in 1990. The dashed diagonal line is the hypothetical relationship we would expect to exist

15. The data set used to construct this scatterplot includes all low- and middle-income countries with more than a million inhabitants for which data were available from the Penn World Tables. Countries with fewer than a million inhabitants were excluded because their economies tend to be unusually volatile, and I did not want the results shown here to depend on unusual cases. The countries for which data are not available include most of those engaged in civil war during these years.

if all the causes of economic performance remained stable from year to year and therefore growth, on average, remained the same from year to year. The part of the regression line that reflects the performance of the countries with the highest growth rates in 1990 lies below the diagonal, showing that they tended to grow less rapidly in 1991 than they had in 1990. Meanwhile, the part of the regression line for countries with the lowest growth rates in 1990 lies above the diagonal, indicating that they grew more rapidly in 1991. Countries growing at above 5 percent per capita in 1990 grew, on average, only 3.7 percent in 1991. At the other extreme, countries with growth declining at 5 percent or more in 1990 were declining at only 2.8 percent per capita, on average, in 1991.

These tendencies were not caused by some vicissitude in the international economy that for once advantaged the poor and disadvantaged the rich. (The reader who suspects that this might be the case is urged to try this regression on other years. In every single pair, the fast-growing countries will do a little less well in the second year, and the slow-growing ones a little better. This result does not mean that growth rates are gradually evening out among countries.)

These tendencies are not caused by anything systematic, but rather by changes in the "error term." The countries with the highest scores at any time are those with not only good systematic economic performance but also, on average, those with positive error terms—either real measurement errors or serendipitous events and luck that cannot be expected again the following year. In the subsequent measurement, economic performance is, on average, still good, but the unsystematic component of the outcome is, on average, neither positive nor negative, and thus the overall score is lower. As a consequence, any time one selects cases for study because they are doing especially well, one can expect that their subsequent performance will decline a bit, and the inverse is true for cases selected because they are doing especially badly.

Regression to the mean is especially likely to interfere with reaching correct conclusions when one is trying to assess the effect of some "treatment," such as structural adjustment loans or aid programs aimed at meeting basic needs. This is because "treatments" are often provided only for those who donors think need them, usually those experiencing some sort of crisis. In such situations, the problem is not that the analyst selects cases from one end of the continuum, but that the agencies supplying the "treatment" do.

Regression to the mean can also affect one's ability to assess the effect of spontaneous "treatments" such as military interventions. If democratic breakdown usually occurs during economic crises, then a research design that compares economic performance before and after military interventions is likely to overestimate the beneficial effects of military rule on the economy, for exactly the same reasons that educational researchers might be tempted to overestimate the beneficial effects of a remedial reading technique. On average, the poor economic performance of the prebreakdown period was caused by both systematic and unfortunate serendipitous factors, but the serendipitous factors that affect performance during the later period under military rule will, on average, be average. If, for example, one compares the growth rate in Argentina, Brazil, Chile, and Uruguay during the year prior to the most recent breakdown of democracy with the average during the first five years of military rule—as a number of authors attempting to assess the effects of bureaucratic authoritarianism did, though usually not quantitatively—one is tempted to conclude that military rulers handle the economy better than do elected politicians. On average, per capita income declined by 1.5 percent during the year prior to breakdown in these countries, but it grew 0.8 percent per year, on average, during the first five years under military rule (not including the breakdown year itself).[16]

One cannot, however, conclude from these figures that military regimes perform better. To assess that question, one would need to model the regression to the mean that would be expected in the relevant years and then compare economic performance under the military with that predicted by the model. Alternatively, one might compare growth during military rule with long-term growth in the same countries, since the ups and downs in the error term would be evened out by averaging over many years. Average growth in these four countries from 1951 to the year before military intervention ranged from 0.9 percent for Uruguay to 3.2 percent for Brazil, all higher than the average during the first five years of military rule.[17] A more careful test could certainly be done, but this simple one is sufficient to sug-

16. These percentages, as well as those in the following paragraph, were calculated from the Penn World Tables.

17. Years included for Argentina are 1951 to 1965, because the military ruled for most of the time after that.

gest that these military governments were not especially successful at delivering rapid growth.

Conclusion

The examples in this chapter have shown that choosing cases for study from among those that cluster at one end of the outcome to be explained can lead to the wrong answers. Apparent causes that all the selected cases have in common may turn out to occur just as frequently among cases in which the effect they are supposed to have caused has not occurred. Relationships that seem to exist between causes and effects in a small sample selected on the dependent variable may disappear or be reversed when cases that span the full range of the dependent variable are examined. Arguments that seem plausible if a historical study or time series begins or ends at a particular date may seem less persuasive if the dates of the study are changed. Regression to the mean can lead the unwary researcher into explaining changes that did not occur. In short, selecting cases without giving careful thought to the logical implications of the selection entails a serious risk of reaching false conclusions.

This is not to say that studies of cases selected on the dependent variable have no place at all in comparative politics. They are useful for digging into the details of how phenomena come about and for developing insights. They identify plausible causal variables. They bring to light anomalies that current theories cannot accommodate. In so doing, they contribute to the creation and revision of proposed theories. By themselves, however, they cannot test the theories they propose (cf. Achen and Snidal 1989). To test theories, one must select cases in a way that does not undermine the logic of inference.

If we want to begin accumulating a body of theoretical knowledge in comparative politics, we need to change the conventions governing the kinds of evidence we regard as theoretically relevant. Conjectures based on cases selected on the dependent variable have a long and distinguished history in the subfield, and they will continue to be important as generators of insights and hypotheses. Regardless of how plausible such conjectures are, however, they retain probationary status as accumulated knowledge until they have been tested, and testing them usually requires the thoughtful selection of cases from the full range of possible outcomes.

CHAPTER 4

How the Evidence You Use Affects the Answers You Get

Rigorous Use of the Evidence Contained in Case Studies

The *New England Journal of Medicine* carries a regular feature called "Case Records from the Massachusetts General Hospital." The articles have titles like "An 80-Year-Old Woman with Sudden Unilateral Blindness" and "A 76-Year-Old Man with Fever, Dyspnea, Pulmonary Infiltrates, Pleural Effusions, and Confusion." These articles explore the progression and pattern of symptoms in cases that are not readily explained by existing medical theory.

That the leading journal in a highly scientific field continues to devote space to case studies suggests that case studies will continue to play a useful role in comparative politics for a long time to come. Comparativists will continue to use case studies to establish facts, delve into anomalies, and try to develop promising theoretical ideas.

In this chapter, I offer advice on how to create and use case study evidence in ways that increase the likelihood of achieving reliable contributions to knowledge. Many of the general methodological prescriptions are the same here as in the rest of the book, but their application to the kinds of arguments and evidence often found in case studies can be tricky. Figuring out the appropriate universe within which to test complicated historical arguments requires more thought than establishing the domain for a simpler argument. Defining complex verbal concepts in ways that allow unambiguous classification of cases into theoretically relevant categories takes more effort than downloading a standard data set from the Internet and choosing which variables to put into a multiple regression. Analysts can sometimes draw on standard nonquantitative operationalizations—for example, the classification of party systems into dominant-party, two-party, multiparty, and fragmented categories—that have been used often enough that they do not need to be reinvented. But much of the time, nonquantitative comparativists must create their own operationalizations and measurements of central concepts. This chapter focuses on the steps necessary to do so.

The chapter has three main parts. The first describes the continuing importance of case studies in comparative politics and reviews the logic of causal analysis as it applies to case study evidence, including the use of such evidence to test complicated historical and path-dependent arguments. The conclusion of this review is that comparativists need more, rather than less, case study evidence—enough that it can be used as the basis of structured comparisons among cases.

Although increasing the number of cases examined is always a good idea, that is not the main emphasis in this chapter. Instead, I focus on the logic of how to select whatever number of cases can feasibly be studied. I emphasize two criteria for selection. First, cases should be representative of the domains of the theories they are intended to test. Second, cases used for testing arguments should be different from the cases from which the arguments were induced, because the analyst would not propose an argument in the first place if it did not fit the cases that generated it.

The second section of the chapter focuses on nonquantitative operationalization and measurement. If case study evidence is to be used to test arguments, complex abstract concepts must be operationalized in concrete ways that reduce the ambiguity surrounding their identification in real-world settings. Concrete and unambiguous criteria for assigning cases to different categories must also be devised. An example may make the potential problems with ambiguity apparent.

A number of arguments in the literature highlight the causal importance of a divided elite in explaining various political outcomes (e.g., Skocpol 1979; Yashar 1997). To test such arguments, the analyst would need, first, concrete criteria usable in multiple settings for identifying which individuals or groups are members of the elite; and, second, unambiguous decision rules for deciding when an elite is divided. The second requirement might be quite difficult in practice, because all groups contain factions, disagreements, and divisions, and the analyst would have to determine the concrete criteria for judging some of these real-world divisions theoretically relevant and others not. Without unambiguous classificatory criteria, we cannot know whether cases fit an argument or not, and thus we cannot use them to test it.

The last and longest part of the chapter is an extended example of how to organize and use historical case study evidence to test a complicated path-dependent argument. This section shows that it is possible to test a path-dependent argument on cases other than those from which it was induced without ignoring the prior sequence of events and context that characterized the original argument. Using Seymour Martin Lipset and Stein Rokkan's hypothesis (1967) about the persistence of historical cleavages in modern party systems as an example, I go through the steps necessary to identify the appropriate universe for testing their hypothesis and demonstrate the operationalization and nonquantitative measurement of concepts embedded in this complicated historical argument.

The Role and Appropriate Use of Case Study Evidence

Case studies, whether single or multiple, continue to be one of the main forms of research in comparative politics. In a review of the contents of the main comparative journals, Adrian Hull (1999) finds that 53.8 percent of articles published between 1983 and 1997 focus on single countries and another 15.7 percent on two to three countries. Case studies remain the primary way that arguments are suggested and evidence collected in the subfield. This is so mainly because much of the evidence used by comparativists must be gathered through fieldwork or the study of archives country by country. Large-*N* data sources are becoming more common and easier to access, but available data sets have little relevance for many subjects and generally contain only superficial information. Many analysts feel the need to collect their own information, and case studies are the most efficient way of doing that.

Case studies have been subjected to considerable methodological criticism. Most of it dwells on the impossibility of testing hypotheses when variables outnumber cases. Even studies based on several case studies typically include more potential causal factors than cases, and, as a result, the evidence marshaled cannot confirm or disconfirm the hypotheses advanced (Lieberson 1991). Other problems identified with the use of case studies include the inability to recognize and ignore idiosyncratic features of the cases chosen—called overfitting theory to data in

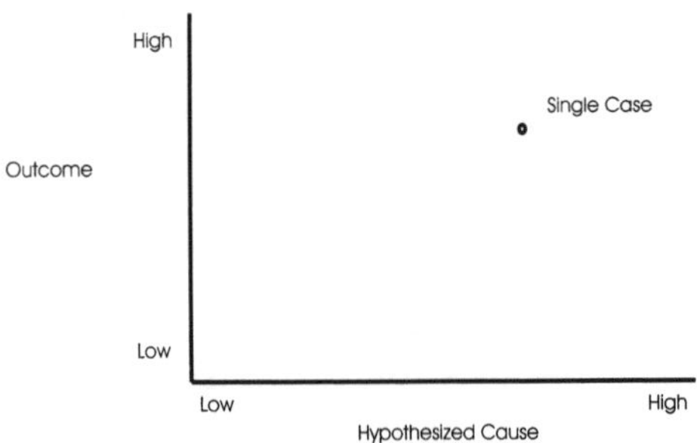

Fig. 4.1. Bivariate hypothesis tested on one case

quantitative work. Though these problems are not inherent in the use of case studies, they occur quite often in practice.

Donald Campbell (1975) suggested that case studies can be made more useful if they are used to test multiple implications of a given theory. Whether the analyst tests one or many implications of the theory, however, the standard and unanswerable criticism of studies based on single cases, or observations, is that they cannot be used to confirm or disconfirm hypotheses. The graph of a hypothesis involving one cause of an outcome for which explanation is sought, tested on one case, makes the problem glaringly clear (see fig. 4.1).

With evidence from only a single case, one has no information at all about whether the universe of cases about which one wants to generalize would, if examined, form a line of points from the origin to the upper right quadrant, a line of points from the upper left to the lower right, an amorphous blob, or any other imaginable shape.[1] In fact, without some knowledge about the values on the outcome and hypothesized causal variables for cases not explicitly examined, one cannot even tell if the case is "high" or "low" on either variable. In practice, of course, the analyst usually has informal knowledge about some other cases, although, as emphasized in chapter 3, it is a good idea to check such informal knowledge and make sure the cases with which the case under study is being implicitly compared are representative of the full universe to which the argument is expected to apply.

Usually, the analyst can identify more than one important causal factor. If so, the single point can no longer be drawn

1. See King, Keohane, and Verba (1994) for a very simple algebraic demonstration and more extensive discussion of this problem.

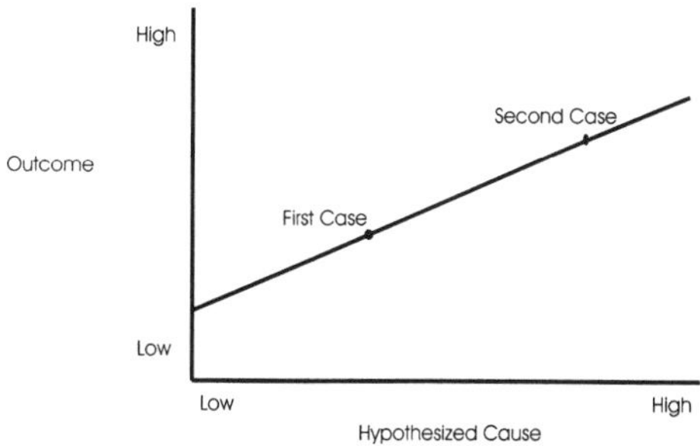

Fig. 4.2. Bivariate hypothesis tested on two cases

easily; but it is still a single point, giving no information about the direction or magnitude of a possible relationship between any hypothesized cause and the outcome.

When only one hypothesized cause is being considered, two cases are sufficient to estimate the relationship between suggested cause and outcome. When shown as a graph, a hypothesis about a single cause tested on two cases yields two points, through which a line can be drawn; the line gives the estimate of the direction and strength of the hypothesized relationship, as shown in figure 4.2. But, of course, a trend based on just two points is not very reliable. Ideally, we would like to see a hypothesis about a trend supported by more data points so that we could feel more sure that we had identified a real trend, not some idiosyncracy of the two cases.

More generally, as long as the analyst has at least one more case than the number of hypothesized causes, estimates of relationships can be made. But, again, an estimate based on only one more case than the number of possible causes will not be reliable. The more additional cases are included, assuming they have not been selected in ways that bias conclusions, the more reliable estimates become.

The analyst who wants to keep the number of cases small might at this point be tempted to test hypotheses one at a time in order to keep the number of cases always larger than the (small) number of potential causes. In general, however, this does not solve the problem. Excluding possible causes that affect the outcome and are also correlated (as they almost always are in social science) with included causal possibilities will bias estimates of the relationship between the included potential cause and the outcome. That is, the cause examined will appear more important than it really is, because some of the effect of the unexamined cause will be attributed to it. An overly simple and unrealistic example may clarify the problem.

Suppose the analyst wants to know what causes school achievement. He plans to examine two individuals, a low-income African American student and a high-income white student. When he looks at the effect of race on achievement, he finds that it fully explains achievement differences. If, however, he had looked at the effect of income on achievement, he would have found that it also fully explained the difference between the two students. For each test, the analyst has more cases (two) than variables (one), but he cannot tell whether race, class, both, or something else that is correlated with race and class explains the difference in achievement. The problem is that testing the effects of correlated variables (race and class) one at a time does not provide a fair test of the effect of either variable. Whichever potential cause is included in the test will appear more important than it is, because it will serve as a partial proxy for the correlated potential cause that was left out.

Nobody would really use case studies as a way of examining the effect of race and class on school achievement, and race and class in the United States are more highly correlated than many other potential causal factors. Nevertheless, many potential causes are correlated, and whenever they are, the same problem arises. It does not matter whether the cases are nations or individuals. To distinguish the effects of race and class on school achievement, the analyst would need to include at least some high-income African Americans and some low-income whites in his study, and he would have to test for the effects of both race and class at the same time on the full set of cases. Only then could he understand the separate effects of each. The surplus of cases over variables must be reasonably large in order to yield reliable results.

The only real solution to the problem of more potential causes than cases is to increase the number of cases. The question for nonquantitative comparativists therefore becomes how to increase the number of cases available for testing relationships without losing the advantages of nuance and descriptive accuracy afforded by case study data.

One simple way to increase the number of cases is to increase the number of observations within the small number of everyday language cases being studied (cf. King, Keohane, and Verba 1994). Recall that the technical definition of a case is different from the everyday language meaning of the word *case.* A case, in methodological terms, is a unit in which each variable takes on only one value or is classified in only one category, otherwise known as an observation. The number of observations within an ordinary language case study can be increased by, for example, looking at states or regions within a country, decisions within an agency, time periods within almost anything, individuals within any organization or territorial entity. Which, if any, of these disaggregations of everyday language cases into multiple observations is reasonable depends on the argument being tested and the unit of analysis implied by it.

In practice, most case studies in the everyday language sense include elements of this kind of disaggregation, though discussion of the multiple observations is often unsystematic in the sense that different potential causes are discussed and "measured" for the different observations. One of the purposes of this chapter is to encourage analysts to make the common practice of including multiple observations in a single everyday language case self-conscious and systematic rather than ad hoc and casual.

When each observation is measured in a different way, no general conclusions can be drawn from the study. Multiple observations within a few everyday language cases can be rendered far more useful by the systematic adherence to what Alexander George and Timothy McKeown (1985) call structured focused comparisons. In more standard language, the analyst examines the same potential causes and the same effects for each observation; uses the same categories for assigning values to variables—that is, measures the same potential causal factors in the same way for each observation; and, in whatever other ways are appropriate in specific studies, strives to make analyses of observations comparable so that generalizations can be drawn from them. In the extended example in the third section of this chapter, I demonstrate the mechanics of carrying out structured focused comparisons in the context of comparative historical research.

In principle, the only constraint on disaggregation as a means of multiplying cases is that the analyst must be sure that the resulting technical cases are all really instances of the same thing.[2] In some investigations, this requirement poses few problems. A scholar interested in the political business cycle might, for example, want to investigate the effect of the legalization of executive reelection on budget deficits in Brazil, but she could not draw robust conclusions from looking at the only instance so far in which a sitting president has run for reelection. By examining all the state races in which sitting governors ran for reelection and comparing them to the earlier period when reelection was forbidden, however, the analyst could increase the number of cases and thus have considerably greater confidence in any conclusions reached in the study. This would be straightforward and unproblematic.

Some research questions, however, pose more difficulties. The analyst trying to explain the effect of interest groups on economic reform policies in a particular country might decide to disaggregate the reform policy package into a set of specific policies and look at what influences each of them separately. In this situation, however, the analyst ends up with many single-case studies of policy decisions rather than a single country study involving many cases, because different elements of reform packages are not usually instances of the same thing. Different specific policies have different costs and benefits to different groups; are made by different political actors, some of whose political careers depend on votes and some of whose do not; require different levels of public support; and differ in the extent of their visibility and intelligibility to affected citizens. For these and other reasons, different variables will be needed to explain outcomes on different policies, and structured focused comparisons will not be possible. The researcher would be better off looking at similar policies in several countries than looking at several different policies within the same country.

To sum up so far, the main shortcoming of case studies is often not the limitation of the study to one or a few everyday language cases, but rather the failure of practitioners to think through the methodological logic of their research strategies.[3] Challenges to

2. The question of whether potential cases are really instances of the same thing also arises in other circumstances. Bartels (1998) has suggested a statistical procedure for weighting the dubious cases more lightly than the unambiguous ones. Such a procedure would be useful for dealing with dubious cases, but not for dealing with cases better explained by a completely different model.

3. A number of articles deal with methodologies for using case studies, especially the issue of choosing cases to use as controls. Among the most frequently cited are Lijphart (1971, 1975); Meckstroth (1975); Skocpol and Somers (1980); Frendreis (1983); and DeFelice (1986).

research designs based on case studies can often be addressed by increasing the number of observations within the everyday language case and by "measuring" the same things in the same way for each observation.

Measurement will be dealt with at length later in this chapter. First, let us consider the special role of case studies in path-dependent arguments.

Case Studies in Path-Dependent Arguments

Although the first step toward more rigorous research strategies using case studies is to increase the number of cases one way or another, not every research design that includes multiple cases is equally useful. A practice that cannot be readily defended is the use of the same case histories to "test" the multiple hypotheses that make up complicated, path-dependent arguments at each of the several nodes of the argument. Typically, the research strategy here involves the selection of several everyday language cases, usually countries. Historical events are then traced in each of the cases, often through centuries, until a final outcome to be explained, such as revolution or democracy, occurs.

At various points, the cases take, or "choose," a particular path, which then precludes a later return to the paths not taken. These choices serve as intervening causes of the next choice points and of the final outcome. The key claim of path-dependent arguments is that these earlier choices create legacies or institutions that last a long time and are very difficult to reverse.

Thus earlier choices change the costs and benefits associated with later choices, and may even determine the existence of later choices. At each choice point, or node, the analyst proposes hypotheses to explain choices. At the extreme, this kind of research design can mean "testing" dozens of hypotheses on the same three cases. It might seem that path-dependent arguments could be disaggregated by treating each node as an observation, but since actors, institutions, and hypotheses change with every node, they are not instances of the same thing. Rather, as in the example above about economic policy, each node can be an instance of something different, and thus many different arguments are tested on the same small number of cases.

Some of the classics of comparative politics use this research strategy: Barrington Moore's *Social Origins of Dictatorship and*

Democracy (1966), Reinhard Bendix's *Nation-Building and Citizenship* (1964), Seymour Martin Lipset and Stein Rokkan's *Party Systems and Voter Alignments* (1967). These are major works of impressive erudition and insight. But although this strategy in the hands of a brilliant practitioner may generate innovative arguments, it runs into limits when trying to test them.

Path-dependent arguments as used in comparative historical analysis face three methodological challenges to the knowledge claims they make. The first involves the question, How do we know that the proposed explanation of the outcome at a particular node is the correct one? This is the same challenge faced by any proposed explanation, and it can be met in the same way. The analyst must compare his proposed explanation with rival ones to see which seems most consistent with evidence. This generally cannot be done, however, without examining more cases than were included in the original study from which the analyst's argument was induced.

A second, closely related challenge is, How do we know that the final outcome we observe (the legacy) was really caused by choices at the series of historical junctures that preceded it, rather than by something else? For example, how do we know that democracy was caused by historical developments in the relationship between lord and peasant, as Moore (1966) argues, rather than by bargaining over taxation, as Robert Bates and Da-Hsiang Lien (1985) and Margaret Levi (1988) suggest? This kind of challenge is also no different from the challenges that any knowledge claim faces, and it also can be met in the same way. Implications can be drawn from both arguments and tested on appropriate sets of cases. Such testing, however, will necessarily involve examining some cases beyond those in which the proposed causal process was originally traced.

The third challenge concerns the identification of "critical junctures," that is, the points in time when choices with long-term consequences were made. If two path-dependent arguments set out to explain the same outcome, and one argument concludes that choices made at one historical juncture determined the final outcome while the other identifies a different juncture as critical, how can we tell which is correct? For example, Deborah Yashar (1997) identifies the Depression as the critical juncture when decisions were made in Costa Rica and Guatemala that determined subsequent outcomes for the rest of the twentieth century, but James Mahoney (2001) disagrees. He thinks that the critical juncture occurred during the liberal period of the nineteenth century and that decisions made during the Depression were already more or less preordained. I do not see how such disagreements can be resolved without the development of measurements of legacies (that is, the interests or institutions created by the earlier choice), a theorization of the effect of these legacies on later choices, and then a test of the theorization on additional cases. Hence, we again run up against a central difficulty in the use of case study evidence—that of simply not having enough of it.

Note that none of these challenges to the knowledge claims advanced in comparative historical arguments arise from the logic of path dependence, which is quite straightforward and widely used in, for example, economics. They arise from two common features of the research design used in comparative historical studies: reliance on small numbers of cases, usually those from which the argument was induced; and vague or ambiguous definitions and measurements, a subject to which I turn in the next section.

What, then, should we do if we believe that complex, path-dependent historical processes cause particular outcomes and we want to overcome these challenges? The first step is to rid ourselves of primordial loyalty to the set of cases with which we began and from which we probably got the idea for the argument in the first place. Whenever possible, the big argument should be broken at its branching points, and hypotheses that purport to explain choices at different nodes should be tested on additional cases that fit appropriate initial conditions. Efforts should be made to see if hypothesized legacies also occur in these other cases.

Authors who use and advocate the comparative historical research strategy often maintain that particular histories determine particular outcomes and that, in consequence, more systematic tests of arguments cannot be used, since they cannot capture the full range of historical nuance (Evans and Stephens 1988). Nevertheless, authors who use this research strategy do make generalizations about the effects of particular historical events and characteristics that they expect will apply to any country that experiences them.

For example, in *Social Origins of Dictatorship and Democracy* (1966), Moore attributes the ultimate choice between dictatorship and democracy to the kind of relationship that had developed through history between lords and peasant village communities. Although Moore's argument takes the reader through a series of historical turning points to explain the rise of commercial agriculture and resulting changes in landlord-peasant relationships in different situations, he concludes with a series of causal generalizations, including:

> [T]he most important causes of peasant revolutions have been the absence of a commercial revolution in agriculture led by the landed upper classes and the concomitant survival of peasant social institutions into the modern era. (477)

From a logical point of view, if a scholar is willing to generalize conclusions drawn from a study, he is implicitly affirming that the same prior historical developments and characteristics have occurred in other cases, since otherwise he would not expect the same outcomes. If such cases exist, then an argument induced from an examination of an original set of cases can and should be tested on those other cases.

When the analyst has proposed a complex, path-dependent argument, it is necessary to find not just shared characteristics but also a shared *sequence* of events and characteristics in order to approximate the initial conditions necessary to test hypotheses about outcomes at particular nodes in the overall argument. This may sound difficult, but it turns out to be feasible more often than one would suspect—if one resolves to do it. The analyst will probably be unable to test the hypotheses proposed at every juncture in a long path-dependent argument, but she should always give serious thought to whether such tests are possible and carry them out whenever they are.

Testing arguments of any kind requires not only appropriately selected cases, but also unambiguous measurements of key concepts. These measurements need not be quantitative, but they do need to be clear. I turn now to the main subject of this chapter: how to operationalize and measure the kinds of concepts frequently used in case studies so that the evidence from them can be used to test arguments as well as propose them.

Nonquantitative Operationalization and Measurement

Most nonquantitative comparativists spend the vast majority of their time "gathering data," though they rarely use this term to describe their activity. Each analyst works within a partly idiosyncratic theoretical perspective, so only some of the "data" collected by one scholar can be used by others. Definitions of the most basic concepts vary across analysts,[4] and most information is buried in long stories that have to be laboriously read in order to retrieve it. In consequence, all of us spend inordinate amounts of time collecting the specialized bodies of evidence needed to propose, and sometimes to test, our arguments.

In response to the difficulty of gathering high-quality information, we have developed a norm in the comparative field that every Ph.D. student should spend at least a year abroad, usually in a single country, gathering his or her own personal "data set," which will be of limited use and only partly accessible to others interested in the same topic. This norm ensures that many of the publications based on dissertations will be case studies. The fieldwork norm contributes to the quality of scholarship in that it helps students to develop a deeper understanding of the societies they study and thus reduces the likelihood of factual and interpretive error. Most importantly, researchers who know their cases intimately may see patterns that would be unlikely to emerge from more superficial examinations.

The fieldwork norm also has disadvantages, however. If a similar norm existed in the political behavior field, every student interested in American political behavior would be expected to develop his or her own survey instrument and then spend a year going door-to-door collecting the responses. If this were the norm, the quality of the surveys would tend to be low due to inexperience; some kinds of information would be collected over and over again; the wording of questions aimed at eliciting the same information would vary from survey to survey, so that it would often be impossible to make comparisons across data sets; the sharing of data would depend on networking; and the field would tend to attract those who enjoy chatting with people at their front doors rather than people who enjoy developing and testing explanations. These consequences of the norm would tend to slow the accumulation of theoretical knowledge.

As long as most comparativists must spend most of their time gathering data, case studies will continue to be used to support most arguments. Case studies dominate the areas of empirical political science that have not developed systematic,

4. See, for example, Collier and Mahon (1993) and Collier and Levitsky (1997) on issues that arise when definitions of concepts vary across analysts.

easily accessible data resources. They make evidence gathering efficient for the individual scholar, at least in the short run. Case studies minimize costs for the analyst, such as acquiring new languages and other context-specific skills and information. Thus, they serve the short-term interests of the data gatherer.

But case studies also have disadvantages. Unless carried out with as much sensitivity to the norms of science as to the particulars of the country under study, case studies may hinder the routinization of data collection and data sharing, and thus the accumulation of knowledge and the development of theory. With the same qualification, they may also discourage rigorous testing and replication.

The purpose of this chapter, however, is to show that reliance on case studies for evidence need not undermine the analyst's ability to share data, test arguments, or replicate earlier tests. But doing so does require changing some practices that are now common. Most arguments that rely on case study evidence involve complex causes, outcomes, and limiting conditions that must be operationalized and measured with great care if tests of the argument are to be persuasive.

Operationalization, as used in quantitative research, refers to the choice of observable indicators that can be used as proxies for abstract and unobservable concepts. The concept of development, for example, means a whole host of things, including the creation of an industrial economy, increased wealth, and a decrease in the ascriptive assignment of occupations, roles, and statuses. The standard operationalization of development, GDP per capita, captures little of the broad meaning of the concept, but it is an appropriate indicator because development implies a high GDP per capita. There are a few countries, mostly high-income oil exporters, that have high GDP per capita without being highly developed in the broader sense of the word, but analysts understand this and can compensate for it in statistical work.

In nonquantitative operationalization, instead of choosing one or a few off-the-shelf indicators to use as proxies for a more complicated concept, the analyst must specify clear, concrete criteria for defining concepts. These criteria then serve as the basis for deciding which cases belong in the study, which time periods in the different cases can be appropriately compared, and how concepts are divided into nominal categories so that cases can be classified in an unambiguous way. Nonquantitative operationalization offers both advantages and disadvantages when compared to quantitative operationalization. On the advantage side, nonquantitative operationalization allows the analyst to stick closer to the original meanings connoted by the concept. On the disadvantage side, carefully figuring out appropriate criteria can be a lot of work.

Measurement involves the assignment of particular cases to particular values or categories of the operationalized concept. In quantitative research, interval or at least ordinal levels of measurement are usually possible. If we take GDP per capita as an indicator of development, for example, each country can be given an interval level value on the indicator. If we were using the Freedom House scale as an indicator of amount of democracy, however, we might not believe that the difference between one and two on the scale was equivalent to the difference between four and five or six and seven, but we would believe that two was higher than one, five higher than four, and seven higher than all the others, so we would be able to give each country an ordinal rank on the indicator. In nonquantitative research, it is often impossible to assign interval or ordinal level values to cases.[5] Thus, nonquantitative measurement usually refers to the classification of cases into nominal (that is, unranked) categories. The purpose of such classification, like the purpose of quantitative measurement, is to permit comparisons across cases and across time. To be useful for this purpose, classification criteria must be concrete, unambiguous, and public, so that other scholars can understand the basis for the analyst's judgments. Much of the discussion in this chapter focuses on measurement in complicated historical arguments, but the issues raised and solutions suggested are relevant for any study in which most of the evidence comes from case histories.

The nominal classification of cases in different time periods or in different parts of the world is often difficult. The absence of quantification makes classification more complicated, more ambiguous, and more subject to dispute among scholars. Disagreements over the use of value-laden labels such as "democracy" probably cannot be avoided. For example, a colleague might object, "What you're calling democracy is not true democracy; true democracy requires adherence to substantive as well

---

5. One can sometimes approach ordinal measurement by developing precise criteria for assignment of cases to categories such as nondemocracy, patrician democracy, bourgeoise democracy, and mass democracy, taking care in the conceptualization to explain why some forms of democracy involve "more democracy" than others.

as procedural norms!" Disagreement over whether a particular case meets criteria for classification into a specified category, however, should be largely avoidable, given clear criteria for measurement. A colleague who disagrees with your conception of democracy should nonetheless be able to say, "If I were to accept your idea of what democracy is, I would agree that this particular case is an example of it." If, having gotten this far, you can go on to show that your classification identifies a difference that helps explain something of interest, your colleague may learn something from your study, even while continuing to disagree with the conceptualization that underlies it.

Measurement issues even affect the establishment of the domains of arguments. When testing any argument, the scholar must first identify the universe of situations in which the argument would be expected to apply. In concrete terms, a set of criteria must be derived from the argument itself that determines the domain of the argument, and then the analyst must assign cases to one of two categories—in the domain or outside it—on the basis of these criteria. In other words, determining the domain of an argument requires measurement. Cases outside the domain get no further attention. The analyst must be careful, however, to select a representative sample from within the domain, as discussed in chapter 3.

The analyst must next decide on the criteria for assigning cases to different categories of outcome. If the outcome of interest is democracy, for example, the analyst must first either choose one of the definitions of democracy available in the literature or devise one. Then he will need to articulate the concrete criteria that cases have to meet in order to be considered democratic. Finally, the cases will have to be assigned to whatever categories are deemed appropriate on a continuum of democracy to nondemocracy. With an outcome such as contemporary democracy, which has been studied by many others, it may be possible to sidestep these measurement decisions by using a publicly available assessment of democracy, such as that provided by Freedom House or the data set of Adam Przeworski et al. (2000). The analyst must compare the sometimes implicit criteria used to classify cases in these data sets with those that make sense for his own argument, however. All classification schemes are useful for some purposes but not others.[6]

6. Elkins (2000) has attempted to show that continuous measures of democracy are better than dichotomous measures such as that used by Przeworski et al. (2000);

Finally, the analyst must decide on criteria for classifying cases with regard to potential causal factors. If, for example, an argument claims that the increasing inability of peasants to rely on landlord patrons for help in times of dire need increases the likelihood of rebellion, then the analyst must find some concrete indicators of reduced landlord help or participation in village life.

If all these measurement issues are considered thoughtfully and reported in published studies so that readers can judge their appropriateness, then the evidence contained in case histories can be deployed in quite persuasive nonquantitative tests of arguments.

Determining criteria to guide the kind of nonquantitative measurement required to deal with the forms of information characteristic of case study–based research can be an arduous task. But it is a task that rewards the effort put into it, because struggling over the conceptual issues raised by trying to measure the same causal factors in the same way across cases often deepens the analyst's understanding of the argument as well as the cases. As a means of disciplining oneself to stick to the same criteria across cases and over time, it is very useful to produce an analogue of the kind of coding scheme used to code open-ended survey questions, as well as a "codebook." The coding scheme is a very specific list of characteristics that will be "counted" as having a particular meaning. It should be sufficiently concrete and precise that if several analysts used it to classify the same phenomena in the same cases, their judgments as to the categories to which instances belonged would be very similar. The codebook is the report of the classification, categorization, or measurement of each potential cause and the outcome in each case. These tools help the analyst maintain the same definitions of basic concepts throughout a study,[7] and they make it possible for others to replicate or extend the study.

They also enable the researcher herself to remember what she has done. Experienced researchers do not need to be reminded how quickly one can forget almost anything, but the young often

---

but which measure is "better" always depends on the theory or hypothesis being tested.

7. Difficulty in maintaining the same definitions of concepts central to an argument might not seem to be a serious problem, but anyone who carefully reads book-length arguments in comparative politics will see that in many of them, the meanings of central ideas vary from one section to another.

labor under the touching illusion that they will not only live forever but will remember everything they now know for the whole time.

As an example of how to deal with the kind of measurement issues that arise in studies based on the comparative historical method, in the final section of this chapter I go through several of the steps involved in testing two of the best-known arguments proposed by Lipset and Rokkan (1967). In the context of this test, I slog through each step of the research process, noting difficult conceptual and nonquantitative measurement decisions and suggesting appropriate ways to handle them. I show how to determine the universe of cases to which a path-dependent argument should apply. I discuss the operationalization of a set of key concepts from Lipset and Rokkan that, like most concepts in comparative politics, originally were expressed with some degree of ambiguity. I demonstrate the creation of a coding scheme as a tool for ensuring that important concepts are handled in the same way in different cases and as an aid to future replication. The purpose of this example is to show how one should go about testing a path-dependent argument induced from one set of cases on another set.

An Example from Lipset and Rokkan

Seymour Martin Lipset and Stein Rokkan's 1967 study explains the emergence of particular cleavage patterns in modern party systems. Their argument about the translation of societal cleavages into party systems prior to mass enfranchisement goes something like the following. The Reformation—the first choice node in the argument—produced three possible outcomes in Christian nations (and proto-nations such as Germany and Italy): an established Protestant church and a predominantly Protestant population; an established Protestant church and a population with a large Catholic minority; or an established Catholic church and a predominantly Catholic population. In Catholic countries, a further struggle occurred during the nineteenth century over the privileges and property of the church and especially over control of education. This is the second node, or branching point. In some countries, secular interests won control of the state and reduced church powers and prerogatives; in others, the state remained allied with the church, and the church retained much of its property and influence. The industrial and commercial

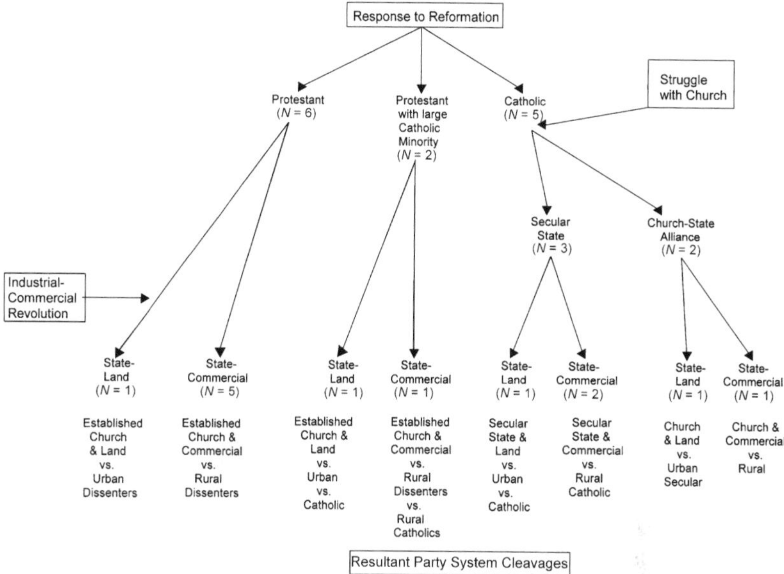

Fig. 4.3. Historical antecedents of party systems. (Based on Lipset and Rokkan 1967.)

revolution brought about the next struggle for dominance, constituting the third node. In some countries, commercial and industrial interests achieved control; in others, traditional landed interests maintained their historic position. In all cases, interests allied with or in control of central governments attempted to achieve a greater centralization and standardization of the nation and faced opposition from left-out groups. These basic oppositions determined which interests coalesced into alliances in different historical settings and where cleavages developed in emerging party systems. A graphical version of this argument is shown in figure 4.3. The countries examined by Lipset and Rokkan can be arrayed in a two-by-four table, as shown in table 4.1.

It might be argued that Lipset and Rokkan's essay is not really an instance of the comparative historical method. They do not, after all, detail the history of each of the cases considered. The logic of the argument, however, is the same as that used in other comparative historical work. Cleavage patterns in twentieth-century party systems depend on the paths "chosen" by countries at several historical junctures over a period of centuries. Case studies of many of the countries considered in the introductory essay are included in the edited volume as support for the argument. I use Lipset and Rokkan's argument for this example, despite this possible objection, because they are more methodologically rigorous than many other practitioners of the comparative historical approach.

Lipset and Rokkan do not lay themselves open to the standard objections. They examine thirteen cases for the core argument and treat several others more briefly. Until the very last stage of the argument, they always have more cases than variables. Their cases span a range of outcomes on the dependent variable. And, compared to other practitioners, they use fairly well defined concepts, so that attempts to test their arguments are not doomed to bog down in futile debates about what they "really" meant. Because Lipset and Rokkan have done so many things carefully, it is possible for us to concentrate on operationalization and measurement without being distracted by other methodological issues.

Lipset and Rokkan make numerous arguments in their densely packed essay. I will concentrate on methodological issues relevant to the two arguments that seem to me most central: that three historical "critical junctures" determine the kind of party system that emerges prior to the extension of mass suffrage, and that "the crucial differences among the party systems emerged in the early phases of competitive politics, before the final phase of mass mobilization" (35).

The reason for giving so much attention to the emergence of party systems prior to widespread participation is the contention, frequently reiterated by Lipset and Rokkan, that these systems persist through time, despite changes in electoral rules, increased mobilization, economic development, economic crisis, and war.

TABLE 4.1. Historical Cleavages in Nineteenth-Century European Party Systems (Lipset and Rokkan)

	Protestant	Protestant with Large Catholic Minority	Catholic with Secular State	Catholic with Church-State Alliance
State-land alliance	1 Britain	2 Prussia/Reich	3 Spain	4 Austria
State-commercial alliance	5 Denmark, Finland, Iceland, Norway, Sweden	6 Netherlands	7 France, Italy	8 Belgium

Suffrage brings the inclusion of working-class voters and in some cases adds an additional cleavage to the original ones, but it does not fundamentally change preexisting cleavages.

Two of the cases examined, Italy and Spain, do not display the expected party system stability over time. To account for outcomes in these cases, Lipset and Rokkan introduce additional hypotheses. After holding out for an admirably long time, they have now reached the point that practitioners of the comparative historical method seem always to reach eventually: the variables outnumber the cases, and explanation degenerates into description.

This degeneration occurs because of the failure to internalize fully the implications of the probabilistic nature of social science theories. We feel an intuitive need to explain outcomes inconsistent with theoretical expectations, even though we know that no theory will explain all the variation that exists in the real world. This need plays a useful role in the development of knowledge in that it spurs examination of anomalous cases. Hypotheses proposed to explain anomalies, however, are just like other hypotheses. They require testing on some other thoughtfully chosen set of cases.

For the example here, I focus on the Lipset and Rokkan hypotheses that (1) "the decisive contrasts among the systems had emerged before the entry of the working-class parties into the political arena" (35); and (2) "the freezing of the major party alternatives [occurred] in the wake of the extension of suffrage" (50).[8] The freezing hypotheses imply, first, that the basic cleavages reflected in the oligarchical system that preceded mass enfranchisement should persist; and, second, that the actual parties that consolidated in the decades immediately after the suffrage extension should survive indefinitely.

Lipset and Rokkan's argument is path-dependent; therefore, in order to test it on cases different from those from which the initial insights were drawn, we need to find some cases that fit the initial conditions set out or implicitly assumed by Lipset and Rokkan.

---

8. Many studies have tested and retested Lipset and Rokkan's arguments on European cases. These studies show substantial stability in European party systems, despite an increase in volatility since about 1970. See, for example, Rose and Urwin (1970); Pedersen (1983); Maguire (1983); and Bartolini and Mair (1990). These excellent studies have refined and developed Lipset and Rokkan's original argument, as well as providing support for, and raising questions about, various aspects of it.

The Potential Universe of Cases

The first step in testing an argument is to determine the domain from which to draw the cases or observations to be used in the test. If we wish to test the argument rather than merely replicate it, we must identify the domain within which we would expect the argument to apply, excluding the cases from which the hypothesis originally drew inspiration. Explicit or implicit initial conditions—including, in some instances, prior sequences of events—as well as attributes implied by the theory itself limit the domain within which we should expect the theory to explain outcomes. For complicated arguments, domain conditions can be extensive and complex, as they are for the Lipset and Rokkan argument that I test below.

Lipset and Rokkan see the cleavages that underlie modern party systems as having arisen during the struggle to consolidate nation-states. The cases they examine had achieved national independence by the early twentieth century, and thus it would seem reasonable to limit the domain within which their argument is tested to countries that became independent before 1940 and remained independent thereafter. The same process that Lipset and Rokkan hypothesized may well be operating in newer states—Lipset and Rokkan themselves certainly believed that it was—but the argument cannot be tested in them. Only in countries with a substantial independent history has a long enough period of independent political activity occurred to test the freezing hypothesis. This restriction eliminates most of Africa and some Asian and Middle Eastern countries from the potential universe, because their party systems have not operated long enough.

Countries in which boundaries changed dramatically at about the time suffrage was extended must also be excluded from tests of the persistence of presuffrage cleavages; and those in which such boundary changes occurred between the extension of suffrage and a time sufficiently recent to test the second element of the freezing hypothesis must be eliminated from both tests. The boundary criterion is included because in situations in which a large piece of territory has been added or subtracted, we would expect that the different interests of often ethnically different citizens in those irredentas might change basic social cleavages in ways not considered by Lipset and Rokkan. This criterion eliminates virtually all of Eastern Europe from the set of countries on which the first hypothesis (persistence of cleavages based in the oligarchical era) can be tested, because the establishment of the borders of most East European countries took place at the same time as the first experiments with mass suffrage. It also eliminates Greece from tests of the first hypothesis, because Greece's boundaries and populations changed repeatedly during the period when suffrage was expanding and immediately thereafter. Greece can, however, be included in tests of the second hypothesis about post-enfranchisement party system stability. Greece's borders have remained stable from about fifteen years after the initiation of mass participation to the present.

As a standard feature of the consolidation of nation-states, Lipset and Rokkan posit a struggle between centralizing nation builders and those defending the prerogatives of often culturally different peripheral localities. The political consequences of this struggle vary depending on the prior outcome of the conflict between Roman Catholicism and its challengers during the Reformation. Consequently, the domain of the Lipset and Rokkan argument must be limited to countries within the Christian historical tradition. Lipset and Rokkan themselves seem to have thought their general argument would apply outside this domain, since studies of Japan and Africa were included in the original edited volume, but neither they nor the authors of these studies give many clues about exactly how the argument would play out in such areas. So I think it fairer to limit the domain for the test to the historically Christian countries. This restriction redundantly eliminates most of the countries of Asia, Africa, and the Middle East.

Lipset and Rokkan's argument also assumes the existence of some degree of political competition—usually the organization of proto-parties, parties of notables, or identifiable parliamentary factions—prior to the extension of political participation to ordinary citizens. We would not expect the period of oligarchic competition prior to mass suffrage to structure politics during subsequent years if there had been no development of oligarchic competition. Thus countries that made a direct transition from despotism to mass democracy should not be expected to fit the argument. To judge by the histories of the countries centrally discussed by Lipset and Rokkan, however, countries need not have had a long or nonviolent period of oligarchic competition in order to be included. Certainly France, Spain, Germany, and Italy did not. The requirement that countries had to have experienced a period of oligarchic competition prior to mass enfranchisement eliminates a few more countries with especially unfortunate histories, though this degree of despotism is somewhat rare among the countries that became independent before 1940.

The freezing hypotheses can be tested only in countries in which suffrage has been extended to most (male) citizens. Since freezing implies stability over a fairly long period of time, to test it we need to eliminate any country in which suffrage had not been extended to most of the urban working class by about 1975. I suggest 1975 as a cutoff date so that we have a long enough time in which to see whether freezing has occurred since then.[9] I focus on working-class rather than universal suffrage because Lipset and Rokkan's argument about freezing is an argument about what happens to party systems when the working class begins to participate.

For suffrage to be meaningful, voters must have some choice among candidates. Thus, we would also want to eliminate countries that, despite broad suffrage, held uncompetitive elections. It is not obvious, however, how much time it takes to develop the party organizations and loyalties that the freezing hypotheses imply. In their discussion of Italy and Spain, Lipset and Rokkan suggest that the failure of those party systems to freeze as expected was caused in part by the very short periods of mass participation (three years in Italy and about five in Spain) before the overthrow of democracy. It is also not clear whether elections need to be fully competitive, free of fraud, and fair, or whether party loyalties and organization also develop when competition is limited and fraud widespread. These are empirical questions that it would be useful to investigate.

In this study, I have included any country that had held two or more at least semicompetitive elections by 1975. These unrestrictive criteria have two purposes: to keep the number of cases as large as possible; and to permit the investigation of whether the degree of competitiveness or length of democratic periods affects the development of stable party systems. Countries need not remain continuously democratic after the extension of suffrage in order to be included in the universe, because Lipset and Rokkan included in their analysis several cases that had experienced periods of authoritarianism, foreign occupation, and chaos.

The final domain condition for testing the freezing hypothesis

9. Rose and Urwin (1970) also used a twenty-five-year period for their assessment of West European party stability.

is that countries that have fulfilled all of the above conditions must also have experienced at least two competitive elections with broad citizen participation since 1985, so that we can assess contemporary party systems.

The countries remaining in the potential universe but not part of Lipset and Rokkan's original study include many in Latin America, Portugal, and Bulgaria for the first test, with Greece added for the second. In all these countries, Lipset and Rokkan's initial conditions are met. Table 4.2 shows the list of countries not discussed by Lipset and Rokkan that are within the Christian historical tradition and had achieved independence by 1940,

TABLE 4.2. The Potential Universe of Cases Not Discussed in Lipset and Rokkan (independent since 1940 and historically Christian)

Country	Reason for Elimination from Universe
Argentina	
Bolivia	
Bulgaria	
Chile	
Colombia	
Costa Rica	
Cuba	No period of democracy since 1985
Czechoslovakia	Border and population changes
Dominican Republic	No period of oligarchic competition before democratization
Ecuador	
El Salvador	
Ethiopia	No period of democracy
Greece	Eliminated from first test because of border changes
Guatemala	
Haiti	No sufficient period of democracy
Honduras	
Hungary	No democratic period prior to 1975
Mexico	
Nicaragua	
Panama	
Paraguay	
Peru	
Poland	Border changes
Portugal	
Romania	Border changes
Uruguay	
USSR	No democratic period prior to 1975; border changes
Venezuela	
Yugoslavia	Border changes

Note: Each of the countries listed had a population greater than one million in 1980. In addition to the countries shown in table 4.1, Lipset and Rokkan discussed Ireland, Switzerland, Germany, Canada, and the United States at various points in their essay. Other studies in their 1967 volume discussed the United States; Britain; Australia; New Zealand; Italy; Spain; West Germany; Finland; Brazil; Norway; Japan; and, more sketchily, several West African countries.

along with the reasons for excluding any that could not be used to retest the Lipset and Rokkan arguments.

A question might be raised about the inclusion of countries that experienced high levels of political violence or long, intense repression either before or after mass enfranchisement. During the nineteenth century, when Latin American countries were consolidating themselves as nation-states, many experienced periods of warlordism, several suffered civil wars, and several became embroiled in territorial wars with their neighbors. Since Lipset and Rokkan did not exclude from their set of cases European countries that had experienced revolution, civil war, and prolonged political violence, I have not excluded such cases either.

Nevertheless, one might argue that political instability was so profound in some Latin American countries and violence so pervasive or dictatorship so oppressive that these countries could not have been expected to develop stable party systems. This is an empirical question that can be investigated within this set of cases, and I will return to it later in the context of conclusions drawn from an examination of the cases. For now, let me note my reason for including in the initial "data set" even the cases that experienced the most violence: several of the countries that suffered the highest levels of violence and oppression have had very stable party systems. In other words, casual observation provides no basis for thinking that a strife-filled history precludes the formation of a stable party system. In fact, Latin Americanists have advanced the hypothesis that long, destructive, and recurrent civil wars between forces led by traditional parties caused mass identification with those parties and thus their perpetuation into the twentieth century (Coppedge 1991).

Early political cleavages in all the countries used for this test reflected struggles of center versus periphery, supporters of the established church versus secularists, and landed versus commercial interests. In many of the countries, some of these fundamental issues had been settled before the extension of suffrage. That is, in many countries either a federal or a unitary system of government had been established and seemed likely to persist, and in most of them the church had lost its privileged position and seemed unlikely to regain it.[10] In some countries, traditional

10. In Bulgaria and Greece, the dominant religion was Orthodox rather than Roman Catholicism. Nevertheless, the struggle between secular and proclerical interests was extremely similar to that occurring in the Roman Catholic parts of Europe and Latin America.

landed interests controlled the state; in others, commercial interests did. If these cases were added to table 4.1, all would fall in either cell 4 or cell 7. In all of them, the earliest principal cleavage embodied in the traditional proto-party system was between traditional, landed, proclerical interests, often called Conservatives, on one side, and commercial, anticlerical interests, often called Liberals, on the other. In several cases, regional hostilities reinforced these basic divisions. In other words, prior to mass enfranchisement, these mostly Latin American cases looked very much like some of the European cases examined by Lipset and Rokkan.

Nonquantitative Measurement

The essence of hypothesis testing is a judgment about whether a set of empirical observations meets theoretically derived expectations. In order to make such a judgment, we must have a way of evaluating the empirical observations that is precise enough for us to feel confident about the judgment and for others to be persuaded by it. This precision is achieved through careful measurement. Nonquantitative measurement usually means the assignment of cases to nominal categories, but complicated historical arguments require some additional measurement decisions. Appropriate time periods within which to compare cases may need to be determined. This is a measurement decision in the sense that identifying the appropriate time also involves putting historical periods into nominal categories, such as oligarchic, on the basis of clear, theoretically relevant criteria.

All these nonquantitative measurement decisions have in common the need for very unambiguous and invariant criteria for assigning cases to categories. Where basic concepts are complicated and have multiple potential meanings, this can be a difficult and time-consuming task. In this section, I plow through a series of such operationalization decisions in detail in order to show the kinds of problems that arise and how they can be dealt with.

Lipset and Rokkan's argument is posed verbally, and little of the evidence supporting it in the case studies is quantitative. The analyst who wants to conduct a test must find ways of assessing key concepts—that is, of "measuring" the variables—that are consistent with the spirit of the Lipset and Rokkan argument but also applicable across cases and capable of replication. This task involves a good deal of thought, because even the simplest and most apparently concrete ideas in the original argument could be operationalized in more than one way.

The theoretical issues involved in determining the domain for a test of the Lipset and Rokkan argument were discussed above. Here I concentrate on how to assess whether those domain conditions have been met. Some of the decisions about whether a country is part of the universe on which the Lipset and Rokkan argument could be tested, such as date of independence, are relatively straightforward.[11] The dates of oligarchic periods, however, are less obvious. To test the Lipset and Rokkan argument, we must have some criteria for determining when government is oligarchic so that we can know which presuffrage cleavages should be expected to persist. The definition of oligarchy used here follows the literature in considering it a period of time during which elite parties or proto-parties structured political competition and in which political participation was limited to a small part of the adult (usually male) population. Some oligarchies were monarchies, some were democracies with extremely restricted suffrage, and some were less institutionalized systems in which executive office was often seized by armed force, though elections were frequently held after seizures of power. As long as competition for high office was structured by somewhat stable proto-parties, the means of choosing the executive does not seem relevant to the definition of oligarchy, and the literature does not distinguish among these types. Periods are here considered oligarchic rather than despotic if elite political competition was public and organized into somewhat stable blocs, rather than occurring entirely within the coterie surrounding the ruler.

In order to test the Lipset and Rokkan argument, it is also necessary to distinguish oligarchy from more competitive periods when the votes of ordinary citizens could be expected to affect politics. Periods were considered oligarchic rather than competitive or semicompetitive if suffrage was legally limited by property qualifications; or suffrage was formally broad but its exer-

11. Even the decision to use date of independence as the beginning of a country's inclusion was not completely unproblematic, however, since a number of countries that had not attained independence by 1940 (e.g., the Philippines and Jamaica) had important functioning party systems well before independence. I decided to use formal independence as the threshold criterion for inclusion in order to keep the decision uncomplicated, but a case could certainly be made for the inclusion of countries that, though not formally independent, had begun developing the party systems that would later structure their politics.

cise was restricted in practice by public voting; or participation was very low because ordinary people simply did not vote; or illiteracy was so extensive that literacy qualifications eliminated nearly all the working class; or heads of government were rarely chosen by voters. Any of these conditions would limit effective participation to a very small proportion of citizens.

Decisions about which parties, proto-parties, and coteries of notables should be expected to persist through time also involve nontrivial problems. In the nineteenth century, as now, parties arose, disappeared, split, merged, and changed their names. Which ones should the analyst informed by the Lipset and Rokkan argument expect to persist? The substance-based strategy for making this decision begins with identifying the parties associated early on with the center-periphery, clerical-secular, and land–commercial interest cleavages and following them through time, being careful not to lose them when they change their names or when one party replaces another representing the same collection of positions on the same basic cleavages. This strategy obviously requires a good deal of digging into the history of each country, but the digging is inherently interesting. It is rarely possible to obtain any kind of quantitative indicator of how much support these parties had, but the main competitors, their socioeconomic position, and the issues they fought over can be identified.

Since we are interested in the effect of the enfranchisement of the working class on the party system, we also want to identify the parties that existed shortly before widespread suffrage. For many countries, quantitative measures of the strength or importance of parties during the last decade or so before enfranchisement are available, which simplifies comparison. Where quantitative measures are not available, verbal descriptions of which parties competed in and won elections can be found.

An extremely difficult measurement issue involves the question of when one party should be treated as a successor or descendant of another. The strict substantive criterion derived from Lipset and Rokkan would require that the descendant represent the same sides of the same cleavages. Where possible, I have used this criterion. I do not, for example, count the Chilean Partido Demócrata Cristiano (PDC) as a successor of the Partido Radical (PR), though both are generally considered middle-class parties, because the PR favored secularization and the PDC has taken a more pro-church stance. On the other hand, I count the Partido de Conciliación Nacional (PCN) in El Salvador as a successor to the Partido Revolucionario de Unificación Democrática (PRUD), because both were military support parties representing similar interests and policy positions. When in doubt, I have tried to err on the side of permissiveness, that is, treating parties as successors when they might not be, in order to be sure that a disconfirmation of Lipset and Rokkan, should one occur, could not be blamed on overly strict criteria for party continuity. If I were testing an original argument of my own, I would try to err on the restrictive side instead, so that a positive finding could not be discounted as due to overly tolerant criteria for what would count as confirmation. (Coding decisions for most parties and countries are shown in appendix C.)

In order to carry out a test of the Lipset and Rokkan hypotheses, it is also necessary to decide on concrete operationalizations of the key outcome ideas: that "the decisive contrasts among the systems had emerged before the entry of the working-class parties into the political arena" (35); and that "major party alternatives" would be frozen "in the wake of the extension of suffrage" (50). Lipset and Rokkan expect one of three outcomes when the working class begins to participate in politics: working-class voters may be incorporated into preexisting parties; new parties may arise to represent working-class voters while the older parties continue to survive; or preexisting parties can fuse into a single party representing elite interests in opposition to new working-class parties. Lipset and Rokkan interpret any of these outcomes as consistent with the notion of freezing.

I have treated cases as conforming to the expectation of cleavage stability if major oligarchic parties (or their descendants) have (1) absorbed new interests and remained major parties; or (2) survived as somewhat important parties while new parties have been added to the system to reflect new interests; or (3) coalesced into a single party, fragmented into multiple parties, or taken on new names yet remained identifiable as representing similar interests, while new parties have been added to the system. This definition is far less restrictive than that used in most studies based on European cases (e.g., Rose and Urwin 1970; Maguire 1983), but I think it captures the various meanings of the idea found in Lipset and Rokkan.

The expression of their ideas in this bald way makes it clear that Lipset and Rokkan conceived of persistence in very broad terms. It also leads to a quite simple way of testing the argument. All of these options imply the persistence of oligarchic parties (or descendants representing the same sides of historical cleavages) and their continued ability to attract votes. If oligarchic parties absorb working-class interests, they will obviously remain large. If, however, competing parties arise to attract the new labor constituency, the traditional parties might attract a much smaller proportion of the total vote while still fulfilling Lipset and Rokkan's expectations. Although Lipset and Rokkan sought to explain the persistence of cleavages, not the vote for traditional parties, their argument implies some degree of continued electoral success for these parties, and that implication can be tested. In the test below, if traditional parties or their descendants still attract a substantial part of the vote, regardless of whether other parties have arisen to compete with them, I will count the case as fulfilling Lipset and Rokkan's expectations.

The definition of a party system frozen in the wake of the extension of suffrage is simpler, since here Lipset and Rokkan seem to be referring to party organizations themselves, rather than cleavages. I define a system as frozen if most of the major parties that emerged or existed during the first ten years after the extension of suffrage still exist as reasonably important parties today, whether or not other parties have arisen since then. Again, this is a less restrictive definition than that usually used by Europeanists.

Operationalizations of other ideas also require careful thought. To begin with one of the apparently most simple, extensions of suffrage are often not clear-cut and unambiguous. Most disturbing, from the perspective of someone trying to test Lipset and Rokkan, the legal extension of suffrage sometimes predates by decades the actual involvement of ordinary citizens in electoral politics or the establishment of competitive electoral regimes. Consequently, the analyst has to make some judgments about what counts as suffrage. The minimum criteria used in the tests below are legal elimination of property qualifications; enfranchisement of at least 10 percent of the population; voter participation by at least 5 percent of the population; use of the secret ballot; and presidents or parliaments chosen by election (by popular election or an elected electoral college, but not some other body) rather than by force more than half the time for at least ten years at some time after the change in the suffrage law.

I did not include the elimination of a literacy requirement because literacy requirements in the second half of the twentieth century restrict the voting rights of the rural poor and the indigenous or otherwise ethnically disadvantaged, not most of the urban working class. In some cases, the extension of suffrage took place in increments, as different qualifications were removed. In some countries, many decades intervened between the elimination of property and literacy qualifications. Where more than one wave of enfranchisement occurred, I have chosen the most important one in terms of numbers of workers affected and thus its expected effect on the party system. Here again, I have tried to follow the usage of Lipset and Rokkan. They emphasize the inclusion of the working class; consequently, where I have had to make a choice, I have treated late eliminations of literacy requirements, which affect primarily the rural poor, as less theoretically relevant than earlier extensions leading to working-class participation.

The Lipset and Rokkan argument assumes that enfranchisement of the working class leads to the participation of a large number of new working-class voters in the political system. If universal suffrage is mandated when a country's economy is so undeveloped that there are few workers, or if literate male suffrage is granted when nearly all workers are illiterate, then the suffrage extension would not be expected by Lipset and Rokkan or anyone else to bring large numbers of workers into the political system. Consequently, we need a rule for deciding when a formal suffrage extension would be sufficiently consequential to have effects. I have chosen a 10 percent enfranchisement threshold. The choice reflects the following logic. In most countries, male workers gained the vote before women did. In such countries, males old enough to vote would make up about 25 percent of the population. Where the vote was limited to the literate, an enfranchisement rate below 10 percent would thus imply an illiteracy rate of more than 60 percent. In such circumstances, it might well be that a literacy requirement would disenfranchise most of the working class. Formal suffrage extensions were also not counted until the working class had become large enough to be modestly influential, which in a number of countries occurred many decades after the initial enfranchisement. Nor were they counted before electoral participation rose to more than 5 percent of the population. Where citizens have the vote but do not use it, whether because they are excluded by coercion or because they live too far from polling places, suffrage would be expected to have little effect on party systems.

The election requirement is included because a few Latin American countries formally extended suffrage several decades before governments actually began to be chosen in elections rather than through violence or elite cabal. We would not expect working-class parties to develop if elections fail to occur or if their outcomes do not affect the composition of government.

I have not taken into consideration whether widespread working-class mobilization actually occurred immediately after suffrage expansion or not. An argument could be made that it would have been more appropriate to consider periods of actual widespread mobilization rather than periods immediately following legal enfranchisement. I have chosen the latter option because it seems to me most consistent with Lipset and Rokkan's actual usage. In discussing Norway, in particular, they begin their discussion with the legal extension of suffrage even though it preceded mass mobilization by several decades.

The various measurement rules used here are summarized in the coding scheme in appendix C. No doubt some readers will disagree with some of these rules. There is no definitive, correct way to translate the kinds of concepts used by Lipset and Rokkan into clear coding criteria, and any particular translation will always provoke some disagreement. But one of the advantages of devising precise criteria, writing them down, and publishing them is that readers who disagree with some of them can check to see what, if any, difference in conclusions would result from changing them.

It is important to maintain a record of all procedures used in creating data, even nonquantitative data. Other scholars, seeking to replicate or simply evaluate your published work, may ask you for details that were too extensive to include in a publication. After a few months have passed, you will find yourself unable to supply these details unless you have written them down.

The record of how data have been created is kept in a codebook. A codebook should document how each variable in each case was coded. It should also contain information about sampling and the universe of cases. In a nonquantitative study such as this one, the codebook allows readers to see how each case was classified. By scrutinizing the codebook, readers can assess the researcher's judgments about the measurement or classification of causal and outcome variables, as well as other key concepts embedded in the argument. In other words, it lays bare an aspect of nonquantitative research that usually remains hidden. If, after considering the codebook, readers find the researcher's judgments biased or uninformed, they will discount conclusions based on those judgments. If, however, readers can find little to object to in the researcher's judgments, their belief in the conclusions will be strengthened.

If case studies are to be used as evidence for testing arguments, they need to contain the same information, measured in the same way, for each case.[12] Creating an explicit codebook helps to maintain that discipline. Appendix C contains the codebook for this study, with country tables showing the information that would need to be included in case studies used to test the Lipset and Rokkan argument. Each country table records the dates of the oligarchic period, formal enfranchisement of the working class, effective suffrage extension—the time after which working-class votes could really be expected to affect political outcomes—and the dates of the first competitive period. It identifies the oligarchic parties or proto-parties, the mass parties that competed during the decades before and after effective enfranchisement, and the main contemporary parties. More recent parties that represent the same ends of the Lipset-Rokkan dichotomies as older ones are treated as descendants or descendant equivalents of the older parties and are not listed separately in the tables. Their votes are included with the votes for the parent parties. Average vote share is recorded wherever available.[13] Only parties that achieved at least 5 percent of the vote or were descended from older parties are included in these tables. Complete election results are available on my web site (see appendix C for further information).

---

12. It would be very unusual to include in a single publication as many case studies as there are countries included here. Where the universe implied by an argument is too large, the analyst can select a sample of cases for inclusion (see chap. 3). Even if the analyst wished to do in-depth narrative case studies of only three countries selected from the full universe, however, the study would be more persuasive if the kind of summary evidence shown in the tables in appendix C were collected and shown for all of the countries in the universe, or a substantially larger sample of them.

13. Some past election results are simply not available by party; apparently they were never recorded in that form. In Peru, for example, contemporary newspapers reported the names of the winners of all legislative seats in the 1939 election, but they did not report their party affiliations. Other sources identify the coalition to which winners belonged, but not the individual parties. Several other countries also record only votes for coalitions as a whole. It is always possible, however, to find out which parties won and which other important parties competed in elections. Although these data are not precise enough to permit a replication of the kind of studies of volatility done by Europeanists, they are adequate for drawing the inferences that need to be drawn in order to test the Lipset and Rokkan argument.

Nonquantitative Hypothesis Testing

Although I have used numbers in the form of vote share to identify which parties attracted at least some mass support during various time periods, the present analysis is not quantitative, and much of it could not be. Some vote share data are missing, though verbal descriptions exist, and presidential vote share or legislative seat share have been substituted for legislative vote share in a number of cases where records of old legislative votes were unavailable. Many of the cases would have had to be eliminated from a quantitative study because of missing or incommensurable data, and the traditional cleavage-persistence argument actually could not have been tested due to insufficient data. So in this instance, a nonquantitative research design allows the test of an argument that otherwise could not have been tested and the inclusion of cases in another test (that of the postsuffrage freezing argument) that otherwise would have to have been left out.

Once the truly difficult operationalization decisions have been made, nonquantitative tests of these arguments are fairly straightforward. Let us consider first whether the historic cleavages that structured proto-party systems during oligarchic periods continued to structure party systems after the enfranchisement of a significant part of the working class. If Lipset and Rokkan's argument concerned only the period immediately after the introduction of mass suffrage, it would not have inspired the lasting interest it has. It is the prediction, apparently consistent with decades of European experience, of the indefinite preservation of a set of pre-twentieth-century social cleavages in contemporary party systems that gives the Lipset and Rokkan argument its fascination for scholars. Table 4.3 shows how the oligarchic parties (including their descendants) fared in the decade prior to effective enfranchisement, the years immediately following it, and the current period.

Lipset and Rokkan note that parties may persist either by absorbing new interests or by successfully competing against new parties that arise to represent new interests. In table 4.3, the top row shows the persistence of parties that absorbed new interests. If we compare the fate of the parties that absorbed new interests (in Colombia, Honduras, Paraguay, and Uruguay) with that of those that had to compete with new parties, we can see that the absorbent parties were much more likely to persist into the late twentieth century than were those that tried to compete. Oligarchic parties were still dominant in all these countries during the postsuffrage period, and they continue to attract over 75 percent of the vote in three of the countries today. Although Uruguay has recently fallen below the 75 percent threshold, the average vote for the combined oligarchic parties during the contemporary period in these four countries remains at 81.1 percent.

TABLE 4.3. Persistence of Traditional Cleavages

	Persistence of Traditional Cleavages from Oligarchic Period to:			
	Just before Suffrage Extension	Shortly after Suffrage Extension	Present	
Absorption of New Interests into Old Parties	Colombia Honduras Paraguay Uruguay	Colombia Honduras Paraguay Uruguay	Colombia Honduras Paraguay	**Old Parties Remain Dominant** (combined vote share greater than 75%)
Addition of New Parties to the Political System	Bulgaria Ecuador Nicaragua Panama Portugal Venezuela[a]	Bulgaria Nicaragua		
	Argentina Bolivia Chile Costa Rica Peru[b]	Argentina Chile Ecuador Panama	Nicaragua Uruguay	**Old Parties Compete with Newer Parties** (combined vote share between 25% and 75%)
	El Salvador Guatemala Mexico	Bolivia Costa Rica El Salvador Guatemala Mexico Peru Portugal Venezuela	Argentina Bolivia Bulgaria Chile[c] Costa Rica Ecuador El Salvador Guatemala Mexico Panama Peru Portugal Venezuela	**Old Parties Passing from the Historical Stage** (combined vote share less than 25%)

[a]No competitive elections, but all seats in legislature held by oligarchic parties.
[b]Seat share 26.4%; only 6.4% if presidential vote share is used.
[c]If the Unión Democrática Independiente (UDI) were also counted as a descendant equivalent of the oligarchic parties, the total vote share for these parties would be 32.1%, which would move Chile to the competitive category above.

The parties that failed to absorb new interests did less well. Even in the decade before effective enfranchisement, they remained dominant in less than half the countries that saw the addition of new parties. By the decade following suffrage extension, parties reflecting traditional cleavages were able to attract less than a quarter of the vote in more than half the countries in which they had to compete with new parties. They have declined still further since then. During the time from 1985 to the present, the average combined vote for oligarchic parties and their descendants in countries in which they had to compete with new parties is 7.7 percent.

In the contemporary period (1985–2000), oligarchic parties continue to dominate the political system in only three countries, all of which had traditional parties able to absorb new interests. An institutionalist might note that the absorption of new interests into old parties was aided in the countries where it happened by such institutional devices as multiple lists or *lemas* within parties, which allowed discontented potential party leaders to get onto the ballot as leaders of their own factions rather than having to organize new parties in order to become candidates; fused ballots that impeded the emergence of small local parties that could not immediately compete in presidential elections; pacts that excluded other parties from participation; and authoritarian rules that prevented the formation of new parties. These observations, however, are peripheral to the Lipset and Rokkan argument and will not be pursued here.

Oligarchic parties still attract more than half the vote, on average, in two additional countries, one of which (Uruguay) is the fourth in which the traditional parties were able to absorb new interests. Among the other thirteen countries, oligarchic parties now attract less than 25 percent of the vote. Where electoral institutions have not created high barriers to the entry of new parties into the political system, traditional cleavages have blurred over time. In short, the Lipset and Rokkan argument about the persistence of historical cleavages does not fare especially well in Latin America and the European periphery. Spain and Italy, as analyzed by Lipset and Rokkan, also fit the pattern shown here. Where cleavages have actually frozen, we can think of institutional reasons for why parties in those countries have been more stable than parties in other countries, but since I have made no effort to test an institutionalist explanation, it remains speculation.

Note that working-class participation is not the only challenge to cleavage stability suggested by the array of cases in table 4.3.

Some of the historical cleavages were headed toward the dustbin of history well before mass suffrage. In eight of the eighteen countries (Argentina, Bolivia, Costa Rica, El Salvador, Guatemala, Mexico, Portugal, and Venezuela), one side of the old liberal-conservative cleavage had ceased to exist as a major political force before working-class participation (see appendix C). In most of these eight countries, upper-class interests were represented either in one party or by multiple ephemeral parties divided by conflicting personal loyalties more than by interests. Both the clerical-secular cleavage and the land-commercial divide had ceased to structure political competition in these countries.

One of the most interesting findings to emerge from this exercise so far is that party systems in this set of cases changed a great deal during the period before mass politics. In 44 percent of the countries, the vote for parties based on traditional cleavages had fallen below 75 percent even before suffrage was extended to the working class. In other words, the cleavage structures identified by Lipset and Rokkan were deteriorating in a number of countries even before the entrance of large numbers of new voters. The average vote for traditional parties that had previously dominated the political arena in all countries for which the presuffrage vote share is available was only 62 percent in the decade before mass suffrage. In short, traditional cleavages themselves seem to have been less stable in these countries than Lipset and Rokkan would have expected.

The second element of the Lipset and Rokkan argument maintains that "the freezing of the major party alternatives [occurred] in the wake of the extension of suffrage" (50). To test this argument, I examine the average vote share won in competitive elections since 1985 by parties that received 5 percent or more of the vote during the first decade after effective suffrage. This tests the organizational continuity of parties, which Lipset and Rokkan expected to be substantial once the working class had been incorporated. As can be seen in table 4.4, the party systems of some countries have certainly frozen. In three out of four of the countries in which old parties absorbed new interests, those same parties still dominate the political system. In only two of the fifteen cases in which the old parties had to compete with new ones, however, do the parties that dominated the political system during the postsuffrage years still attract more than 50 percent of the vote. The average vote share of all combined postsuffrage parties in countries in which the old parties had to compete is 26.1

percent during the current period. The pattern of organizational persistence thus looks similar to the pattern of cleavage persistence shown in table 4.3. Where parties were able to absorb new interests, they survived from the oligarchic period to the present. Where they had to compete, not only did many of them not survive as organizations, but the cleavage structures underlying the parties also tended to shift.

TABLE 4.4. "Frozen in the Wake" of Working-Class Enfranchisement: Organizational Persistence

		Combined Average Vote Share since 1985 for Postsuffrage Parties (%)
Absorption of new interests into old parties	Colombia	81.9
	Honduras	95.3
	Paraguay	89.1
	Uruguay	61.9
	Average	82.1
Addition of new parties to the political system	Argentina	29.5
	Bolivia	29.8
	Bulgaria	14.0[a]
	Chile	14.4
	Costa Rica	42.8
	Ecuador	14.5
	El Salvador	33.6
	Greece	7.2[b]
	Guatemala	0.0
	Mexico	73.4
	Nicaragua	2.3
	Panama	19.9
	Peru	23.2
	Portugal	32.1
	Venezuela	54.1
	Average	26.1

[a]Includes votes for the Bulgarian National Peasants Union (BZNS), BZNS–Nicola Petkov, and People's Union (NS), and half the votes for the electoral alliance between the NS and the SDS (Union of Democratic Forces). The various permutations are generally considered successors of the postsuffrage Agrarian Union. The total also includes votes for the Bulgarian Social Democratic Party, successor of the postsuffrage Social Democratic Party. After World War II, the Social Democrats split under pressure from Soviet occupation forces, and the larger faction became the ruling Communist Party. A small faction continued to exist as Social Democrats. The small faction seems to reflect better Lipset and Rokkan's idea of organizational persistence. If, however, one were to treat the Bulgarian Socialist Party, the former Communists, as the successor of the Social Democrats, the total average vote share for successors of postsuffrage parties in the contemporary period would be 45 percent.

[b]Includes votes for the Communist Party of Greece (KKE), KKE-NS, and half the vote for the Coalition of the Left (SIN).

Although the postsuffrage parties still play a role in most countries—a large role in about a third of them—the amount of persistence shown here does not seem sufficient to support the idea that the parties have been frozen in the wake of working-class suffrage. Indeed, these figures do not convey the full fluidity of postsuffrage party systems in these countries. Only forty-six of the eighty-three parties that attracted at least 5 percent of the vote in a postsuffrage election even survived into the contemporary period.

The two countries with the most solidly frozen party systems and cleavage structures are Paraguay and Honduras, in both of which traditional parties still get over 85 percent of the vote. Note that these are two of the poorest, least developed countries in the group considered here. Both have had extensive experience with dictatorship. Paraguay did not democratize until 1993 and has held only two fully competitive elections with full suffrage in its entire history. The experience of these countries suggests that poverty, lack of education, and a history of repression do not explain the more recent democratizers' lesser party stability relative to Western European party systems.

On the other hand, a long, mostly democratic history may contribute modestly to the persistence of party organizations. In the countries with the most democratic experience (Colombia, Uruguay, Chile, Costa Rica, and Venezuela), postsuffrage parties still attract slightly more than half the vote, on average. Postsuffrage parties in countries with less democratic experience, in contrast, attract a bit more than a third. Of course, we do not know the direction of the causal arrow. It may be that institutionalized parties contribute to democratic stability, as, for example, Scott Mainwaring and Timothy Scully (1995) have argued; but it seems equally plausible that stable democracy helps parties to remain stable. Even in the most democratic countries, however, the party systems can hardly be called frozen, with only about half the contemporary vote captured by postsuffrage parties.

The evidence summarized here shows that party systems in these countries are much more fluid than those in Western Europe. Richard Rose and Derek Urwin (1970) consider that a party fulfills Lipset and Rokkan's expectations if its share of the vote changes, on average, less than a quarter of a percentage point per year, and most parties in West European countries met this criterion from 1945 to 1970. The only countries in the set used for this test in which the main parties meet it are Paraguay and Honduras.

This exercise has involved only the most preliminary and rudimentary test of Lipset and Rokkan. It might be that if appropriate controls were added, their claim about the lasting legacies of the historical junctures they identified as critical would appear stronger. It might be argued, for example, that some countries included in this test had experienced so little electoral competition both before the extension of suffrage and since that they should not be expected to have developed stable party cleavages. A preliminary assessment of that possibility can be undertaken here. In the countries that have endured the longest periods of dictatorship (Bolivia, Bulgaria, El Salvador, Guatemala, Honduras, Mexico, Nicaragua, Paraguay, Peru, and Portugal), oligarchic parties (and their descendants) attracted 24.6 percent of the vote, on average, in elections after 1985. In countries with more democratic experience, they attracted 24 percent. Postsuffrage parties (and their descendants) in countries with more authoritarian experience got 48.7 percent of the vote in recent elections, compared with 50.1 percent in the other countries. These very small differences do not support the conjecture that long periods of authoritarianism undermine cleavage stability. Although postsuffrage party organizations are somewhat more stable in the five countries with the longest democratic histories (Colombia, Uruguay, Chile, Costa Rica, and Venezuela), underlying cleavage stability seems unaffected by regime experience.

Other arguments might also be tested, of course. One of the advantages of having carefully defined and measured the concepts used by Lipset and Rokkan is that quite a few other hypotheses can now be tested that we would not previously have been able to assess in a systematic way.

The findings above must be considered tentative. But until future work demonstrates otherwise, we will have to consider the Lipset and Rokkan hypothesis about the persistence of historical cleavages as largely disconfirmed outside the set of cases from which it was induced. The postsuffrage party systems in these other countries tend to be slushy rather than frozen.

The discovery that an argument generally considered to hold in Western Europe cannot be confirmed outside that area should not necessarily lead to its rejection, even if much more thorough and persuasive tests than those discussed above were done. Rather, the disconfirmation should lead to a search for the characteristics of West European countries conducive to party system stability. Such a search might lead to the discovery of causes of freezing unnoticed by Lipset and Rokkan because these causes did not vary within the set of cases they had selected for observation. It might also eventually lead to challenges to the original Lipset and Rokkan argument if causes were discovered that had nothing to do with historical critical junctures or the configuration of societal cleavages in particular countries.

Conclusion

This chapter began by noting that although case studies have attracted a great deal of methodological criticism, they are the major source of evidence in most studies in the comparative field, and that they need not have many of the shortcomings for which they have been criticized. It is possible to use them in a more methodologically careful way. The test of Lipset and Rokkan demonstrated some of the features that should characterize analyses based on case studies: the inclusion of as many cases as possible in order to increase the robustness of findings; the use of "structured focused comparison," that is, measuring the same causal factors and outcomes in the same way in each case; and the use of cases other than those from which hypotheses have been induced to test arguments.

The purpose of this exercise has been to demonstrate several widely known but often disregarded lessons. First, if one "tests" hypotheses on the same cases used to develop them, one will certainly confirm them. Such research designs do not subject arguments to the possibility of falsification. Second, the need to rely on "data" from case studies does not require reliance on vague or ambiguous measurement of basic concepts. Finally, when assessing a path-dependent argument, all stages of the argument need not always be tested on the same cases. It is often possible to find cases other than those in which the analyst was originally interested that have the initial conditions that make it possible to use them to test arguments advanced at particular nodes of path-dependent arguments. Such tests are not always possible, but a conscientious effort to find such cases should always be made.

Often, analysts will know little about such cases—just as Lipset and Rokkan probably had little information about Latin

America—and may be reluctant to spend time learning about cases in which they feel no particular interest. Some would perhaps go further, arguing that the exercise above is unfair, since it subjects an argument developed to apply to European cases to a set of cases mostly from a different region. I would take the opposite position. The compartmentalization of comparative politics into geographical areas may once have been necessary to facilitate gathering information that could be found nowhere but in the countries themselves, but it has no theoretical justification and, in fact, hinders the development of theory. To the extent that the field develops a norm that hypotheses need to be tested on cases different from those that inspired them, practitioners will be induced to transcend this compartmentalization and take a step toward becoming broad comparativists rather than specialists in regional detail.

Such tests would make a twofold contribution to the development of hardier theories. First, "theories" capable of explaining only the few cases from which they were induced could be discarded quickly—a major efficiency gain for the field. Second, modification and the specification of theoretical, not geographical, domains will improve theories such as Lipset and Rokkan's that seem to fit cases in one region pretty well (Rose and Urwin 1970; Bartolini and Mair 1990), but do not fit other cases that it seems they should. Analysts will search for the *general* conditions that limit the domain of the theory, rather than offering case-specific reasons for exceptions, as Lipset and Rokkan do for Spain and Italy. The result will be better and more durable theories.

CHAPTER 5

How the Approach You Choose Affects the Answers You Get

Rational Choice and Its Uses in Comparative Politics

As the new millennium begins, feuding seems to be dying down between advocates of traditional comparative approaches and those who have embraced rational choice. Those of us who use rational choice learn continuously from those who do not, and many of those who find the approach uncongenial have nevertheless been influenced by the insights it has brought to light. This interaction among approaches has been fruitful, if occasionally acrimonious.

Nevertheless, a tension remains between the traditional values of the comparative field and rational choice scholarship as it is usually practiced. Rational choice arguments are being applied in more and more substantive areas, a development that has been seen as threatening to the most basic values of the comparative field by some and as scientific progress by enthusiastic converts. Comparativists have always prized the acquisition of deep and thorough knowledge of the politics, society, and history of the countries they study, and they have invested heavily in the fieldwork and language training necessary to gain this depth of understanding. This kind of knowledge, however, often seems to have no place in rational choice arguments. Nothing in the rational choice approach requires ignoring context or relying on superficial knowledge of politics and history, but both often occur in practice, as comparativists have noticed. This is a real shortcoming in a good deal of the rational choice literature and one that comparativists cannot take lightly.

On the other side of the scales, however, rational choice provides some intellectual tools for theory building that are currently unmatched by other commonly used approaches. Although imaginative scholars can build theories within any research tradition, the tools of rational choice make it easier. Rational choice has spread from one research domain to another in the same way that other efficiency-enhancing innovations spread, and for the same reasons. It helps those who use it accomplish something they want to accomplish: creating theoretically cogent and empirically testable arguments. In addition, it is relatively easy to use. It requires only a little specialized knowledge and no great mathematical ability, so the "start-up" costs are low.

Decisions about what approach to take to particular research questions should be based on assessments of what kind of leverage different approaches offer for answering the question of interest. Research approaches are not religions or parties to which we owe lifelong loyalty. They are tools we should pick up as needed and lay down when they do not suit the task at hand. All have strengths and weaknesses. Of the sets of research tools currently used in comparative politics, rational choice seems to be the one most often misunderstood by those who do not use it (and by some of those who do).

The reason for this misunderstanding is largely accidental. Rational choice entered political science through the study of democratic politics in general and American politics in particular, at a time when many comparativists were focused on countries mired in poverty and authoritarian rule. Although issues relevant to developing countries have always been amenable to research using the rational choice approach,[1] they are quite different from those studied by most early rational choice scholars. Only a decade or so ago, Robert Bates (1990, 46) lamented that due to the dearth of democracies in the developing world, knowledge of the advances made by rational choice theorists in explaining democratic politics merely added to the frustrations facing students of developing countries. Now, however, with democratic processes squarely at the center of politics in most of Latin America and Eastern Europe and becoming important in more and more parts of Africa and Asia, many more students of developing countries have begun to find rational choice a useful way to approach the study of politics.

The main purpose of this chapter is to offer a clear introduc-

---

1. See North (1979); Levi (1988); and Olson (1993) for examples of important rational choice arguments about economic transformation and the development of democracy. But the immense proliferation of rational choice explanations has occurred in the context of democratic politics. These theories have only recently been applied to current political processes in developing countries.

tory description of the rational choice approach, in the process dissipating some widespread misunderstandings. The first section of the chapter concentrates on this. Rational choice arguments offer more leverage for answering some kinds of questions than others, and the discussion below shows how these differences derive from the assumptions on which rational choice arguments are based. The next section describes some of the most important contributions of rational choice to the study of political science and offers some suggestions for their further extension into areas of interest to comparativists. The last section addresses the question, What characteristics should an approach possess in order to be useful? This chapter is not intended to proselytize for rational choice, but rather to explain its appeal, give it its due (but no more than its due), and note the substantive areas in which it has been especially fruitful.

Distinguishing Features of Rational Choice

In contrast to most arguments in the dependency, historical institutionalist (as defined by March and Olsen 1984), and comparative historical sociology traditions, rational choice arguments use the individual, or some analogue of the individual, as the unit of analysis. They assume that individuals, including politicians, are rational in the sense that, given goals and alternative strategies from which to choose, they will select the alternatives that maximize their chances of achieving their goals. Institutions, other structural characteristics such as ethnic divisions or the size of the peasantry, and immediate political circumstances enter rational choice arguments as factors that shape second-order preferences (that is, strategies employed to attain goals). These contextual factors determine the alternatives from which individuals may choose their strategies and the costs and benefits associated with strategies. Factors that shape first-order preferences—what I am here calling goals—are outside the deductive structure of rational choice models (that is, the models do not attempt to explain their origins), but goals nevertheless play a crucial role in rational choice arguments. The most compelling use of this approach results from the creative synthesis of the rational actor assumptions with, first, a plausible attribution of goals and, second, a careful interpretation of the effects of institutions and other factors on the feasible strategies available to actors for achieving these goals.

Misperceptions about Rational Choice

Many who have worked outside the rational choice tradition hold misperceptions of it that interfere with their ability to use the insights and methods associated with it. So, before considering the applicability of some of these ideas outside the context in which they emerged, I discuss some of the most common misperceptions so that they can be set aside. They include contentions that rational choice arguments

- are inherently conservative;
- assume that all people are motivated by material interests (the economists' famous *homo economicus*);
- assume that people's preferences are stable or unchanging;
- are based on unrealistic assumptions, since people are not really rational, and they lack the information and calculating ability assumed by rational choice theory;
- are ahistorical and fail to take context into account;
- are deterministic; and
- cannot be used to explain path-dependent situations.

In the following paragraphs, I discuss each of these misperceptions in turn, including the grain of truth upon which each pearl of misperception has been accreted. This section aims to clear away some misunderstandings and to delimit the domain in which rational choice arguments are likely to be useful. Although none of the statements listed above is generally true, some are true in some instances; and, when they are true, rational choice arguments are not likely to provide much leverage for understanding events.

Ideology

Although a number of scholars whose sympathies cluster to the left of the political spectrum use rational choice models (e.g., John Roemer, Amartya Sen, Michael Taylor, Adam Przeworski, David Laitin, and Michael Wallerstein), one continues to hear the claim that rational choice arguments have a conservative bias. Apparently, this stems from the prominence of University of Virginia and University of Chicago economists in the development of the public choice subfield, which often focuses on the economic inefficiencies caused by government interventions in markets. It is true that many economists, especially those associated with the public choice literature, show a touching faith in markets and a deep suspicion of government involvement in economic matters. And some of these economists have helped to build the current economic liberalization orthodoxy that is having such a major impact on developing-country economies. Public choice is only one subfield, however, in what has become a very large field of rational choice arguments applied to many aspects of politics. As the work of the individuals listed above shows, the tools of the rational choice approach can be used to serve many different ideals (cf. Barry 1982).

Goals

A second misperception is that rational choice arguments assume that material interests motivate human beings. This is simply false. The "rationality" assumed by rational choice arguments is of the narrowest means-ends kind. Assumptions about the goals held by individuals are supplied by the analyst, not by the approach. The approach only assumes that people (1) choose the means they consider most likely to result in desired ends; (2) can weakly order their goals (that is, given any set of alternatives, they will prefer one to the other or be indifferent between the two); and (3) hold consistent preferences (that is, if they prefer chocolate to strawberries and strawberries to cabbage, then they prefer chocolate to cabbage). Although one can think of situations in which the second or third condition might not hold, they are not common. If one limits the domain of rational choice arguments to areas in which these conditions seem plausible, the domain remains extremely broad.

Because the rational choice approach makes no assumptions about goals, the analyst who seeks to apply it to a particular problem must identify the goals of the actors involved. The analyst cannot usually offer direct proof, such as survey data, to show that actors really do have the goals imputed to them, since such data may not be available and, even if it is, actors may have good reasons to lie about their goals. Nevertheless, checks on the analytic imagination are built into the rational choice approach: if the analyst misspecifies actors' goals, then their behavior will differ from that predicted. Inconvenient facts will cast doubt on the argument, as they would within the framework of any other approach.

In practice, analysts often make plausible assumptions about the goals of actors, but these assumptions are supplied by analysts, not by the approach per se. For most arguments in economics, and for some in political science, it is entirely plausible to attribute goals of material self-interest to actors. If one wants to explain how firms set their prices or which industries lobby for tariffs, it is reasonable to assume that material interests shape these decisions. There is, of course, nothing unique to rational choice in the idea that material interests motivate much of human behavior. It is an idea shared by most Marxist, neo-Marxist, pluralist, corporatist, ad hoc, and journalistic accounts of political behavior.

Many of the most interesting rational choice arguments about democratic politics, however, do not conceptualize the salient actor as *homo economicus.* Instead, they attribute to democratic politicians the goals of reelection, political survival, and career advancement. In some countries, the advancement of a political career may be the surest road to amassing a fortune, but, more commonly, officeholders could make more money doing something else. A rational choice argument might not offer a satisfactory account of why certain individuals choose politics while others choose business or professional careers. Once the choice has been made, however, it seems reasonable to attribute the goal of survival in office to those who have previously demonstrated a preference for officeholding, and rational choice arguments have had substantial success using this assumption to explain the behavior of politicians.

The theoretical bite of rational choice arguments depends both on the plausibility of the goals attributed to actors and on the ability of analysts to identify the goals a priori, that is, without reference to the specific behavior to be explained. Most of the time, analysts are on firm ground when they assume that actors prefer more material goods to less or that politicians prefer continuing their careers to ending them. It is obviously not true that all politicians prefer continuing their careers, since some retire before every election; but if the average politician has this goal, then the argument that assumes this goal will explain average behavior. Rational choice arguments tend to become less persuasive and less useful as the real goals of actors become more idiosyncratic. Thus, rational choice arguments do a good job of explaining why most members of the U.S. Congress cater to the interests of their constituents; but they would not, in my view, do a good job of explaining why a few Russian intellectuals joined Lenin in his apparently hopeless struggle to overthrow the czar. It is possible to construct a rational choice explanation for this behavior if one begins by attributing to the followers some very idiosyncratic goals. Such an explanation is not satisfying, however, because it leaves unexplored one of the most puzzling factors needed to explain Lenin's followers: the origin of their unusual goals.

The ability of the analyst to attribute plausible goals to actors a priori thus limits the domain within which rational choice arguments are useful. Because the approach sets no limits on what the goals may be, it is possible to construct rational choice explanations for apparently irrational (in the everyday sense of the word) behavior by claiming that actors were rationally pursuing their own (peculiar) goals. The person who, for instance, gives all his or her possessions to a religious cult can be said to be rationally pursuing the goal of self-abnegation. But when goals are directly inferred from observed behavior, rational choice arguments slide from "creative tautology," to use Brian Barry's phrase (1970), into mere tautology.

Rational choice arguments are not usually useful for explaining acts of extraordinary heroism, stupidity, or cruelty, which are often motivated either by highly idiosyncratic goals or by lapses of means-ends rationality. (They can, however, deal reasonably well with run-of-the-mill cruelty and stupidity, such as that which occurred during the war in Bosnia.) They are not useful in situations in which goals must be inferred from the specifics of the behavior one seeks to explain. Such "explanations" are vacuous.

Some examples from the study of revolution may help to clarify when plausible goals can be attributed to actors a priori, thus making rational choice arguments useful, and when they cannot. Powerful rational choice arguments have been suggested to explain why peasants, who can plausibly be assumed to wish to maximize their own welfare, sometimes join revolutionary movements (Popkin 1979); why members of radical organizations, who can plausibly be assumed to try to maximize their chance of achieving power, choose particular political strategies (DeNardo 1985); and why postrevolutionary regimes, which can plausibly be assumed to seek to maximize survival in power, choose particular economic policies (Colburn 1986). In these instances, the analyst can identify goals that, on the one hand, are plausible and that, on the other, motivate many behaviors besides the one the analyst seeks to explain.

In contrast, there is, to my knowledge, no rational choice argument to explain why a few educated, comfortably middle-class individuals ignore family responsibilities and more secure and lucrative career opportunities in order to join nascent revolutionary movements in which the likelihood of achieving power is far lower than the likelihood of ending up dead or in jail. We know that such individuals play an important role in the early stages of revolutionary movements, regardless of objective chances for the movement's success. They can be incorporated within the rational choice framework as people who have unusual goals, and they are sometimes taken as a given in rational choice arguments that explain why people with more average goals sometimes join movements (e.g., Lohmann 1992, 1993). But rational choice arguments have not offered, and I suspect never will offer, a persuasive explanation for the behavior of such exceptional individuals. Only their strategies, given their goals, are grist for the rational choice mill.

Stable Preferences

The claim that rational choice arguments assume unchanging preferences is a misunderstanding born of a failure to distinguish everyday language from technical language. Rational choice arguments require only that preferences or goals remain stable during the time it takes actors to choose strategies. This can be for the minute or two it takes an actor to decide how to vote in a committee, or it can be for a period that covers many years, if the analyst believes that actors faced the same situation repeatedly over a long period of time. The duration of stable preferences depends on how the analyst interprets the situations facing actors. If the analyst's reading of history suggests that goals changed over time or in reaction to external shocks, then he could incorporate such change into the rational choice argument through a change in payoffs. Since the preferences that are assumed—for example, the preference for more over less material goods or for remaining in power as opposed to losing office—are so basic, however, they actually tend to remain stable.

Many discussions of the implausibility of unchanging preferences arise from a confusion between the term *preferences* as used in the rational choice idiom—what I call "goals" here in order to avoid this confusion—and the everyday language use of the word *preferences.* The latter has a much broader meaning than the rational choice word *preferences.* The everyday meaning includes both the kinds of underlying goals that are referred to as preferences in the rational choice idiom and also attitudes toward (preferences about) choices or activities that would help achieve the goals. These attitudes are not referred to as preferences in the rational choice idiom; they are called strategies, strategic choices, or, occasionally, second-order preferences. They include policy preferences, institutional preferences, and most other preferences about real-life choices. Second-order preferences are choices of strategies for achieving first-order preferences. Within rational choice arguments, politicians' policy and institutional preferences (in everyday language) are strategic behaviors aimed at achieving their goal of remaining in office. Policy preferences may alter radically in response to changed circumstances, but this does not imply that preferences, in the rational choice sense, have changed. The politician's first-order preference for remaining in office remains unchanged, but he rationally picks the policy or institutional strategy he considers most likely, in the circumstances he faces, to help him achieve that goal. Policy and institutional preferences are virtually always endogenous in rational choice arguments, as critics claim they should be; but they are called strategies, not preferences.

In short, the objection that rational choice arguments make implausible assumptions about unchanging preferences arises from a misunderstanding. The assumptions actually necessary to rational choice arguments about the stability of preferences are minimal and substantively innocuous in most situations.

Information and Calculating Requirements

A fourth objection to the use of rational choice arguments is that they make unrealistic assumptions about human calculating ability and information acquisition; it is argued that although people may try to pursue their goals efficiently, they lack sufficient information and calculating ability to do it. There is a sizable grain of truth in these claims, but it is mitigated by three circumstances. First, the information requirements are more implausible in some situations than others. Rational choice arguments are most likely to be useful in situations in which these requirements do not strain credulity, and it is in these areas, as I show below, that they have been most successful. Second, for several reasons (also discussed below), people can sometimes behave as if they had sufficient information and calculating ability even when they do not. That is, they make the same choices they would have made if they had had full information and unlimited mental ability. Rational choice arguments also work pretty well when the analyst can demonstrate reasons to believe that people behave as if they were making rational calculations even if they are not. Finally, although the simplest rational choice arguments usually assume complete information, techniques exist for incorporating incomplete information into models. Models that assume incomplete information can get complicated, but they pose no problem in principle.

Rational choice arguments are easiest to devise in situations in which actors can identify other actors and know their goals, and in which the rules that govern interactions among actors are precise and known to all (Tsebelis 1990, 32). Many situations in democratic politics exhibit these characteristics; consequently, rational choice arguments have successfully explained a number of democratic processes. Interactions in legislatures, between legislatures and the bureaucracy, within party leaderships, within ruling coalitions, and in other political bodies established in democratic settings tend to involve easily identifiable actors whose goals are easy to establish and whose interactions are governed by precise, well-known procedural rules.

Rational choice arguments can even be used successfully in democracies that differ substantially from the ideal, as do many of the democracies in developing countries. Limitations on effective participation, representation, or party competition do not reduce the usefulness of rational choice arguments, as long as there is some competition in the system and as long as interactions among political actors remain reasonably predictable and transparent to all involved.

Rational choice arguments are also more likely to be useful when explaining outcomes of high salience to the individuals involved. People spend more time and effort acquiring information when the results of their decisions have important consequences. The average citizen is often "rationally ignorant" about politics; her vote will have almost no effect on political outcomes, and therefore it would not be rational to spend time learning all about the issues and candidates. In contrast, the average legislator, whose career depends on making electorally correct choices, has good reason to use time and energy to stay well informed. Because of the visible and well-structured nature of governing institutions in established democracies and the importance to the careers of elected officials of making the right decisions, rational choice arguments have proved especially useful in explaining behaviors in these institutions.[2]

Whether rational choice arguments can be used successfully to explain decision making within authoritarian regimes depends on the regime's level of transparency, stability, and predictability.[3] Rational actor assumptions are likely to be plausible in regimes in which the rules governing survival and advancement are clear to both participants and observers and are relatively unchanging, but not in regimes in which many decisions are made in secret by a small group of individuals and in which rules and rulers change frequently, radically, and unpredictably.[4]

Rational choice arguments can be useful in some circumstances even when actors lack crucial information. Actors can sometimes learn through trial and error to choose the same strategies that they would have chosen if they had had full information and an unlimited ability to calculate. Thus, if situations are repeated over and over again, people can be expected to learn over time to understand them and to make more effective decisions. The more important the outcome to the person, the more effort will be expended on learning. It has been suggested that rational choice arguments will not work in very new or transitional democracies, because the rules and players have not become established and actors have had no time to learn about the new system. Recent research suggests that this concern is overstated. The electoral incentives created by democracy are so powerful and transparent, and the results of decisions so important to hopeful politicians at the birth of democracy, that they spend

2. See, for example, Ferejohn (1974); Fiorina (1977); Fiorina and Noll (1978); Hammond and Miller (1987); Mayhew (1974); and Shepsle and Weingast (1981b).

3. The point being made here has to do with the plausibility of the information requirements of the rational choice model for individuals operating in different kinds of political systems. When the analyst treats the state itself as a rational actor, authoritarianism has little effect on the plausibility of assumptions about information and may make more plausible the unitary actor assumption implied by treating the state as an actor.

4. Smith (1979), for example, has used motivational assumptions consistent with the rational choice approach (though without explicit rational choice jargon) to explain the behavior of officials in Mexico's PRI (Institutional Revolutionary Party). The Idi Amin government in Uganda, at the opposite end of the predictability continuum, would have been much harder to analyze in this way.

whatever effort is necessary to acquire information and update it constantly to keep up with the fluidity of the political situation. To judge by their decisions, they are about as well informed and can calculate about as well as politicians in more institutionalized democracies (Frye 1997; Geddes 1995, 1996).

A plausible argument can be made, however, that voters in new democracies have fewer incentives than would-be politicians to learn about the options available in the new system and thus learn more slowly. As a result, substantial numbers of new voters may fail to vote for the parties that would best represent their interests in early elections. Modest support for this argument can be found in analyses of early electoral behavior in Eastern Europe. Before the first democratic election in Hungary, voters told survey researchers that they preferred social democratic policies, but they did not vote for parties that offered this option (Kolosi et al. 1992). Most Russian voters polled before the 1993 parliamentary elections preferred centrist policy options, but centrist parties lost to more extreme parties on both the left and right (Treisman 1998). The strongest vote for communist successor parties in Bulgaria, Romania, and Poland has come from the most backward rural areas, not from the regions with a concentrated blue-collar vote that former communist parties have tried hardest to attract. In general, the association between socioeconomic status and party vote is substantially lower in Eastern Europe than in Western Europe. Although the evidence is not strong enough to prove that this is caused by incomplete information, and various other explanations have been suggested, incomplete information is a plausible contender.[5] If so, then the general tendency of rational choice arguments to be more useful for predicting elite behavior (because elites are more likely to approximate the information requirements of the model) than mass

5. Some have contended that East European voters have longer time horizons than are usually attributed to voters in the West, and that they vote for candidates who offer radical reform despite short-term costs because they expect that they or their children will benefit in the long run. This argument seems less plausible now than it did a couple of years ago, since the vote for candidates and parties that actively support radical economic reform during their campaigns has fallen in more recent elections. Other analysts, most notably Jowitt (1992), argue that citizens in the new democracies of Eastern Europe have goals different from the essentially materialist ones usually attributed to voters in established democracies. If Jowitt's view is correct, East European voters are not inefficiently pursuing the goal of policies that will improve their material situations because they lack sufficient information about the new system; rather, they are pursuing, perhaps efficiently, other goals.

behavior may be more marked in transitional or fluid political situations.

Actors may also behave as if they were rational without conscious learning if some selection mechanism exists to weed out behaviors that lead to outcomes different from those a rational actor would have chosen. Just as differential survival rates eliminate less-efficient mutations in evolutionary theories, they can eliminate actors in other arenas who follow strategies that fail to converge with the outcomes that would have been produced by rational (that is, efficient) choices. It has been argued, for example, that firm managers do not actually think about profits when they make most decisions (Nelson and Winter 1982). Nevertheless, existing firms behave as though they were profit maximizers, because competition drives out of business those that deviate too far from profit-maximizing behavior (Alchian 1950; Winter 1964). The same kind of argument can be made for politicians. Politicians may sincerely believe that they are ignoring constituency and interest group pressures and voting according to conscience, but if they deviate too far from behavior that maximizes their chances for reelection, they are likely to be defeated in the next election. As with learning, natural selection requires repetitions. Neither learning nor evolution can be used to support a claim that actors behave as if they were rational in unrepeated situations.

To summarize, the information and calculation requirements of the rational choice model are stiff. Rational choice arguments are more likely to succeed in explaining behavior when actors closely approximate these requirements. The appropriate domain of rational choice arguments thus includes situations in which outcomes are very important to actors, since that impels the gathering of knowledge; situations in which the rules governing interactions are clear and precise; and situations that occur repeatedly so that actors can learn or so that efficient strategies can evolve even in the absence of conscious learning (Tsebelis 1990, 31–39). Where choices have few consequences (e.g., "cheap talk," such as survey responses) or little effect on overall outcomes (votes in elections), we should expect scant investment in information gathering, and rational choice arguments may not predict actors' behavior very well. Where information is kept hidden from actors or the rules that govern interactions change frequently and unpredictably (as in some dictatorships), rational choice arguments will probably not be useful. When it is not reasonable to think that individuals can actually figure out their own best strategy, when situations are not repeated, and when no plausible selection mechanism can be identified, rational choice arguments are likely to offer less explanatory leverage. Despite these numerous limitations, however, much of politics remains inside the rational choice domain.

History and Context

The claim that rational choice theories ignore history and context is true to the same degree that it is true of all theories. All theories identify causes that can be expected to have the same effect, with some probability, within a specified domain. History and context may determine the domain within which a theory is useful. Or they may determine the values of the variables that enter the theory as purported causes. Or they may supply the other variables that impinge on the relationship of interest and thus affect the probability that the cause will actually have the predicted effect. History and context enter into rational choice arguments in the same ways. If there is any difference, it is that the rational choice approach provides criteria for selecting specific elements from the vast rococo of reality for use in arguments, rather than leaving the choice entirely to the observer's intuitions.

Contrary to the claims of critics, most rational choice arguments about political behavior actually give primacy to institutions and other contextual circumstances as causes of outcomes. "The rational-choice approach focuses its attention on the constraints imposed on rational actors—the institutions of a society. . . . Individual action is assumed to be optimal adaptation to an institutional environment, and interaction between individuals is assumed to be an optimal response to each other. Therefore, the prevailing institutions . . . determine the behavior of the actors, which in turn produces political or social outcomes" (Tsebelis 1990, 40).

A couple of examples may clarify the integral relationship between context and rational choice arguments. In an article that treats Catholic hierarchies as rational actors attempting to maximize the number of the faithful, Anthony Gill (1994) finds that the amount of competition from Protestant evangelists, along with a few characteristics of the historic church-state relationship in each country, predicted whether the Catholic Church opposed authoritarianism. In other words, the behavior of interest (opposition to authoritarianism) is explained by a circumstance (level of Protestant competition) and a small set of institutions (that structure church-state relations) in conjunction with the assumption that the church hierarchy acts rationally to pursue its goal (of maximizing the faithful). The goal is shared by church leaders in all countries. Their strategies for achieving it, however—support for or opposition to military governments—depend on circumstances and institutions that vary across countries and affect the costs, benefits, and feasibility of different strategies. These circumstances and institutions thus cause differences in behavior.

A second example explains the initiation of land reform. Using an argument that treats Latin American legislators as rational actors bent on reelection, Nancy Lapp (1997) finds that institutional changes that increase the importance of the peasant vote (e.g., illiterate suffrage, secret ballot, or easy registration) increase the likelihood of land reform. The goal of legislators in all countries is assumed to be the same: remaining in office. They attempt to do this by voting for policies for which constituents will reward them at election time. When literacy requirements prevent most peasants from voting, rational politicians have no reason to provide them with policies that would benefit them, but when peasants are enfranchised, incentives change. An institutional change thus leads to a change in legislators' strategies for pursuing an unchanging goal.

In these and other rational choice explanations of political phenomena, variations in institutions (in the example above, changes in electoral laws) and other contextual circumstances (in the first example, the amount of competition from Protestants) cause differences in the incentives faced by rational actors, who then make decisions in accordance with the incentives they face. Far from being ahistorical and acontextual, rational choice arguments about politics depend heavily on context.

Determinism

The rational choice model, that is, the deductive logic that connects the choice of means to preexisting goals, is deterministic. This does not, however, imply that rational choice arguments make deterministic predictions of behavior. The most useful way to think of rational choice arguments is as if-then statements with the following form: *if* the actors have the goals the observer claims, and *if* the information and calculation requirements are plausible (for any of the reasons noted above), and *if* the actors actually face the rules and payoffs the observer claims they do, *then* certain behavior will occur.

Some slippage can occur at each *if* without necessarily eviscerating the whole argument. A few actors may have goals that differ from the majority's. For example, a few members of Congress may not care about reelection. If most do, however, the argument will still explain the behavior of most of them and therefore the outputs of the legislature. Some actors may lack information or the ability to calculate. For example, freshman legislators may not yet have learned the ropes, but if most legislators are not freshmen, the argument will still hold, on average. Or the observer may misunderstand the situation that faces some actors even though the situation facing most of them has been correctly interpreted. For example, the observer may incorrectly assume that payoffs to members of small parties are the same as payoffs to members of large parties. If so, the argument will still explain the behavior of members of large parties. In all of these examples, an empirical test of the argument (if one is possible) should show that the argument explains a substantial part of the outcome, though not every individual action. In other words, the argument results in probabilistic predictions and explanations, just as other social science arguments do.

Path Dependence

The concept of path dependence was invented in economics to explain situations in which choices at time 1 affect the costs, benefits, and availability of options at time 2. It thus offers a rational explanation for behavior at time 2 that at first glance appears irrational. It is rather ironic, given the genesis of the idea, that the notion has arisen that rational choice is not useful for explaining path-dependent phenomena. The claim that path-dependent situations require a different form of argument seems to have sprung from a combination of two of the misperceptions noted above: the idea that rational choice approaches ignore history and context, and the misunderstanding of the meaning of the word *preference* in the rational choice idiom. Once these two misperceptions are abandoned, it is clear that rational choice arguments often provide sufficient leverage for explaining path-dependent outcomes.

This section has dealt with a series of misconceptions about rational choice arguments. It has shown that several of them are simply that: misunderstandings that should not be permitted to muddy the waters any longer. Other misperceptions bring to light serious impediments to using rational choice arguments to explain all conceivable human behaviors. I have argued that these objections should be taken seriously and used to delimit the domain within which rational choice arguments can be expected to be useful. I now turn to a different question: What distinguishes the rational choice approach from others?

What Really Distinguishes the Rational Choice Approach

The defining features of the rational choice approach are (1) methodological individualism, usually applied to individual people but sometimes also to organizations that can plausibly be expected to behave as unitary rational actors;[6] (2) explicit identification of actors and their goals or preferences; (3) explicit identification of the institutions and other contextual features that determine the options available to actors and the costs and benefits associated with different options; and (4) deductive logic. The rational choice approach has no monopoly on any of these features. Furthermore, most arguments originally posed within other frameworks can be translated into rational choice idiom. Advocates of structuralist arguments, for example, believe that structural conditions such as terms of trade or the distribution of income cause outcomes. They consider it unnecessary to spell out explicitly how

6. In my judgment—not shared by all practitioners—a further limitation on the appropriate domain of rational choice arguments is that they are only likely to be useful when the unit of analysis is either the individual or a hierarchical and well-organized group. The reason for the need for hierarchy and organization is that, as Arrow (1950) and McKelvey (1976) have shown, nondictatorial methods for aggregating preferences within groups lead to cycles and thus violate the consistency requirement of rationality. See also Elster (1986, 3–4). Extensive research on the U.S. Congress shows that institutional arrangements within groups can prevent cycling and lead to stable outcomes, and thus it may be reasonable to treat even democratic states as unitary actors in some circumstances. But these kinds of institutions do not exist in unorganized groups such as classes. It seems reasonable to treat unions, states in the international arena, and parties (in some circumstances) as rational unitary actors, since the analyst can usually discover the institutions that lead to preference stability. In general, however, unorganized groups such as classes or interest groups do not behave as rational unitary actors. One can use rational choice arguments to explain the behavior of members of these groups and the behavior of groups as aggregates of these individuals, but not the behavior of such groups as though they were corporate units.

structures determine the incentives facing particular individuals and thus determine their choices and, through their choices, social outcomes. Nevertheless, the analyst who wants to incorporate these intervening steps into a structuralist argument usually has no trouble doing so.

In short, there is nothing very unusual about the assumptions or structure of rational choice arguments. Nevertheless, the focus on the incentives facing individuals, the ruthless pruning of extraneous complexity, and the use of deductive logic have together resulted in a cluster of theoretical results both novel and fruitful (discussed below).

The Uses of Rational Choice

The rational choice literature in political science is now so enormous that it is impossible to catalog it even briefly. One major strand uses economic incentives to explain economic and political outcomes. This strand simply extends standard economic theories into areas where their implications had not previously been fully understood (e.g., Przeworski and Wallerstein 1988). Many Marxist and pluralist arguments, if carefully articulated, could be subsumed into this category of rational choice, since they expect people to pursue their material interests through political action. Standard spatial models of policy choice, a rigorous articulation of the pluralist conception of politics, fit within this strand. Recent creative applications of this venerable approach often highlight the implications of some hitherto underappreciated element of economic theory. Thus, for example, Ronald Rogowski (1989) derives expectations about coalition formation and change from the Stolper-Samuelson Theorem about the differential effect of changes in international prices on the political interests of holders of scarce and abundant factors. Jeffry Frieden (1991) argues that asset specificity, that is, the costliness of moving capital or skills from one use to another, explains why some business interests have more policy influence than others.

Other applications of the rational choice approach depart further from its roots in economics. Rather than attempting a comprehensive survey, I focus here on the developments within rational choice theory that demonstrate the kinds of insights that emerge as a consequence of the rigor and deductive logic of rational choice arguments. The applications of rational choice that have most changed the way political scientists think about the world have been those that show the nonobvious effects of aggregation and interaction among rational individuals. It was not the assumptions about self-interest and the rational pursuit of goals that distinguished the analyses that produced these worldview-changing ideas, but rather the careful articulation of the logic that underlies aggregation and interaction. Many other analyses have assumed, though often implicitly, that people are rational and self-interested, but they lacked the conceptual tools to see that the behavior of groups cannot be directly inferred from the interests of individuals in the group.

I deal here with three categories of argument: those that demonstrate the unintended and nonobvious results of aggregating individually rational choices; those that unpack the black box of the state by looking explicitly at the individuals who actually make state decisions, at the goals that shape their behavior, and at the incentives they face; and those that treat political decisions as strategic interactions among actors rather than decisions under external constraint. There is a great deal of overlap among these categories; in fact, nearly all the studies discussed below treat political outcomes as the result of strategic interactions among actors. For substantive reasons, however, it seems useful to discuss some strategic interactions under the rubric of aggregation and others elsewhere.

The Consequences of Aggregation

The theoretical development within the rational choice framework that has had the most radical and far-reaching effect on our understanding of the political world is the series of proofs that group decisions will not necessarily, or even usually, reflect the interests of the majority in the group, even if members of the group are entirely equal and decisions are arrived at democratically. Among a number of nonobvious and sometimes perverse aggregation effects, two stand out in terms of their political and theoretical consequences: the proof that majority rule does not necessarily result in policies that reflect majority preferences; and the demonstration that individuals who would benefit from public goods usually will not, if they are rational, help achieve them.[7]

7. See Schelling (1978) for other aggregation effects.

Cycles under Majority Rule and the Effects of Intralegislative Institutions

Kenneth Arrow (1950) developed the original proof that the aggregation of preferences through majority rule (given a set of plausible and unrestrictive conditions) may lead to policy cycles.[8] The theoretical work in this area is mathematical, and I am not the person to summarize it adequately. Instead, let me note some of the substantive implications that flow from it.

First, majority rule is no guarantee that the interests of the majority will be reflected in policy. A series of votes in a representative institution, such as a legislature, can result in any possible policy outcome, depending on the *sequencing* of votes on different options (McKelvey 1976; Schofield 1976). Hence the importance of agenda control, since those who control the agenda control the order in which measures are brought to a vote. Given the Arrow and McKelvey results, one need not posit powerful interest groups that buy votes through campaign contributions or hegemonic classes that control governments to explain the failure of legislatures to represent the interests of the majority of voters. Powerful groups *may* greatly influence policy—whether they do is an empirical question—but the mere existence of unrepresentative policies does not demonstrate that they do. The consequence of this result is to focus attention on the leadership and institutions within representative bodies in order to figure out who controls the agenda and how, and to figure out what causes policy stability when Arrow's proof leads to the expectation of cycling.

An enormous rational choice literature has arisen, most of it focused on the U.S. Congress, that seeks to explain how congressional institutions and procedures lead to relatively stable policy outcomes (Shepsle 1979; Shepsle and Weingast 1984, 1987a, 1987b; Denzau and MacKay 1981, 1993).[9] Implicitly or explicitly, these arguments also address the question of how representative legislatures are likely to be under different institutional arrangements (especially rules governing the role of committees, assignment to committees, and amendments from the floor). Some comparative work on the effects of intralegislative institutions

8. These ideas are further developed in McKelvey (1976, 1979); Sen (1970); and Schwartz (1986).

9. See Krehbiel (1988) for an extremely useful review of some of the most important arguments and how they fit together.

has been done (e.g., Huber 1992; Tsebelis 2002), but not much on legislatures in developing or former communist countries.[10]

Research in this area could help to explain differences in representativeness across countries, tendencies toward immobilism versus legislative effectiveness, and biases in policy outcomes. It would also, by broadening the range of institutions across which comparisons could be made, make an important contribution toward the development of theories about the effects of intralegislative institutions. In order to apply these models to legislatures in developing countries, assumptions about the functioning of the institutions themselves would obviously have to be revised. Since a number of presidential systems in new democracies resemble the U.S. system in terms of the fundamental division of power between the president and legislature, however, there is reason to believe that models developed to explain outcomes in the United States would provide a useful starting point for the study of intralegislative institutions in the new systems.

Collective Action Problems

More than thirty years ago, Mancur Olson (1965) demonstrated the political consequences of combining standard assumptions about individual rationality with the notion of public goods developed by economists. Public goods have the following properties: once supplied to a target group, no member of the group can be excluded from enjoying them, whether the person helped to create them or not; and use of the good by one individual does not reduce its availability or usefulness to others. The standard example is clean air. Once laws limiting pollution have been passed, clean air (the public good) can be enjoyed by all. Whether or not specific people do anything to bring it about—work to pass a clean-air law, for example, or pay for antipollution devices for their cars—they cannot be denied its use, and, in most circum-

10. The first steps in this direction have been taken by Londregan (2000); Ames (1995a, 1995b); Remington and Smith (1998a, 1998b, 1998c, 2000); and Baldez and Carey (1999). Ames (1987) contains some discussion of the committee system and procedures for appointing committee members and chamber leadership in Brazil between 1946 and 1964. A number of descriptive studies of Latin American legislatures were carried out during the 1970s—for example, Hoskin, Leal, and Kline (1976); Agor (1971, 1972); Packenham (1970); and Smith (1974). Many observers currently follow legislative activities closely in their respective countries. Only a few efforts have begun, however, to adapt the models developed to explain the effects of legislative institutions in the United States to conditions in the legislatures of developing and former communist countries.

stances, the fact that many other people are breathing it does not crowd anyone out or reduce the air's healthful effects. Consequently, it is not rational for any individual to contribute toward attaining the good. If, on the one hand, enough people are already willing to do the work or pay the cost to bring about the public good, there is no reason to do anything oneself, since one will enjoy its benefits when it arrives regardless of whether one worked for it. If, on the other hand, there are not presently enough individuals at work to produce the public good, there is still no reason to contribute, since any one person's efforts are extremely unlikely to make the difference in whether the public good will be produced. There are, as it turns out, certain conditions under which it is rational for individuals to band together in collective action, but the conditions are somewhat stringent and often go unmet. Hence, effective collective action toward a commonly held goal often fails to develop, even when it seems to a casual observer that it would be in everyone's interest to cooperate.

The logic of collective action leads to devastating revisions of some standard ideas about politics. It breaks the link between individual interests and group political action that underlies virtually all interest-based understandings of politics, from Marxist to pluralist. The failure of lower-class groups to organize to defend their interests, for example, is transformed from an anomaly to be explained by false consciousness or Gramscian hegemony into the behavior expected of rational lower-class actors.

The effects for democratic theory are equally serious. The logic of collective action leads to the expectation that the interests of average citizens are unlikely to influence policy-making, since ordinary people are unlikely to organize to express their interests effectively. In general, government policies that supply benefits to groups are public goods for the group, even if the goods themselves are privately consumed. Organizing to press for benefits is costly to the individuals who could benefit from the goods if they were supplied, and, because the goods are public, it is not rational for individuals to bear these costs if they can free ride instead.

The logic of collective action has a number of frequently observed but—prior to Olson—misunderstood substantive consequences. Groups in which resources are distributed unequally, for example, are more likely to be able to organize than are groups in which members are more equal; inequality increases the likelihood that one member of the group will receive enough benefits from a public good to be willing to shoulder the costs of lobbying, regardless of the free riding of others. This argument has been used to explain why industries that contain one or a few very large firms are more likely to be protected by tariffs.

Small groups are more likely to be able to organize to press for the policies they prefer than are larger groups. In small groups, members can recognize whether others are contributing and punish those who free ride. As a result, they can solve the collective action problem by changing the incentives facing individual members. This explains why special interest groups are often effective in the policy arena even when most citizens disagree with them or could benefit from different policies. The relationship between group size and the ability to organize also helps explain the prevalence of agricultural pricing policies in Africa that benefit the relatively small number of urban consumers (and their employers, since low food prices reduce the demand for wages) at the expense of large numbers of rural producers (Bates 1981).

Previously organized groups are more likely to achieve the policies they want than are the unorganized. Because organization is costly, groups that have already paid start-up costs have an advantage over groups that have not. It is easier to change the purpose of an existing group than to form a new one. This argument has been used to explain why political leaders in new states often mobilize followers along ethnic lines. It is more difficult to form new groups than to turn existing ethnically based organizations to new purposes (Bates 1990).

Most of these substantive arguments were originally made in the context of either the United States or Africa. Nevertheless, their implications for other countries are obvious. Tariffs elsewhere have also tended to protect large industries. Pricing and other policies affecting the relative welfare of urban and rural dwellers have, on average, disadvantaged the less well organized rural inhabitants of most developing countries. Barriers to the entry of new parties representing recently enfranchised groups have, on average, been high. The logic of collective action implies that policies, *even in fair and competitive democracies,* will tend to benefit the rich and well organized at the expense of the more numerous poor and unorganized, simply because the former are more likely to be able to exercise their rights effectively; it thus offers a possible explanation for one of the central characteristics of policy choice in most of the world.

The closely related tragedy of the commons, or common pool,

logic explains why resources held in common by a group will often be overexploited. Unless institutions have been established and enforced to allocate rights and responsibilities, rational individuals will use as much as they can of the common pool, since they know that if they do not, others will; and they will not invest in maintaining it, since the fruits of their investment would be shared with many others. The obvious examples of common pool problems come from the environment. Common pool logic explains why the oceans tend to be overfished, why lands bordering the Sahel are overgrazed and turning into desert, and why many large mammals were hunted to extinction by early humans. As with Arrow's paradox, understanding the common pool problem has led to an interest in discovering how people have solved common pool problems (Ostrom 1990; Ostrom, Schroeder, and Wynne 1993; Ostrom, Gardner, and Walker 1994). Recently, this logic has been used to show why tax collection is inefficient in Russia (Treisman 1999) and in Argentina (Jones, Sanguinetti, and Tommasi 2000). Although the details differ because of differences in political system and circumstances, in both cases, access to the common pool of revenue via revenue sharing creates incentives for provincial governments to overspend and to underinvest in revenue collection.

Inside the Black Box of the State

Most of the paradoxical effects of aggregation result from the pursuit of individual interests by actors in society. Their representatives in government are either assumed simply to reflect constituency interests (as in the cycling and intralegislative institutional literature) or never discussed with care (as in the collective action literature). In the collective action literature, elected representatives are usually assumed to reflect the interests of whichever groups lobby hardest or make the largest campaign contributions.

A second stream of rational choice theorizing focuses explicitly on the actors inside the black box of the state.[11] This strand differs from the first in that political leaders are not assumed to reflect the interests of constituents or dominant coalitions. In-

11. The word *state* is not often used in literature dealing with the United States. Within the standard terminology of comparative politics, however, the kinds of arguments prominent in the study of politics in the United States that focus on the causes of decisions by presidents, legislators, and government bureaucrats open up the black box of the state to see how the mechanisms inside work.

stead, explicit attention is given to the ways that institutions affect which interests politicians find it politically useful to represent and how the struggle for survival in office affects not only policy choice but institutional choice and other behavior of political leaders. Societal interests form a backdrop to the interactions among politicians but do not dominate them.

Despite the emphasis placed on the state by new institutionalists and others, rational choice arguments are more likely to make systematic links between particular institutional characteristics of states and the behavior of elected and appointed officials. Practitioners of rational choice were not the first to notice the autonomy of the political realm (or the state), but they have been quite successful at producing theories that use state or political characteristics to explain policy outcomes. Two major research traditions have provided the intellectual foundations for much of the current work in this vein: Douglass North's seminal arguments (1981, 1985, 1989a, 1989b, 1990) situating the causes of institutional change in the struggle over revenue between rulers and major economic interests; and work aimed at explaining the behavior of legislators in the United States (e.g., Downs 1957; Mayhew 1974; Fiorina 1977; Jacobson and Kernell 1983; Shepsle and Weingast 1981b, 1987a, 1987b).

Rational choice arguments about state or government actors begin with explicit attention to their goals and then consider the ways that various behaviors and choices can affect the achievement of goals in given institutional settings. The keystone of the approach is a simple model of politicians as rational individuals who attempt to maximize career success. In the U.S. context, this is often simplified to maximizing the probability of reelection, but somewhat broader conceptions of what it is that politicians maximize have been suggested and successfully used by comparativists (Rogowski 1978; Ames 1987). Using this one simple assumption about goals and a small number of characteristics of the U.S. political system, rational choice arguments have explained many of the behaviors that characterize members of Congress: the devotion of large amounts of resources to constituency service; the preference for pork; position taking and credit claiming; the avoidance of votes on controversial issues; and the assiduous pursuit of media coverage (Mayhew 1974; Ferejohn 1974; Shepsle and Weingast 1981a).

Other rational choice arguments link election seeking or survival maximizing to particular kinds of policy outcomes. Anthony

Downs (1957) has argued that parties trying to maximize the probability of election in a two-party system offer policy platforms that converge to the center of the electorate's preferences. James Buchanan and Gordon Tullock (1962), followed by a long series of books and articles in the public choice tradition, have claimed that various inefficient government interventions in the economy can be explained as results of the efforts of election-seeking politicians to secure support from constituents and campaign contributions from special interests.

Comparativists have built on, extended, and adapted these arguments to other political contexts with different and often more fluid institutions. The literature on rent seeking (Krueger 1974) uses politicians' interest in holding on to office to explain why they choose policies that create rent-seeking opportunities that reduce growth. Certain government policies create monopoly rents by limiting competition in certain endeavors, and rent seekers attempt to buy their way into these protected niches through campaign contributions and bribes. These attempts divert resources out of productive investment and result in an inefficient allocation of scarce resources (Buchanan, Tollison, and Tullock 1980). Robert Bates (1981, 1983) shows that agricultural policies chosen to consolidate political support lead to reduced food production, reduced agricultural exports, and recurring balance of payments crises. His argument that the fall in African agricultural production can be explained by government policies aimed at keeping the price of food low and at capturing the surplus generated by production for export has been one of the most influential in this category. Recent work by Bates (1989) and Michael Lofchie (1989) has further explored the nuances of African agricultural policy using the same logic and assumptions. Forrest Colburn's explanation (1986) of postrevolutionary agricultural policy in Nicaragua follows a similar line of argument. In short, politicians' interest in political survival explains why in both Africa and Latin America, policies have been pursued that have impoverished peasant farmers and reduced food production. Politicians have courted the support of urban dwellers, who have more political clout than rural people, by keeping food prices low. These low prices reduce the income of small farmers and decrease their incentives to produce for the market. In all these cases, analysts have shown how political incentives lead state actors to adopt economically inefficient policies. Barry Ames (1987) goes a step further to claim that presidents in Latin

American countries generally choose policies in order to maximize their chances of survival in office. Similar arguments have been used to explain policy choices in communist countries (Anderson 1993) and in Japan (Ramsayer and Rosenbluth 1993; Noll and Shimada 1991; Cox and Thies 1998, 2000; Cox, Rosenbluth, and Thies 1999, 2000).

An important innovation in rational choice explanations of policy outcomes is the veto players model developed by George Tsebelis (1995, 2002), which shows how political institutions change the policy outcomes expected in standard spatial models. Each branch of government that must agree to a policy before it can become law and each party that is a member of the ruling coalition and must therefore also agree to a policy is counted as a veto player. Tsebelis shows that the more veto players there are in the political system and the more dispersed they are in the policy space, the less likely it is, all else being equal, that policy will be changed.

The comparative study of the effects of political institutions has a long and distinguished history (Duverger 1954; Lijphart 1990; Lijphart and Grofman 1984; Rae 1967; Taagepera and Shugart 1989). But until recently, most of this literature focused on the effect of electoral institutions on either the number of parties in the system or the fairness of the translation of votes into seats,[12] and these were not issues of great interest outside Western Europe. Now, since democratization and other constitutional changes have taken place in so many developing and former communist countries, institutional questions have taken on new salience among scholars who work on these areas.

The literature on the effects of political institutions in new democracies that has blossomed so profusely since the "third wave" implicitly, though not always explicitly, assumes rational office-seeking politicians (e.g., Shugart and Carey 1992; Carey and Shugart 1998; Jones 1995; Ordeshook and Shvetsova 1994; Remington and Smith 1998b). It investigates the effects of different electoral rules and other political institutions on the kinds of parties that develop and the behavior of politicians. Virtually all of these studies, contrary to claims made by Green and Shapiro (1994), include serious empirical tests of arguments. Although some of these arguments are not expressed in rational choice

12. Exceptions are Cain, Ferejohn, and Fiorina (1987); Cox (1990); Shugart (1995, 1998); and Shugart and Carey (1992).

idiom, their logic depends on implicit assumptions that politicians seek office and rationally choose strategies for achieving it. Electoral rules and political institutions have the effects they do because they determine the feasible set of strategies for seeking office and the costs and benefits of each option. This literature extends arguments originally developed to account for party systems in Western Europe to new, mostly presidential systems in developing countries. These analyses offer general answers to questions about how many parties are likely to exist in particular systems, how easy it is for new parties to form, and how broad a range of interests is likely to be represented in legislatures.

Another strand of rational choice literature addresses the question of why ethnic parties have become so important in a number of newly independent or democratizing countries. Several observers have argued that would-be political leaders make ethnic identity salient and mobilize it because the preexisting organizations and personal networks within ethnic groups reduce the cost of organizing from scratch (Cohen 1974; Laitin 1986, 1998; Bates 1990). Where many members of an ethnic group feel disadvantaged and discriminated against because of their ethnicity, or where stories of violence and atrocities committed against members of the group remain vivid in the memories of many, members of the group would be especially responsive to these efforts. The point of the arguments, however, is that lasting ethnic mobilization is rarely spontaneous. It is fomented and institutionalized by politicians who see it as the best strategy by which to pursue their own quest for political power.

Still other rational choice arguments examine coalition formation. William Riker's seminal analysis (1962) of coalition formation began a long and fruitful inquiry into the study of coalitions. Most of this work focused on European parliamentary systems, but it is now being extended to Japan and, with some revisions, to presidential government in multiparty systems.

A variety of rational choice arguments have shown that the relationship of election-oriented politicians to self-interested bureaucrats affects legislative oversight, policy implementation, and the supply of both public goods and constituency services (Niskanen 1971; Arnold 1979; Fiorina and Noll 1978; McCubbins and Schwartz 1984; Geddes 1994). Other studies have explained government corruption and reforms aimed at ending it (Manion 1996; Shleifer and Vishny 1993; Geddes and Ribeiro 1992; Geddes 1999b).

Buchanan and Tullock (1962) were the first to argue explicitly that political institutions are politically motivated creations, and that their establishment and operation can be understood only by understanding the individual purposes they serve. Since then, changes in many other political institutions—innovations in the committee system of the U.S. Congress (Cox and McCubbins 1993), changes in nominating procedures for British members of Parliament and in French electoral laws (Tsebelis 1990), and the choice of representative institutions and electoral rules in West Germany (Bawn 1993), Latin America, and Eastern Europe (Frye 1997; Geddes 1995, 1996)—have been explained as results of the efforts of politicians to maximize their long-term electoral success.

In short, a set of extremely simple arguments that begin with the assumption that politicians are self-interested maximizers of the probability of political success, along with a context supplied by the institutions of a given political system, provide explanations of many of the political outcomes scholars would most like to understand. Solid empirical evidence supports most of these arguments.

Strategic Interactions among Political Actors

Most of the arguments discussed above examined the interactions of rational actors, even though most did not explicitly use game theory to do it. In this section, I describe game theory as an additional tool for illuminating the logic of interactions among rational actors. To the standard apparatus of rational choice arguments, in which individuals respond to a particular set of institutional incentives, game theory adds the idea that individuals strategically interact with each other to produce social outcomes. That is, game theory "seeks to explore how people make decisions if their actions and fates depend on the actions of others" (Ordeshook 1986, xii). In non–game theoretic arguments, individuals are assumed to pursue their goals within constraints imposed by the environment. In game theory, actors decide how best to pursue their goals after taking into account both environmental constraints and the equally rational and strategic behavior of other actors. Since strategic behavior and interdependence are fundamental characteristics of politics, game theory offers a particularly useful approach to understanding political actors and processes.[13]

13. Extremely good, moderately technical introductions to game theory can be found in Ordeshook (1986) and Moulin (1982).

Game-theoretic explanations of politics have emerged from the study of elections and legislative decision making, mostly in the United States. Much of this literature, like that on intra-legislative institutions, is both abstract and highly technical, and I do not discuss it here. Indeed, a shortcoming of many game-theoretic studies is that, because of the great complexity of interactions among strategic players, they are heavy on mathematical theorizing and short on credible empirical results. Thus, I focus here on less technical and less abstract applications of game theory that have proved fruitful in substantive terms.

One of the most important contributions of game theory to thinking about politics is the prisoner's dilemma, which is a generalization of the collective action problem discussed above (Hardin 1982). The prisoner's dilemma describes the logic of situations in which two or more individuals would all end up better off if they could agree among themselves to cooperate, but if binding agreements are impossible, each will be better off if he or she chooses not to cooperate. Since it is rational for each individual to refuse to cooperate, none do; the goal is not achieved, and all are worse off than they might have been had they cooperated. Much of the work on prisoner's dilemma games has focused on the difference between single interactions and interactions that are repeated (or iterated) over time. Although it is always rational for all players to defect in single games, under some circumstances cooperation is rational when games are repeated.

Prisoner's dilemma games have been used to explain many situations in international relations. They can also offer leverage for explaining domestic political outcomes—for example, interactions among coalition partners; pacts such as the Colombian National Front, in which traditional enemies agree to cooperate to limit competition in order to secure the democratic system that benefits both and to exclude other potential competitors; and the pervasiveness of patron-client relationships. Other simple games illuminate the logical structure of other situations.[14]

One of the earliest nontechnical game-theoretic arguments of relevance for students of developing countries is Guillermo O'Donnell's analysis (1973) of the game between Argentine parties between 1955 and 1966, in which he demonstrates the per-

14. See Tsebelis (1990) for a description of the most commonly used simple games and the relationships among them.

verse consequences of the military's ban on the Peronist party. Tsebelis's game-theoretic analysis (1990) of interactions first between party elites and masses and then among elites of different parties, though focused on Belgium, has clear implications for understanding politics in other divided societies. It can be used both where divisions are ethnic and where they are based on class. His treatment of electoral coalitions in France should be read by anyone interested in countries that have multiparty systems and runoff elections, such as Poland and Brazil. Game theory has also been used to illuminate aspects of regime change (Przeworski 1986, 1991, 1992; Colomer 1995; Cohen 1994; Geddes 1999a, 1999c).

In my opinion, game theory is the most potentially fruitful strand of the rational choice approach. Its strategic and interactive image of politics is realistic, and it can be used to illuminate political situations without recourse to advanced mathematics. Although theoretical developments in game theory will continue to be made by the mathematically gifted and trained, interesting substantive insights can arise from quite simple and tractable games.

Rational Choice and the Research Frontier in Comparative Politics

To some extent, the choice of which intellectual perspective to embrace is simply a matter of taste. A taste for rational choice arguments may involve little more than a preference for the austere over the rococo. It is often suggested that an attraction to the rational choice approach implies a (naïve) belief in human rationality, or at least a belief that if people are not rational, they should be. Some practitioners may feel this way, but I, at any rate, do not. The appeal of the rational choice approach, in my view, lies in its substantive plausibility in numerous political situations; its theoretical coherence; the fruitful simplification of "buzzing blooming" reality it offers, which facilitates comparative work; and its capacity to explain puzzling outcomes and generate nonobvious conclusions.

Rational choice arguments deal only with systematic patterns of incentives that lead to systematic patterns in outcomes. In contrast, more contingent political arguments, such as those that characterize the Juan Linz and Alfred Stepan series (1978) on the breakdown of democracy and the Guillermo O'Donnell, Philippe Schmitter, and Laurence Whitehead series (1986) on redemocratization, focus on the specific conjunctural circumstances that make particular decisions understandable. The strength of such contingent political explanations is that they offer a very complete description of events. Their weakness is that they do not easily lend themselves to the construction of general theories because they do not distinguish between systematic and idiosyncratic causes. Rational choice arguments have the opposite strengths and weaknesses. They invariably omit from the analysis colorful and arresting details that some observers consider important. But by abstracting from the specifics of particular cases, they make theory building possible and facilitate comparisons across cases that may at first appear too different to compare.

Many criticize rational choice models on the grounds that they simplify reality to such a degree that the model seems to bear no resemblance at all to the real world. And some work unquestionably deserves this stricture. Rational choice arguments can easily cross the line from simple to simplistic. Persuasive and useful applications of the rational choice approach, however, take into account the most important features of the social and institutional setting. They also draw insights from important abstract arguments. The bite of good rational choice arguments comes from the synthesis of empirical evidence from the cases under examination and abstract deductive logic.

Using rational choice models requires the analyst to identify relevant actors, to determine their preferences, and to present a plausible justification for the attribution of preferences. Observers can, of course, make mistakes in their attribution of preferences, but rational choice models do "have the advantage of being naked so that, unlike those of some less explicit theories, [their] limitations are likely to be noticeable" (Schelling 1984). The rational choice approach does not prescribe any particular methodology for testing hypotheses, but persuasive work combines deductive rational choice arguments with examinations of evidence to see if it conforms to the expectations generated by the deductive model.

This summary of rational choice explanations has dealt only with some of the best-known arguments that directly address questions fundamental to understanding politics. Even this brief survey shows that there is a well-developed rational choice literature replete with theories that have only begun to be extended and modified for use in newly democratic countries. Analysts have so far made use of only the simplest of the theories about parties and legislatures that have been proposed in the context of U.S. and West European politics. With spreading democratization, this literature has begun to seem more relevant to scholars interested in understanding politics in countries outside the North Atlantic core.

Recent events have set the agenda for future applications of the rational choice approach. Because institutions determine available options and affect strategic choices, the institutional fluidity of democratizing and recently democratized countries poses a challenge and an opportunity for the rational choice approach. Two areas seem to me especially overdue for systematic attention from rational choice practitioners.

The first is the emergence and consolidation of democratic political processes. The analysis of legislatures and party systems in new democracies is at the forefront of the research agenda in comparative politics. The institutionalist approach to post-transition politics takes the transitions as given, thus bypassing the consolidology cul-de-sac, and seeks to analyze current political processes. One of the advantages of this approach to thinking about the development of democratic processes is that it avoids the value-laden arguments about what consolidated democracy should be and how far some competitive but flawed real political systems deviate from whichever definition is chosen. Instead, analysts draw expectations about the effects of particular political practices from theories developed in the study of democratic politics elsewhere; if outcomes in new democracies differ from expectations, existing theories must be modified. This more detailed and theoretically informed examination of political processes results in a more accurate assessment of exactly how and why the differences affect outcomes, if they do.

Scholars writing about many different countries have produced an impressive body of literature on the effects of the institutional variation in new democracies, in the process adding considerably to preexisting literature on the consequences of electoral institutions.[15] Most new democracies have presidential or semipresidential systems. Presidential elections create centripetal incentives in party systems in the same way that single-member legislative

15. For a very useful summary, see Carey (1998).

districts do.[16] Where legislators are elected by proportional representation (PR), as they are in most new democracies, the electoral system is pulled in both directions—toward a two-party centrism by presidential elections and toward more ideologically dispersed multipartism by PR legislative elections.

Work on the Latin American presidential systems has discovered that rules that affect the size of presidential coattails determine which pull is stronger. Where presidential and legislative elections occur at the same time, presidential coattails are strong, and parties that cannot compete for the presidency tend to fade away; in these cases, two-party systems tend to emerge. Where elections for different offices occur on different schedules, parties that have no hope of winning presidential elections can nevertheless continue to do well in legislative and municipal elections, and thus they can survive (Shugart 1995; Shugart and Carey 1992). Presidential runoffs also encourage the persistence of small parties. Rather than forming preelection coalitions, small parties enter the first round in order to establish their bargaining power as coalition partners for the second round. Moreover, legislative elections occur at the same time as the first round of the presidential election (if they are concurrent), which means that small parties run in them as well. For these reasons, party fragmentation tends to be greater in countries with presidential runoffs.[17] In parliamentary systems, district magnitude has the greatest effect on party fragmentation, but in presidential systems, district magnitude has less effect than runoffs and election schedules (Jones 1995).

The effects of a number of electoral rules have been pretty thoroughly worked out. These include, as noted, the effect of presidential runoffs and different election schedules on party fragmentation; the effect of ethnic heterogeneity on party fragmentation (Ordeshook and Shvetsova 1994); and the effect of preference voting, term limits, and running multiple lists under the same party label on party discipline in the legislature and on candidate campaign strategies (e.g., Ames 1995a, 1995b, 2001; Carey 1996; Taylor 1992; Archer and Shugart 1997; Cox and

16. But see Ordeshook, Shvetsova, and Filippov (1999) for a more nuanced view.

17. There has been some controversy over the effects of runoffs, but the balance of the evidence at this point supports the claim that they encourage party fragmentation. It is very hard to disentangle this question empirically, because runoffs have generally been initiated in countries with fragmented party systems, so it is hard to judge whether the runoffs are cause or effect.

Shugart 1995; Morgenstern 1999). These are the nuts and bolts of democratic politics, and a great deal of progress has been made in figuring them out.

The first steps have also been taken toward figuring out some more complex institutional issues. Scholars are beginning to build an understanding of presidential powers and the relationship between presidents and legislatures. Many of these studies begin from the premise that the probability of democratic breakdown is increased by conflict between the president and the legislature.[18] Scholars have explored two factors that might contribute to potential conflict or stalemate. The first is divided or minority government. Conflict or stalemate is obviously less likely if the president's party has a majority in the legislature, so analysts pursuing this line of thought emphasize the electoral rules that increase fragmentation in the party system, which in turn increases the likelihood of minority presidents.

The second involves the president's constitutional powers to set the legislative agenda, veto legislation, and issue decrees, that is, the president's power to pursue his own agenda even without legislative support. The implicit idea here is that stalemate is less likely if the president can do much of what he wants without legislative support. John Carey and Matthew Shugart (1998) have proposed an index to measure these presidential powers, though they have not shown what effects they have. A recent discussion of presidential powers by Scott Mainwaring and Matthew Shugart (1997a, 1997b) attempts to combine the constitutional powers emphasized by Carey and Shugart in earlier work with what Mainwaring and Shugart call partisan powers, meaning essentially the amount of support the president has in the legislature. This addition brings the notion of presidential powers closer to what we think of intuitively as strong presidents. At this point, these arguments have not gone very far either in terms of theorization of the relationship between presidents and legislatures or in terms of showing clear empirical effects of different arrangements, and this subject remains central to the research agenda.

Legislatures in developing and ex-communist presidential systems have received much less attention than presidents because analysts have considered them less influential. Legislatures are

18. This is a widely believed but, until recently, untested idea. Cheibub (2001) shows that party fragmentation in presidential systems, contrary to much that has been written, does not increase the likelihood of democratic breakdown.

beginning to be taken more seriously, however, and some path-breaking work has recently appeared. John Londregan's study (2000) of the Chilean Senate is the first to offer an in-depth analysis of legislative committees in a contemporary Latin American legislature.[19] Thomas Remington and Steven Smith have done a series of studies (1995, 1998a, 1998c, 2000) that draw on the literature on the U.S. Congress in order to analyze the Russian Duma and its relationship to the president. Legislative studies are on the research frontier for those working on new democracies.

The work noted above focuses on the effects of political institutions, but such analyses always lead back to the prior question: What caused the institutions in the first place? The second area for new research seeks to explain the creation of new institutions. Rational choice arguments about the creation of institutions are in their infancy. Most explanations of institutional change by economists assume that efficiency gains explain changes, without considering who reaps the benefits of efficiency gains and who loses. The challenge for rational choice theorists is to revise such economic arguments by incorporating the effects of different actors' pursuit of their own, often inconsistent, goals and the nonobvious effects of the aggregation of multiple individual choices.

The period of transition has been a good time to investigate this question, because a large number of countries have chosen new democratic institutions or modified old ones. Scholars analyzing these choices have shown that in both Latin America and Eastern Europe, new political institutions have been chosen to further the electoral interests of those who served on the roundtables, legislatures, and constituent assemblies that picked them (e.g., Frye 1997; Remington and Smith 1996; Colomer 1997; Geddes 1995, 1996). These studies are a beginning, but a great deal remains to be done.

The convergence to mainstream theories and methodologies for analyzing politics in democratic developing countries is occurring because a very large body of theory on democratic politics exists, and those who are making use of it can see that it gives them leverage for understanding a good deal of what is going on. Once the countries that analysts were interested in had democratized and politics had become more rule bound and transparent,

19. Ames (1987) analyzes the role of committees in the Brazilian Chamber of Deputies between 1946 and 1964.

useful theories were available as a starting point for understanding political processes. Democratization opened up niches for certain kinds of work, and scholars, many of them young and well-trained, moved into them. As the tools of rational choice have become more familiar, scholars have also found other creative uses for them, outside the areas with long traditions of rational choice scholarship.

CHAPTER 6

Conclusion

Creating theories that will explain aspects of the real world is the central task for social scientists. We may at times think it useful or enjoyable to describe important events or create elegant theories with no relevance to the particular planet we live on, but these activities are peripheral to the main task. Theory building requires interaction between theoretical speculation and reality checks. This book has discussed both.

Much of the book has focused on the importance of trying to test arguments so that the theories we propose and come to believe will have some lasting value. Of course, all theories are eventually challenged, revised, and discarded. But they should be challenged by evidence discovered later, not by evidence available at the time they were proposed. With this goal in mind, I have emphasized very basic features of research design: the routine search for observable implications of arguments so that empirical tests can be devised, regardless of whether the argument as a whole can be tested; the selection of cases to use for tests from the full range of possible outcomes for the implication being tested;[1] testing arguments on cases different from those from which the arguments were induced; the careful and concrete operationalization of concepts; the development of concrete criteria for non-quantitative measurement; and the publication of criteria for operationalizing and classifying, or measuring, concepts along with research conclusions.

The parts of the book that deal with efforts to check theoretical speculations against reality draw their arguments directly from the logic of statistics, but this should not be taken to imply that problems arising from the need to test arguments can be

1. Implications do not always refer to the same set of cases as the original argument. Sometimes theories imply particular outcomes for subsets of cases, and sometimes they imply outcomes for cases at different levels of analysis or aggregation. In such situations, the implication must be tested on the set of cases to which it applies, not the set to which the theory applies; but the principle that the full range of variation in outcomes should be considered remains the same.

solved by quantification. Quantification by itself solves few of the problems discussed in this book. In fact, quantitative work in practice very often suffers from weaknesses analogous to those discussed here.

The operationalization of complex or nuanced concepts can be problematic in both quantitative and nonquantitative research. In nonquantitative studies, the most common problem, as noted in chapter 4, is insufficiently precise indicators that undermine the ability to assess whether cases fit theoretical expectations. Quantitative work, in contrast, has most often been criticized for its tendency to use easily available indicators that measure precisely but fail to capture the full meaning of concepts. This problem is not the most serious to arise from operationalization in quantitative studies, however. If we remember that what we are testing is not the argument itself but implications of the argument, then an indicator's failure to reflect all aspects of a concept need not trouble us as long as we think the argument in which the concept is embedded implies a relationship between the indicator and a particular outcome. For example, the argument that modernization increases the likelihood of democratic governance implies that as GDP per capita rises, the probability of democracy should also rise. If a statistical test of the relationship between GDP per capita and some measure of democracy shows that a relationship does indeed exist, we should take this result as modest confirmation of the argument, even though GDP per capita is, as many have noted, a very imperfect indicator of modernization. We should not, however, take it as the be-all and end-all of confirmations. We should see it as a confirmation of one implication, and we should try to think of other implications—preferably, others that are not so closely correlated with GDP per capita that we can be certain how they will come out before we start.

The more serious danger that arises from operationalization decisions in quantitative work is that off-the-shelf indicators, used because they are readily available, may in fact mainly measure something *other* than the concept of interest. In statistical terms, the indicator is highly correlated with a left-out variable. Researchers believe they have found a relationship between an outcome and the concept for which the indicator has been used as a proxy, but in reality it is the left-out factor that is responsible for the correlation found. In other words, the analyst has a particularly insidious problem with spurious correlation.

Consider this example from the study of the effects of ethnic conflict. Analysts have hypothesized that countries in which ethnicity is highly politicized will experience especially intense, even violent, distributional struggles, and that growth will be reduced in consequence. The image of politics in this argument is one of fierce competition between two or three large ethnic groups. The argument is supported by a number of quantitative studies of economic development that have shown that ethnic heterogeneity seems to reduce growth.[2] The measure of ethnic heterogeneity used, however, is the one produced by Soviet researchers in the 1960s, and it identifies dozens of language-based ethnic groups in some countries. This measure has been criticized on the grounds that it does not measure the kind of ethnic differences that are politically relevant. Concerns about what this indicator really measures have been reinforced by the finding that if a dummy variable for Africa is added to the regressions, the effect of ethnic heterogeneity disappears. One possible interpretation is that ethnic heterogeneity is one of the underlying causes of slow growth in Africa. Another, however, is that African economies have grown slowly for reasons unrelated to ethnic differences, but that because African countries have more different language groups on average than countries in other regions, ethnic heterogeneity appears to slow growth. To discover which of these possibilities is correct would require other tests of the various arguments about the effects of ethnic heterogeneity, including intraregional tests. Until these are done, the possibility that the ethnic heterogeneity index is really serving as a proxy for some collection of left-out causal factors cannot be ruled out.

Of course, quantitative studies have no monopoly on spurious correlation. In fact, spurious correlation is even harder to guard against in small-*N* studies. It might be the case, for example, that the European party stability that Lipset and Rokkan attributed to the persistence of historical cleavages was really caused by a set of stability-inducing electoral institutions. If so, then the relationship they found is spurious. In both kinds of research, spurious correlations are often uncovered by other researchers whose intuitions suggest different causes of the outcome being explained. In large-*N* research, the next step is to add variables reflecting the rival argument to the statistical model. In small-*N*

2. See, for example, Easterly (2001) and studies he cites.

research, it may be necessary to add more cases to the research design before rival hypotheses can be assessed.

Measurement problems also affect both quantitative and nonquantitative studies. Large-*N* studies had a bad reputation among comparativists for a long time because of the poor quality of most of the data available and because of the feeling that most quantitative work was mechanistic, with values assigned to variables failing to reflect what the analyst claimed to be measuring. These issues remain challenges with which those doing large-*N* cross-national studies must contend. Some of the off-the-shelf data sets available have flaws that should, but do not always, give analysts pause when they decide to use them. The Soviet measure of ethnic heterogeneity referred to above is a case in point. Those who are familiar with it note that different counting rules seem to have been used in different countries, and that a number of country scores seem surprising (Laitin and Posner 2001). Nevertheless, it is the only measure of ethnic heterogeneity available for a large number of countries, and it continues to be used.

The measurement problem in the Soviet ethnic heterogeneity index is the same as that facing scholars doing nonquantitative research. Potential causal factors, such as ethnic heterogeneity, need to be measured in the same way in each case or each time. If the Soviet researchers had been able to follow the advice given in chapter 4 about creating clear coding criteria and a written coding scheme to be used by all researchers who take on the task of assigning cases to measurement categories, their index would have fewer problems.[3] Nonquantitative researchers do not have the luxury of using off-the-shelf data sets, so they are not tempted to ignore measurement problems known to exist in them; but unclear, nonpublic criteria for classifying cases—that is, "measurement" rules that seem to vary across cases or over time—are a common failing of nonquantitative work.

Quantitative studies also face case selection problems. Although outright selection on the dependent variable is rare, the exclusion of a few cases—often because data are not easily available—from one end of the distribution of outcomes can bias results. We might wonder, for example, whether the inclusion of a couple of additional European countries that were growing very rapidly during the period under study would have changed

3. Soviet researchers could not use the same coding criteria in each case because they relied on census data, and countries do not use the same rules for judging languages and ethnicity in their censuses.

the conclusions reached by Geoffrey Garrett and Peter Lange (1986) about the relationship between the partisan composition of government and growth rates. Quantitative studies, like nonquantitative ones, can be unpersuasive when we suspect that if the author had included other cases or a different time period, the results would have been different.

In short, quantitative and qualitative studies suffer from some of the same kinds of weaknesses. Those who do quantitative work also need to think through the issues of case selection and measurement emphasized in this book. Off-the shelf data sets may need to be revised or even rejected. At the very least, the probable effects of their deficiencies need to be considered and reported in conclusions drawn from analyses that use them.

Plodding through all the steps of doing nonquantitative tests of the Lipset and Rokkan hypotheses had two goals: to illuminate some of the measurement and coding issues that arise in both quantitative and nonquantitative research; and to show that even if one cannot, for whatever reason, carry out statistical tests of an argument, some kind of test of its implications is nearly always possible. Nonstatistical tests provide less information and less clear decision rules about whether to reject arguments than do statistical tests. They are not as precise. They cannot tell if chance can be ruled out as the cause of differences in outcomes between cases that have some antecedent condition and cases that do not. They do not provide a precise estimate of the size of the effect of the antecedent condition on the outcome. Often, they cannot hold constant irrelevant factors that affect the outcomes so that the independent effect of the factor of interest can be assessed. Nevertheless, they can demonstrate in a broad-brushstroke way whether the theoretical speculation seems to be consistent with reality. They can thus be used to eliminate some theoretical speculations that imply outcomes inconsistent with the pattern of real-world events. This might sound like a modest accomplishment, but I believe that a number of the arguments most of us read in graduate school would have been disconfirmed by such nonquantitative tests.

Although nonstatistical tests provide what is in some ways a weak foundation for theory building, they have two points in their favor. First, they are better than nothing. They facilitate the elimination of unviable theoretical speculations, and they encourage further and more rigorous examination of arguments that survive these tests. Perhaps if we did not require graduate students to spend their time reading and thinking about untested arguments on this side and that side, the time it takes to finish a Ph.D. in political science could fall below its current average of about seven years. In short, nonstatistical tests of arguments, though time-consuming for the analyst, would increase aggregate efficiency in the discipline.

Second, carrying out nonstatistical tests requires so much digging into the details and circumstances of each case that the problems that arise in statistical work from the use of quantitative indicators that measure something other than the concept the analyst wants to measure are unlikely to occur. Where the analyst has undertaken this digging, defining, and categorizing, he could then carry out some statistical tests if the study included enough cases. Since time and resources are scarce, however, analysts may feel that they cannot make a major investment in digging up information and then also learn statistical methods. In less accessible research areas, there may be exactly the trade-off that traditional comparativists have always emphasized between precise statistical tests using imprecise and possibly biased indicators of underlying concepts, on the one hand, and imprecise tests using more carefully devised indicators on the other. Where the analyst faces such a trade-off, an argument can be made for the nonstatistical test using high-quality indicators. Serious nonstatistical reality checking, however, is quite different from what has sometimes passed for evidence, namely, descriptions of the way purported cause and effect unfolded in the cases that inspired the argument.

The strictly methodological suggestions in this book are quite simple and are drawn from some of the most basic insights of statistics. I expect them to be uncontroversial,[4] even if difficult to carry out in practice. In contrast, I have no shoulders of giants to stand on when addressing the question of how to increase the likelihood of generating fruitful theoretical speculations. I have tried to articulate an alternative to what I think is the dominant but unspoken model of explanation in comparative politics: a multivariate regression equation. It is one of the ironies of contemporary comparative politics that although many have resisted the pressure to use statistics in their research, regression as a model of explanation nevertheless permeates the field.

By a regression model of explanation, I mean an understand-

4. But see Rogowski (1995) and Collier and Mahoney (1996).

ing of explanation as the discovery and listing of all the causal factors that contribute to some outcome. The causal factors are usually discovered through an inductive search during fieldwork or immersion in archives, guided by some loose theoretical expectations. These qualitative inductive searches resemble the atheoretical search for patterns in statistical data referred to as data grubbing. If the analyst were doing statistics, all the possible causal factors would be shoveled into a regression as independent variables, and those that achieved statistical significance would be reported as causes.

The alternative understanding of theory creation I suggest has two elements, one having to do with how we approach big questions and the other being a more general strategy for disciplining speculations into more fully coherent theories. Chapter 2 suggested a shift in focus from attempting to identify factors that contribute to outcomes to trying to explain the relationships among the moving parts of the processes leading to outcomes. My attempt to articulate this shift in focus stresses the need for a new way of thinking about "big questions," but others have expressed what I think are the same concerns in different ways. The *Analytic Narratives* of Robert Bates and his colleagues (1998) are efforts to articulate a different model of explanation that focuses on process rather than outcome. Andrew Abbott complains that "'theory' comprises only a few narratives of 'possible mechanisms'. . . . [A]ction and contingency disappear into the magician's hat of variable-based causality, where they hide during the analysis, only to be reproduced with a flourish in the article's closing paragraphs" (2001, 98). Elinor Ostrom thought in 1982 that the era of the dominance of what I am calling the regression model of explanation, which she associated with the hegemony of behavioralism and quantitative methods, was ending with "a whimper." Whimpering or not, however, the regression model still seems to be going strong. Much of the discomfort with standard methods expressed by champions of the small-*N* approach also arises from a feeling that process is being shortchanged in large-*N* studies (for example, Mahoney, 2000).

Both Ostrom and Bates et al. emphasize the failure to theorize processes leading to outcomes, a failure that, I claim, arises from the conception of explanation as a list of causes. Neither rejects the testing of theories, but both prioritize the careful elaboration of theory. Bates et al. stress the usefulness of theories drawn from economics in explaining a wide range of nonobvious subjects. Ostrom, in contrast, emphasizes the possibility and need to develop theories of individual decision making that rely on more realistic assumptions about motivation, information, and calculating ability than do rational choice arguments. Both express a concern that the emphasis on falsificationism in social science leads to a rejection of theories that cannot be translated directly into regression equations, and this leads both scholars to give little attention to testing.

My own view, which will come as no surprise at this point, is that testing is an essential aspect of theory building. Sturdy theories are created through the repeated interaction between deductively rigorous theoretical speculations and careful reality checks. In contrast to what I think has become the standard unexamined idea of testing, however, I emphasize the importance of looking for implications of arguments that can be tested rather than assuming that arguments themselves must be tested.

One of the problems with seeing explanation as analogous to a multivariate regression is that this view confuses tests of arguments with the arguments themselves. Some arguments can be translated directly into regressions and tested, but others cannot. In general, analysts seeking to test arguments should try to discover as many observable implications of the argument as possible and then test whether the pattern of real-world events is consistent with multiple outcomes implied by these implications. One of the observable implications of an argument may be a simple restatement of the argument itself, but this is unlikely to be the only implication. Some of the implications of an argument will be much simpler and easier to test than the argument itself—as, for example, the implication of my argument about authoritarian breakdown that military regimes should last for shorter periods than other kinds of authoritarianism.

The larger the number of implications that are tested and shown to be consistent with reality, the more persuasive an argument becomes. Given the poor quality of data and measurement we comparativists have to deal with, it is often more persuasive to show multiple flawed tests of an argument than to aim for one perfect one. Each flawed test may be a weak reed to lean on, but eventually a hut that will withstand a mild storm can be built of them.

I am certainly not the first to articulate this understanding of testing. It is a standard idea in economic modeling and game theory and is expressed very clearly in King, Keohane, and

Verba (1994), but it does not seem to have percolated through the comparative field. I emphasize this idea here because, once internalized, it opens up many possibilities for testing and can have a dramatic effect on research design.

Up to this point, I have emphasized tests of theoretical speculations, but we would also like to improve the quality of the speculations we test. The standard line on theoretical speculations is that they can come from anywhere: they can arise from unstructured inductive research; they can be derived from other theories; they can pop into the mind during a shower. The standard line is, of course, true. But I believe that some ways of approaching the research enterprise are more likely to be theoretically fruitful than others. I suggest that the likelihood of making progress in theory building can be increased by going through the following conscious steps aimed at turning casual speculations into more disciplined ideas about cause and effect: Begin with the basic units of action and decision making—usually individuals, but if not, be explicit about what the unit is. If the unit is an aggregate of individuals, think about how the group is organized and whether there are formal or informal rules for aggregating preferences into choices. Make explicit statements about the motivations and capacities of the units of action. If you believe choices are not goal-oriented, describe in a logically rigorous way what is going on instead. Think through the logic of how contextual factors such as institutions are likely to affect choices. In addition, think through the logic of how other units with whom actors interact will affect their choices and the effects of their choices.

Currently, the easiest way to follow this advice is to adopt the rational choice approach. The advice can be followed without using rational choice, however, and I would urge those working on subjects that do not seem amenable to the rational choice approach to resist the temptation to follow the well-trodden path. The important features of the advice are the following.

- Methodological individualism, unless there is a good reason to use some other unit of analysis and the mechanisms that allow the alternative unit to make decisions as though it were an individual can be described. The reason for prioritizing individuals is that arguments that turn out not to make sense at the individual level, regardless of how plausible they otherwise seem, never survive the test of time and closer scrutiny.

- Explicit attention to the psychological and cognitive mechanisms that underlie individual action. Within the rational choice tradition, this means making explicit statements about actors' motivations. If the analyst believes the action under investigation is not goal-oriented—as in most learning models of how values are acquired, for example—then she needs to make clear what actors are doing instead. If the analyst believes action is goal-oriented but that the self-interest assumption used in the rational choice approach does not describe reality, then she needs to articulate explicitly what does motivate actors and think through how these motivations will affect decisions in different circumstances. If the analyst believes that actors are self-interested but, in the situation under investigation, pursue goals other than the standard rational choice goals of increasing their wealth or maximizing the likelihood of winning the next election, the analyst needs to show evidence to support the attribution of a nonstandard goal. The more idiosyncratic the goal, the more evidence is needed. Goals cannot be inferred from actions taken. To do so renders the explanation built on this inference vacuous.
- Explicit attention to the attributes of actors that affect decision making—notably, access to information, cost of information, capacity for processing information, and attitude toward risk. Rational choice arguments usually assume that individuals are risk-neutral, but considerable research in psychology suggests that most people's attitude toward risk depends on circumstances. Prospect theory models individual behavior using an assumption, more consistent with research findings, that individuals are more risk-accepting when facing losses than when contemplating the possibility of gain. Prospect theory can be used in situations in which the assumption of risk neutrality seems implausible.
- Identification of contextual factors that systematically influence actors' behavior and an explanation of how and why these factors affect actors.
- Consideration of the effect of other actors' behavior on the actions and decisions of the actors under scrutiny.
- Investigation of whether unforeseen outcomes occur as

a result of the aggregation of many individual choices or actions.

If the analyst takes a somewhat inchoate speculation—the sort likely to pop into the head during a shower—and subjects it to serious thought along the lines noted above, with luck by the end of an hour or so, a clear speculation with lots of moving parts from which implications may be derived will have emerged. The speculation will contain holes, but they will be obvious and can be patched by a very focused search for information. The speculation will also contain mistakes, some of which will be discovered as the analyst hunts up evidence to use for testing various implications. It will gradually be improved, even before explicit testing. The tests themselves will probably lead to at least minor revisions, if not total rejection of the idea. It is both useful and possible to get into the habit of going through these steps whenever an interesting idea appears on the horizon.

In this book, I have approached theory building from two directions, neither of which can be neglected if we wish to improve our understanding of the world. On the one hand, I have urged that attention be focused in a disciplined way on building theories of the processes that contribute to the complicated, compound outcomes we hope to explain. On the other hand, I have argued that we need to abide by standard norms of research design if we want our theories to be more than artful sand castles.

Though the sand-castle metaphor emphasizes the transitory nature of untested theories and the paradigms to which they contribute, their short life spans are not the real problem. The real problem is that when one untested theory succeeds another, we do not get closer to truth over time. Instead, we waste our lives in fruitless, often ideologically weighted debates, and we make little contribution to the human community. We were called to science as a vocation for something better.

Appendix A

Classification Scheme for Coding Authoritarian Regimes

Each regime used in the data analysis receives a score between zero and one for each regime type; this score is the sum of "yes" answers divided by the sum of both "yes" and "no" answers. A regime's classification into a nominal category (see the next section in this appendix) depends on which score is significantly higher than the other two. Hybrids are regimes with similar scores for two or more regime types.

Is it a single-party regime?

Did the party exist prior to the leader's election campaign or accession to power?

Was the party organized in order to fight for independence or lead some other mass social movement?

Did the first leader's successor hold, or does the leader's heir apparent hold, a high party position?

Was the first leader's successor, or is the current heir apparent, from a different family, clan, or tribe than the leader?

Does the party have functioning local-level organizations that do something reasonably important, such as distribute seeds or credit or organize local government?

Does the party either face some competition from other parties or hold competitive intraparty elections?

Is party membership required for most government employment?

Does the party control access to high government office?

Are members of the politburo (or its equivalent) chosen by routine party procedures?

Does the party encompass members from more than one region, religion, ethnic group, clan, or tribe (in heterogeneous societies)?

Do none of the leader's relatives occupy very high government office?
Was the leader a civilian before his accession?
Was the successor to the first leader, or is the heir apparent, a civilian?
Is the military high command consulted primarily about security matters?
Are most members of the cabinet or politburo-equivalent civilians?

Is it a military regime?
Is the leader a retired or active general or equivalent?
Was the successor to the first leader, or is the heir apparent, a general or equivalent?
Is there a procedure in place for rotating the highest office or dealing with succession?
Is there a routine procedure for consulting the officer corps about policy decisions?
Has the military hierarchy been maintained?
Does the officer corps include representatives of more than one ethnic, religious, or tribal group (in heterogeneous countries)?
Have normal procedures for retirement been maintained for the most part? (That is, has the leader refrained from or been prevented from forcing his entire cohort or all officers from other tribal groups into retirement?)
Are merit and seniority the main bases for promotion, rather than loyalty or ascriptive characteristics?
Has the leader refrained from having dissenting officers murdered or imprisoned?
Has the leader refrained from creating a political party to support himself?
Has the leader refrained from holding plebiscites to support his personal rule?
Do officers occupy positions in the cabinet other than those related to the armed forces?
Has the rule of law been maintained? (That is, even if a new constitution has been written and laws decreed, are decrees, once promulgated, followed until new ones are written?)

Is it a personalist regime?

Does the leader lack the support of a party?

If there is a support party, was it created after the leader's accession to power?

If there is a support party, does the leader choose most of the members of the politburo-equivalent?

Does the country specialist literature describe the politburo-equivalent as a rubber stamp for the leader?

If there is a support party, is it limited to a few urban areas?

Was the successor to the first leader, or is the heir apparent, a member of the same family, clan, tribe, or minority ethnic group as the first leader?

Does the leader govern without routine elections?

If there are elections, are they essentially plebiscites, that is, without either internal or external competition?

Does access to high office depend on the personal favor of the leader?

Has normal military hierarchy been seriously disorganized or overturned?

Have dissenting officers or officers from different regions, tribes, religions, or ethnic groups been murdered, imprisoned, or forced into exile?

Has the officer corps been marginalized from most decision making?

Does the leader personally control the security apparatus?

Coding of Regimes

Afghanistan
- 1973–78, personalist, Daoud
- 1979–92, personalist/single-party (foreign maintained), Karmal/Najibullah
- 1992–95, personalist, Rabbani

Albania
- 1946–91, single-party

Algeria
- 1963–92, military/single-party
- 1992–, military

Angola
- 1976–, single-party (free and fair elections, 1992)

Argentina
- 1943–46, military
- 1949–55, personalist, Perón
- 1955–58, military
- 1966–73, military
- 1976–83, military

Bangladesh
- 1971–75, personalist/single-party, Mujib
- 1975–82, personalist, Zia

1982–90, personalist, Ershad

Benin

1965–68, military

1972–91, personalist, Kerekou

Bolivia

1943–46, military

1952–64, single-party

1964–69, personalist, Barrientos

1971–78, military/personalist, Banzer

Botswana

1966–, single-party (free and fair elections, 1966)

Brazil

1964–85, military

Bulgaria

1947–90, single-party (foreign maintained)

Burkina Faso

1966–80, personalist, Lamizana

1983–87, personalist, Sankara

1987–, personalist, Campaoré

Burundi

1966–87, military/single-party

1987–93, military

1996–, military/personalist, Buyoya

Cambodia

1953–67, personalist, Sihanouk

1967–75, personalist, Lon Nol

1975–79, single-party

1979–90, single-party (foreign maintained)

1997–, personalist/single-party, Hun Sen

Cameroon

1961–83, single-party

1983–, personalist, Biya

Central African Republic

1960–66, personalist, Dacko

1966–79, personalist, Bokassa

1981–94, military/personalist, Kolingba

Chad

1960–75, personalist/single-party, Tombalbaye

1975–79, military

1982–90, personalist, Habre

1990–, personalist, Deby

Chile

1973–89, military/personalist, Pinochet

China

1949–, single-party

Colombia

1953–58, military/personalist, Rojas Pinilla

Congo

1963–68, personalist/single-party, Massamba-Debat

1968–92, military/single-party

1997–, personalist, Sassou-Nguesso

Cuba

1952–59, personalist, Batista

1959–, personalist/single-party, Castro

Czechoslovakia
1948–90, single-party (foreign maintained)
Dominican Republic
1930–61, personalist, Trujillo
1966–78, personalist, Balaguer
Ecuador
1963–66, military
1972–79, military
Egypt
1952–, military/personalist/single-party, Nasser/Sadat/Mubarak
El Salvador
1931–48, military
1948–84, military/single-party
Ethiopia
1974–91, military/personalist, Mengistu
1991–, single-party
Gabon
1960–, personalist/single-party, Bongo
German Democratic Republic
1945–90, single-party (foreign maintained)
Ghana
1960–66, personalist/single-party, Nkrumah
1966–69, military
1972–79, military
1981–2000, personalist, Rawlings (free and fair elections, 1996)
Greece
1967–74, military
Guatemala
1954–58, personalist, Castillo Armas
1963–66, military
1970–85, military
Guinea
1958–84, single-party
1984–, personalist, Conté
Guinea-Bissau
1974–80, single-party
1980–99, personalist, Vieira
Haiti
1950–56, personalist, Magloire
1957–86, personalist, Duvalier family
1991–94, military
1995–, personalist/single-party, Aristide
Honduras
1933–56, personalist/single-party, Carías/Gálvez/Lozano
1963–71, military/single-party
1972–81, military
Hungary
1949–90, single-party (foreign maintained)
Indonesia
1949–65, personalist, Sukarno
1967–98, military/personalist/single-party, Suharto
Iraq
1958–63, personalist, Qasim
1963–68, personalist, Arif
1968–79, personalist/single-party, Takriti clan
1979–, personalist, Saddam Hussein
Ivory Coast
1960–99, single-party

Kenya
1963–, single-party
Korea, North
1948–, personalist/single-party, Kim family
Korea, South
1961–87, military
Laos
1975–, single-party
Liberia
1944–80, personalist, Tubman/Tolbert
1980–90, personalist, Doe
Libya
1969–, personalist, Qadhafi
Madagascar
1960–72, single-party
1972–75, military
1975–93, personalist, Ratsiraka
Malawi
1964–94, personalist, Banda
Malaysia
1957–, single-party
Mali
1960–68, single-party
1968–91, personalist, Traoré
Mauritania
1960–78, personalist, Daddah
1980–, military/personalist, Taya
Mexico
1929–2000, single-party (free and fair elections, 1997)
Mozambique
1975–, single-party (free and fair elections, 1994)
Myanmar
1962–88, military/personalist/single-party, Ne Win
1988–, military
Nicaragua
1936–79, personalist, Somoza family
1979–90, single-party
Niger
1960–74, single-party
1974–93, military/personalist, Kountché/Saïbou
1996–99, personalist, Mainassara
Nigeria
1966–79, military
1983–93, military
1993–99, military/personalist, Abacha/Abubakar
Pakistan
1958–69, personalist, Ayub Khan
1971–77, personalist, Bhutto
1977–88, military/personalist, Zia
Panama
1968–81, personalist/single-party, Torrijos
1981–89, military/personalist, Noriega
Paraguay
1940–47, personalist, Morínigo
1949–54, personalist, Chávez
1954–93, military/personalist/single-party, Stroessner

Peru
1948–56, military/personalist, Odría
1968–80, military
Philippines
1972–86, personalist, Marcos
Poland
1947–89, single-party (foreign maintained)
Portugal
1932–74, personalist, Salazar/Caetano
Romania
1945–90, personalist/single-party, Gheorghiu-Dej/Ceauşescu
Rwanda
1962–73, single-party
1973–94, military/single-party
1994–, military
Senegal
1960–2000, single-party
Sierra Leone
1968–92, single-party
1992–96, military/personalist, Strasser
Singapore
1965–, single-party
Somalia
1969–90, personalist, Siad Barré
Soviet Union
1917–91, single-party
Spain
1939–79, personalist, Franco
Sudan
1958–64, military
1969–85, personalist, Nimeiri
1989–, military/personalist, Bashir
Syria
1949–54, military
1963–, military/personalist/single-party, Asad family
Taiwan
1949–2000, single-party (free and fair elections, 1996)
Tanzania
1964–, single-party (free and fair elections, 1995)
Thailand
1948–57, military
1958–73, military
1976–88, military
Togo
1967–, personalist, Eyadema
Tunisia
1957–, single-party
Turkey
1923–46, single-party
1980–83, military
Uganda
1966–71, personalist, Obote
1971–79, personalist, Amin
1986–, personalist, Museveni
Uruguay
1973–84, military
Venezuela
1948–58, military/personalist, Pérez Jiménez
Vietnam
1954–, single-party

Vietnam, South
1955–63, personalist, Diem
Yemen
1962–78, military
1978–, personalist, Salih
Yemen, South
1967–90, single-party
Yugoslavia
1945–89, single-party
Zaire (Congo after 1997)
1965–97, personalist, Mobutu
1997–, personalist, Kabila family
Zambia
1964–91, single-party
Zimbabwe
1979–, single-party

Appendix B

Labor Repression Coding

A labor repression score was calculated for each year for each of eighty-four developing countries. The factors that contribute to the labor repression score are shown below on the labor repression information sheet. This information sheet was used to keep track of data on a large number of countries from multiple sources, but also to ensure that the same criteria would be used to assess all the countries.

The information thus collected was transformed into numbers using the coding rules. For each of the five separate elements that contribute to the final labor repression score, each country was given a score between zero and one, with one meaning more repression and zero meaning that unions are more able to represent workers' interests. Not all information was available for all countries for all years, but estimates could be made from what was available. The five scores were then added to create the final labor repression score.

Labor Repression Information Sheet

Country name____________________________________
Date__________ Source_______________________________

1. **Are unions legal and free to function?**
   Unions legal?
   All unions legal, or only those affiliated with the government or ruling party?
   Are they actually allowed to meet and carry out normal day-to-day activities?
   Can government dissolve unions?
   Are registration rules, if any, intrusive or used to control, fragment, or eliminate unions?

2. **Are unions autonomous from the government and ruling party?**
   Are independent unions free to organize?
   Are unions free to choose their own leaders?
   Must union leaders be members of the ruling party?
   Are unions dependent on the government or ruling party for finance?
   Are unions free to affiliate with the confederation they choose, or must they affiliate with one linked to the ruling party?
   Are unions controlled by the government or ruling party?

3. **Can unions use the customary methods for pursuing the interests of workers, that is, collective bargaining and strikes?**
   Is collective bargaining legal?
      For which unions?
   Does it actually occur, and are bargains enforced?
   Are areas subject to collective bargaining unduly limited by government regulation?
   Is collective bargaining legal at the industry level?
   Are strikes legal?
      For which unions?
   Do government regulations or compulsory arbitration unduly limit strikes?
   Does fear of death, torture, beatings, or imprisonment undermine the right to strike?
   Do strikes actually occur?

4. **Can labor participate in politics (not simply as an affiliate of the ruling party)?**
   Is it possible to form a labor party?
   Is it possible for unions to endorse nonincumbent candidates?
   Are peaceful demonstrations legal?
   Even if it cannot participate autonomously, is labor part of the ruling coalition, and can union leaders express labor interests within the ruling party?
   Is participation in peaceful opposition demonstrations dangerous?

5. Is violence used by the government, ruling party, unions affiliated with the ruling party, or private actors to intimidate, harass, or punish strikers, union leaders, or workers?
Murders?
Approximate number:
Who is targeted (leaders, strikers, ordinary union members)?
In what circumstances (during police efforts to break up strikes, in prison, extrajudicial execution, legal execution)?
Torture?
Routine or occasional?
Arrests and detention?
How many?
How long, on average?
Who is targeted?
Legal or arbitrary?
Detention without trial?
Strikes broken up by police, army, or private guards?

Coding Rules

1. Legality and freedom to function

1.0 Unions are illegal, and the ban is enforced; or there are virtually no unions.

0.9 Unions are formally legal, but all activities are banned; or one union confederation affiliated with the ruling party is legal, but virtually all activity is prohibited.

0.8 Unions are formally legal, but functioning is nearly prohibited by rules (e.g., meetings require prior permission, which is rarely or never granted); or special rules applicable to the largest ethnic group nearly prohibit union activity within that group.

0.7 Only unions affiliated with the ruling party are legal.

0.6 Both government employees and agricultural workers are prohibited from organizing.

0.5 Government registration rules can be and are used to eliminate unions or to prevent them from forming; or registration rules cause severe fragmentation; or government harassment impedes union functioning but does not prevent it;

or the government favors affiliated unions but does not prevent others.

0.4 Government employees are prohibited from unionizing (no other restrictions).

If there are other restrictions, add .2 to base score if government employees are prohibited from organizing.

Subtract .2 from base score if government employees are in fact organized even though it is illegal.

0.3 There are tedious registration rules (no other restrictions).

0.2 Government can legally dissolve unions but does not do it often (no other restrictions).

If there are other restrictions, add .1 to base score if government can and does dissolve unions.

0.1 Unions are illegal in some "essential services" (no other restrictions).

2. Autonomy

1.0 Unions are controlled by the ruling party or government, their leaders are appointed or subject to veto, their funding is controlled, and they show no sign of independent activity or their activities are banned.

0.8 Unions can be dissolved, leaders can be replaced, and funding is controlled, but unions continue to elect their own leaders and struggle against government control.

0.6 There is only one union confederation and it is affiliated with the ruling party, but its leaders sometimes advocate policies in opposition to the government.

0.5 The largest confederation is affiliated with the ruling party or government, and other unions exist but are disadvantaged by intimidation or exclusion from benefits available to affiliates of the ruling party;

or the government sets up competing subsidized unions to draw support from others.

0.4 Unions are formally independent, but there is extensive government interference;

or company unions are strongly encouraged.

0.2 Unions are independent, but union leaders can be purged.

3. Collective bargaining and strikes

1.0 Collective bargaining and strikes are illegal.

0.9 Collective bargaining is very restricted, and strikes are illegal;
or bargaining is informal, there are no written contracts, contracts are not legally enforced, there are many restrictions on the right to strike, and strikes are very rare.

0.8 Bargaining is only through a single-party controlled union and strikes are illegal or virtually illegal, but wildcat strikes occur and are tolerated;
or virtually all bargaining and strikes are prohibited, but wildcat strikes occur and are tolerated;
or all bargaining is handled through government bodies, wages are fixed by the government, there is compulsory arbitration, and strikes do not occur.

0.7 Collective bargaining is suspended, wages are frozen, and strikes are illegal.

0.6 Collective bargaining is legal, but strikes are banned (disputes are settled by government- or party-influenced labor courts or by compulsory arbitration);
or collective bargaining occurs only through a union affiliated with the ruling party, and strikes are legal only when approved by the party;
or collective bargaining is legal only in the private sector, and there are many restrictions on the right to strike.

0.5 Unions are so weak that collective bargaining and strikes are very rare.

0.4 Collective bargaining is legal, and strikes are legal only after very lengthy government procedures;
or collective bargaining and strikes are legal in the private but not the public sector;
or collective bargaining and strikes are legal except in "essential services," very broadly defined.

0.3 Collective bargaining is legal, but strikes are legal only in the private sector.

0.2 Collective bargaining is legal, and strikes are legal after notification and moderate procedures.
Add .2 to base score if employers often disregard agreements reached through collective bargaining,

arbitration, or labor courts; or if strikes are legal, but employers can legally dismiss striking workers.

Add .1 to base score if strikes are extremely rare, even though formally legal.

Subtract .1 from base score if strikes are common in some areas even though formally prohibited.

Add .6 to base score if strikes are legal but very dangerous (i.e., likely to lead to death, torture, or serious beatings).

4. **Political participation**

1.0 No participation is permitted, that is, there is no labor party, demonstrations are not permitted, and public expressions of workers' interests do not occur within the ruling party.

0.8 Mass participation is restricted and dangerous, but some labor leaders can express their views in public.

0.7 Participation is not autonomous, but labor is part of the dominant party coalition, and labor leaders are able to represent workers' interests within the party.

0.6 Participation is legal but discouraged, and very little occurs.

0.5 Participation is legal, but dangerous.

0.3 Participation is discouraged, but it occurs.

5. **Violence**

1.0 Hundreds are executed or disappeared, whether legally or not, whether by government or paramilitary forces (routine torture and mass detentions usually accompany large numbers of executions but are not required).

0.9 Many executions occur (but less than 100 per year), and torture is routine.

0.8 Some executions occur, torture is common, and there are many long detentions.

0.7 Some executions or deaths occur in clashes with police or military, torture is reported but not routine, and there are arrests and detentions.

0.6 There are assassinations and intimidation by paramilitary forces, but the number of deaths is not very large.

0.5 Few, if any, executions occur; torture is reported but not routine; there are many detentions, but most are for a short time;
or a few deaths and many injuries to strikers occur during clashes with police or military, but violence is not systematic (arrests usually also occur but are not required).

0.4 Few, if any, executions occur; torture is not routine; beatings are reported; there are some arrests or detentions.

0.3 Executions and torture are rare or nonexistent; there are a large number of arrests, most for a short time.

0.2 Executions and torture are rare or nonexistent, and there are some detentions of strikers or union leaders for short periods;
or long-term detention continues of moderate numbers of union leaders or members arrested in the past.

Add .4 to base score if Amnesty International reports many executions or disappearances, routine torture, and many detentions, but unions and workers are not among the main targets of repression. (The rationale here is that such punishments deter the expression of labor grievances even where workers have not been the main victims.)

Average Labor Repression Scores (1970–81)

Algeria	3.3	Costa Rica	0.8
Argentina	3.5	Cyprus	0.3
Bangladesh*	2.1	Dominican Rep.	1.5
Benin	2.8	Ecuador	1.6
Bolivia	3.2	Egypt	3.1
Botswana	0.7	El Salvador	3.1
Brazil	3.4	Ethiopia	3.8
Burkina Faso	1.4	Fiji	0.2
Cameroon	3.6	Gabon	3.4
Central African Rep.	4.0	Gambia	0.9
Chile	3.0	Ghana	1.2
Colombia	0.7	Greece	2.1
Congo	3.2	Guatemala	3.8

(continues)

Guinea	4.3	Pakistan	2.6
Guyana	1.2	Panama	0.8
Haiti	4.5	Paraguay	2.7
Honduras	0.9	Peru	2.0
India	1.1	Philippines	2.3
Indonesia	2.6	Portugal	1.7
Iran	4.2	Rwanda	3.8
Iraq	4.4	Senegal	2.4
Israel	0.0	Sierra Leone	1.1
Ivory Coast	2.8	Singapore	2.9
Jamaica	0.2	Somalia	4.2
Jordan	1.6	South Africa	3.1
Kenya	2.6	Sri Lanka	1.0
Korea (South)	3.0	Sudan*	3.8
Lesotho	2.8	Swaziland	2.5
Liberia	3.2	Syria	4.2
Madagascar	1.4	Taiwan	3.4
Malawi	4.0	Tanzania	3.0
Malaysia	2.3	Thailand*	2.1
Mali	4.0	Togo	3.4
Mauritania	4.0	Trinidad & Tobago	0.4
Mauritius	0.4	Tunisia	3.2
Mexico	2.4	Turkey	1.8
Morocco	0.6	Uganda	4.7
Myanmar	4.0	Uruguay	3.4
Nepal	3.7	Venezuela	1.5
Nicaragua*	2.4	Yemen	4.2
Niger	2.5	Zaire	3.7
Nigeria	1.8	Zambia	0.7

*Excluded from most scatterplots and all regressions because economic data are not available.

Sources Used in Labor Repression Coding

Abós, Alvaro. 1984. *Las Organizaciones Sindicales y el Poder Militar (1976–1983)*. Buenos Aires: Biblioteca Política Argentina.

African Trade Union News (Lomé, Togo). 1975–81. Various issues.

Akhter, Mahmood. 1975. "Patterns and Directions of Growth of Trade Unions and Employers' Organisations in Pakistan." In CENTO Seminar, *Patterns and Directions of Growth of Trade Unions and Employers' Organizations in the Development of the CENTO Region*. Tehran: CENTO.

Albornoz Peralta, Osvaldo. 1983. *Breve Síntesis: Historia del Movimiento Obrero Ecuatoriano.* Quito: LeiraNueva.

Amnesty International. 1973–82. *Amnesty International Report.* London: Amnesty International Publications.

Ananaba, Wogu. 1979. *The Trade Union Movement in Africa: Promise and Performance.* London: C. Hurst & Company.

Anderson, Rodney. 1987. "Mexico." In *Latin American Labor Organizations,* edited by Gerald Michael Greenfield and Sheldon Maram. Westport, Conn.: Greenwood Press.

Arudsoth, Ponniah, and Craig Littler. 1993. "State Regulation and Union Fragmentation in Malaysia." In *Organized Labor in the Asia-Pacific Region: A Comparative Study of Trade Unionism in Nine Countries,* edited by Stephen Frenkel. Ithaca: ILR Press.

Bahan, Della, William Bollinger, Darline Alvarez, and Sandra Gain. 1985. *El Salvador Update: Labor under Siege: A Report on the Salvadoran Trade Union Movement.* Los Angeles: El Rescate.

Baloyra, Enrique. 1982. *El Salvador in Transition.* Chapel Hill: University of North Carolina Press.

Barrera, Manuel, and J. Samuel Valenzuela. 1986. "The Development of Labor Movement Opposition to the Military Regime." In *Military Rule in Chile: Dictatorship and Oppositions,* edited by J. Samuel Valenzuela and Arturo Valenzuela. Baltimore: Johns Hopkins University Press.

Berik, Günseli, and Chihan Bilginsoy. 1996. "The Labor Movement in Turkey: Labor Pains, Maturity, Metamorphosis." In *The Social History of Labor in the Middle East,* edited by Ellis Goldberg. Boulder: Westview.

Bianchi, Robert. 1984. *Interest Groups and Political Development in Turkey.* Princeton: Princeton University Press.

Bienefeld, M. A. 1975. "Socialist Development and the Workers in Tanzania." In *The Development of an African Working Class: Studies in Class Formation and Action,* edited by Richard Sandbrook and Robin Cohen. Toronto: University of Toronto Press.

Brown, Andrew, and Stephen Frenkel. 1993. "Union Unevenness and Insecurity in Thailand." In *Organized Labor in the Asia-Pacific Region: A Comparative Study of Trade Unionism in Nine Countries,* edited by Stephen Frenkel. Ithaca: ILR Press.

Camacho, Daniel. 1985. *Desarrollo del Movimiento Sindical en Costa Rica.* San José: Editorial Universidad de Costa Rica.

CENTO Seminar. 1975. *Patterns and Directions of Growth of Trade Unions and Employers' Organizations in the Development of the CENTO Region.* Tehran: CENTO.

Chagas, Jorge, and Mario Tonarelli. 1989. *El Sindicalismo Uruguayo: Bajo la Dictadura (1973–1984).* Montevideo: Ediciones del Nuevo Mundo.

Cho, Changwa. 1978. "Labour Movement in Korea." *Journal of Labour Economics* 2:73–86.

Choi, J. J. 1989. *Labor and the Authoritarian State: Labor Unions in South Korean Manufacturing Industries.* Seoul: Korea University Press.

Ciencia y Tecnología para Guatemala. 1989. *El Movimiento Sindical en Guatemala (1975–1985).* Mexico City: CITGUA.

Compa, Lance. 1989. *Labor Rights in Haiti.* Washington, D.C.: International Labor Rights Education and Research Fund.

Conference on Trade Union, Human, and Democratic Rights in Bangladesh, India, Nepal, Pakistan, and Sri Lanka. 1991. *Rights of Workers in South Asia.* New Delhi: Friedrich-Ebert Foundation.

Cook, Maria Lorena. 1990. "Organizing Opposition in the Teachers' Movement in Oaxaca." In *Popular Movements and Political Change in Mexico,* edited by Joe Foweraker and Ann Craig. Boulder: Lynne Rienner.

Covell, Maureen. 1987. *Madagascar: Politics, Economics, and Society.* London: Frances Pinter.

Damachi, Ukandi. 1975. "The Internal Dynamics of Trade Unions in Ghana." In *The Development of an African Working Class: Studies in Class Formation and Action,* edited by Richard Sandbrook and Robin Cohen. Toronto: University of Toronto Press.

Dekker, L. Douwes, D. Hemson, J. S. Kane-Berman, J. Lever, and L. Schlemmer. 1975. "Case Studies in African Labour Action in South Africa and Namibia (South West Africa)." In *The Development of an African Working Class: Studies in Class Formation and Action,* edited by Richard Sandbrook and Robin Cohen. Toronto: University of Toronto Press.

Delgado, Alvaro. 1984. *Política y Movimiento Obrero, 1970–1983.* Bogotá: Editorial Colombia Nueva.

Delgado González, Trifonio. 1984. *100 Años de Lucha Obrera en Bolivia.* La Paz: Ediciones ISLA.

Diallo, Garbo. 1993. *Mauritania—The Other Apartheid?* Current African Issues 16. Uppsala, Sweden: Nordiska Afrikainstitutet.

Donato M., Elisa, and Manuel Rojas B. 1987. *Sindicatos, Política y Economía, 1972–1986.* San José: Editorial Alma Mater.

Doronio, Catalino M. 1976. "Industrial Relations in the Philippines." *Asian Labour* 24, no. 125 (January): 20–26.

El Jack, Ahmed Hassan, and Chris Leggett. 1980. *Industrial Relations and the Political Process in the Sudan.* Research Series No. 49. Geneva: International Institute for Labour Studies.

Ellner, Steve. 1993. *Organized Labor in Venezuela, 1958–1991: Behavior and Concerns in a Democratic Setting.* Wilmington: SR Books.

Erickson, Kenneth. 1977. *The Brazilian Corporative State and Working-Class Politics.* Berkeley: University of California Press.

Falabella, Gonzalo. 1981. *Labour in Chile under the Junta, 1973–1979.* Working Papers No. 4. London: University of London, Institute of Latin American Studies.

Frenkel, Stephen, Jon-Chao Hong, and Bih-Ling Lee. 1993. "The Resurgence and Fragility of Trade Unions in Taiwan." In *Organized Labor in the Asia-Pacific Region: A Comparative Study of Trade Unionism in Nine Countries,* edited by Stephen Frenkel. Ithaca: ILR Press.

Ghotbi, Ahmad. 1977. *Workers Say No to the Shah.* London: CRTURI.

Goldberg, Ellis. 1996. "Reading from Left to Right: The Social History of Egyptian Labor." In *The Social History of Labor in the Middle East,* edited by Ellis Goldberg. Boulder: Westview.

Guyana. Ministry of Information. 1981. *Action in Partnership: Trade*

Unions and the People's New Constitution. Georgetown: Publications Division, Ministry of Information.

Hadiz, Vedi R. 1994. "The Political Significance of Recent Working Class Action in Indonesia." In *Indonesia's Emerging Proletariat: Workers and Their Struggles,* edited by David Bourchier. Clayton, Victoria (Australia): Centre of Southeast Asian Studies, Monash Asia Institute, Monash University.

Handelman, Howard. 1976. "The Politics of Labor Protest in Mexico: Two Case Studies." *Journal of Inter-American Studies and World Affairs* 18: 167–94.

———. 1979. *Organized Labor in Mexico: Oligarchy and Dissent.* Hanover, N.H.: American Universities Field Staff.

Handy, Jim. 1984. *Gift of the Devil: A History of Guatemala.* Pp. 223–30. Toronto: Between the Lines.

Hernández, Héctor. 1991. *Solidarismo y Sindicalismo en Honduras.* Tegucigalpa: Federación Unitaria de Trabajadores de Honduras.

Herrera Torres, Juvenal. 1976. *La Situación Actual del Movimiento Obrero Colombiano.* Medellín: Editorial La Gaitana.

Ihonvbere, Julius O., and Timothy M. Shaw. 1988. "Petroleum Proletariat: Nigerian Oil Workers in Contextual and Comparative Perspectives." In *Labour and Unions in Asia and Africa,* edited by Roger Southall. Hong Kong: Macmillan Press.

International Labour Office. 1980. *Year Book of Labour Statistics.* Pp. 627–40. Geneva: ILO.

———. 1989–90. *Year Book of Labour Statistics.* Pp. 997–1039. Geneva: ILO.

International Labour Organisation. 1987. *Labour Administration: Profile on Bangladesh.* Bangkok: ILO Asian and Pacific Regional Centre for Labour Administration.

Jeffries, Richard D. 1975. "Populist Tendencies in the Ghanaian Trade Union Movement." In *The Development of an African Working Class: Studies in Class Formation and Action,* edited by Richard Sandbrook and Robin Cohen. Toronto: University of Toronto Press.

Jelin, Elizabeth. 1977. *Conflictos Laborales en la Argentina, 1973–1976.* Estudios Sociales No. 9. Buenos Aires: Centro de Estudios de Estado y Sociedad.

Jomo, K. S., and Patricia Todd. 1994. *Trade Unions and the State in Peninsular Malaysia.* Kuala Lumpur: Oxford University Press.

Karnik, V. B. 1982. *Trade Union Movement and Industrial Relations.* Bombay: Somaiya.

Kim, Hwang-Joe. 1993. "The Korean Union Movement in Transition." In *Organized Labor in the Asia-Pacific Region: A Comparative Study of Trade Unionism in Nine Countries,* edited by Stephen Frenkel. Ithaca: ILR Press.

Kraus, Jon. 1988. "The Political Economy of Trade Union–State Relations in Radical and Populist Regimes in Africa." In *Labour and Unions in Asia and Africa,* edited by Roger Southall. Hong Kong: Macmillan Press.

Ladjevardi, Habib. 1985. *Labor Unions and Autocracy in Iran.* Syracuse: Syracuse University Press.

Leitner, Kerstin. 1977. *Workers, Trade Unions, and Peripheral Capitalism in Kenya after Independence.* Frankfurt: Peter Lang.

Liauzu, Claude. 1996. "The History of Labor and the Workers' Movement in North Africa." In *The Social History of Labor in the Middle East,* edited by Ellis Goldberg. Boulder: Westview.

Library of Congress. Congressional Research Service. Foreign Affairs and National Defense Division. 1977. *The Status of Human Rights in Selected Countries and the U. S. Response.* Washington, D.C.: U.S. Government Printing Office.

Longuenesse, Elisabeth. 1996. "Labor in Syria: The Emergence of New Identities." In *The Social History of Labor in the Middle East,* edited by Ellis Goldberg. Boulder: Westview.

López Larrave, Mario. 1979. *Breve Historia del Movimiento Sindical Guatemalteco.* Guatemala: Editorial Universitaria.

Lora, Guillermo. 1977. *A History of the Bolivian Labour Movement, 1848–1971.* Translated by Christine Whitehead, edited and abridged by Laurence Whitehead. Cambridge: Cambridge University Press.

Luke, David Fashole. 1984. *Labour and Parastatal Politics in Sierra Leone: A Study of African Working-Class Ambivalence.* New York: University Press of America.

Mabry, B. D. 1977. "The Thai Labour Movement." *Asian Survey* 17:931–51.

———. 1987. "The Labour Movement and the Practice of Professional Management in Thailand." *Journal of Southeast Asian Studies* 17: 303–26.

Mabry, B. D., and K. Srisermbhok. 1985. "Labor Relations under Martial Law: The Thailand Experience." *Asian Survey* 25:613–37.

Martens, George R. 1978. *Trade Unions and Nation Building in Francophone Africa.* Special issue of *Labor and Development.* Lomé, Togo: Regional Economic Research and Documentation Center.

Menjívar, Rafael. 1982. *Formación y Lucha del Proletariado Industrial Salvadoreño.* 2d ed. San José: Editorial Universitaria Centroamericana.

Mericle, Kenneth. 1977. "Corporatist Control of the Working Class: Authoritarian Brazil since 1964." In *Authoritarianism and Corporatism in Latin America,* edited by James Malloy. Pittsburgh: University of Pittsburgh Press.

Meza, Victor. 1980. *Historia del Movimiento Obrero Hondureño.* Tegucigalpa: Editorial Guaymuras.

Middlebrook, Kevin, ed. 1991. *Unions, Workers, and the State in Mexico.* La Jolla: University of California, San Diego Center for U.S.-Mexican Studies.

Mogalakwe, Monageng. 1997. *The State and Organised Labour in Botswana: "Liberal Democracy" in Emergent Capitalism.* Aldershot, England: Ashgate.

Moghadam, Valentine. 1996. "Making History, but Not of Their Own Choosing: Workers and the Labor Movement in Iran." In *The Social History of Labor in the Middle East,* edited by Ellis Goldberg. Boulder: Westview.

Moncaya, Victor Manuel, and Fernando Rojas. 1978. *Luchas Obreras y Política Laboral en Colombia.* Bogotá: La Carreta.

Moreira Alves, Maria Helena. 1985. *State and Opposition in Military Brazil.* Austin: University of Texas Press.

Muase, Charles Kabeya. 1989. *Syndicalisme et Démocratie en Afrique Noire: L'expérience du Burkina Faso (1936–1988).* Paris: Éditions Karthala.

National Union of Mineworkers. 1978. *Report of the National Union of Mineworkers Delegation: Trade Union and Human Rights in Chile and Bolivia.* London: National Union of Mineworkers.

Nye, Roger Paul. 1974. "The Military in Turkish Politics." Ph.D. diss., Washington University, St. Louis.

O'Brien, Leslie. 1988. "Between Capital and Labour: Trade Unionism in Malaysia." In *Labour and Unions in Asia and Africa,* edited by Roger Southall. Hong Kong: Macmillan Press.

Park, Young-Ki. 1979. *Labor and Industrial Relations in Korea: System and Practice.* Labor and Management Studies No. 6. Seoul: Sogang University Press.

Peace, Adrian. 1975. "The Lagos Proletariat: Labour Aristocrats or Populist Militants." In *The Development of an African Working Class: Studies in Class Formation and Action,* edited by Richard Sandbrook and Robin Cohen. Toronto: University of Toronto Press.

Peña Sánchez, Julián. 1986. *Debilidad del Movimiento Sindical en la República Dominicana.* Santo Domingo: Ediciones de Taller.

Pérez Arce, Francisco. 1990. "The Enduring Union Struggle for Legality and Democracy." In *Popular Movements and Political Change in Mexico,* edited by Joe Foweraker and Ann Craig. Boulder: Lynne Rienner.

Perspectives on Caribbean Labour. Various years. Barbados: Caribbean Congress of Labour.

Posas, Mario. 1987. *Breve Historia de las Organizaciones Sindicales de Honduras.* Tegucigalpa: Friedrich Ebert.

Priestley, George. 1986. *Military Government and Popular Participation in Panama: The Torrijos Regime, 1968–1975.* Boulder: Westview.

Roxborough, Ian. 1984. *Unions and Politics in Mexico.* Cambridge: Cambridge University Press.

Sallahuddin. 1992. *Labour at the Crossroads.* Georgetown: New Guyana Co.

Schmitter, Philippe. 1973. "The 'Portugalization' of Brazil?" In *Authoritarian Brazil: Origins, Policies, and Future,* edited by Alfred Stepan. New Haven: Yale University Press.

Shalev, Michael. 1996. "The Labor Movement in Israel: Ideology and Political Economy." In *The Social History of Labor in the Middle East,* edited by Ellis Goldberg. Boulder: Westview.

U.S. Department of State. 1978–82. *Country Reports on Human Rights Practices.* Washington, D.C.: U.S. Government Printing Office.

Williams, Philip J., and Knut Walker. 1997. *Militarization and Demilitarization in El Salvador's Transition to Democracy.* Pp. 71–113. Pittsburgh: University of Pittsburgh Press.

Zapata, Francisco. 1989. "Labor and Politics: The Mexican Paradox." In *Labor Autonomy and the State in Latin America,* edited by Edward Epstein. Boston: Unwin Hyman.

Zelaya, Irma Raquel, Arnoldo Kuestermann, and Carlos Escobar Armas, eds. 1991. *Mas de 100 Años del Movimiento Obrero Urbano en Guatemala.* Vol. 3, *Reorganización, Auge y Desarticulación del Movimiento Sindical (1954–1982).* Guatemala City: Asociación de Investigación y Estudios Sociales (ASIES).

Appendix C

Coding Scheme for Test of the Lipset and Rokkan Freezing Hypotheses

Domain Implied by the Argument

To be included in the set of cases for the tests, countries must have

- Achieved independence by 1940
- Experienced no major boundary changes or transfers of population in the period between the measured starting points (i.e., the oligarchic or postsuffrage period) and endpoints (i.e., later elections)
- Been part of the Christian historical tradition
- Experienced at least minimal political competition during the period of elite rule preceding broad political participation
  - Descriptions of competition between proto-parties, parties of notables, or parliamentary factions in the country specialist historical literature are interpreted as indicating the existence of competition.
  - The competition need not have been peaceful or fully institutionalized.
- Crossed the "effective suffrage threshold" by 1975, defined as:
  - suffrage extended to most of the (male) working class; and
  - two or more at least semicompetitive elections held after enfranchisement.
  - Continuous democracy after suffrage extension not required.
- Held at least two competitive elections with broad citizen participation since 1985

Operationalization of Central Concepts

Oligarchy

A period is interpreted as oligarchic if the following conditions hold:

- Elite parties or proto-parties are described in the country specialist historical literature as structuring political competition.
- Competition is public and organized into somewhat stable blocs, not limited to intrigue within the clique surrounding the ruler.
- Meaningful political participation is limited to a small part of the (male) population via
  - property qualifications; and/or
  - public voting; and/or
  - literacy requirements when more than 60 percent of the population is illiterate; and/or
  - voting participation by less than 5 percent of the population for whatever reason.

Effective Suffrage Threshold

Suffrage extension is defined as meaning that enough of the population is enfranchised that observers would expect working-class voters to affect political outcomes. For this to be true, the following conditions must hold:

- The legal elimination of property qualifications for voting
- The legal enfranchisement of at least 10 percent of the total population[1]
- Voting participation by at least 5 percent of the total population
- The use of a secret ballot

---

1. These figures are expressed in terms of total population because that is the most readily available form of data. The working assumption here is that adult males made up about 25 percent of the population of most countries at the time of enfranchisement. If 10 percent of the population were enfranchised, that would imply that 40 percent of adult males were allowed to vote. Given the level of development in most countries at the time of the first suffrage extensions, 40 percent would include most urban dwellers.

- A literacy rate of at least 40 percent where illiterates are denied suffrage
- Presidents and parliaments chosen by election (either direct election or via electoral college, but not by some other body) rather than by force more than half the time during the ten years after the extension of suffrage
- Elections need not be fully free and fair, but there must be some degree of partisan competition and some possibility that a nonincumbent can win

Identification of Relevant Parties

Oligarchic parties. The identity of oligarchic parties, proto-parties, and blocs is drawn from the historical literature on the oligarchic period in each country, which describes competing elite groups in terms of interests, ideology, faith, and sometimes regional concentration. In some cases, the main parties during the oligarchy differ from those during earlier periods. For this study, each elite proto-party is classified—when the literature indicates that such classification is salient—as falling at one end or the other of the following Lipset and Rokkan cleavage dimensions:

- Center versus periphery (unitarist versus federalist, centrist versus decentralist)
- Landed wealth versus commercial wealth (sometimes traditional economics versus free trade)
- Clerical versus secular

Factions are not counted as separate parties. Factions are defined as ephemeral political groups, loyal to a particular leader or small group of leaders, that run candidates in one or a few elections but cannot be distinguished on grounds of ideology or interest from other factions within the same party or bloc.

Presuffrage parties. Presuffrage parties are nontraditional parties that attracted 5 percent or more of the vote in any legislative election held during the ten years prior to passage of the effective suffrage threshold. The 5 percent rule for new parties aims to include parties after they have achieved at least a small mass following. Where it is impossible to get actual election results for legislative elections, the following can be used as approximations:

- Presidential election returns
- Distribution of seats in the lower chamber[2]
- Election returns from the capital city
- Election returns from a slightly earlier period
- Descriptions in the literature of which parties participated in elections[3]

Parties descended from oligarchic parties are treated as continuations of those parties even if their names have changed. Votes for all descendants of oligarchic parties are counted, regardless of how small the parties are, so as to avoid underestimating their persistence when they have fragmented into many small parties.

Postsuffrage parties. Postsuffrage parties are new parties that attracted 5 percent or more of the vote in any legislative election held within ten years after the extension of suffrage. Where legislative election results are not available, the following can be used as approximations:

- Presidential election returns
- Distribution of seats in the lower chamber

Later parties. Later parties are parties not descended from traditional, presuffrage, or postsuffrage parties that attracted at least 5 percent of the vote in any legislative election after 1985.

Persistence of Traditional Cleavages

Traditional cleavages are interpreted as persisting if any of the following conditions hold for 1985–2000:

- Oligarchic parties (or their descendants) have absorbed new interests and continue to dominate the political space.
- Oligarchic parties (or their descendants) have survived as important political actors while new parties have emerged to represent new interests.
- Oligarchic parties (or their descendants) have coalesced

2. Where only the distribution of legislative seats is available, 3 percent was used as the lower threshold for counting parties because it is common for small parties to be disadvantaged by the translation of votes into seats.

3. Since the only purpose of these data is to identify the parties that existed prior to suffrage expansion, exact figures are not important.

into a single party to compete against the new parties that have emerged.
- Oligarchic parties (or their descendants) have split into multiple identifiable descendants, whether or not new parties have also entered the political arena.

Parties are defined as *descendants* of earlier ones if they are described in the country specialist literature as

- representing the same interests that were represented by an earlier party; and
- falling at the same ends of all the Lipset and Rokkan cleavage dimensions identified as salient for the original parties.

In some countries, there are other long-standing cleavages in addition to those identified by Lipset and Rokkan—for example, inclusive versus racial-cultural definitions of citizenship in Panama. In the spirit of Lipset and Rokkan, these cleavages are treated in the same way as those they identified.

Most parties are founded by dissidents from older parties, but that by itself does not make them descendants within the Lipset-Rokkan framework. They are considered new if they represent or appeal to different sides of the Lipset-Rokkan dichotomies, different combinations of sides, or new interests or ideologies that did not exist previously. If the offshoot appeals to the same ends of the Lipset-Rokkan dichotomies as did the root party but differs primarily over leadership, then the offshoot is considered a descendant. Parties that do not emerge as splits from older parties but that nevertheless appeal to the same sides of the Lipset-Rokkan dichotomies are considered *descendant equivalents*. They are not organizational descendants, but they represent the same underlying social forces.

Frozen in the Wake of Suffrage Extension

"Frozen in the wake" seems to mean to Lipset and Rokkan the actual organizational persistence of particular parties.

Organizational persistence. Party organizations that competed during the decade after effective enfranchisement and have persisted through time, though their names may have changed.

Information Used in Tests of the Lipset and Rokkan Arguments

The tables that follow are the rough equivalent of a codebook for the information used to test the Lipset and Rokkan arguments about the persistence of cleavage structures and the freezing of party alternatives. Each table shows the coding decisions made for a particular country. The tables include the following elements:

- Date identified as the endpoint of the period of oligarchic competition
- The date of formal suffrage extension to the majority of the working class
- Dates of the first competitive political system, that is, the period within which postsuffrage vote share would be measured
- The date of effective enfranchisement, that is, when working-class votes would have been expected to actually affect political outcomes
- Date of the most recent democratization
- Names and average vote shares of the principal oligarchic parties or proto-parties (average vote includes that of all factions and descendants)
- Names and average vote shares of presuffrage parties that received 5 percent or more of the vote or 3 percent or more of seats in any election during the decade prior to effective enfranchisement (average vote includes that of all factions and descendants)
- Names and average vote shares of postsuffrage parties that received 5 percent or more of the vote or 3 percent or more of the seats in any election during the decade after effective enfranchisement (average vote includes that of all factions and descendants)
- Names and average vote shares of later parties that received 5 percent of the vote in any election since 1985
- Dates of elections included in the vote averages and notes about any elections that were unusual

The average vote shares combine votes for all factions and descendants of the parties to which they are attributed as well as for the named party itself. For example, in a number of countries, different ephemeral factions of one of the oligarchic parties ran in almost every election. I have not treated these as separate parties. Instead, I have treated them—as the country specialist literature does—as factions of the same root party having many interests in common. I have also included parties considered descendants of earlier ones in the combined vote for the root parties in later elections. Descendants are parties that represent the same combination of ends of the Lipset-Rokkan dichotomies as did the earlier party. Sometimes they have split from the earlier party, but sometimes they are new. Since the first Lipset and Rokkan argument is about the persistence of cleavages, the important thing is that they represent the same interests as did the older party. If the reader does not see a party that he knows competed during a certain time period, it is because it has been treated as a faction or descendant. Notes in each table identify most factions and descendants that have been included with each of the root parties.

Where parties ran as parts of electoral alliances or coalitions and their legislative votes were not reported separately, I followed one of two rules. Where the members of the alliance were relatively equal, I split the vote equally among them. For example, half of the vote for the Alianza Frente del País Solidario in Argentina is attributed to the Unión Cívica Radical. Where one party in an alliance was much larger than its allies, however, all the votes were attributed to it. All the votes for the Alianza por Cambio in Mexico, for example, were attributed to the PAN (Partido Acción Nacional). Because they are so numerous, not all alliance partners and descendant parties are identified in the notes to the tables, but most of the important ones are. Others can be found on my website <www.polisci.ucla.edu/faculty/geddes>.

Whenever doubts arose about whether to classify parties as descendants or how to attribute votes within an alliance, I tried to err on the side of cleavage persistence or organizational continuity. I wanted to be as sure as possible that coding mistakes would not cause disconfirmation of the Lipset and Rokkan argument.

The tables also list the main interests with which the parties are identified, privileging interests relevant to the Lipset and Rokkan argument. The full election returns from which these tables were made can be found on my website, along with data sources and sources consulted in making judgments about the interests represented by different parties.

Argentina

Oligarchic period	1861–1912	Semicompetitive elections; fraud
Formal suffrage extension	1853	Universal male; public vote
First competitive period	1912–30	Secret vote; competitive elections
Effective suffrage date	1912	
Current competitive period	1983–	Democratization[a]

Main Political Parties (includes factions and descendants)	Presuffrage Average Vote[b] (%)	Postsuffrage Average Vote (%)	Average Vote since 1985 (%)	Vote in Most Recent Election (%)
Oligarchic parties				
P. Autonomista Nacional[c]	75.3	26.1	1.0	
Presuffrage parties				
Unión Cívica[d]	n/a	2.1		
Unión Cívica Radical	40.2[e]	46.0	29.0	11.6
P. Socialista	16.5	9.0	2.6	4.2
Unión Patriótica	1.7			
Postsuffrage parties				
P. Demócrata Progresista		5.4	1.4	1.7
Demócrata		1.9		
Later parties				
P. Justicialista (Peronista)			38.2	37.4
Alianza Frente del País Solidario			8.4	11.6
Unión de Centro Democrático			3.7	3.0
Alternativa por una República de Iguales			0.8	7.2
Movimiento por la Dignidad y la Independencia			0.9	
Acción por la República			1.3	
Others	5.2	9.4	12.8	23.3

Elections included:

Presuffrage average vote	1904, 1906, 1908, 1910 (city of Buenos Aires only)
Postsuffrage average vote	1912, 1914, 1916, 1918, 1920, 1922
Average vote since 1985	1985, 1987, 1989, 1991, 1993, 1995, 1997, 1999, 2001
Most recent election	October 14, 2001

Party interests

P. Autonomista Nacional[f] (PAN)	Secular, land, and commercial. Called Unión Electoral in 1906, P. Autonomista y Nacional in 1908, and Unión Nacional in 1910.
Unión Cívica (UC)	Secular, upper and middle class
Unión Cívica Radical[g] (UCR)	Secular, middle class. This includes UCR vote and vote for UCR provincial parties.
P. Socialista[h] (PS)	Secular, workers and intellectuals
Unión Patriótica (UP)	Clerical, middle class
P. Demócrata Progresista (PDP)	Upper-class reformist, protectionist, decentralist, support especially in southern region. In the current period, Alianza Sur and P. Demócrata in Mendoza province treated as descendants.

P. Demócrata (PD)	Upper-class center-right, Córdoba
P. Justicialista (Peronista)[i] (PJ)	Multiclass with emphasis on labor, originally state interventionist, now neoliberal
Alianza Frente del País Solidario[j] (FrePaSo)	Middle class and intellectuals, Peronist dissidents, opposes extreme neoliberalism, strongest in Buenos Aires. Formed by Frente Grande (center-left, formed by some Peronist dissidents and independents), some Socialists, and small parties.
Unión de Centro Democrático (UCeDe)	Modern upper and middle class, free market. Includes Alianza del Centro vote.
Alternativa por una República de Iguales (ARI)	Social democratic dissidents from both UCR and FrePaSo
Movimiento por la Dignidad y la Independencia (MODIN)	Military, far right, supporters of coup attempts
Acción por la República (AporR)	Modern upper and middle class, free enterprise, center-right electoral vehicle for Cavallo

[a]Earlier democratizations occurred in 1958, 1962, and 1973, but each was followed by only one competitive election prior to renewed military intervention.

[b]Election results are available only for the city of Buenos Aires.

[c]By the 1890s, PAN had factionalized into many different ephemeral parties. All the factions are added together here. The "PAN" vote in later periods is the sum of votes for a number of small, mostly provincial parties that seem descended from the old PAN.

[d]UC (or UC Nacional in the earliest elections) had a significant existence during the 20 or so years before 1912 and was a frequent coalition partner with PAN factions, but its vote is not reported separately for the presuffrage period.

[e]UCR abstained during 1904–12. This is the average vote for 1892, 1994, 1895, 1896, and 1898 elections in the city of Buenos Aires.

[f]For names of factions and descendants, see author's website.

[g]Votes shown also include Concentración Cívica, Unión Cominal, and Unión Democrática in the early periods; and P. Intransigente (PI) and Movimiento de Integración y Desarrollo (MID) in the later period. Includes half the votes for Alianza Trabajo, Justicia y Educación (UCR's alliance with FrePaSo).

[h]Early factions and descendants include Socialismo Argentino and P. Socialista Internacional (PSI). PSI went on to become the P. Comunista in 1912. Current descendants include P. Socialista Democrático (PSD) and P. Socialista Popular (PSP) and their alliance, Alianza Unidad Socialista; P. Comunista and Movimiento al Socialismo and their alliances, Alianza Izquierda Unida and Alianza Frente del Pueblo; P. de Trabajadores por el Socialismo; Movimiento Social de los Trabajadores; and P. Socialista Auténtico.

[i]PJ competed as the P. Laborista in 1946 and offered candidates as Unión Popular in 1962 and 1965. In 1973, it was part of the coalition Frente Justicialista de Liberación (FreJuLi), which also included MID, PCP, P. Popular Cristiano (PPC), and small socialist and regional parties. In 1983–87, FreJuLi included the PJ, MID, and Frente de Izquierda Popular. In 1989, PJ was part of Frente Justicialista Popular (FreJuPo), along with P. del Trabajo y del Pueblo, P. Demócrata Cristiano (PDC), MID, and Movimiento Patriótico de Liberación (MPL). Average vote also includes separate votes for Frente Justicialista del Chubut, P. del Trabajo y del Pueblo, and Movimiento Unión Popular.

[j]Figures include half the votes for Alianza Trabajo, Justicia y Educación (FrePaSo's alliance with UCR). In 1995–97, they also include Frente Grande (FG), Alianza Cruzada Frente Grande, and Alianza Frente País. In 2001, they also include FG, Nuevo Espacio, Nuevo Movimiento, PDC, PI, PSD, and PSP.

Bolivia

Oligarchic period	1884–1952	Competitive; limited suffrage
Formal suffrage extension	1952	Universal
First competitive period	1956–62	Flawed elections
Effective suffrage date	1952	
Current competitive period	1985–	Democratization[a]

Main Political Parties (includes factions and descendants)	Presuffrage Average Vote (%)	Postsuffrage Average Vote (%)	Average Vote since 1985 (%)	Vote in Most Recent Election (%)
Oligarchic parties				
P. Republicano	52.9		0.5	
P. Liberal	9.0			
P. Conservador[b]				
Presuffrage parties				
Acción Cívica Boliviana (Aramayo)	1.8			
Falange Socialista Boliviana	3.5	10.4	0.8	
Federación Universitaria Boliviana, Frente de Izquierda Boliviana	5.7			
Movimiento Nacionalista Revolucionario	18.6	87.3	27.6	18.2
P. de la Izquierda Revolucionaria	8.6			
Postsuffrage parties				
P. Social Cristiano		0.6	0.4	
P. Comunista de Bolivia		1.5	0.3	
P. Obrero Revolucionario		0.2	0.2	
Later parties				
Acuerdo Patriótico			5.3	
Alianza Demócrata Nacionalista			20.1	22.3
Frente del Pueblo Unido			0.3	
Izquierda Unida			3.4	3.7
Movimiento de Izquierda Revolucionario, MIR–Nueva Mayoría			12.2	16.8
MIR–Bolivia Libre, Movimiento Bolivia Libre			2.1	3.1
Movimiento Nacionalista Revolucionario de Izquierda			1.4	
MNR Vanguardia, Conciencia de Patria			12.1	17.2
Unión Cívica Solidaridad			7.5	16.1
Others			5.9	2.7

Elections included:

Presuffrage average vote	1940, 1947, 1951 (presidential)
Postsuffrage average vote	1956, 1958, 1960, 1962
Average vote since 1985	1985, 1989, 1993, 1997
Most recent election	June 1, 1997

Party interests

P. Republicano (PR)	Alliance of land and artisans. Descendants include Concordancia, an alliance of Republican factions including P. Republicano-Socialista and P. Republicano-Genuino (conservative, mining); and P. de la Unión Republicana Socialista (itself an alliance of the two Republican factions with P. Socialista Unificado).
P. Liberal (PL)	Secular, middle class, free market
Acción Cívica Boliviana (Aramayo) (ACB)	Vehicle for Aramayo
Falange Socialista Boliviana (FSB)	Military and middle-class opposition to traditional parties, originally national socialist, urban middle class, Santa Cruz region.
Federación Universitaria Boliviana, Frente de Izquierda Boliviana (FUB, FIB)	Students, workers, leftist. Includes vote for other leftist organizations.
Movimiento Nacionalista Revolucionario (MNR)	Multiclass, populist originally. In 1993, in alliance with Movimiento Revolucionario Tupaj Katari de Liberación (indigenous interests).
P. de la Izquierda Revolucionaria (PIR)	Alliance of unions and small leftist parties, including FIB; communist; electoral vehicle for Arze.
P. Social Cristiano (PSC)	PSC became P. Demócrata Cristiano (PDC) in 1965, joined with P. Revolucionario Barrientista (PRB) in 1978. Clerical, middle class.
P. Comunista de Bolivia (PCB)	Communists, split from PIR. Part of Frente de Liberación Nacional, 1966; Unidad Democrática y Popular, 1978–80; FPU, 1985; IU, 1989.
P. Obrero Revolucionario (POR)	Trotskyist, support from miners
Acuerdo Patriótico (AP)	1993 election: MIR and ADN
Alianza Demócrata Nacionalista (ADN)	1980: includes Alianza Popular de Integración Nacional, Movimiento Agrario Revolucionario Campesino, PIR; 1989: also PDC. Conservative, Christian, urban business, especially in Santa Cruz. Vehicle for Banzer.
Frente del Pueblo Unido (FPU)	1985: includes PCB and MIR-BL
Izquierda Unida (IU)	1989: includes Eje, MBL, P. Socialista Uno, PCB, MIR-Masas, and others. Alliance of small left parties, *cocaleros,* especially in Chaparé, anti-U.S.
Movimiento de Izquierda Revolucionario, MIR–Nueva Mayoría (MIR, MIR-NM)	MIR: young militants split from PDC. Name changed to MIR-NM in 1989, when joined by middle-class professionals and factions from

	MNR and the left. Provincial middle class, social democratic.
MIR–Bolivia Libre, Movimiento Bolivia Libre (MIR-BL, MBL)	Split from MIR in 1985, name change in 1986. Centrist, eastern region
Movimiento Nacionalista Revolucionario de Izquierda (MNRI)	Split from MNR. Left, workers. Principal party in UDP.
Movimiento Nacionalista Revolucionario Vanguardia, Conciencia de Patria (MNRV, CONDEPA)	Aymará, urban lower class and marginalized, recent migrants. La Paz and El Alto. Many members moved to CONDEPA after 1988.
Unión Cívica Solidaridad (UCS)	Conservative, populist, urban lower class and marginalized. Law and order.

[a]Competitive elections were held in 1978, 1979, and 1980, but the military prevented the winners from taking power until 1982. I count 1985 as the first unfettered election.

[b]P. Conservador disappeared prior to presuffrage period.

Bulgaria

Oligarchic period	1878–1901	Constitutional monarchy; limited participation; fraud
Formal suffrage extension	1878	Universal male
First competitive period	1901–26	Competitive elections; participation threshold passed[a]
Effective suffrage date	1901	
Current competitive period	1990–	

Main Political Parties (includes factions and descendants)	Presuffrage Average Vote (%)	Postsuffrage Average Vote (%)	Average Vote since 1985 (%)	Vote in Most Recent Election (%)
Oligarchic parties				
Liberal	59.2	67.6		
Conservative	29.2	12.7		
Presuffrage parties				
Agrarian Union	3.2	9.5	11.4	9.1
Postsuffrage parties				
Social Democrats		3.7	33.6	17.1
Later parties				
Union of Democratic Forces			26.0	9.1
Movement for Rights and Freedom			6.8	7.5
National Movement Simeon II			8.5	42.7
Bulgarian Euro-Left			1.3	1.0
Bulgarian Business Bloc			2.2	
Others	8.4	6.5	10.1	13.5

Elections included:

Presuffrage average vote	1894, 1899
Postsuffrage average vote	1901, 1902, 1908, 1911
Average vote since 1985	1990, 1991, 1994, 1997, 2001
Most recent election	June 17, 2001

Party interests

Liberal	Secular, republican, nationalist. Vote share is the total for many competing factions, including the Democrats, National-Liberals, Progressive Liberals, and Young Liberals (all factionalized among themselves).
Conservative	Clerical, monarchist, Russophile. Vote share is the total for competing factions, the National P., and Unionists.
Agrarian Union	Peasants. In current period, descendants include the People's Union (NS) and its factions.
Social Democrats	Urban workers, socialist. In current period, descendants include Bulgarian Social Democratic P. (BSDP) and Bulgarian Socialist P. (BSP).
Union of Democratic Forces (SDS)	Alliance of democratic parties in opposition to ex-communists, multiclass. In 1997–2001, partici-

	pated in United Democratic Forces, a coalition with NS.
Movement for Rights and Freedom (DPS)	Descendant of the Ethnic Turkish Party, which got a few votes in the pre- and postsuffrage period but never passed the 5% threshold.
National Movement Simeon II (NDS)	Monarchist
Bulgarian Euro-Left (BE)	Urban middle class, social democratic
Bulgarian Business Bloc (BBB)	Nationalist, free enterprise

Note: In contrast to other East European countries, Bulgaria's boundary changes did not occur at the same time as the actual suffrage extension and do not seem to have affected the party system. Bulgaria gained Eastern Rumelia in 1885, before widespread lower-class participation in politics. Other boundary changes occurred as a result of the Balkan Wars and World War I, but they had little effect on the party system. Bulgaria won Thrace in 1913 but only controlled it during one election. I can find no evidence, either in the country specialist literature or voting patterns, that Bulgaria's other losses—the Dobruja to Romania and a small western strip to Yugoslavia—affected the party system.

[a]Turnout in the towns rose beginning in 1901, and 50% of the enfranchised in the towns voted in the 1902 election (Kostadinova 1995, 25).

Chile

Oligarchical period	1858–1900	Limited participation
Formal suffrage extension	1874	Literate male
First competitive period	1900–1924	Participation threshold passed
Effective suffrage date	1900	Illiterate suffrage in 1970
Current competitive period	1989	Democratization

Main Political Parties (includes factions and descendants)	Presuffrage Average Seat Share[a]	Postsuffrage Average Seat Share[a]	Average Vote since 1985 (%)	Vote in Most Recent Election (%)
Oligarchic parties				
P. Conservador	34.6	24.3		
P. Liberal	33.5	18.0		
Descendants of PC and PL combined			16.7	13.8
P. Nacional (1)	1.8	10.2		
P. Radical	18.3	18.0	3.5	4.1
Presuffrage parties				
P. Liberal-Democrático	11.2	24.3		
Postsuffrage				
P. Demócrata	0.7	3.5		
Later parties				
P. Comunista de Chile			5.4	5.2
P. Socialista de Chile			8.3	10.0
P. por la Democracia			12.1	12.7
P. Demócrata Cristiano			23.8	18.9
Unión Democrática Independiente			15.4	25.2
Others		1.6	14.9	10.0

Elections included:

Presuffrage average seat share[a]	1891, 1894, 1897
Postsuffrage average seat share[a]	1900, 1903, 1906, 1909, 1912
Average vote since 1985	1989, 1993, 1997, 2001
Most recent election	January 16, 2001

Party interests

P. Conservador (PC)	Originally centralist, clerical, land, especially in central Chile; later also attracted votes from peasants and middle class. In 1966, P. Conservador, P. Liberal and other conservative elements formed P. Nacional (2). After 1989, these interests are represented mainly by Renovación Nacional, with a few votes going to P. Liberal and P. Nacional (2).
P. Liberal (PL)	Pragmatic secular, commercial, industrialists, land. Includes Doctrinario, Unionista and Aliancista factions. For current period, see above.
P. Nacional (1) (PN1)	Secular, centralist, banking, high bureaucracy; supported strong presidency

P. Radical (PR)	Secular, northern mining interests, middle class; favored decentralization. Over time, free public education, social welfare. Currently called P. Radical de Chile.
P. Liberal-Democrático (PLD)	Pragmatic secular, centralist; public officials, army officers, mining interests
P. Demócrata (PD)	Secular, middle class, urban workers, nitrate miners, domestic industrialists; protectionist, social welfare
P. Comunista de Chile (PCdeCh)	Secular, intellectuals, urban workers, and miners. In 1989, also includes P. Amplio de la Izquierda Socialista as a descendant.
P. Socialista de Chile (PSdeCh)	Secular, workers, and intellectuals. Includes votes for P. Socialista Chileno in 1989.
P. por la Democracia (PPD)	Moderate wing of the pre-1973 P. Socialista de Chile
P. Demócrata Cristiano (PDC)	Clerical, multiclass, reformist
Unión Democrática Independiente (UDI)	Centralist, neoliberal; officials and interests closely allied with Pinochet

[a]Seats are used because the cumulative vote system operating during this period renders voting data misleading.

Colombia

Oligarchic period	1849–1936	Limited suffrage; periods of violence and one-party rule
Formal suffrage extension	1853	Universal male[a]
First competitive period	1939–50	Universal male, competitive elections
Effective suffrage date	1939	
Current competitive period	1958–	Democratization;[b] 1978, full competition

Main Political Parties (includes factions and descendants)	Presuffrage Average Vote (%)	Postsuffrage Average Vote (%)	Average Vote since 1985 (%)	Vote in Most Recent Election (%)
Oligarchic parties				
P. Conservador	43.1	34.6	28.3	27.0
P. Liberal	56.8	63.9	53.6	54.0
Later parties				
Alianza Democrática M-19[c]			2.6	
Others		1.6	15.4	19.0

Elections included:

Presuffrage average vote	1931, 1933
Postsuffrage average vote	1939, 1941, 1943, 1945
Average vote since 1985	1986, 1990, 1991, 1994, 1998
Most recent election	March 8, 1998

Party interests

P. Conservador (PC)	Centralist, clerical, alliance of land, high clergy, and military; multiclass in twentieth century. Includes Movimiento de Salvación Nacional as descendant equivalent.
P. Liberal (PL)	Federalist, secular, free trade, antislavery; multiclass in twentieth century. Includes Nuevo Liberalismo as descendant equivalent.
Alianza Democrática M-19 (ADM-19)	Former revolutionaries, urban popular sector. In 1991, includes Frente Democrático, Frente Popular, and sectors of Unión Patriótica. Joined by Esperanza, Paz y Libertad and P. Revolucionario de los Trabajadores in 1994.

[a]In 1863, the power to establish suffrage laws was devolved to the states, and most introduced restrictions.

[b]Return to competitive elections and civilian government, but competition limited to the two traditional parties, between which legislative seats were divided equally regardless of the vote.

[c]The figures shown underestimate the vote for ADM-19 because sources lump the vote under "others" for some elections.

Costa Rica

Oligarchic period	1849–1936	Limited suffrage; indirect elections; public vote
Formal suffrage extension	1913	Universal male
First competitive period	1940–	Competitive elections; secret vote[b]
Effective suffrage date	1940	
Current competitive period	1940–	

Main Political Parties (includes factions and descendants)	Presuffrage Average Vote (%)	Postsuffrage Average Vote (%)	Average Vote since 1985 (%)	Vote in Most Recent Election (%)
Oligarchic parties				
P. Liberal, many factions	66.9	20.6	5.0	12.8
P. Conservador[c]				
Presuffrage parties				
P. Republicano Nacional	26.7	64.3	42.5	41.2
P. Comunista	1.3	3.4		
P. Reformista	5.1			
Postsuffrage parties				
P. Demócrata		11.7	0.3	1.2
P. Socialdemócrata/P. Liberación Nacional		3.0[d]	42.5	35.3
Later parties				
Fuerza Democrática			2.8	5.8
Others			6.9	3.7

Elections included:

Presuffrage average vote	1923, 1928, 1932, 1936 (presidential)
Postsuffrage average vote	1940, 1944, 1948 (presidential)
Average vote since 1985	1986, 1990, 1994, 1998
Most recent election	February 1, 1998

Party interests

P. Liberal (PL)	Secular, commercial and landowning (coffee). Total shown here combines the vote of several Liberal factions. P. Republicano, P. Unidad Nacional, and P. Nacional treated as factions or descendants of PL. Current vote share attributed to them is the combined vote of a large number of very small parties whose antecedents cannot be traced. They have been treated as remnants of the traditional parties to make certain they are not undercounted.
P. Conservador (PCon)	Clerical, land
P. Republicano Nacional (PRN)	Clerical, Christian reformist, middle class and workers. The contemporary P. Unidad Social Cristiana is treated as its descendant.
P. Comunista (PCom)	Socialist, urban and banana workers. Changed name to Bloque de Obreros y Campesinos, then to P. Vanguardia Popular.

P. Reformista (PR)	Clerical, reformist, workers
P. Demócrata (PD)	Land, coffee interests, extreme right
P. Socialdemócrata/P. Liberación Nacional (PSD/PLN)	Secular, reformist, middle class. Name changed to P. Liberación Nacional.
Fuerza Democrática (FD)	A leftist coalition in 1994–98 that includes P. del Progreso, Pueblo Unido (itself a coalition), and P. Revolucionario de los Trabajadores.

[a]Direct vote for president established in 1913.

[b]The secret ballot was introduced in principle in 1925, but its use did not become mandatory until September 1936 (after the February elections).

[c]Conservatives were defeated in battle early in the nineteenth century.

[d]PSD was founded in 1945 and did not run in the presidential election, but it won 8.9% of the seats in the Constituent Assembly elected in 1948. I have used that as a proxy measure of its support in that year and therefore consider it a postsuffrage party.

Ecuador

Oligarchic period	1861–1924	High illiteracy; illegal seizures of power; dictatorships
Formal suffrage extension	1861	Literate male
First competitive period	1947–63	Competitive elections; literacy threshold passed
Effective suffrage date	1947	
Current competitive period	1978–	Democratization; illiterate suffrage[a]

Main Political Parties (includes factions and descendants)	Presuffrage Average Vote (%)	Postsuffrage Average Vote[b] (%)	Average Vote since 1985 (%)	Vote in Most Recent Election (%)
Oligarchic parties				
P. Liberal Radical Ecuatoriano	27.4	17.1	4.5	
P. Conservador Ecuatoriano	50.1	26.9	3.7	1.8
Presuffrage parties				
P. Socialista Ecuatoriano	8.5	1.7	4.2	3.4
Postsuffrage parties				
Movimiento Cívico Democrático Nacional		5.5		
Frente Popular Democrático		3.0		
Concentración de Fuerzas Populares		6.5	24.0	19.6
Federación Nacional Velasquista — Acción Revolucionaria Nacionalista Ecuatoriana		10.8[c]		
Later parties				
P. Social Cristiano			23.9	21.9
Frente Radical Alfarista			3.6	3.0
Izquierda Democrática			12.7	12.3
Democracia Popular — Unión Demócrata Cristiana			11.7	24.3
Frente Amplio de Izquierda			1.9	0.8
Movimiento Popular Democrático			5.6	3.9
Movimiento Unidad Plurinacional Pachakutik — Nuevo País			1.4	2.5
Others	14.1	28.7	2.3	6.7

Elections included:

Presuffrage average vote	1933, 1940 (presidential)
Postsuffrage average vote	1947, 1950, 1952, 1954
Average vote since 1985	1986, 1988, 1990, 1992, 1994, 1996, 1998
Most recent election	May 31, 1998

Party interests

P. Liberal Radical Ecuatoriano (PLRE) — Secular, commercial, financial, coast. Descendants include the Coalición Institucionalista Demócrata (which became C. Nacional Re-

	publicana in 1985 and P. Republicano in 1986) and P. Democrático.
P. Conservador Ecuatoriano (PCE)	Clerical, land, highlands
P. Socialista Ecuatoriano (PSE)	Secular, intellectuals, some workers after World War II, socialist. Allied with FADI, 1996.
Movimiento Cívico Democrático Nacional (MCDN)	Alliance of dissident Liberals and opponents of the traditional parties. Supported Galo Plaza presidential campaign in 1948. Alianza Democrática Nacional, which supported the Larrea presidential campaign in 1952 and was made up of many of the same people, treated as descendant.
Frente Popular Democrático (FPD)	Temporary alliance of opponents of main parties
Concentración de Fuerzas Populares (CFP)	Guayaquil, popular classes. Descendants include P. Assad Bucaram, P. Roldosista Ecuatoriano, Pueblo, Cambio y Democracia, and Acción Popular Revolucionaria Ecuatoriana.
Federación Nacional Velasquista, Acción Revolucionaria Nacionalista Ecuatoriana (FNV/ARNE)	FNV: personalist vehicle of Velasco Ibarra. ARNE: Falange, Hispanidad, nationalism, promilitary.
P. Social Cristiano (PSC)	Clerical, upper and middle class, originally close ties to PCE. Rejuvenated by Febres Cordero as Frente de Reconstrucción Nacional, in alliance with Liberals, Conservatives, and the Coalición Institucionalista Demócrata. Conservative, free enterprise, coast.
Frente Radical Alfarista (FRA)	Multiclass reformist. Split from PLRE in 1978 over collaboration with military.
Izquierda Democrática (ID)	Middle class and workers, socialist, Quito and Guayaquil
Democracia Popular—Unión Demócrata Cristiana (DP)	Middle class, clerical, conservative, social Christian, Sierra and Oriente. Alliance of P. Democrático Cristiano (which split from Social Christians) and PCE splinter.
Frente Amplio de Izquierda (FADI)	Christian left. Former Unión Democrática Popular.
Movimiento Popular Democrático (MPD)	Students, intellectuals, leftist. Split from P. Comunista Marxista Leninista (itself a split from P. Comunista Ecuatoriano, which competed in presuffrage period but never got above 5% of the vote).
Movimiento Unidad Plurinacional Pachakutik—Nuevo País (MUPP-NP)	Indigenous party, joined by Freddy Ehlers, a TV personality. Ehlers (Nuevo País) left MUPP after 1996.

[a]Illiterates first voted in 1984.

[b]Data sources have large "others" sections.

[c]FNV/ARNE coalition got 43% of the presidential vote in 1952, but sources do not show it as having won any legislative seats that year. They show 57.1% of the vote going to "others," however. On the assumption that many of these others were Velasco supporters, I have attributed 43% of the 1952 legislative vote to FNV/ARNE and reduced the "others" category to 14.1% for calculating this average.

El Salvador

Oligarchic period	1911–31	Semicompetitive
Formal suffrage extension	1883	Universal male
First competitive period	1964–84	Flawed elections;[a] fraud
Effective suffrage date	1964	
Current competitive period	1989–	Competitive elections

Main Political Parties (includes factions and descendants)	Presuffrage Average Vote (%)	Postsuffrage Average Vote (%)	Average Vote since 1985 (%)	Vote in Most Recent Election (%)
Oligarchic parties				
P. Liberal (idealist faction)[b]	8.6			
P. Liberal (pragmatic faction)[b]	14.1			
P. Conservador[c]				
Presuffrage parties				
P. Laborista Salvadoreño	23.4			
P. Fraternal Progresista	4.0			
P. Revolucionario de Unificación Democrática	28.2	56.4	9.8	12.5
P. Acción Renovadora	21.8	8.8	0.5	
Postsuffrage parties				
Unión Democrática Nacionalista		1.5	0.5	
P. Demócrata Cristiano		31.9	26.3	9.1
Later parties				
Alianza Republicana Nacional			39.6	36.0
Frente Farabundo Martí para la Liberación Nacional			14.7	35.2
Convergencia Democrática			3.3	
Centro Democrático Unido			0.9	5.4
Others		1.4	4.3	1.7

Elections included:

Presuffrage average vote	1931, 1950 (presidential)
Postsuffrage average vote	1964, 1966, 1968, 1970
Average vote since 1985	1985, 1988, 1991, 1994, 1997, 2000
Most recent election	March 12, 2000

Party interests

P. Liberal (idealist faction)	Decentralist, secular, free market, coffee growers and exporters, artisans. Idealist Liberal descendants included P. Evolución Nacional and P. Constitucionalista.
P. Liberal (pragmatic faction)	Centralist, state intervention, industrialization, middle class and public employees. P. Zaratista was a descendant of the pragmatic PL.
P. Conservador (PC)	Clerical, land
P. Laborista Salvadoreño (PLS)	Peasants, radicalized workers, and indigenous; social welfare, land reform

P. Fraternal Progresista (PFP)	Popular sector, populist
P. Revolucionario de Unificación Democrática (PRUD)	Military-civilian coalition; public employees, retired military, traditional labor leaders, agricultural workers. Succeeded by P. de Conciliación Nacional. P. Republicano de Evolución Nacional treated as descendant.
P. Acción Renovadora (PAR)	Upper class, civilian opposition to military rule
Unión Democrática Nacionalista (UDN)	Socialist, dissident reformist officers, unions, agrarian leaders, professors and students
P. Demócrata Cristiano (PDC)	Clerical, reformist, middle class, professionals, teachers, white-collar employees, urban workers, some peasants
Alianza Republicana Nacional (ARENA)	Clerical, land, far right, anticommunist
Frente Farabundo Martí para la Liberación Nacional (FMLN)	Former revolutionary left; workers, peasants, intellectuals. In 1994, allied with CD and Movimiento Nacionalista Revolucionario.
Convergencia Democrática (CD)	Alliance of Christian and secular social democrats. Includes Movimiento Popular Cristiano, P. Social Demócrata (PSD), and UDN.
Centro Democrático Unido (CDU)	Alliance of reformist left. In 1999, alliance of CD, P. Democrático, and P. Popular Laborista; in 2000, of CD and PSD.

[a]Competition during this period was limited by the military, and fraud was widespread. Nevertheless, after the introduction of proportional representation in 1963, opposition parties were able to win seats in the legislature, and parties developed that have shown some capacity for survival over time.

[b]The Idealist and Pragmatic wings of the Liberal Party were long-standing rivals to which strong loyalties were felt, not primarily personalist factions like those in so many of the oligarchic parties in other countries.

[c]Conservatives had disappeared by the early twentieth century.

Greece

Oligarchic period	1864–1911	Constitutional monarchy
Formal suffrage extension	1822	Universal male
First competitive period	1910–36[a]	Also 1950–67; flawed elections
Effective suffrage date	1910	
Current competitive period	1974–	Democratization

Main Political Parties (includes factions and descendants)	Presuffrage Average Vote[a] (%)	Postsuffrage Average Seat Share[b] (%)	Average Vote since 1985 (%)	Vote in Most Recent Election (%)
Oligarchic parties				
New P.	not used			
National P.	not used	30.3		
Presuffrage parties				
Liberal P. (Venizelos)	not used	62.7		
People's P.	not used			
Communist Party of Greece	not used	1.2	10.4	8.7
Postsuffrage parties				
Agrarians		1.2		
Later parties				
Pan Hellenic Socialist Movement			42.3	43.8
New Democracy			42.6	42.7
Democratic Social Movement			1.0	2.6
Political Spring			1.1	
Others		4.6	2.4	2.2

Elections included:

Presuffrage average vote	Not included[a]
Postsuffrage average seat share[b]	1926, 1928, 1933
Average vote since 1985	1985, 1989 (1), 1989 (2), 1990, 1993, 1996, 2000
Most recent election	April 9, 2000

Party interests

New P. (NK)	Secular, commercial, reformist, cautious economic policies, westernizing, moderate about Greek expansionism. Founded and led by Trikoupis.
National P. (EK)	Proclerical, expansionist economic and foreign policy, nationalist. Led by Deliyannis.
Liberal P. (Venizelos) (KP)	Republican, supported by immigrants and recently acquired territories and modernizing capitalist middle class; social reform, land reform, Anglophile. Also called Progressive Republican.
People's P. (LK)	Royalist (or Populist), proclerical, supported by Greek heartland, lower middle class, anticapitalist, xenophobic
Communist Party of Greece (KKE)	Communist, urban workers and intellectuals. Includes votes for Coalition of the Left (SIN).
Agrarians	Thessaly

Pan Hellenic Socialist Movement (PASOK)	Social democratic, middle class and workers, state interventionist
New Democracy (ND)	Centrist, neoliberal, upper and middle class
Democratic Social Movement (DIKKI)	Socialist
Political Spring (POLA)	Modern conservative

[a]Because of boundary changes and the enormous exchange of populations during the early part of this period, only elections from 1926 on are used in this study.

[b]Vote share data are incomplete in data sources used for this period.

Guatemala

Oligarchic period	1871–1931	Dictatorship; illegal seizures of power
Formal suffrage extension	1921	Literate male, high illiteracy
First competitive period	1944–54	Competitive elections
Effective suffrage date	1945	1965, universal suffrage[a]
Current competitive period	1985–	Competitive elections[b]

Main Political Parties (includes factions and descendants)	Presuffrage Average Vote (%)	Postsuffrage Average Vote (%)		Average Seat Share since 1985[c] (%)	Vote in Most Recent Election (%)
		Seats	Pres		
Oligarchic parties					
P. Conservador and P. Liberal combined	7.1	14.5		2.6	
P. Liberal Progresista				4.3	
P. Conservador, P. Liberal, and P. Liberal Progresista combined			18.7		
Presuffrage parties					
F. Popular Libertador		21.1	5.5		
Renovación Nacional		15.1	65.4	0.9	
F. Popular Libertador and Renovación Nacional combined	86.3				
P. Acción Revolucionaria[d]		32.7			
P. Socialista[d]		4.0			
Postsuffrage parties					
P. Popular			7.1		
P. Comunista		4.1			
Unión Patriótica		2.1			
P. de Integridad Nacional		1.1			
Later parties					
Democracia Cristiana Guatemalteca				19.9	
Unión del Centro Nacional				15.9	1.0
Movimiento de Acción Solidaria				3.9	2.1
P. Democrático de Co-operación Nacional—P. Revolucionario				2.8	
Frente Democrático Nueva Guatemala				1.9	1.3
Alianza Nación Nueva				2.0	12.3
P. de Avanzada Nacional				23.9	30.3
Frente Republicano Guatemalteco				20.2	47.8
Alianza Nacional				0.6	
Others	6.7	5.2	3.2	1.0	5.2

Elections included:

Presuffrage average vote	1944 presidential
Postsuffrage average vote	1948, 1950, 1953 (seats); 1950 (presidential)
Average vote since 1985	1985, 1990, 1995, 1999 (seats)[c]
Most recent election	November 7, 1999 (presidential, first-round)

Party interests

P. Conservador (PC)	Clerical, anticommercial. During pre- and postsuffrage period, included in the alliance of F. Nacional Democrático and P. Demócrata Central, P. Republicano-Democrático, and various opposition alliances. Also included in Unión Nacional Electoral, along with P. Unidad Democrática, P. Unificación Anticomunista and REDENCIÓN. Current descendant equivalents: Unión Nacionalista Organizada and Movimiento de Liberación Nacional (previously Movimiento Democrático Nacionalista: clerical, planters, far right, free enterprise, violently anticommunist).
P. Liberal (PL)	Secular, free market. During pre- and postsuffrage period, same as above.
P. Liberal Progresista (PLP)	Ubico support party. Centrist, secular, upper class, state interventionist. REDENCIÓN, electoral vehicle of Ydígoras Fuentes, treated as descendant equivalent. Included in Unión Nacional Electoral (see above). Current descendants: P. Institucional Democrático (party of the military government, state interventionist, support from military, bureaucracy, commercial) and Central Auténtico Nacionalista.
F. Popular Libertador (FPL)	Nationalist left and center-left, students, middle class. Part of Arévalo coalition, F. Unido de Partidos Arevalistas (FUPA) in 1944 presidential election. Reported seat share includes parties that split from FPL but remained allied with it, such as P. Social Revolucionario and P. Revolucionario de Unión Nacional.
Renovación Nacional (RN)	Center and center-left, commercial, middle class. Part of FUPA in 1944 presidential election and Frente Electoral, coalition supporting Arbenz in 1950. Current descendants: P. Revolucionario (the fragment of Arévalo supporters allowed to participate during military rule: middle class, reformist), Frente Unido de la Revolución, and P. Socialista Democrático (PSD).
P. Acción Revolucionaria (PAR)	Merger of FPL and RN. RN withdrew from PAR in 1946 and FPL withdrew in 1947, but PAR continued. Peasant support.
P. Socialista (PS)	Base in peasant organizations; split from PAR
P. Popular (PP)	"Neo-Peronist" center-left opposition to Arbenz; antimilitary

P. Comunista (PC)	Urban intellectuals, labor. Split from PAR in 1950; PC changed name to P. Guatemalteco del Trabajo (PGT) in 1952.
Unión Patriótica (UP)	Opposition to Arévalo and Arbenz, electoral vehicle for Marroquín
P. de Integridad Nacional (PIN)	Regional party from Quetzaltenango, Arbenz's home state. Arbenz vehicle.
Democracia Cristiana Guatemalteca (DCG)	Clerical, social democratic, urban middle class, peasants
Unión del Centro Nacional (UCN)	Centrist, free enterprise, modern business, urban. Electoral vehicle for Carpio.
Movimiento de Acción Solidaria (MAS)	Modern conservative, evangelicals; renamed Acción Reconciliadora Democrática (ARDE) in 1996. Electoral vehicle for Serrano.
P. Democrático de Cooperación Nacional – P. Revolucionario (PDCN-PR)	Alliance of PDCN (modern conservatives, evangelicals, personalist vehicle of Serrano) and PR (a descendant of RN)
Frente Democrático Nueva Guatemala (FDNG)	Peasants and indigenous; peace, demilitarization, indigenous rights, land reform. Alliance of populist organizations, unions, and various RN descendants.
Alianza Nación Nueva (ANN)	Coalition of Desarrollo Integral Auténtico (organized by community leaders from Sacatepéquez and Chimaltenango, base in rural NGOs and university, human rights, peace) and Unidad Revolucionaria Nacional Guatemalteca (formerly guerrillas and PGT). FDNG was also part of ANN but left in 1999. Implementation of peace accords.
P. de Avanzada Nacional (PAN)	Urban middle class, modern business, sugar, neoliberal, Guatemala City. Electoral vehicle for Arzú.
Frente Republicano Guatemalteco (FRG)	Military, Protestants, peasants in scorched-earth areas, export sector. Support vehicle for Rios Montt.
Alianza Nacional (AN)	Alliance of UCN, DCG, and PSD

[a]Beginning with the 1945 constitution, voting was obligatory and secret for literates but optional and public for illiterates.

[b]Elections have been honest, but the left side of the political spectrum was legally proscribed until the 1999 elections.

[c]Legislative elections are two-tiered in Guatemala, and data sources differ in how they report these results. For some years, total vote share is reported; for others, separate national and district vote shares are reported. For the most recent elections, only seat share is available. Seat share is used to indicate support in the current period in order to keep results comparable across elections.

[d]PAR and P. Socialista are listed as presuffrage parties, even though they did not exist prior to 1945, because they were factions of the presuffrage FPL-RN coalition that elected Arévalo in 1944.

Honduras

Oligarchic period	1876–1924	Illegal seizures of power; dictatorship
Formal suffrage extension	1894	Universal male
First competitive period	1924–32	Competitive elections
Effective suffrage date	1924	
Current competitive period	1981	Democratization

Main Political Parties (includes factions and descendants)	Presuffrage Average Vote (%)	Postsuffrage Average Vote (%)	Average Vote since 1985 (%)	Vote in Most Recent Election (%)
Oligarchic parties				
P. Nacional	33.1	49.6	46.9	52.2
P. Liberal	66.9	49.9	48.4	44.3
Others			4.7	3.6

Elections included:

Presuffrage average vote	1919, 1923
Postsuffrage average vote	1928, 1932
Average vote since 1985	1985, 1989, 1993, 1997, 2001
Most recent election	November 25, 2001

Party interests

P. Nacional (PN) Clerical, centralist, protectionist. Vote share includes P. Nacional Democrático and P. Nacional de Honduras (current name).

P. Liberal (PL) Secular, multiclass. Vote share includes P. Liberal Republicano, P. Liberal Constitucionalista, and P. Liberal de Honduras (current name).

Mexico

Oligarchic period	1857–1912	Violence; dictatorship; indirect elections
Formal suffrage extension	1857	Universal
First competitive period	1967–88	Flawed elections; fraud
Effective suffrage date	1967	
Current competitive period	1988–	Competitive elections

Main Political Parties (includes factions and descendants)	Presuffrage Average Vote (%)	Postsuffrage Average Vote (%)	Average Vote since 1985 (%)	Vote in Most Recent Election (%)
Oligarchic parties				
P. Conservador[a]				
P. Liberal[b]				
Presuffrage parties				
P. Revolucionario Institucional	88.3	82.4	48.0	37.8
P. Acción Nacional	9.8	13.0	25.4	39.2
Later parties				
P. Popular Socialista			2.4	
P. Auténtico de la Revolución Mexicana			2.0	0.7
P. de Frente Cardinista de Reconstrucción Nacional			3.0	
P. Revolucionario Democrático			14.0	19.1
Others	2.0	4.7	5.8	3.1

Elections included:

Presuffrage average vote	1958, 1961, 1964
Postsuffrage average vote	1967, 1970, 1973, 1976
Average vote since 1985	1988, 1991, 1994, 1997, 2000
Most recent election	July 7, 2000

Party interests

P. Conservador (PC)	Centralist, clerical, protectionist, developmentalist
P. Liberal (PL)	Federalist, secular, free trade
P. Revolucionario Institucional (PRI)	Secular, officialist, multiclass, state interventionist until the 1980s
P. Acción Nacional (PAN)	Clerical, upper and middle class, free market. In 2000, PAN led an alliance with small parties, Alianza por Cambio.
P. Popular Socialista (PPS)	Dissident labor, communist. Competed in pre- and postsuffrage periods but did not pass 5% threshold until current period.
P. Auténtico de la Revolución Mexicana (PARM)	PRI dissidents. Competed in pre- and postsuffrage periods but did not pass 5% threshold.
P. de Frente Cardinista de Reconstrucción Nacional (PFCRN)	Dissident labor and intellectuals. Formed from P. Socialista de los Trabajadores.

P. Revolucionario Democrático (PRD)	Multiclass populist, state interventionist. Alliance of PRI dissidents with P. Mexicano Socialista (formed by merger of P. Socialista Unificado de México—itself an electoral alliance of P. Comunista Mexicano, P. Mexicano de los Trabajadores, P. del Pueblo Mexicano, P. Socialista Revolucionario, and Movimiento de Acción y Unidad Socialista—and P. Mexicano de los Trabajadores) and the Frente Democrático Nacional coalition. In 2000, PRD led an alliance with small parties, Alianza por México.

[a]Defeated in battle in 1866 and disappeared within a decade.
[b]Dominated Mexican politics from 1876 to the Revolution in 1917.

Nicaragua

Oligarchic period	1858–93	Semicompetitive; indirect elections
Formal suffrage extension	1893	Universal male
First competitive period	1928–74	Flawed elections; fraud
Effective suffrage date	1928	
Current competitive period	1990–	Democratization

Main Political Parties (includes factions and descendants)	Presuffrage Average Vote[a] (%)	Postsuffrage Average Vote[b] (%)	Average Vote since 1985 (%)	Vote in Most Recent Election (%)
Oligarchic parties				
P. Liberal Nacionalista	not used	58.0		
P. Conservador	not used	42.0		
Descendants of P. Liberal Nacionalista and P. Conservador, combined			54.0	57.8
Later parties				
Frente Sandinista de Liberación Nacional			39.9	42.2
Others			5.9	

Elections included:

Presuffrage average vote	Not included[a]
Postsuffrage average vote	1928, 1932 (presidential)[b]
Average vote since 1985	1990, 1996, 2001
Most recent election	November 4, 2001

Party interests

P. Liberal Nacionalista (PLN)	Secular, free trade, commercial; under Somoza, developmentalist, multiclass. Descendants include P. Liberal and P. Liberal Independiente de Unión Nacional; included in Unión Nacional Opositora (UNO), Alianza Liberal (AL), and P. Liberal Constitucionalista (PLC).
P. Conservador (PC)	Clerical, protectionist, land and commercial. Descendants include P. Conservador de Nicaragua and P. Conservador Demócrata de Nicaragua; included in UNO, AL, and PLC.
Frente Sandinista de Liberación Nacional (FSLN)	Workers and peasants, originally much of the middle class, socialist

[a]Presuffrage elections are excluded from this study because of rampant electoral fraud.

[b]Postsuffrage legislative vote share is not available. The 1928 and 1932 presidential elections are considered the only fair Nicaraguan elections prior to 1990. An alternative indicator—average seat share for the 1928, 1930, 1932, and 1934 Chamber of Deputies—is 35% for the PLN and 65% for the PC.

Panama

Oligarchic period	1903–30	Semicompetitive elections
Formal suffrage extension	1904	Universal male; direct elections in 1920
First competitive period	1932–40	Competitive elections; fraud; illegal seizures of power
Effective suffrage date	1932	
Current competitive period	1994–	Competitive elections

Main Political Parties (includes factions and descendants)	Presuffrage Average Seat Share[a] (%)	Postsuffrage Average Seat Share[a] (%)	Average Vote since 1985[b] (%)	Vote in Most Recent Election[b] (%)
Oligarchic parties				
P. Conservador	20.7	8.3		
P. Liberal	73.9	54.2	13.7	9.7
Postsuffrage parties				
P. Nacional Revolucionario		27.1	19.9	25.4
Democratic P.	1.1	6.3		
Agrarian P.	1.1	1.0		
Unionist P.		1.0		
Socialist P.		1.0		
Later parties				
P. Revolucionario Democrático			34.8	46.7
P. Demócrata Cristiano			6.7	7.1
P. Solidaridad			6.0	5.5
Movimiento de Renovación Nacional			4.0	1.4
P. Renovación Civilista			3.5	1.4
Movimiento Papa Egoró			4.9	
Others	3.3	1.0	6.4	2.8

Elections included:

Presuffrage average seat share[a]	1924, 1928
Postsuffrage average seat share[a]	1932, 1936, 1940
Average vote since 1985	1994, 1999[b]
Most recent election	May 2, 1999

Party interests

P. Conservador (PC)	Inherited from Colombia, centralist, clerical, landlords. From 1916 on, main competition among Liberal factions.
P. Liberal (PL)	Inherited from Colombia, secular, urban, commercial. Seat share includes all Liberal factions, reform Liberals, national Liberals, P. Liberal Renovador, P. Liberal Doctrinario, and P. Liberal Doctrinario Democrático. Currently includes P. Liberal Nacional, MOLIRENA, and P. Liberal Auténtico.

P. Nacional Revolucionario (PNR)	Popular classes, anti-U.S., racist, xenophobic; electoral vehicle for Arias. P. Arnulfista, main party in Unión por Panamá (UP) alliance (1999), treated as descendant.
Democratic P.	Reformist multiclass
Agrarian P.	Ephemeral
Unionist P.	Ephemeral
Socialist P. (PS)	Socialist
P. Revolucionario Democrático (PRD)	Officialist, multiclass, populist, allied with military, nationalist. Main party in Nueva Nación (NN) alliance (1999).
P. Demócrata Cristiano (PDC)	Clerical, urban middle class, antimilitary. Main party in Acción Opositora (AO) alliance (1999).
P. Solidaridad (P Sol)	Centrist, nationalist. Participated in NN (1999).
Movimiento de Renovación Nacional (MORENA)	Business interests, pro-U.S. Participated in UP alliance (1999).
P. Renovación Civilista (PRC)	Antimilitary, centrist. Participated in AO (1999).
Movimiento Papa Egoró (Papa Egoró)	Indigenous, green, support in urban slums. (Name means "Mother Earth" in the indigenous Emera language.)

[a]Vote share is not available for pre- or postsuffrage periods.

[b]1999 vote shares are estimates. For 1999, vote is given for alliances only. Seat breakdown, however, is by party. For the estimate used here, I attribute to each party the share of the total alliance vote equivalent to its share of the total alliance seats.

Paraguay

Oligarchic period	1870–1936	Indirect elections; illegal seizures of power
Formal suffrage extension	1870	Universal; direct elections since 1940
First competitive period	1968–73	Semicompetitive elections
Effective suffrage date	1968	
Current competitive period	1993–	Democratization

Main Political Parties (includes factions and descendants)	Presuffrage Average Vote[a] (%)	Postsuffrage Average Vote (%)	Average Vote since 1985 (%)	Vote in Most Recent Election (%)
Oligarchic parties				
P. Colorado	not used	78.2	51.8	53.8
P. Liberal	not used	20.6	37.3[b]	
Later parties				
Encuentro Nacional			9.7[b]	
Alliance of PLRA (descendant of PL) and EN				42.7[b]
Others		1.3	0.3	0.5

Elections included:

Presuffrage average vote	Not included[a]
Postsuffrage average vote	1968, 1973
Average vote since 1985	1993, 1998
Most recent election	May 10, 1998

Party interests

P. Colorado (PC)	Centralist, clerical, officialist party under Stroessner. Currently, official name is Asociación Nacional Republicana.
P. Liberal (PL)	Decentralist, secular. Includes P. Liberal Radical and P. Liberal Radical Auténtico.
Encuentro Nacional (EN)	Social democratic, young urban middle-class support.

[a]Presuffrage average not recorded because of limitations on competition during the authoritarian period preceding 1967.

[b]In 1998, P. Liberal Radical Auténtico, a descendant of the PL, and EN formed an electoral alliance. The calculation of the current average attributes the 1998 vote to the two parties according to each party's share of their combined vote in 1993, when they competed separately.

Peru

Oligarchic period	1872–1931	Limited suffrage; illegal seizures of power
Formal suffrage extension	1931	Literate male
First competitive period	1939–45	Competitive elections
Effective suffrage date	1939	
Current competitive period	1980–	Democratization; illiterate suffrage

Main Political Parties (includes factions and descendants)	Presuffrage Average Vote[a] (%) Seats	Presuffrage Average Vote[a] (%) Pres	Postsuffrage Average Vote[b] (%)	Average Vote since 1985 (%)	Vote in Most Recent Election (%)
Oligarchic parties					
P. Civilista					
P. Constitucional	18.2				
P. Demócrata	8.2				
P. Liberal					
Combined oligarchic parties and descendants		13.8	5.6		
Presuffrage parties					
P. Democrático Reformista	71.4		5.6		
Unión Revolucionaria		50.8	16.5		
Alianza Popular Revolucionaria Americana[c]		35.4	33.5	22.2	19.7
Concentración Nacional de Partidos			38.8		
P. Comunista Peruano[d]	NA			0.1	
Later parties					
CAMBIO 90, Nueva Mayoría, Perú 2000				23.3	4.8
Frente Democrático				6.0	
Acción Popular				3.7	4.2
Partido Popular Cristiano				2.8	
Izquierda Socialista				1.1	
Izquierda Unida				7.3	
Frente Independiente Moralizador				6.0	11.0
Perú Posible				9.9	26.3
Somos Perú				2.6	5.8
Unidad Nacional				2.8	13.8
Others	2.3			12.3	14.4

Elections included:

Presuffrage average vote	1924, 1929 (seats), 1931 (presidential)
Postsuffrage average vote	1939, 1945 (presidential)[b]
Average vote since 1985	1985, 1990, 1995, 2000, 2001
Most recent election	April 8, 2001

Party interests

P. Civilista (P Civil) — Decentralization, secular, civilianist, modern plantations, mining, finance, manufacturing, Lima. Major party in 1872–1915 but did not run separate presidential candidates in later years.

P. Constitucional (P Const)	Centrist, church-state status quo, protectionist, nationalist, electoral vehicle for military
P. Demócrata (PD)	Clerical, middle class and artisans, interior, Arequipa
P. Liberal (PL)	Extremely anticlerical, free market
Combined oligarchic parties	P. Constitucional Renovador del Perú and Acción Republicana, which ran in the presuffrage presidential elections, treated as descendants of the combined oligarchic parties
P. Democrático Reformista (PDR)	Clerical, developmentalist, social reforms, protectionist. Leguía support vehicle.
Unión Revolucionaria (UR)	Maintenance of church-state status quo, developmentalist, social reforms, integration of indigenous, balanced budget and stable money, nationalist, decentralization. Electoral vehicle for Sánchez Cerro.
Alianza Popular Revolucionaria Americana (APRA)	Advanced social reforms, developmentalist, state interventionist, land reform, multiclass, northern region.[c]
Concentración Nacional de Partidos (CNP)	Coalition to elect Prado. Twelve parties, including PCP, a faction of UR, and Coalición Conservadora. (APRA was illegal, but APRA voters supported Prado in return for his promise to relegalize the party.)
P. Comunista Peruano (PCP)	Workers, miners, intellectuals. Communist.
CAMBIO 90, Nueva Mayoria, Perú 2000 (C90, NM, P2000)	Multiclass, populist, neoliberal. Fujimori electoral vehicles.
Frente Democrático (FD)	Upper and middle class, neoliberal. Vargas Llosa electoral vehicle. Alliance of AP, PPC, Movimiento Libertad, and Solidaridad y Democracia.
Acción Popular (AP)	Moderate reformist, educated urban, middle class, southern region. Belaúnde electoral vehicle.
Partido Popular Cristiano (PPC)	Clerical, upper and middle class, Lima
Izquierda Socialista (IS)	Alliance of leftist parties, socialist
Izquierda Unida (IU)	Unions, social movements. Alliance of leftist parties.
Frente Independiente Moralizador (FIM)	Populist, anticorruption
Perú Posible (PP)	Multiclass, populist. Toledo electoral vehicle.
Somos Perú (SP)	Centrist, especially in Lima. Electoral vehicle for Andrade Carmona.
Unidad Nacional (UN)	Christian, center-right, alliance of PPC and Unión de Centro Democrático.

[a]The presuffrage period includes both the end of the Leguía administration and the 1931 presidential election, and the party system changed dramatically between the two. For this reason, seat share (legislative vote share by party is not available) during the last years of the Leguía government and presidential vote share for 1931 (no legislative elections were held until 1939) are used as the basis for assessing the strength of the presuffrage parties.

[b]Data sources for legislative results (even Peruvian newspapers at that time) show candidates elected but do not indicate their party affiliations.

[c]APRA was proscribed during part of the presuffrage period but was nevertheless politically active and highly influential.

[d]The PCP is included here as a presuffrage party, even though information about its seat share in the legislature is unavailable, because the literature includes descriptions of it as having elected deputies in both the Constituent Assembly of 1931 and the legislature of 1945.

Portugal

Oligarchic period	1822–1910	Constitutional monarchy
Formal suffrage extension	1911[a]	
First competitive period	1915–26	Literate male; flawed elections
Effective suffrage date	1915	
Current competitive period	1974–	Democratization

Main Political Parties (includes factions and descendants)	Presuffrage Average Vote (%)	Postsuffrage Average Seat Share (%)	Average Vote since 1985 (%)	Vote in Most Recent Election (%)
Oligarchic parties				
P. Regenerador and P. Progressista,[b] combined	n/a	2.4		
Presuffrage parties				
P. Republicano Português[c]	n/a	88.7		
Postsuffrage parties				
P. Socialista Português		2.5	32.1	44.1
P. Católico		2.2		
União dos Interesses Econômicos		1.2		
Later parties				
P. Social Demócrata			39.3	32.3
Coligação Democrática Unitária			10.8	9.0
P. Popular			7.2	8.3
P. Renovador Democrático			4.6	
Bloco de Esquerda			0.5	2.4
Others		3.0	4.6	4.0

Elections included:

Presuffrage average vote	Not available
Postsuffrage average seat share	1915, 1919, 1921, 1922, 1925
Average vote since 1985	1985, 1987, 1991, 1995, 1999
Most recent election	October 10, 1999

Party interests

P. Regenerador (PR) — Secular, constitutional monarchy, land and commercial. By the end of the monarchy, it had split into several factions. Causa Monárquica treated as descendant equivalent during postsuffrage period.

P. Progressista (PP) — Secular, constitutional monarchy, land and commercial, broader suffrage. By the end of the monarchy, it had split into several factions.

P. Republicano Português (PRP) — Secular, republican, middle class. Split into three factions shortly after the 1910 revolution: P. Democrático, P. Republicano Evolucionista, and União Republicana. Later descendants include Acção de Reconstitução Nacional, P. Governamentais, and Esquerda Democrática.

	Conjunção Republicano Socialista (CRS) included PRP interests, along with others.
P. Socialista Português (PSP)	Socialist, originally working class in Lisbon and Oporto. PSP interests included in CRS, along with others. Current name: P. Socialista.
P. Católico (PC)	Clerical, middle and upper class
União dos Interesses Econômicos (UIE)	Land, commercial, finance, procapitalist
P. Social Demócrata (PSD)	Centrist, multiclass
Coligação Democrática Unitária (CDU)	Communist and green. Alliance of P. Comunista Português and Os Verdes.
P. Popular (PP)	Free market, upper and middle class. PP is the former Coligação Democrática Social.
P. Renovador Democrático (PRD)	Nationalist, right, anti-EU
Bloco de Esquerda (BE)	Communist

[a]Suffrage was extended to literate males in 1822, but literacy was so restricted that only 1 percent of the population could vote. The 1911 constitution gave the vote to literate males and heads of households, and although some restrictions were subsequently reimposed, over 40 percent of adult males remained eligible to vote (calculated from Oliveira Marques 1978, 610).

[b]P. Regenerador and P. Progressista were both descendants of the early P. Liberal. Conservatives were defeated in the mid-nineteenth century and disappeared. Election results for the presuffrage period are unavailable, but these parties and their factions won about 90 percent of seats.

[c]Complete election results are unavailable for the presuffrage period, but literature reports that PRP won about 10 percent of the seats in the 1908 and 1910 parliamentary elections.

Uruguay

Oligarchic period	1875–1918	Indirect elections
Formal suffrage extension	1918	Universal; direct elections
First competitive period	1919–73	Competitive elections
Effective suffrage date	1919	
Current competitive period	1984–	Democratization

Main Political Parties (includes factions and descendants)	Presuffrage Average Vote	Postsuffrage Average Vote	Average Vote since 1985	Vote in Most Recent Election
Oligarchic parties				
Lemas Colorados/P. Colorado	59.7	49.9	31.4	31.3
Lemas Blancos/P. Nacional	36.3	46.7	30.5	21.3
Presuffrage parties				
P. General Fructuoso Rivera	2.9			
Later parties				
Encuentro Progresista (includes Frente Amplio)[a]			30.2	38.5
Nuevo Espacio			6.2	4.4
Others	1.0	3.4	0.2	

Elections included:

Presuffrage average vote	1907, 1913, 1917
Postsuffrage average vote	1919, 1922, 1925, 1928
Average vote since 1985	1989, 1994, 1999
Most recent election	October 31, 1999

Party interests

Lemas Colorados/P. Colorado (PC)	Centralist, Montevideo; in twentieth century, multiclass
Lemas Blancos/P. Nacional (PN)	Federalist, land, interior; in twentieth century, multiclass
P. General Fructuoso Rivera (G. Rivera)	Personalist vehicle
Encuentro Progresista (includes Frente Amplio) (EP)	Middle class and labor, Montevideo, social democratic
Nuevo Espacio (NE)	Intellectuals and labor, Montevideo, left

[a]Frente Amplio competed in 1989 and 1994. It was part of Encuentro Progresista in 1999.

Venezuela

Oligarchic period	1935–45	Semicompetitive
Formal suffrage extension	1858	Literate male
First competitive period	1958–[a]	Competitive elections
Effective suffrage date	1947	Universal
Current competitive period	1958–	Democratization

Main Political Parties (includes factions and descendants)	Presuffrage Average Vote[b]	Postsuffrage Average Vote	Average Vote since 1985[c]	Seat Share in Most Recent Election[c]
Oligarchic parties				
P. Liberal[d]	n/a			
Presuffrage parties				
Acción Democrática[b]	n/a	45.5	30.6	19.1
Postsuffrage parties				
Movimiento Electoral del Pueblo		3.2	0.6	
Comité de Organización Política Electoral Independiente		19.4	22.1	4.5
Unión Republicana Democrática		14.4	0.6	
Cruzada Cívica Nacionalista		2.7		
Frente Democrático Popular		3.7		
Independientes Pro Frente Nacional		3.3		
P. Comunista Venezolano		2.5	0.2	
Later parties				
Convergencia Nacional			5.3	
La Causa Radical			8.6	3.0
Movimiento V República			6.6	46.1
Movimiento al Socialismo			10.1	12.7
Proyecto Venezuela			3.3	4.2
Primero Justicia				3.0
Others		5.2	12.3	7.3

Elections included:

Presuffrage average vote	Not included[a]
Postsuffrage average vote	1947, 1958, 1963, 1968
Average vote since 1985	1988, 1993, 1998[c]
Most recent election	July 30, 2000 (seats)[c]

Party interests

P. Liberal (PL)	Centrist, secular, upper class, developmentalist, officialist
Acción Democrática (AD)	Secular, multiclass, populist
Movimiento Electoral del Pueblo (MEP)	Social democratic, originally left wing of AD. Part of Patriotic Pole (PP) in 1998.
Comité de Organización Política Electoral Independiente (COPEI)	Clerical, middle class
Unión Republicana Democrática (URD)	Former supporters of Medina Angarita government; free market, close to military, populist

Cruzada Cívica Nacionalista (CCN)	Conservative, military, supporters of former dictator Pérez Jiménez
Frente Democrático Popular (FDP)	Electoral vehicle for Admiral Larrazábal
Independientes Pro Frente Nacional (IPFN)	Electoral vehicle for Uslar Pietri
P. Comunista Venezolano (PCV)	Secular, labor, intellectuals; part of PP 1998
Convergencia Nacional (CN)	Multiclass populist alliance of a faction of COPEI, MAS, MEP, and thirteen tiny parties. Electoral vehicle for Caldera.
La Causa Radical (LCR)	Independent labor, support especially in industrial areas of Guyana and Bolívar
Movimiento V República (MVR)	Chávez supporters, lower and middle class, populist; part of PP in 1998
Movimiento al Socialismo (MAS)	Socialist (originally split from PCV), now left wing of Chávez supporters. Part of PP in 1998.
Proyecto Venezuela (PV)	Middle class reformist, Carabobo region. Electoral vehicle for Salas.
Primero Justicia (PJ)	Reformist opposition to Chávez

[a]Competitive elections were held between 1946 and 1948, but this period is not long enough to be used here. See coding scheme.

[b]Before 1947, Venezuela had indirect elections for both Congress and the president, so no presuffrage results are available for either office. In 1942, however, in the last election under the old regime, government candidates won 70 percent of the municipal council races they contested and 94.7 percent of seats in state legislative assemblies. AD was the best organized of the opposition forces, and it is therefore listed as a presuffrage party.

[c]Vote share data are not available for the most recent legislative election.

[d]Conservatives were defeated in battle during the Federal War in the 1860s.

Bibliography

Abbott, Andrew. 2001. *Time Matters: On Theory and Method.* Chicago: University of Chicago Press.

Achen, Christopher. 1986. *The Statistical Analysis of Quasi-Experiments.* Berkeley: University of California Press.

Achen, Christopher, and Duncan Snidal. 1989. "Rational Deterrence Theory and Comparative Case Studies." *World Politics* 41:143–69.

Agor, Westin. 1971. *The Chilean Senate: Internal Distribution of Influence.* Austin: Institute of Latin American Studies, University of Texas Press.

———, ed. 1972. *Latin American Legislative Systems: Their Role and Influence.* New York: Praeger.

Alchian, Armen. 1950. "Uncertainty, Evolution, and Economic Theory." *Journal of Political Economy* 58:211–22.

Alesina, Alberto, and Allan Drazen. 1991. "Why are Stabilizations Delayed?" *American Economic Review* 81:1170–88.

Allen, William Sheridan. 1973. *The Nazi Seizure of Power: The Experience of a Single German Town, 1930–1935.* New York: New Viewpoints.

Ames, Barry. 1987. *Political Survival: Politicians and Public Policy in Latin America.* California Series on Social Choice and Political Economy. Berkeley: University of California Press.

———. 1995a. "Electoral Rules, Constituency Pressures, and Pork Barrel: Bases of Voting in the Brazilian Congress." *Journal of Politics* 57: 324–53.

———. 1995b. "Electoral Strategy under Open List Proportional Representation." *American Journal of Political Science* 39:406–33.

———. 2001. *The Deadlock of Democracy in Brazil.* Ann Arbor: University of Michigan Press.

Amnesty International. Various years. *Amnesty International Report.* London: Amnesty International Publications.

Anderson, Richard. 1993. *Public Policy in an Authoritarian State: Making Foreign Policy during the Breznev Years.* Ithaca: Cornell University Press.

Archer, Ronald, and Matthew Shugart. 1997. "The Unrealized Potential of Presidential Dominance in Colombia." In *Presidentialism and Democracy in Latin America,* edited by Scott Mainwaring and Matthew Shugart. Cambridge: Cambridge University Press.

Arnold, Douglas. 1979. *Congress and the Bureaucracy: A Theory of Influence.* New Haven: Yale University Press.

Arrow, Kenneth. 1950. *Social Choice and Individual Values.* New Haven: Yale University Press.

Baldez, Lisa, and John Carey. 1999. "Presidential Agenda Control and

Spending Policy: Lessons from General Pinochet's Constitution." *American Journal of Political Science* 43:29–55.

Baran, Paul. 1957. *The Political Economy of Growth.* New York: Monthly Review Press.

Barro, Robert. 1999. "Determinants of Democracy." *Journal of Political Economy* 107, no. 6, pt. 2:158–83.

Barros, Alexandre. 1978. "The Brazilian Military: Professional Socialization, Political Performance, and State Building." Ph.D. diss., University of Chicago.

Barry, Brian. 1970. *Sociologists, Economists, and Democracy.* London: Collier-Macmillan.

———. 1982. "Methodology versus Ideology: The 'Economic' Approach Revisited." In *Strategies of Political Inquiry,* edited by Elinor Ostrom. Beverly Hills: Sage.

Bartels, Larry. 1998. "Electoral Continuity and Change, 1868–1996." *Electoral Studies* 17:301–26.

Bartolini, Stefano, and Peter Mair. 1990. *Identity, Competition, and Electoral Availability: The Stabilisation of European Electorates, 1885–1985.* Cambridge: Cambridge University Press.

Bates, Robert. 1981. *Markets and States in Tropical Africa: The Political Basis of Agricultural Policies.* California Series on Social Choice and Political Economy. Berkeley: University of California Press.

———. 1983. *Essays on the Political Economy of Rural Africa.* Berkeley: University of California Press.

———. 1989. *Beyond the Miracle of the Market: The Political Economy of Agrarian Development in Kenya.* Political Economy of Institutions and Decisions series. Cambridge: Cambridge University Press.

———. 1990. "Macropolitical Economy in the Field of Development." In *Perspectives on Positive Political Economy,* edited by James Alt and Kenneth Shepsle. Cambridge: Cambridge University Press.

Bates, Robert, Avner Greif, Margaret Levi, Jean-Laurent Rosenthal, and Barry Weingast. 1998. *Analytic Narratives.* Princeton: Princeton University Press.

Bates, Robert, and Anne Krueger, eds. 1993. *Political and Economic Interactions in Economic Policy Reform.* Cambridge, Mass.: Blackwell.

Bates, Robert, and Da-Hsiang Donald Lien. 1985. "A Note on Taxation, Development and Representative Government." *Politics and Society* 14: 53–70.

Bawn, Kathleen. 1993. "The Logic of Institutional Preferences: The German Electoral Law as a Social Choice Outcome." *American Journal of Political Science* 37:965–89.

Bendix, Reinhard. 1964. *Nation-Building and Citizenship: Studies of Our Changing Social Order.* New York: Wiley.

Ben-Dor, G. 1975. "Civilianization of Military Regimes in the Arab World." *Armed Forces and Society* 1:317–27.

Bermeo, Nancy. 1997. "Myths of Moderation: Confrontation and Conflict during Democratic Transitions." *Comparative Politics* 29:305–22.

Bienen, Henry. 1978. *Armies and Parties in Africa.* New York: Africana Publishing.

Binder, Leonard. 1986. "The Natural History of Development Theory." *Comparative Studies in Society and History* 28:3–33.

Bollen, Kenneth. 1979. "Political Democracy and the Timing of Development." *American Sociological Review* 44:572–87.

Bollen, Kenneth, and Robert Jackman. 1985. "Economic and Non-Economic Determinants of Political Democracy in the 1960s." *Research in Political Sociology* 1:27–48.

Bornschier, Volker, Christopher Chase-Dunn, and Richard Rubinson. 1978. "Cross-National Evidence of the Effects of Foreign Investment and Aid on Economic Growth and Inequality: A Survey of Findings and a Reanalysis." *American Journal of Sociology* 84:651–83.

Bratton, Michael, and Nicolas van de Walle. 1992. "Popular Protest and Political Reform in Africa." *Comparative Politics* 24:419–42.

———. 1994. "Patrimonial Regimes and Political Transitions in Africa." *World Politics* 46:453–89.

———. 1997. *Democratic Experiments in Africa: Regime Transitions in Comparative Perspective.* Cambridge: Cambridge University Press.

Braumoeller, Bear F., and Gary Goertz. 2000. "The Methodology of Necessary Conditions." *American Journal of Political Science* 44:844–58.

Brown, Michael Barratt. 1963. *After Imperialism.* London: Heinemann.

———. 1974. *The Economics of Imperialism.* London: Penguin.

Buchanan, James, Robert Tollison, and Gordon Tullock, eds. 1980. *Toward a Theory of the Rent-Seeking Society.* Economics Series No. 4. College Station: Texas A & M Press.

Buchanan, James, and Gordon Tullock. 1962. *The Calculus of Consent.* Ann Arbor: University of Michigan Press.

Burkhart, Ross, and Michael Lewis-Beck. 1994. "Comparative Democracy: The Economic Development Thesis." *American Political Science Review* 88:903–10.

Cain, Bruce, John Ferejohn, and Morris Fiorina. 1987. *The Personal Vote.* Cambridge: Harvard University Press.

Campbell, Donald. 1975. "'Degrees of Freedom' and the Case Study." *Comparative Political Studies* 8:178–93.

Campbell, Donald, and H. Laurence Ross. 1968. "The Connecticut Crackdown on Speeding: Time Series Data in Quasi-Experimental Analysis." *Law and Society Review* 3:33–53. Reprinted in *The Quantitative Analysis of Social Problems,* edited by Edward R. Tufte. Reading, Mass.: Addison-Wesley.

Cardoso, Fernando Henrique. 1973a. "Associated-Dependent Development: Theoretical and Practical Implications." In *Authoritarian Brazil: Origins, Policies, and Future,* edited by Alfred Stepan. New Haven: Yale University Press.

———. 1973b. "Imperialism and Dependency in Latin America." In *Structures and Dependency,* edited by Frank Bonilla and Robert Girling. Stanford: Institute of Political Studies.

———. 1977. "The Consumption of Dependency Theory in the U.S." *Latin American Research Review* 12:38–53.

———. 1986. "Entrepreneurs and the Transition Process: The Brazilian Case." In *Transitions from Authoritarian Rule: Comparative Perspec-*

tives, edited by Guillermo O'Donnell, Philippe Schmitter, and Laurence Whitehead. Baltimore: Johns Hopkins University Press.

Cardoso, Fernando Henrique, and Enzo Faletto. 1979. *Dependency and Development in Latin America.* Translated by Marjorie Mattingly Urquidi. Berkeley: University of California Press.

Carey, John. 1996. *Term Limits and Legislative Representation.* New York: Cambridge University Press.

———. 1998. "Institutional Design and Party Systems." In *Consolidating the Third Wave Democracies,* edited by Larry Diamond, Marc Plattner, Yun-han Chu, and Hung-mao Tien. Baltimore: Johns Hopkins University Press.

Carey, John, and Matthew Shugart, eds. 1998. *Executive Decree Authority: Calling Out the Tanks or Just Filling Out the Forms?* New York: Cambridge University Press.

Casper, Gretchen, and Michelle Taylor. 1996. *Negotiating Democracy.* Pittsburgh: University of Pittsburgh Press.

Chase-Dunn, Christopher. 1975. "The Effects of International Economic Dependence on Development and Inequality: A Cross-National Study." *American Sociological Review* 40:720–38.

Chehabi, H. E., and Juan Linz, eds. 1998. *Sultanistic Regimes.* Baltimore: Johns Hopkins University Press.

Cheibub, José Antonio. 2002. "Minority Governments, Deadlock Situations, and the Survival of Presidential Democracies." *Comparative Political Studies* 35:284–312.

Clapham, Christopher, and George Philip. 1985. *The Political Dilemmas of Military Regimes.* London: Croom Helm.

Cohen, Abner. 1974. *Two-Dimensional Man.* Berkeley: University of California Press.

Cohen, Youssef. 1994. *Radicals, Reformers, and Reactionaries: The Prisoner's Dilemma and the Collapse of Democracy in Latin America.* Chicago: University of Chicago Press.

Colburn, Forrest. 1986. *Post-revolutionary Nicaragua: State, Class, and the Dilemmas of Agrarian Policy.* California Series on Social Choice and Political Economy. Berkeley: University of California Press.

Collier, David, ed. 1979. *The New Authoritarianism in Latin America.* Princeton: Princeton University Press.

Collier, David, and Ruth Berins Collier. 1979. "Inducements versus Constraints: Disaggregating 'Corporatism.'" *American Political Science Review* 73:967–86.

Collier, David, and Steven Levitsky. 1997. "Democracy with Adjectives: Conceptual Innovation in Comparative Research." *World Politics* 49: 430–51.

Collier, David, and James E. Mahon, Jr. 1993. "Conceptual Stretching Revisited: Adapting Categories in Comparative Analysis." *American Political Science Review* 87:845–55.

Collier, David, and James Mahoney. 1996. "Insights and Pitfalls: Selection Bias in Qualitative Research." *World Politics* 49:56–91.

Collier, Ruth Berins. 1999. *Paths toward Democracy: Working Class and Elites in Western Europe and South America.* Cambridge: Cambridge University Press.

Collier, Ruth Berins, and James Mahoney. 1997. "Adding Collective Actors to Collective Outcomes: Labor and Recent Democratizations in South America and Southern Europe." *Comparative Politics* 29:285–303.

Colomer, Josep. 1995. *Game Theory and the Transition to Democracy: The Spanish Model.* Aldershot, England: Edward Elgar.

———. 1997. "Strategies and Outcomes in Eastern Europe." *Journal of Democracy* 6:72–86.

Coppedge, Michael. 1998. "The Evolution of Latin American Party Systems." In *Politics, Society and Democracy: Latin America,* edited by Scott Mainwaring and Arturo Valenzuela. Boulder: Westview.

Corbo Loi, Vittorio. 1974. *Inflation in Developing Countries: An Econometric Study of Chilean Inflation.* New York: American Elsevier.

Cox, Gary. 1990. "Centripetal and Centrifugal Incentives in Electoral Systems." *American Journal of Political Science* 34:903–35.

Cox, Gary, and Mathew McCubbins. 1993. *Legislative Leviathan: Party Government in the House.* Berkeley: University of California Press.

Cox, Gary, Frances Rosenbluth, and Michael Thies. 1999. "Electoral Reform and the Fate of Factions: The Case of Japan's Liberal Democratic Party." *British Journal of Political Science* 29:33–56.

———. 2000. "Electoral Rules, Career Ambitions, and Party Structure: Comparing Factions in Japan's Upper and Lower Houses." *American Journal of Political Science* 44:115–22.

Cox, Gary, and Matthew Shugart. 1995. "In the Absence of Vote Pooling: Nomination and Vote Allocation Errors in Colombia." *Electoral Studies* 14:441–60.

Cox, Gary, and Michael Thies. 1998. "The Cost of Intraparty Competition: The Single, Nontransferable Vote and Money Politics in Japan." *Comparative Political Studies* 31:267–91.

———. 2000. "How Much Does Money Matter? 'Buying' Votes in Japan, 1967–1990." *Comparative Political Studies* 33:37–58.

Decalo, Samuel. 1976. *Coups and Army Rule in Africa: Studies in Military Style.* New Haven: Yale University Press.

DeFelice, Gene. 1986. "Causal Inference and Comparative Methods." *Comparative Political Studies* 19:415–37.

DeNardo, James. 1985. *Power in Numbers.* Princeton: Princeton University Press.

Denzau, Arthur, and Robert MacKay. 1981. "Structure-Induced Equilibria and Perfect-Foresight Expectations." *American Journal of Political Science* 25:762–79.

———. 1993. "Gatekeeping and Monopoly Power of Committees: An Analysis of Sincere and Sophisticated Behavior." *American Journal of Political Science* 27:740–61.

Deyo, Frederic. 1984. "Export Manufacturing and Labor: The Asian Case." In *Labor in the Capitalist Economy,* edited by Charles Bergquist. Beverly Hills: Sage.

———. 1987. "State and Labor: Modes of Political Exclusion in East Asian Development." In *The Political Economy of the New Asian Industrialism,* edited by Frederic Deyo. Ithaca: Cornell University Press.

Diamond, Larry, Juan Linz, and S. M. Lipset, eds. 1989. *Democracy in Developing Countries.* Boulder: Lynne Rienner.

Dion, Douglas. 1998. "Evidence and Inference in the Comparative Case Study." *Comparative Politics* 30:127–45.

Dogan, Mattei. 2001. "Paradigms in the Social Sciences." *International Encyclopedia of Social Sciences* 16:11023–27.

dos Santos, Theotônio. 1970. "The Structure of Dependence." *American Economic Review* 60:235–46.

Downs, Anthony. 1957. *An Economic Theory of Democracy.* New York: Harper.

Duval, Raymond. 1978. "Dependence and Dependencia Theory: Notes toward Precision of Concept and Argument." *International Organization* 32:51–78.

Duverger, Maurice. 1954. *Political Parties: Their Organization and Activity in the Modern State.* New York: Wiley.

Easterly, William. 2001. *The Elusive Quest for Growth: Economists' Adventures and Misadventures in the Tropics.* Cambridge, Mass.: MIT Press.

Eckstein, Harry. 1975. "Case Study and Theory in Political Science." In *Handbook of Sociology,* edited by Neil Smelser. Beverly Hills: Sage.

Elkins, Zachary. 2000. "Gradations of Democracy? Empirical Tests of Alternative Conceptualizations." *American Journal of Political Science* 44: 287–94.

Elster, Jon, ed. 1986. *Readings in Social and Political Theory.* New York: New York University Press.

Evans, Peter. 1979. *Dependent Development: The Alliance of Multinational, State, and Local Capital in Brazil.* Princeton: Princeton University Press.

Evans, Peter, and John Stephens. 1988. "Studying Development since the Sixties: The Emergence of a New Comparative Political Economy." *Theory and Society* 17:713–45.

Ferejohn, John. 1974. *Pork Barrel Politics: Rivers and Harbors Legislation, 1947–1968.* Stanford: Stanford University Press.

Fernández, Raquel, and Dani Rodrik. 1991. "Resistance to Reform: Status Quo Bias in the Presence of Individual Specific Uncertainty." *American Economic Review* 81:1146–55.

Finer, S. E. 1975. *The Man on Horseback: The Role of the Military in Politics.* 2d ed. Harmondsworth, U.K.: Penguin.

Fiorina, Morris. 1977. *Congress, Keystone of the Washington Establishment.* New Haven: Yale University Press.

Fiorina, Morris, and Roger Noll. 1978. "Voters, Bureaucrats, and Legislators: A Rational Choice Perspective on the Growth of Bureaucracy." *Journal of Public Economy* 9:234–59.

Fishlow, Albert. 1971. "Origins and Consequences of Import Substitution in Brazil." In *International Economics and Development,* edited by Luis DiMarco. New York: Academic Press.

Fontana, Andrés. 1987. "Political Decision-Making by a Military Corporation: Argentina, 1976–1983." Ph.D. diss., University of Texas.

Frank, Andre Gunder. 1967. *Capitalism and Underdevelopment in Latin America: Historical Case Studies of Chile and Brazil.* New York: Monthly Review Press.

———. 1970. "The Development of Underdevelopment." In *Imperialism and Underdevelopment,* edited by Robert I. Rhodes. New York: Monthly Review Press.

Frendreis, John. 1983. "Explanation of Variation and Detection of Covariation: The Purpose and Logic of Comparative Analysis." *Comparative Political Studies* 16:255–72.

Frieden, Jeffry. 1989. "Winners and Losers in the Latin American Debt Crisis: The Political Implications." In *Debt and Democracy in Latin America,* edited by Barbara Stallings and Robert Kaufman. Boulder: Westview.

———. 1991. *Debt, Development, and Democracy: Modern Political Economy and Latin America, 1965–1985.* Princeton: Princeton University Press.

Frye, Timothy. 1997. "The Politics of Institutional Choice: Post-Communist Presidencies." *Comparative Political Studies* 30:523–53.

Garrett, Geoffrey, and Peter Lange. 1986. "Performance in a Hostile World." *World Politics* 38:517–45.

Geddes, Barbara. 1994. *Politician's Dilemma: Building State Capacity in Latin America.* Berkeley: University of California Press.

———. 1995. "A Comparative Perspective on the Leninist Legacy in Eastern Europe." *Comparative Political Studies* 28:239–74.

———. 1996. "The Initiation of New Democratic Institutions in Eastern Europe and Latin America." In *Institutional Design in New Democracies,* edited by Arend Lijphart and Carlos Waisman. Boulder: Westview.

———. 1999a. "Authoritarian Breakdown: Empirical Test of a Game Theoretic Argument." Paper presented at the annual meeting of the American Political Science Association, Atlanta.

———. 1999b. "Douglass North and Institutional Change in Contemporary Developing Countries." In *Competition and Cooperation: Conversations with Nobelists about Economics and Political Science,* edited by James Alt, Margaret Levi, and Elinor Ostrom. New York: Russell Sage.

———. 1999c. "What Do We Know about Democratization after Twenty Years?" *Annual Review of Political Science* 2:115–44.

Geddes, Barbara, and Artur Ribeiro Neto. 1992. "Institutional Sources of Corruption in Brazil." *Third World Quarterly* 14:641–61.

Geddes, Barbara, and John Zaller. 1989. "Sources of Popular Support for Authoritarian Regimes." *American Journal of Political Science* 33: 319–47.

George, Alexander, and Timothy McKeown. 1985. "Case Studies and Theories of Organizational Decision Making." *Advances in Information Processing in Organizations* 2:21–58.

Gill, Anthony. 1994. "Rendering unto Caesar? Religious Competition and Catholic Political Strategy." *American Journal of Political Science* 38: 403–25.

Gonçalves, Reinaldo, and Amir Coelho Barros. 1982. "Tendências dos Termos de Troca: A Tese de Prebisch e a Economia Brasileira—1850/1979." *Pesquisa e Planejamento Econômico* 12:109–31.

Green, Donald, and Ian Shapiro. 1994. *Pathologies of Rational Choice Theory: A Critique of Applications in Political Science.* New Haven: Yale University Press.

Haberler, Gottfried. 1961. "Terms of Trade and Economic Development." In *Economic Development for Latin America,* edited by Howard S. Ellis and Henry C. Wallich. London: Macmillan.

Haggard, Stephan. 1986. "The Newly Industrializing Countries in the International System." *World Politics* 38:343–70.

———. 1990. *Pathways from the Periphery: The Policies of Growth in Newly Industrializing Countries.* Ithaca: Cornell University Press.

Haggard, Stephan, and Robert Kaufman. 1995. *The Political Economy of Democratic Transitions.* Princeton: Princeton University Press.

———, eds. 1992. *The Politics of Economic Adjustment: International Constraints, Distributive Conflicts, and the State.* Princeton: Princeton University Press.

Haggard, Stephan, and Steven Webb. 1994. *Voting for Reform: Democracy, Political Liberalization, and Economic Adjustment.* New York: Oxford University Press.

Hammond, Thomas, and Gary Miller. 1987. "The Core of the Constitution." *American Political Science Review* 81:1155–74.

Hardin, Russell. 1982. *Collective Action.* Baltimore: Johns Hopkins University Press.

Higley, John, and Richard Gunther, eds. 1992. *Elites and Democratic Consolidation in Latin America and Southern Europe.* Cambridge: Cambridge University Press.

Hinnebusch, Raymond. 1985. *Egyptian Politics under Sadat: The Post-populist Development of an Authoritarian-Modernizing State.* Cambridge: Cambridge University Press.

Hirschman, Albert. 1968. "The Political Economy of Import-Substituting Industrialization in Latin America." *Quarterly Journal of Economics* 82:2–32.

———. 1973. "Inflation in Chile." In *Journeys Toward Progress: Studies of Economic Policy Making in Latin America.* New York: Norton.

———. 1979. "The Turn to Authoritarianism in Latin America and the Search for Its Economic Determinants." In *The New Authoritarianism in Latin America,* edited by David Collier. Princeton: Princeton University Press.

Hopwood, D. 1988. *Syria, 1945–1986: Politics and Society.* London: Unwin Hyman.

Hoskin, Gary, Francisco Leal, and Harvey Kline. 1976. *Legislative Behavior in Colombia.* Buffalo: Council on International Studies, State University of New York at Buffalo.

Huber, John. 1992. "Restrictive Legislative Procedures in France and the United States." *American Political Science Review* 86:675–87.

Hull, Adrian Prentice. 1999. "Comparative Political Science: An Inventory and Assessment since the 1980's." *PS* 32:117–24.

Hunter, Wendy. 1997. *Eroding Military Influence in Brazil: Politicians against Soldiers.* Chapel Hill: University of North Carolina Press.

Huntington, Samuel. 1991. *The Third Wave: Democratization in the Late Twentieth Century.* Norman: University of Oklahoma Press.

Ianni, Octávio. 1968. *O Colapso do Populismo no Brasil.* Rio de Janeiro: Editorial Civilização Brasileira.

Jackman, Robert. 1973. "On the Relation of Economic Development to Democratic Performance." *American Journal of Political Science* 17: 611–21.

———. 1982. "Dependence on Foreign Investment and Economic Growth in the Third World." *World Politics* 34:175–96.

Jacobson, Gary, and Samuel Kernell. 1983. *Strategy and Choice in Congressional Elections.* 2d ed. New Haven: Yale University Press.

Janowitz, Morris. 1960. *The Professional Soldier: A Social and Political Portrait.* Glencoe, Ill.: Free Press.

———. 1977. *Military Institutions and Coercion in the Developing Nations.* Chicago: University of Chicago Press.

Johnson, Chalmers. 1987. "Political Institutions and Economic Performance: The Government-Business Relationship in Japan, South Korea, and Taiwan." In *The Political Economy of the New Asian Industrialism,* edited by Frederic Deyo. Ithaca: Cornell University Press.

Jones, Mark. 1995. *Electoral Laws and the Survival of Presidential Democracies.* Notre Dame: University of Notre Dame Press.

Jones, Mark, Pablo Sanguinetti, and Mariano Tommasi. 2000. "Politics, Institutions, and Fiscal Performance in a Federal System: An Analysis of the Argentine Provinces." *Journal of Development Economics* 61: 305–34.

Jowitt, Kenneth. 1992. *The New World Disorder: The Leninist Extinction.* Berkeley: University of California Press.

Kalyvas, Stathis. 1999. "The Decay and Breakdown of Communist One-Party Systems." *Annual Review of Political Science* 2:323–43.

Karl, Terry. 1986. "Petroleum and Political Pacts: The Transition to Democracy in Venezuela." In *Transitions from Authoritarian Rule: Latin America,* edited by Guillermo O'Donnell, Philippe Schmitter, and Laurence Whitehead, vol. 3. Baltimore: Johns Hopkins University Press.

———. 1990. "Dilemmas of Democratization in Latin America." *Comparative Politics* 23:1–21.

Kaufman, Robert, Harry Chernotsky, and Daniel Geller. 1975. "A Preliminary Test of the Theory of Dependency." *Comparative Politics* 7:303–30.

Kennedy, Gavin. 1974. *The Military in the Third World.* New York: Charles Scribner's Sons.

King, Gary. 1989. *Unifying Political Methodology: The Likelihood Theory of Statistical Inference.* New York: Cambridge University Press.

King, Gary, Robert Keohane, and Sidney Verba. 1994. *Designing Social Inquiry: Scientific Inference in Qualitative Research.* Princeton: Princeton University Press.

Kolosi, Tamás, Iván Szelényi, Szonja Szelényi, and Bruce Western. 1992. "The Making of Political Fields in Post-Communist Transition (Dynamics of Class and Party in Hungarian Politics, 1989–90)." In *Post-Communist Transition: Emerging Pluralism in Hungary,* edited by András Bozóki, András Körösényi, and George Schöpflin. New York: St. Martin's Press.

Koo, Hagen. 1987. "The Interplay of State, Social Class, and World System in East Asian Development. In *The Political Economy of the New Asian Industrialism,* edited by Frederic Deyo. Ithaca: Cornell University Press.

Kostadinova, Tatiana Pentcheva. 1995. *Bulgaria 1879–1946: The Challenge of Choice.* East European Monographs. New York: Columbia University Press.

Krehbiel, Keith. 1988. "Spatial Models of Legislative Choice." *Legislative Studies Quarterly* 13:259–319.

Krueger, Anne. 1974. "The Political Economy of the Rent-Seeking Society." *American Economic Review* 64:291–303. Reprinted in James Buchanan, Robert Tollison, and Gordon Tullock, eds., *Toward a Theory of the Rent-Seeking Society,* Economics Series No. 4. College Station: Texas A & M University Press, 1980.

Kuczynski, Pedro-Pablo. 1977. *Peruvian Democracy under Economic Stress: An Account of the Belaúnde Administration, 1963–1968.* Princeton: Princeton University Press.

Kuhn, Thomas. 1970. *The Structure of Scientific Revolutions.* 2d ed. International Encyclopedia of Unified Science 2:2. Chicago: University of Chicago Press.

Laitin, David. 1986. *Hegemony and Culture.* Chicago: University of Chicago Press.

———. 1998. *Identity in Formation: The Russian-Speaking Populations in the Near Abroad.* Ithaca: Cornell University Press.

Laitin, David, and Daniel Posner. 2001. "The Implications of Constructivism for Constructing Ethnic Fractionalization Indices." *APSA-CP* (winter): 13–17.

Lapp, Nancy. 1997. "Landing Votes: Expansion of Suffrage and Land Reform in Latin America." Ph.D. diss., University of California, Los Angeles.

Lave, Charles, and James March. 1975. *Introduction to Models in the Social Sciences.* New York: Harper & Row.

Leff, Nathanial. 1968. *Economic Policy-Making and Development in Brazil, 1947–1964.* New York: Wiley.

Lenin, V. I. [1916] 1968. "Imperialism, the Highest Stage of Capitalism." In *Lenin on Politics and Revolution: Selected Writings,* edited by James E. O'Connor. New York: Pegasus.

Levi, Margaret. 1988. *Of Rule and Revenue.* Berkeley: University of California Press.

Levy, Marion J. 1966. *Modernization and the Structure of Societies: A Setting for International Affairs.* Princeton: Princeton University Press.

Leys, Colin. 1974. *Underdevelopment in Kenya: The Political Economy of Neo-colonialism, 1964–1971.* Berkeley: University of California Press.

Lieberson, Stanley. 1991. "Small N's and Big Conclusions: An Examination of the Reasoning in Comparative Studies Based on a Small Number of Cases." *Social Forces* 7 (December): 307–20.

Lijphart, Arend. 1971. "Comparative Politics and Comparative Method." *American Political Science Review* 65:682–95.

———. 1975. "The Comparable Cases Strategy in Comparative Research." *Comparative Political Studies* 8:158–77.

———. 1990. "The Political Consequences of Electoral Laws, 1945–85." *American Political Science Review* 84:481–96.

Lijphart, Arend, and Bernard Grofman, eds. 1984. *Choosing an Electoral System: Issues and Alternatives.* New York: Praeger.

Linz, Juan, and Alfred Stepan. 1996. *Problems of Democratic Transition and Consolidation: Southern Europe, South America, and Post-Communist Europe.* Baltimore: Johns Hopkins University Press.

———, eds. 1978. *The Breakdown of Democratic Regimes.* 4 vols. Baltimore: Johns Hopkins University Press.

Lipset, Seymour Martin. 1959. "Some Social Requisites of Democracy: Economic Development and Political Legitimacy." *American Political Science Review* 52:69–105.

Lipset, Seymour Martin, and Stein Rokkan. 1967. "Cleavage Structures, Party Systems, and Voter Alignments: An Introduction." In *Party Systems and Voter Alignments,* edited by Seymour Martin Lipset and Stein Rokkan. New York: Free Press.

Lofchie, Michael. 1989. *The Policy Factor: Agricultural Performance in Kenya and Tanzania.* Boulder: Lynne Rienner.

Lohmann, Susanne. 1993. "A Signaling Model of Informative and Manipulative Political Action." *American Political Science Review* 87:319–33.

———. 1994. "Dynamics of Informational Cascades: The Monday Demonstrations in Leipzig, East Germany, 1989–1991." *World Politics* 47: 42–101.

Londregan, John. 2000. *Legislative Institutions and Ideology in Chile.* New York: Cambridge University Press.

Londregan, John, and Keith Poole. 1990. "Poverty, the Coup Trap, and the Seizure of Executive Power." *World Politics* 42:151–83.

———. 1996. "Does High Income Promote Democracy?" *World Politics* 49:1–30.

Maguire, Maria. 1983. "Is There Still Persistence? Electoral Change in Western Europe, 1948–79." In *West European Party Systems: Continuity and Change,* edited by Hans Daalder and Peter Mair. Beverly Hills: Sage.

Mahoney, James. 2000. "Strategies of Causal Inference in Small-N Analysis." *Sociological Methods and Research* 28:387–424.

———. 2001. *The Legacies of Liberalism: Path Dependence and Political Regimes in Central America.* Baltimore: Johns Hopkins University Press.

Mainwaring, Scott. 1994. "Explaining Choices of Political Institutions: Interests and Ideas in Brazil, 1985–1988." Paper prepared for presentation at the annual meeting of the American Political Science Association, New York City.

Mainwaring, Scott, and Timothy Scully, eds. 1995. *Building Democratic Institutions: Party Systems in Latin America.* Stanford: Stanford University Press.

Mainwaring, Scott, and Matthew Shugart. 1997a. "Conclusion: Presidentialism and the Party System." In *Presidentialism and Democracy in Latin America,* edited by Scott Mainwaring and Matthew Shugart. Cambridge: Cambridge University Press.

———. 1997b. "Presidentialism and Democracy in Latin America: Rethinking the Terms of the Debate." In *Presidentialism and Democracy in Latin America,* edited by Scott Mainwaring and Matthew Shugart. Cambridge: Cambridge University Press.

Manion, Melanie. 1996. "Corruption by Design: Bribery in Chinese Enterprise Licensing." *Journal of Law, Economics, and Organization* 12: 167–95.

Ma'oz, M. 1986. "The Emergence of Modern Syria." In *Syria under Assad: Domestic Constraints and Regional Risks,* edited by M. Ma'oz and A. Yaniv. London: Croom Helm.

———. 1988. *Assad: The Sphynx of Damascus.* New York: Weidenfeld and Nicholson.

March, James, and Johan P. Olsen. 1984. "The New Institutionalism: Organizational Factors in Political Life." *American Political Science Review* 78:734–49.

Mayhew, David. 1974. *Congress: The Electoral Connection.* New Haven: Yale University Press.

McClelland, David C. 1961. *The Achieving Society.* New York: Van Nostrand.

McCubbins, Mathew, and Thomas Schwartz. 1984. "Congressional Oversight Overlooked: Police Patrols vs. Fire Alarms." *American Journal of Political Science* 28:165–79.

McGowan, Patrick, and Dale Smith. 1978. "Economic Dependency in Black Africa: An Analysis of Competing Theories." *International Organization* 32:179–235.

McKelvey, Richard. 1976. "Intransitivities in Multidimensional Voting Models and Some Implications for Agenda Control." *Journal of Economic Theory* 12:472–82.

———. 1979. "General Conditions for Global Intransitivities in Formal Voting Models." *Econometrica* 48:1085–1111.

Meckstroth, Theodore. 1975. "'Most Different Systems' and 'Most Similar Systems': A Study in the Logic of Comparative Inquiry." *Comparative Political Studies* 8:132–57.

Merton, Robert. 1957. *Social Theory and Social Structure.* New York: Free Press.

Moore, Barrington. 1966. *Social Origins of Dictatorship and Democracy: Lord and Peasant in the Making of the Modern World.* Boston: Beacon Press.

Moore, Wilbert E. 1963. "Industrialization and Social Change." In *Industrialization and Society,* edited by Bert Hoselitz and Wilbert E. Moore. New York: UNESCO-Mouton.

Morgenstern, Scott. 2001. "Organized Factions and Disorganized Parties: Electoral Incentives in Uruguay." *Party Politics* 7:235–56.

Moulin, Herve. 1982. *Game Theory for the Social Sciences.* New York: New York University Press.

Nelson, Richard R., and Sidney G. Winter. 1982. *An Evolutionary Theory of Economic Change.* Cambridge: Harvard University Press.

Niskanen, William. 1971. *Bureaucracy and Representative Government.* Hawthorne, N.Y.: Aldine.

Noll, Roger, and Haruo Shimada. 1991. "Comparative Structural Policies." In *Parallel Politics: Economic Policymaking in Japan and the United States,* edited by Samuel Kernell. Washington, D.C.: Brookings.

Nordlinger, Eric. 1977. *Soldiers in Politics: Military Coups and Governments.* Englewood Cliffs, N.J.: Prentice-Hall.

North, Douglass. 1979. "Framework for Analyzing the State in Economic History." *Explorations in Economic History* 16:249–59.

———. 1981. *Structure and Change in Economic History.* New York: Norton.

———. 1985. "Transaction Costs in History." *Journal of European Economic History* 14:557–76.

———. 1989a. "Institutions and Economic Growth: An Historical Introduction." *World Development* 17:1319–32.

———. 1989b. "A Transaction Cost Approach to the Historical Development of Polities and Economies." *Journal of Institutional and Theoretical Economics* 145:661–68.

———. 1990. *Institutions, Institutional Change, and Economic Performance.* Political Economy of Institutions and Decisions series. Cambridge: Cambridge University Press.

Obasanjo, Olusegun. 1998. "The Country of Anything Goes." *New York Review of Books* (Sept. 24): 55–57.

O'Donnell, Guillermo. 1973. *Modernization and Bureaucratic-Authoritarianism: Studies in South American Politics.* Politics of Modernization, no. 9. Berkeley: Institute of International Studies.

———. 1978. "Reflections on the Patterns of Change in the Bureaucratic-Authoritarian State." *Latin American Research Review* 13:3–38.

———. 1979. "Tensions in the Bureaucratic-Authoritarian State and the Question of Democracy." In *The New Authoritarianism in Latin America,* edited by David Collier. Princeton: Princeton University Press.

O'Donnell, Guillermo, and Philippe Schmitter. 1986. *Transitions from Authoritarian Rule: Tentative Conclusions about Uncertain Democracies.* Baltimore: Johns Hopkins University Press.

O'Donnell, Guillermo, Philippe Schmitter, and Laurence Whitehead, eds. 1986. *Transitions from Authoritarian Rule.* 4 vols. Baltimore: Johns Hopkins University Press.

Oliveira Marques, A. H. de. 1978. *História da Primeira República Portuguesa: As Estruturas de Base.* Lisbon: Iniciativas Editoriais.

Olson, Mancur. 1965. *The Logic of Collective Action: Public Goods and the Theory of Groups.* Cambridge: Harvard University Press.

———. 1993. "Dictatorship, Democracy, and Development." *American Political Science Review* 87:567–76.

Ordeshook, Peter. 1986. *Game Theory and Political Theory: An Introduction.* Cambridge: Cambridge University Press.

Ordeshook, Peter, and Olga Shvetsova. 1994. "Ethnic Heterogeneity, District Magnitude, and the Number of Parties." *American Journal of Political Science* 38:100–123.

Ordeshook, Peter, Olga Shvetsova, and Mikhail Filippov. 1999. "Party Fragmentation and Presidential Elections in Post-Communist Democracies." *Constitutional Political Economy* 10:1–24.

Ostrom, Elinor. 1982. "Beyond Positivism: An Introduction to This Volume." In *Strategies of Political Inquiry,* edited by Elinor Ostrom. Beverly Hills: Sage.

———. 1990. *Governing the Commons: The Evolution of Institutions for Collective Action.* Cambridge: Cambridge University Press.

Ostrom, Elinor, Roy Gardner, and James Walker. 1994. *Common-Pool Resources.* Ann Arbor: University of Michigan Press.

Ostrom, Elinor, Larry Schroeder, and Susan Wynne. 1993. *Institutional Incentives and Sustainable Development: Infrastructure Policies in Perspective.* Boulder: Westview.

Packenham, Robert. 1970. "Legislatures and Political Development." In *Legislatures in Developmental Perspective,* edited by Alan Kornberg and Lloyd Musolf. Durham: Duke University Press.

Pedersen, Morgens. 1983. "Changing Patterns of Electoral Volatility: Explorations in Explanation." In *West European Party Systems: Continuity and Change,* edited by Hans Daalder and Peter Mair. Beverly Hills: Sage.

Penn World Tables. See <http://pwt.econ.upenn.edu>.

Perlmutter, Amos. 1969. "From Obscurity to Rule: The Syrian Army and the Ba'th Party." *Western Political Quarterly* 22:827–46.

Popkin, Samuel. 1979. *The Rational Peasant: The Political Economy of Rural Society in Vietnam.* Berkeley: University of California Press.

Powell, John Duncan. 1971. *Political Mobilization of the Venezuelan Peasant.* Cambridge: Harvard University Press.

Prébisch, Raúl. 1950. *The Economic Development of Latin America and Its Principal Problems.* New York: United Nations.

Przeworski, Adam. 1986. "Some Problems in the Study of the Transition to Democracy." In *Transitions from Authoritarian Rule,* edited by Guillermo O'Donnell, Philippe Schmitter, and Laurence Whitehead. Vol. 3, *Comparative Perspectives.* Baltimore: Johns Hopkins University Press.

———. 1991. *Democracy and the Market: Political and Economic Reforms in Eastern Europe and Latin America.* Cambridge: Cambridge University Press.

———. 1992. "Games of Transition." In *Issues in Democratic Consolidation,* edited by Scott Mainwaring, Guillermo O'Donnell, and Samuel Valenzuela. Notre Dame: University of Notre Dame Press.

———. 1995. Contribution to "The Role of Theory in Comparative Politics: A Symposium." *World Politics* 48:16–21.

Przeworski, Adam, and Fernando Limongi. 1993. "Political Regimes and Economic Growth." *Journal of Economic Perspectives* 7:51–71.

———. 1997. "Modernization: Theories and Facts." *World Politics* 49: 155–83.

Przeworski, Adam, Michael Alvarez, José Antonio Cheibub, and Fernando Limongi. 2000. *Democracy and Development: Political Institutions and Well-Being in the World 1950–1990.* Cambridge: Cambridge University Press.

Przeworski, Adam, and Michael Wallerstein. 1988. "Structural Dependence of the State on Capital." *American Political Science Review* 82: 11–30.

Rabinovich, I. 1972. *Syria under the Ba'th, 1963–66: The Army-Party Symbiosis.* Jerusalem: Israel Universities Press.

Rae, Douglas. 1967. *The Political Consequences of Electoral Laws.* New Haven: Yale University Press.

Ramsayer, Mark, and Frances Rosenbluth. 1993. *Japan's Political Marketplace.* Cambridge: Harvard University Press.

Remington, Thomas, and Steven Smith. 1995. "The Development of Parliamentary Parties in Russia."*Legislative Studies Quarterly* 20:457–89.

———. 1996. "Political Goals, Institutional Context, and the Choice of an Electoral System: The Russian Parliamentary Election Law." *American Journal of Political Science* 40:1253–79.

———. 1998a. "Decrees, Laws, and Inter-branch Relations in the Russian Federation." *Post-Soviet Affairs* 14:287–322.

———. 1998b. "Electoral Institutions and Party Cohesion in the Russian Duma." *Journal of Politics* 60:417–39.

———. 1998c. "Theories of Legislative Institutions and the Organization of the Russian Duma." *American Journal of Political Science* 42:545–72.

———. 2000. *The Politics of Institutional Choice: The Formation of the Russian State Duma.* Princeton: Princeton University Press.

Remmer, Karen. 1989. *Military Rule in Latin America.* New York: Unwin Hyman.

———. 1995. "New Theoretical Perspectives on Democratization." *Comparative Politics* 28:103–22.

Richards, A., and John Waterbury. 1990. *The Political Economy of the Middle East: State, Class, and Economic Development.* Chaps. 11–13. Boulder: Westview.

Riker, William. 1962. *The Theory of Political Coalitions.* New Haven: Yale University Press.

Rodrik, Dani. 1994. "The Rush to Free Trade in the Developing World: Why So Late? Why Now? Will It Last?" In *Voting for Reform: Democracy, Political Liberalization, and Economic Adjustment,* edited by Stephan Haggard and Steven Webb. Oxford: Oxford University Press.

Rogowski, Ronald. 1978. "Rationalist Theories of Politics: A Midterm Report." *World Politics* 40:296–323.

———. 1989. *Commerce and Coalitions: How Trade Affects Domestic Political Alignments.* Princeton: Princeton University Press.

———. 1995. "The Role of Theory and Anomaly in Social-Scientific Inference." *American Political Science Review* 89:467–70.

Rose, Richard, and Derek W. Urwin. 1970. "Persistence and Change in Western Party Systems since 1945." *Political Studies* 18:287–319.

Ross, Michael. 2001. "Does Oil Hinder Democracy?" *World Politics* 53: 325–61.

Rueschemeyer, Dietrich, Evelyne Huber Stephens, and John D. Stephens. 1992. *Capitalist Development and Democracy.* Chicago: University of Chicago Press.

Sandbrook, Richard. 1986. *The Politics of African Economic Stagnation.* New York: Cambridge University Press.

Schelling, Thomas. 1978. *Micromotives and Macrobehavior.* New York: Norton.

———. 1984. *Choice and Consequence: Perspectives of an Errant Economist.* Cambridge: Harvard University Press.

Schofield, Norman. 1976. "Instability of Simple Dynamic Games." *Review of Economic Studies* 45:575–94.

Schwartz, Thomas. 1986. *The Logic of Collective Choice.* New York: Columbia University Press.

Scott, James C. 1976. *The Moral Economy of the Peasant: Rebellion and Subsistence in Southeast Asia.* New Haven: Yale University Press.

———. 1985. *Weapons of the Weak: Everyday Forms of Peasant Resistance.* New Haven: Yale University Press.

Sen, Amartya. 1970. *Collective Choice and Social Welfare.* San Francisco: Holden Day.

Shelley, Percy Bysshe. 1817. "Ozymandias." In *John Keats and Percy Bysshe Shelley: Complete Poetical Works.* New York: Modern Library.

Shepsle, Kenneth. 1979. "Institutional Arrangements and Equilibrium in Multidimensional Voting Models." *American Journal of Political Science* 23:27–36.

Shepsle, Kenneth, and Barry Weingast. 1981a. "Political Preferences for the Pork Barrel: A Generalization. *American Journal of Political Science* 25:96–111.

———. 1981b. "Structure-Induced Equilibrium and Legislative Choice." *Public Choice* 37:503–19.

———. 1984. "Uncovered Sets and Sophisticated Voting Outcomes with Implications for Agenda Institutions." *American Journal of Political Science* 28:49–74.

———. 1987a. "The Institutional Foundations of Committee Power." *American Political Science Review* 81:85–104.

———. 1987b. "Reflections on Committee Power." *American Political Science Review* 81:935–45.

Shleifer, Andrei, and Robert Vishny. 1993. "Corruption." *Quarterly Journal of Economics* 108:599–617.

Shugart, Matthew. 1995. "The Electoral Cycle and Institutional Sources of Divided Government." *American Journal of Political Science* 89:327–43.

———. 1998. "The Inverse Relationship between Party Strength and Executive Strength: A Theory of Politicians' Constitutional Choices." *British Journal of Political Science* 28:1–29.

Shugart, Matthew, and John Carey. 1992. *Presidents and Assemblies: Constitutional Design and Electoral Dynamics.* New York: Cambridge University Press.

Singer, Hans. 1950. "The Distribution of Gains between Investing and Borrowing Countries." *American Economic Review* 40:472–99.

Skidmore, Thomas. 1967. *Politics in Brazil, 1930–1964: An Experiment in Democracy.* New York: Oxford University Press.

Sklar, Richard. 2002. "The New Modernization." In *African Politics in Postimperial Times: The Essays of Richard L. Sklar.* Trenton, NJ: Africa World Press.

Skocpol, Theda. 1979. *States and Social Revolutions: A Comparative Analysis of France, Russia, and China.* Cambridge: Cambridge University Press.

Skocpol, Theda, and J. Goodwin. 1994. "Explaining Revolutions in the Contemporary Third World." In *Social Revolutions in the Modern World,* edited by Theda Skocpol. Cambridge: Cambridge University Press.

Skocpol, Theda, and Margaret Somers. 1980. "The Uses of Comparative History in Macrosocial Inquiry." *Comparative Studies in Society and History* 22:174–97.

Smith, Peter. 1974. *Argentina and the Failure of Democracy: Conflict among Political Elites, 1904–1955.* Madison: University of Wisconsin Press.

———. 1979. *Labyrinths of Power: Political Recruitment in Twentieth Century Mexico.* Princeton: Princeton University Press.

Snyder, Richard. 1998. "Paths out of Sultanistic Regimes: Combining Structural and Voluntarist Perspectives." In *Sultanistic Regimes,* edited by H. E. Chehabi and Juan Linz. Baltimore: Johns Hopkins University Press.

Snyder, Richard, and James Mahoney. 1999. "The Missing Variable: Institutions and the Study of Regime Change." *Comparative Politics* 32: 103–22.

Springborg, R. 1989. *Mubarak's Egypt: Fragmentation of the Political Order.* Boulder: Westview.

Stallings, Barbara, and Robert Kaufman, eds. 1989. *Debt and Democracy in Latin America.* Boulder: Westview.

Stepan, Alfred. 1971. *The Military in Politics: Changing Patterns in Brazil.* Princeton: Princeton University Press.

Sunkel, Osvaldo. 1972. "National Development Policy and External Dependence in Latin America." In *Contemporary Inter-American Relations,* edited by Yale Ferguson. Englewood Cliffs, N.J.: Prentice-Hall.

———. 1973. "Transnational Capitalism and National Disintegration in Latin America." *Social and Economic Studies* 22:132–76.

Taagepera, Rein, and Matthew Shugart. 1989. *Seats and Votes: The Effects and Determinants of Electoral Systems.* New Haven: Yale University Press.

Taylor, Michelle. 1992. "Formal versus Informal Incentive Structures and Legislator Behavior: Evidence from Costa Rica." *Journal of Politics* 54:1055–73.

Tella, Torcuato di. 1965. "Populism and Reform in Latin America." In *Obstacles to Change in Latin America,* edited by Claudio Véliz. London: Oxford University Press.

Tilly, Charles. 1984. *Big Structures, Large Processes, Huge Comparisons.* New York: Russell Sage.

Treisman, Daniel. 1998. "Between the Extremes: Moderate Reforms and Centrist Blocs in the 1993 Election." In *Growing Pains: Russian Democracy and the Election of 1993,* edited by Timothy Colton. Washington, D.C.: Brookings Institution Press.

———. 1999. "Russia's Tax Crisis: Explaining Falling Revenues in a Transitional Economy." *Economics and Politics* 11:145–69.

Tsebelis, George. 1990. *Nested Games: Rational Choice in Comparative Politics.* Berkeley: University of California Press.

———. 1995. "Decision Making in Political Systems: Veto Players in Presidentialism, Parliamentarism, Multicameralism, and Multipartism." *British Journal of Political Science* 25:289–325.

———. 2002. *Veto Players: How Political Institutions Work.* Princeton: Princeton University Press and Russell Sage.

Tucker, Robert. 1969. *The Marxian Revolutionary Idea.* New York: Norton.

U.S. Department of State. 1979–83. *Country Reports on Human Rights Practices.* Washington, D.C.: U.S. Government Printing Office.

Valenzuela, Arturo. 1978. *The Breakdown of Democratic Regimes: Chile.* Baltimore: Johns Hopkins University Press.

van de Walle, Nicolas, and Kimberly Butler. 1999. "Political Parties and

Party Systems in Africa's Illiberal Democracies." *Cambridge Review of International Affairs* 12:761–87.

Van Doorn, Jacques, ed. 1968. *Armed Forces and Society: Sociological Essays.* The Hague: Mouton.

———. 1969. *Military Profession and Military Regimes: Commitments and Conflicts.* The Hague: Mouton.

Waterbury, John. 1973. "Endemic and Planned Corruption in a Monarchical Regime." *World Politics* 25:533–55.

———. 1983. *The Egypt of Nasser and Sadat: The Political Economy of Two Regimes.* Princeton: Princeton University Press.

Weber, Max. 1958. *From Max Weber: Essays in Sociology.* Translated and edited by H. H. Gerth and C. Wright Mills. New York: Oxford University Press.

Weffort, Francisco. 1965. "Estado y Masas en el Brasil." *Revista Latinoamericana de Sociología* 65:53–71.

Winter, Sidney G. 1964. "Economic 'Natural Selection' and the Theory of the Firm." *Yale Economics Essays* 4:225–72.

World Bank. 1980, 1981, 1984, 1988. *World Development Report.* New York: Oxford University Press.

World Bank. 2002. World Development Indicators. CD-Rom.

Yashar, Deborah. 1997. *Demanding Democracy: Reform and Reaction in Costa Rica and Guatemala, 1870s–1950s.* Stanford: Stanford University Press.

Index

Abacha, Sani, 52. *See also* Nigeria
Abbott, Andrew, 219
Africa, 13–14, 18, 32, 41, 48, 66, 67, 79, 126, 152, 153, 176, 197, 200, 215. *See also names of individual countries*
Aggregation, consequences of, 193–98, 221, 223
Albania, 80, 83
Alessandri, Jorge, 120. *See also* Chile
Allen, William Sheridan, 95
Allende, Salvador, 122. *See also* Chile
Ames, Barry, 200
Amin, Idi, 52. *See also* Uganda
Analytic narratives, 38, 219
Angola, 75
Argentina, 13, 32, 52, 53, 57, 128, 168, 204–5. *See also* Perón, Juan; Peronist party
Arrow, Kenneth, 194, 198
Asad, Hafez al, 74. *See also* Ba'ath Party; Syria
Asia, 14, 16–18, 41, 101, 111, 126, 152–53, 176. *See also names of individual countries*
Austria, 109
Austro-Hungarian Empire, 109
Authoritarianism: opposition to, 189; and party development, 154, 171; relationship with development, 15–16, 20; transitions from, 2, 40, 44–88, 220; transitions to, 1, 2. *See also* Authoritarian regime; Cadre-interests argument; Coup; Coup conspiracy; Democratic breakdown; Democratization; Dictator; Dictatorship; Elite splits; Factions and factionalization; Military regime; Personalist regime; Single-party regime; Transition
Authoritarian regime, 41; breakdown of, 44–88; classification of, 50–53, 69–77; criteria for inclusion in data set, 71–72; politics in, 43–53, 64, 185; survival of, 69, 78–87. *See also* Authoritarianism; Bureaucratic authoritarian regime; Cadre-interests argument; Coup; Coup conspiracy; Democratic breakdown; Democratization; Dictator; Dictatorship; Elite splits; Factions and factionalization; Military regime; Personalist regime; Single-party regime; Transition

Ba'ath Party (Syria), 74. *See also* Asad, Hafez al; Syria
Bangladesh, 77
Bargaining, 44–46, 99. *See also* Authoritarianism, transitions from; Authoritarian regime, breakdown of; Democratization; Negotiation; Transition
Barrientos, René, 77. *See also* Bolivia
Barry, Brian, 25, 181
Bates, Robert, 38, 40, 140, 176, 200, 219–20
Battle-of-the-sexes game, 55–58, 62, 65
Belgium, 109, 205
Bendix, Reinhard, 140
Benin, 58
Bolivia, 32, 54, 77, 111, 113, 168, 171. *See also* Barrientos, René
Bosnia, 181

Botswana, 71, 72
Bratton, Michael, 48, 65, 66
Braumoeller, Bear, 90, 116
Brazil, 32, 52, 57, 93–94, 100, 128, 138, 205
Britain. *See* England
Buchanan, James, 200, 203
Bulgaria, 48, 155, 171, 186
Bureaucratic authoritarian regime, 15–17, 128. *See also* Authoritarian regime; Military regime
Burkina Faso, 64
Burma (Myanmar), 75

Cadre-interests argument, 53–68, 77–85, 87, 97. *See also* Military regime; Personalist regime; Single-party regime
Caetano, Marcello, 48. *See also* Portugal
Cambodia, 80–81
Campbell, Donald, 134
Cardoso, Fernando Henrique, 94. *See also* Brazil
Carey, John, 209
Case, definition of, 96
Cases: classification of, 50–53, 69–77, 131–32, 145–47, 157–63, 216; missing, 80–81, 86. *See also* Domain; Measurement; Operationalization; Universe
Case selection, 5, 16, 23–25, 42, 47, 86, 89–97, 105, 111, 125–35, 139, 142, 151–52, 213, 216. *See also* Domain; Selection; Selection bias; Universe
Case studies, 11, 24, 42, 47, 96, 117–18, 123, 131–49, 164, 172
Central America, 32. *See also* *names of individual countries*
Chile, 32, 52, 57, 119–23, 128, 170–71, 210. *See also* Alessandri, Jorge; Allende, Salvador; Partido Demócrata Cristiano; Partido Radical; Pinochet, Augusto
China, 106, 107, 109, 110
Clapham, Christopher, 2
Cleavage, in Lipset and Rokkan, 148–52, 156–61, 165–71, 215
Coding, 71–72, 99, 160, 163–64, 216–17; codebook, 147, 163–64; coding scheme, 72, 99, 147–48, 163–64, 216; coding sheet, 99–100. *See also* Cases, classification of; Domain; Measurement; Operationalization; Universe
Colburn, Forrest, 200
Collective action, 7, 33, 195–98, 204
Colombia, 165, 170–71, 204
Colomer, Josep, 57
Common pool, 197–98
Comparative historical analysis, 140–41. *See also* Comparative historical method; Comparative historical sociology; Historical institutionalism
Comparative historical method, 22, 148, 149. *See also* Comparative historical analysis; Comparative historical sociology; Historical institutionalism
Comparative historical sociology, 22, 177. *See also* Comparative historical analysis; Comparative historical method; Historical institutionalism
Compound outcome, 23, 27–28, 37–40, 43–44, 87–88, 223
Congo (Zaire), 54
Corruption, 11, 66, 202
Costa Rica, 140, 168, 170–71
Coup, 55–56, 66, 72, 76. *See also* Authoritarianism, transitions to; Coup conspiracy; Democracy, transitions from; Democratic breakdown; Transition
Coup conspiracy, 54–57. *See also* Authoritarianism, transitions to; Coup; Democracy, transitions from; Democratic breakdown; Transition
Creativity, 30–35
Credible first move (first-mover strategy), 57–58, 63, 66
Cuba, Cuban, 80, 112–13

Democracy, 139–40, 176; causes of, 39; classification or measurement of, 72, 76, 86, 145–46; development of parties and, 153, 154, 158, 170; economic performance in, 128; politics in, 184–86, 195, 201, 210; relationship with development, 6, 8–16, 83; transitions from, 2; transitions to, 2, 41–44, 48, 58, 63, 79. *See also* Authoritarianism, transitions from; Authoritarian regime, breakdown of; Coup conspiracy; Democratic breakdown; Transition

Democratic breakdown, 27, 128, 206. *See also* Authoritarianism, transitions to; Coup; Coup conspiracy; Transition

Democratization, 1–4, 17, 23, 27, 37, 41–45, 48–49, 63–64, 67, 84, 87–88, 201, 206, 207, 211. *See also* Authoritarianism, transitions from; Authoritarian regime, breakdown of; Bargaining; Cadre-interests argument; Democracy; Negotiation; Transition

Dependency, 2, 6, 7, 11–20, 177

Deyo, Frederic, 94

Dictator, 81; personalist, 52–53, 60–63, 66–69, 73. *See also* Authoritarianism; Authoritarian regime; Democratic breakdown; Dictatorship; Personalist leader; Personalist regime; Transition

Dictatorship, 15, 41, 48–49, 75; personalist, 63, 65. *See also* Authoritarianism; Authoritarian regime; Democratic breakdown; Dictator; Military regime; Personalist leader; Personalist regime; Regime, breakdown of; Single-party regime; Transition

Dion, Douglas, 114

Dogan, Mattei, 6

Domain (of a theory or argument), 90, 94–98, 109–11, 113, 115, 131–32, 146, 152–55, 158–63, 173, 181–82, 187–88. *See also* Cases, classification of; Case selection; Coding; Universe

Dominican Republic, 52. *See also* Trujillo, Rafael

Downs, Anthony, 199–200

Eastern Europe, 3, 41, 52, 83, 152–53, 176, 186, 203, 210. *See also names of individual countries*

Economic crisis, 45, 50, 65–66, 128

Economic development, 6, 8–9, 18, 23, 27, 80, 150, 215

Economic liberalization, 2, 3–4, 179. *See also* Economic reform

Economic reform, 4, 50, 138. *See also* Economic liberalization

Ecuador, 32, 111

Egypt, 74–75. *See also* Naguib, Muhammed; Nasser, Gamal Abdel; Sadat, Anwar

Electoral institutions, 201–3, 207–9, 215

Elite splits, 45, 47–48, 58, 62–65, 87, 106. *See also* Authoritarianism, transitions from; Authoritarian regime, breakdown of; Cadre-interests argument; Factions and factionalization; Transition

Elkins, Zachary, 70

El Salvador, 111, 113, 168, 171. *See also* Partido de Conciliación Nacional; Partido Revolucionario de Unificación Democrática

England, 10, 107, 109–11, 203

Europe, 9–10, 41, 83, 156–57, 160, 165, 167, 173, 202, 215, 216. *See also names of individual countries;* Eastern Europe; Western Europe

Evans, Peter, 94

Evolutionary selection, 33, 187. *See also* Selection

Eyadema, Etienne, 53. *See also* Togo

Factions and factionalization, 47, 55–63, 132. *See also* Authoritarianism, transitions from; Authoritarian regime, breakdown of; Cadre-interests argument; Elite splits; Transition

Fiji, 99

France, 106–9, 112, 115, 153, 203, 205

Frieden, Jeffry, 192

Game theory, 34, 55–62, 65, 203–5. *See also* Battle-of-the-sexes game; Prisoner's dilemma
Garrett, Geoffrey, 217
George, Alexander, 137
Germany, 107, 109–10, 148, 153, 203
Germany, East, 48
Gill, Anthony, 188
Goertz, Gary, 90, 116
Greece, 83, 153, 155
Green, Donald, 25, 201
Guatemala, 111, 113, 140, 168, 171

Haiti, 99
Hirschman, Albert, 119–22
Historical institutionalism, 21, 177. *See also* Comparative historical analysis; Comparative historical method; Comparative historical sociology
Honduras, 111, 165, 170–71
Hull, Adrian, 133
Hungary, 186
Huntington, Samuel, 41

Implications, observable or testable, 23, 28, 38–40, 43, 64–69, 73, 78, 85–86, 96–97, 134, 192, 213–14, 217, 220–21
Import-substitution industrialization, 15, 20, 94, 121–22
Indonesia, 54, 75. *See also* Suharto
Inductive research strategy, 5, 37–38, 42, 87–88, 219, 221
Institutional change, 44, 68, 189, 199, 203, 210. *See also* Institutional choice
Institutional choice, 46, 199, 210. *See also* Institutional change
Institutional Revolutionary Party (Partido Revolucionario Institucional, PRI, Mexico), 52, 71. *See also* Mexico
Iran, 48, 103
Iraq, 99
Italy, 148, 151, 153, 154, 167

Jamaica, 99
Japan, 107, 109–10, 153, 201, 202
Johnson, Chalmers, 73
Juncture, critical or historical, 140–41, 149–50, 171, 172

Keohane, Robert, 28, 96, 220–21
King, Gary, 28, 96, 220–21
Koo, Hagen, 94
Korea. *See* North Korea; South Korea
Kuhn, Thomas, 5, 6–7, 38

Labor repression, 93–95, 98–105; measurement of, 98–100
Laitin, David, 178
Lange, Peter, 217
Laos, 64
Lapp, Nancy, 189
Latin America, 13, 16, 18, 32, 41, 79, 112, 155–57, 162, 167, 172–73, 176, 189, 200–201, 203, 208, 210. *See also names of individual countries*
Legislative institutions, 194–95, 198, 203, 204, 210
Lenin, V. I., 181. *See also* Revolution; Russia; Soviet Union
Leninist party, 52. *See also* Eastern Europe; Revolution
Levi, Margaret, 140
Libya, 80
Lien, Da-Hsiang, 140
Limongi, Fernando, 80
Linz, Juan, 205–6
Lipset, Seymour Martin, 133, 140, 148–65, 167–68, 170–73, 215, 217
Lithuania, 109
Lofchie, Michael, 200
Londregan, John, 83, 210

Mahoney, James, 140
Mainwaring, Scott, 170, 209
Majority rule, 193–94
Malaysia, 72. *See also* United Malay National Organization
Marx, Karl, 9, 10, 13, 20
Mauritius, 99
McKelvey, Richard, 194
McKeown, Timothy, 137
Means-ends rationality, 179–82

Measurement, 70–71, 98–100, 124–27, 132, 137, 139, 142, 144–47, 172, 216–18, 220; nonquantitative, 5, 51, 132, 142, 145–49. *See also* Cases, classification of; Coding; Operationalization
Mentor, 35–37
Merton, Robert, 18
Mexico, 52, 70, 71, 93–94, 100, 111, 114, 168, 171. *See also* Institutional Revolutionary Party
Middle East, 32, 74, 84, 152–53, 200. *See also* Egypt; Iran; Iraq; Syria; Yemen, South
Military: elite splits in, 62–63; factions in, 62–63; interests of officers, 49, 53–58, 60, 62–63; intervention by, 11, 16, 53, 55–57, 77, 128; opposition to, 189; role in democratic breakdown, 16, 44, 48; role in transitions from authoritarianism, 66–68; rule by, 77, 128; threats by, 106, 111–12; type of authoritarianism, 51–52, 76–77. *See also* Authoritarianism; Authoritarian regime; Coup; Coup conspiracy; Democratic breakdown; Dictator; Dictatorship; Elite splits; Factions and factionalization; Military regime; Transition
Military regime: classification of, 51–53, 72–74, 77; durability of, 3, 69, 77–79, 81–82, 85, 220; interests of officers in, 53–58, 60; transitions from, 2, 63–69. *See also* Authoritarianism; Authoritarian regime; Dictator; Dictatorship; Elite splits; Factions and factionalization; Military; Transition
Model, 32–34, 40, 58. *See also* Signaling model
Modernization, 6, 7–12, 16–20
Moore, Barrington, 39, 139–40, 141–42

Naguib, Muhammed, 74. *See also* Egypt
Nasser, Gamal Abdel, 74. *See also* Egypt
Necessary condition or cause, 90, 114–17
Negotiation, 44, 57, 66, 68, 69, 75, 97–98. *See also* Authoritarianism, transitions from; Authoritarian regime, breakdown of; Bargaining; Democratization; Transition
Netherlands, 109
Ne Win, 75. *See also* Burma
Nicaragua, 48, 54, 76, 111, 114, 171. *See also* Sandinistas; Somoza regime
Niger, 64
Nigeria, 52, 54. *See also* Abacha, Sani
Nordlinger, Eric, 55
North, Douglass, 199
North Africa, 83–84. *See also* Libya
North America, 10, 12, 20. *See also* United States
North Korea, 80
Norway, 163

O'Donnell, Guillermo, 2, 45, 47, 48, 94, 98, 204, 206
Oligarchy, 151, 153, 157–58, 160, 164–69, 171
Olson, Mancur, 195, 196
Operationalization, 24–25, 131–33, 142, 144–45, 213–16; of authoritarianism, 50–53, 69–77; of concepts used by Lipset and Rokkan, 157–63, 165; of democracy, 72, 76, 86, 145–46; of military regimes, 51–53, 72–74, 77; of personalist regimes, 51–53, 72, 77–79; of single-party regimes, 51–53, 72–75; of threat, 112–14. *See also* Cases, classification of; Coding; Measurement
Ostrom, Elinor, 219–20
Ottoman Empire, 109. *See also* Turkey

Paradigm, 4, 6–8, 10, 12–13, 15–22, 223
Paraguay, 32, 75, 111, 165, 170–71. *See also* Stroessner, Alfredo

Partido de Conciliación Nacional (PCN, El Salvador), 159. *See also* El Salvador
Partido Demócrata Cristiano (PDC, Chile). *See also* Chile
Partido Radical (PR, Chile), 159. *See also* Chile
Partido Revolucionario de Unificación Democrática (PRUD, El Salvador), 160. *See also* El Salvador
Partido Revolucionario Institucional (PRI, Mexico). *See* Institutional Revolutionary Party
Party system, 149–51, 154–72
Path dependence, 133, 139–42, 148, 151, 172, 178, 190
Perón, Juan, 53. *See also* Argentina; Peronist party
Peronist party, 205. *See also* Argentina; Perón, Juan
Personalist leader (or dictator): allies of, 50, 60–63, 74; during transitions, 60–63, 66. *See also* Authoritarianism; Authoritarian regime; Dictator; Dictatorship; Personalist regime; Transition
Personalist regime: cases left out, 81; classification of, 51–53, 72, 77–79; politics in, 60–63; transitions from, 65–69, 82. *See also* Authoritarianism; Authoritarian regime; Dictator; Dictatorship; Personalist leader; Transition
Peru, 32, 111, 171
Philip, George, 2
Pinochet, Augusto, 52, 58, 122. *See also* Chile
Pluralist theories, 8, 19, 180, 192, 196
Poland, 109, 186, 205
Poole, Keith, 83
Portugal, 48, 83, 109, 155, 168, 171. *See also* Caetano, Marcello; Salazar, António de Oliveira
Preferences, as used in rational choice arguments, 177, 179–83
Presidential institutions, 195, 202, 205, 207–8
Prisoner's dilemma, 32, 204
Prospect theory, 34, 222
Prussia, 107, 109
Przeworski, Adam, 76, 80, 146, 178
Public choice, 178–79, 200
Public goods, 33, 193, 195–97, 202

Rational choice, 6, 22, 25–26, 175–211, 221–22; distinguishing features of, 191–92; misperceptions about, 178–91
Rebellion, 10, 66, 69, 112, 147
Reformation, 148, 153
Regime: breakdown of, 3, 62, 65–66, 79–80, 83, 85–87, 97–98; change in, 43–45, 50, 73–87, 205; definition of, 70. *See also* Authoritarianism; Authoritarian regime; Cadre-interests argument; Coup; Coup conspiracy; Democracy; Democratic breakdown; Democratization; Dictatorship; Military regime; Personalist regime; Single-party regime; Transition
Regression to the mean, 24, 123–29
Remington, Thomas, 210
Rent seeking, 200. *See also* Public choice
Research design, 4–5, 20, 22–24, 26, 42, 117, 128, 139, 141, 149, 165, 172, 213, 216, 223
Research frontier, 7, 29
Research topic, choosing a, 27–37
Revolution, 10, 27, 37, 44, 68, 73, 89, 103, 139, 181–82; Skocpol's argument about, 106–15
Revolutionary Party of Tanzania (CCM, Tanzania), 52, 75. *See also* Tanzania
Riker, William, 202
Roemer, John, 178
Rogowski, Ronald, 192
Rokkan, Stein, 133, 140, 148–65, 167–68, 170–73, 215, 217
Romania, 83, 186
Rose, Richard, 170
Ross, Michael, 84
Russia, 106–7, 109, 110, 181, 186, 210. *See also* Soviet Union

Sadat, Anwar, 74. *See also* Egypt
Salazar, António de Oliveira, 48. *See also* Portugal
Sand castles, 4, 6, 37, 223
Sandinistas, 76. *See also* Nicaragua
Schmitter, Philippe, 2, 45, 47, 48, 206
Scully, Timothy, 170
Selection: by nature, 97; on the dependent variable, 89–94, 97, 102–7, 116–19, 127–29, 216. *See also* Case selection; Domain; Selection bias; Universe
Selection bias, 23–24, 47, 65, 89–105, 117–18, 123. *See also* Case selection; Domain; Selection; Universe
Sen, Amartya, 178
Shapiro, Ian, 25, 201
Shugart, Matthew, 209
Signaling model, 34
Singapore, 93–94, 100
Single-party regime: cadres in, 49–50, 58–60; classification of, 51–53, 72–75; factions in, 59–60; politics in, 58–60, 61; transitions from, 63–64, 67–69, 78–85. *See also* Authoritarianism; Authoritarian regime; Dictatorship; Regime; Transition
Sklar, Richard, 21
Skocpol, Theda, 106–15
Smith, Steven, 210
Somoza regime, 48, 76. *See also* Nicaragua
South Korea, 93–94, 100, 103
Soviet Union, 3, 70, 83; collapse of, 1, 3. *See also* Russia
Spain, 32, 57, 83, 109, 151, 153, 154, 167
Stepan, Alfred, 55, 205–6
Strategy, as used in rational choice arguments, 177, 183
Stroessner, Alfredo, 75. *See also* Paraguay
Suffrage, 151–71, 189; definition of effective, 161–63
Suharto, 75. *See also* Indonesia
Sweden, 109
Syria, 58, 74. *See also* Asad, Hafez al; Ba'ath Party

Taiwan, 72, 93–94, 100
Tanzania, 52, 72. *See also* Revolutionary Party of Tanzania
Taylor, Michael, 178
Thailand, 54
Theory building, 4–5, 22–23, 27–28, 43–44, 87–88, 129, 173, 175–76, 206, 213, 217, 219–23
Time series, 24, 117–19, 123, 129
Togo, 53. *See also* Eyadema, Etienne
Transition: between different kinds of authoritarianism, 73; classification of, 75–77, 79; from authoritarianism, 2–3, 32, 40–50, 61–68, 75, 78–88, 98; institutional choice during, 210; to authoritarianism, 2, 94. *See also* Authoritarianism, transitions from; Authoritarian regime, breakdown of; Bargaining; Cadre-interests argument; Coup; Coup conspiracy; Credible first move; Democracy, transitions to; Democratic breakdown; Democratization; Elite splits; Factions and factionalization; Military; Military regime, transitions from; Negotiation; Personalist leader, during transitions; Personalist regime, transitions from; Regime; Single-party regime, transitions from
Trujillo, Rafael, 52. *See also* Dominican Republic
Tsebelis, George, 201, 205
Tucker, Robert, 20
Tullock, Gordon, 200, 203
Turkey, 70. *See also* Ottoman Empire

Uganda, 52, 99. *See also* Amin, Idi
United Malay National Organization (UMNO, Malaysia), 75. *See also* Malaysia
United States, 10, 113–14, 180,

United States (*continued*)
194–95, 197, 199, 203, 204, 207, 210. *See also* North America
Universe (of cases), 24–25, 86, 90, 95–97, 111, 115–18, 131, 134, 146, 148, 152–55, 158, 163. *See also* Case selection; Coding; Domain
Uruguay, 128, 165–67, 170, 171
Urwin, Derek, 170

Van de Walle, Nicolas, 48, 65, 66
Venezuela, 168, 170, 171
Verba, Sidney, 28, 96, 220–21
Vietnam, 80

Wallerstein, Michael, 178
Weber, Max, 30–31
Western Europe, 9, 170, 171–72, 201–2, 207. *See also names of individual countries*
Whitehead, Laurence, 206

Yashar, Deborah, 140
Yemen, South, 80
Yugoslavia, 83